A SHARE IN THE KINGDOM

A Commentary on the Rule
of St. Benedict for Oblates

Benet Tvedten, O.S.B.

THE LITURGICAL PRESS
Collegeville, Minnesota 56321

The text of the *Rule* quoted throughout this work is *RB 1980: The Rule of St. Benedict,* edited by Timothy Fry, O.S.B., The Liturgical Press.

The quotes from the Second Book of Dialogues of St. Gregory the Great are from *Life and Miracles of St. Benedict,* translated by Odo J. Zimmermann, O.S.B., and Benedict R. Avery, O.S.B., The Liturgical Press.

Cover illustration by Ade Bethune.

Library of Congress Cataloging-in-Publication Data

Tvedten, Benet.
    A share in the kingdom : a commentary on the rule of St. Benedict for Oblates / Benet Tvedten.
      p. cm.
    ISBN 0-8146-1808-1
    1. Benedict, Saint, Abbot of Monte Cassino. Regula.
2. Monasticism and religious orders—Rules. 3. Oblates of St.
Benedict. I. Benedict, Saint, Abbot of Monte Cassino. Regula.
English. II. Title.
BX3004.T94 1989   89-35509
255'.106—dc20   CIP

Acknowledgements

Bede: Lives of the Abbots of Wearmouth and Jarrow from THE AGE OF BEDE translated by D. H. Farmer (Penguin Classics, 1983), copyright © D. H. Farmer, 1983, pp. 189 and 196–197. Reproduced by permission of Penguin Books Ltd.

BEDE: A HISTORY OF THE ENGLISH CHURCH AND PEOPLE translated by Leo Sherley-Price, revised by R. E. Latham (Penguin Classics, 1968), copyright © Leo Sherley-Price, 1955, 1968, p. 336. Reproduced by permission of Penguin Books Ltd.

The Rule of Taize, © Ateliers et Presses de Taize.

Basil, *Ascetical Works: The Long Rules,* Fathers of the Church, translated by M. Monica Wagner, C.S.C., The Catholic University of America Press.

The Letters of St. Bernard of Clairvaux, translated and edited by Bruno Scott James, Henry Regnery Company.

Thomas Merton, *The Wisdom of the Desert.* Copyright © 1960 by the Abbey of Gethsemani, Inc. Reprinted by permission of New Directions Pub. Corp.

David Knowles, *Christian Monasticism.* Weidenfeld and Nicolson.

Sacred Art at St. John's Abbey. The Liturgical Press.

The Rule of the Master, translated by Luke Eberle, O.S.B. Cistercian Publications.

Aelred of Rievaulx, *Treatises, The Pastoral Prayer,* introduction by David Knowles, Cistercian Publications.

Aelred of Rievaulx, *On Spiritual Friendship,* translated by Mary Eugenia Loher, S.S.N.D., Cistercian Publications-Consortium Press.

Besa, *The Life of Shenoute,* translated by David N. Bell. Cistercian Publications.

Pachomius, *Pachomian Koinonia,* translated by Armand Veilleux. Cistercian Publications.

Stephen of Lexington, *Letters from Ireland, 1228–1229,* translated by Barry W. O'Dwyer, Cistercian Publications.

Hubert Van Zeller, *The Rule of St. Benedict,* Sheed & Ward.

Aelred of Rievaulx, *The Mirror of Charity,* translated by Geoffrey Webb and Adrian Walker, Mowbray.

Maurus Wolter, O.S.B., *The Principles of Monasticism,* edited and translated by Bernard Sause, O.S.B. B. Herder Book Company.

Colman J. Barry, O.S.B., *Worship and Work.* St. John's Abbey Press.

Frank Bottomly, *The Explorer's Guide to the Abbeys, Monasteries, and Churches of Great Britain.* Kaye & Ward, Ltd.

Book of Prayer. St. John's Abbey Press.

Contents

Foreword

"Listen carefully," St. Benedict says in the beginning of the Prologue to his *Rule*. Although he wrote a rule for monks, monks have not retained the exclusive rights to it. Nuns have also accepted the *Rule of St. Benedict* as their guide to Christian living. Lay people and secular priests who are Oblates of St. Benedict also follow the *Rule* in a manner that is adaptable to their vocations.

The *Rule* was written for a community, but the individual Benedictine is formed by both the *Rule* and the community. Therefore I cannot avoid mentioning monks with whom I have lived, to whom I have listened, and from whom I have learned.

This book is for the benefit of Oblates of St. Benedict, who are also listeners and learners. It attempts to explain some things that may have remained a mystery to Oblates over their years of affiliation with Benedictine communities. Although their spirituality is nourished by the *Rule*, there are particular chapters in it which seem to have no bearing on their lives. Some chapters have little or no bearing on the lives of modern Benedictine monks and nuns, but St. Benedict, in his time, had reasons for including them in the *Rule*. I have looked at the *Rule* as it was written for monks and from my own experience of having lived under it as a monk for thirty years. But, to repeat what was observed above, the *Rule* belongs to all of us: monks, nuns, and Oblates.

It is my hope that this book will also interest the person who is presently a stranger to St. Benedict and the *Rule*. If anyone will listen, there is so much to be learned from St. Benedict. Although I am neither a monastic historian nor a *Rule* exegete, I hope what I have written will be helpful to all of you.

Benet Tvedten, O.S.B.

Oblates of St. Benedict

Benedictine abbots from around the world, assembled in Rome for a congress, made this statement about Oblates of St. Benedict:

> The Congress wishes to express its deep appreciation of the role of Oblates, and indeed the role of all those Christians who are united with us in prayer and aspire to a form of life inspired by the Rule of St. Benedict. We thank them for their loyal association with us, an association which in some cases stretches back over many years; we thank them, because it is not only they who receive blessings from the monastery, but they are also a source of blessings and help for the monastery. We ask them to continue steadfast in the way they have chosen, placing their trust in their Benedictine vocation. . . . May the efforts which all are making assist both Oblates and their monastic communities ''to set out on the way of the Lord, with the Gospel as our guide'' (The Prologue), so that all may contribute towards the attainment of peace, unity, and the coming of the Kingdom of God.[1]

This message from the world's abbots refers to your Benedictine oblation as a vocation, a calling. Most of the people we know are doing all right without being affiliated with the Benedictines. But some people wish to apply St. Benedict's teachings to their way of Christian life. You felt called to do this. I began my relationship with the Benedictines as an Oblate and ended up in a monastery. Like the people who asked Jesus where he lived, you and I accepted the invitation to "come and see." We went to where the monks or nuns live and what we saw there made us want to attach ourselves to that kind of life in some way. You cannot live where the monks or nuns live, but you take home their Benedictine ideals. You carry them to work. You practice them in your parish and in your neighborhood.

Isn't it amazing how people keep discovering the *Rule?* A few years ago I received a letter from a woman who had been the guest of a Benedictine community of women. She wrote:

> I read The Rule for the first time when I was there. I think there is a terrific need for nuns and monks. You stand for something, you represent something the world really needs. To me your Rule has offered all kinds of extremely practical advice about how one should live in the heart. And that there are people like you consciously trying to live it day in, and day out, is very important.[2]

Today this woman is an Oblate of St. Benedict.

Introduction

St. Benedict

Pope St. Gregory the Great (A.D. 604), in his biography of St. Benedict, concludes that "Anyone who wishes to know more about his life and character can discover in his *Rule* exactly what he was like as an abbot, for his life could not have differed from his teaching."

St. Gregory's *Life* of St. Benedict is hagiographic, a style whose purpose is to edify the reader rather than to provide accurate and detailed biographical data. This does not mean, however, that hagiography is useless. Beneath the hyperbole, there are truths to be learned. In the case of St. Benedict, we have his *Rule*, which reveals more truth about him than the biography by his saintly admirer.

St. Benedict was born in 480 at Nursia in Umbria. His biographer assures us that the boy Benedict "showed mature understanding, and strength of character far beyond his years" and that he "kept his heart detached from every pleasure." Isn't there something formidable about a boy like that? I'm disturbed by saints who were ascetics before the age of puberty. St. John Bosco had a problem with St. Dominic Savio, a boy who wanted to practice excessive mortification. Don Bosco says, "Religion must be around us like the air we breathe, but boys must not be wearied by too many devotions and observances."

St. Gregory tells us that St. Benedict went to school in Rome when he was in his late teens. His parents wanted him to receive a liberal education, but Benedict saw the danger of his becoming a libertine instead of being liberally educated:

> When he found many of the students there abandoning themselves to vice, he decided to withdraw from the world he had been preparing to enter; for he was afraid that if he acquired any of its learning, he would be drawn down with them to his eternal ruin. In his desire to please God alone, he turned his back on further studies, gave up home and inheritance and resolved to embrace the religious life. He took this step, fully aware of his ignorance; yet he was truly wise, uneducated though he may have been.

St. Gregory informs us that St. Benedict experienced temptations while living as a hermit. One of them was "a violent temptation of the flesh." At this age it apparently wasn't easy to keep "his heart detached from *every pleasure.*" St. Gregory writes: "He had once upon a time seen a certain woman and now the evil spirit pictured her to his fancy. The memory of her wrought so powerfully upon his mind that he could scarcely bear the fire of lust burning within him and he was on the point of yielding to it to leave the wilderness." This is how the young Benedict overcame the temptation: "Seeing a thorny shrub close by, he cast off his garment, threw himself into the brambles and rolled about in them until every part of his body was suffering torture." St. Gregory, in the tradition of hagiography, assures us that St. Benedict never had another lustful thought. It's to St. Gregory's credit that he has told us about that one instance. I think all of us like our saints to be human.

St. Benedict saw how demoralizing it was to live in a secularistic society. He saw how people were destroying themselves by living undisciplined lives. So he ran away. I suspect he ran away because he realized how easy it would be to succumb to all those temptations. No doubt his peers ridiculed him, but he wanted to set his life on a different course. And when he did, St. Gregory tells us, "Soon after many forsook the world to place themselves under his guidance, for now that he was free from these temptations he was ready to instruct others in the practice of virtue."

Subiaco is the place where Benedict found his vocation. He tried to live there in solitude, but it became apparent that he was not called to the life of a hermit. It was here that he discovered the disadvantage of being a solitary. On Easter a priest from nearby came to the cave in which Benedict was living and advised him that he shouldn't be fasting. "Today you may not fast, it is Easter Day." Benedict had become too much out of touch. He was called from the cave to be the abbot in Vicovaro, a town on the way to Subiaco. The monks there tried to kill him. "Look for an abbot after your own hearts," St. Benedict told the monks of Vicovaro as he fled from them. He returned to Subiaco and set about organizing monastic life for people who were genuinely interested in reforming their lives. Later he moved to Monte Cassino where he wrote the *Holy Rule,* grew old, and died. Fortunately for all of us, he did not leave his talent hidden under a bushel basket in the cave for the rest of his life.

The *Rule*

In 1937, a French monk who had been working on a new edition of the *Holy Rule* revealed that St. Benedict had drawn upon another monastic rule in the composition of his own. It is only in recent years that the Benedictine Order has accepted the fact that St. Benedict based his *Rule* on the Rule of the Master, which was written at the end of the fifth century in the neighborhood of Rome.

St. Benedict condensed the Rule of the Master. He discarded whole chapters and toned down others. Benedict could not rule a monastery in the same way the Master did. Benedict says an abbot should not be "excitable, . . . obstinate, jealous or oversuspicious"—everything the Master is. The Master's Rule is long and repetitious. He labors over trivialities. He expects his monks to be perfect.

St. Benedict's *Rule* is written for a monastery of imperfect monks. He presumes there will be misbehavior and complaints in his monastery. He is willing to acknowledge human nature, to work with it, and to improve it.

Prologue

St. Benedict had a lot of common sense. He knew he was writing a rule for ordinary people. St. Benedict asks that the *Rule* be read to the novice three times in the course of the novitiate, and in chapter 66 he says, "We wish this rule to be read often in the community, so that none of the brothers can offer the excuse of ignorance." St. Benedict realized, and so has every abbot after him, that monks need to be reminded over and over again. No matter how closely we listen, the message has to be repeated constantly. We don't achieve perfection merely by reading the *Holy Rule* once. We don't necessarily earn it by practicing the *Rule* throughout our lives. St. Benedict would be the first to admit that nobody is perfect. He wrote a rule for imperfect monks, for ordinary people.

A retreat master once told us, "Benedictines are like an old pair of shoes." Sometimes we are reluctant to throw away an old pair of shoes and buy a new pair. Old shoes, no matter how scruffy they look, are comfortable. Soon after I entered the monastery, I discovered how comfortable I felt because everything was so ordinary. The monks, especially, were ordinary. I knew I was at home.

I think more people would enter Benedictine communities if they didn't have the misconception that they must be exceptionally holy to become monks or nuns. They don't have to be. As a matter of fact, they don't even have to be exceptionally holy after they've become monks or nuns. All that is required is that they keep trying to improve their lives.

St. Benedict teaches all of us how to be practical, moderate, steadfast. He shares his good common sense with us. An Oblate promises to dedicate himself or herself to the service of God and humankind according to the *Rule of St. Benedict*, insofar as his or her state in life permits. You aren't expected to be a monk or nun, but you are expected to be something like those of us who are. St. Benedict wants all of us to love the liturgy, to pray the psalms and meditate on scripture, to see Christ in the guests who come to our homes, to take good care of the property we own, to take good care of our bodily needs as well as our spiritual needs, to be kind and helpful to one another. There are many ways in which we are supposed to be alike.

The *Rule* is centered on Christ and the Christian life. The ordinary Christian can accept this rule of life as an aid to living a virtuous life within the Church. *The Rule of St. Benedict* reminds us of the order we should have in our lives, the priorities, and the discipline.

St. Benedict realizes that we have already been called to the Christian life by baptism, but if we've become lethargic in living out that commitment, this Rule is for us:

> This message of mine is for you, then, if you are ready to give up your own will, once and for all, and armed with the strong and noble weapons of obedience to do battle for the true King, Christ the Lord. . . .
>
> Let us get up then, at long last, for the Scriptures rouse us when they say: *"It is high time for us to arise from sleep* (Rom 13:11). Let us open our eyes to the light that comes from God, and our ears to the voice from heaven that every day calls out this charge: *If you hear his voice today, do not harden your hearts* (Ps 94[95]:8) (Prologue).

St. Benedict tells us to begin this manner of following Christ right now, today. "The Lord waits for us daily to translate into action, as we should, his holy teachings." We all pray to be given "our daily bread." Yesterday's bread has lost its freshness, and tomorrow's bread is not yet baked. We can't live in the past or in the future. "While we are in this body and have time to accomplish all these things by the light of life—we must run and do now what will profit us forever." What are we expected to accomplish right now? *"Keep your tongue free from vicious talk and your lips from all deceit; turn away from evil and do good; let peace be your quest and aim* (Ps 33[34]:14-15)."

St. Benedict is establishing a school in which we will learn how to do all these things. He promises us "nothing harsh, nothing burdensome." He knows we are just ordinary people. Although he "may prompt us to a little strictness," he asks us not to become discouraged. We will learn to appreciate the discipline imposed on us by the *Rule*. In time, "we shall run on the path of God's commandments, our hearts overflowing with the inexpressible delight of love."

"Never swerving from his instructions, then, but faithfully observing his teaching in the monastery until death, we shall through patience share in the sufferings of Christ that we may deserve also to share in his kingdom. Amen." If the monastery is the school of the Lord's service, Oblates are students in its extension program. The *Rule* is their textbook. It is read frequently. It is lived faithfully.

CHAPTER 1

The Kinds of Monks

"There are clearly four kinds of monks." Cenobites are the kind St. Benedict favors most. Cenobites live in a family. The word "cenobite" means "common life." All families have a head, and within a family there are certain customs to which all the members conform. St. Benedict calls this "living under a rule and an abbot in a monastery." Everyone else calls it "living at home."

The second kind of monk is the hermit. This is the monk who has gone off to live by himself after having been formed by a community. He can leave the monastic family because he is "self-reliant now." Parents expect their children to reach an age of self-reliance. So does St. Benedict. "Thanks to the help and guidance of many, they are now trained to fight against the devil. They have built up their strength and go from the battle line in the ranks of their brothers to the single combat of the desert." We have all been formed by the family into which we were born or adopted. Parents, brothers, and sisters have all contributed to our development. When the time comes to face life on our own, however, we do not go to the desert. We go to work or to college. Children leave home one by one, and when the last one is out the door, it is the parents who have the desert experience. They are the ones who feel like hermits when the family is raised and gone.

Some people live alone because they have never married or because they have been left alone after the death of a spouse or the separation from one. No matter how intimate we are with neighbors and friends, we can never have the same relationship with them that we have had with the people in our own *cenobium,* our own family. If we become hermits by choice or by circumstance, St. Benedict tells us that we can count on God's assistance to see us through life.

Cenobites and hermits are, in St. Benedict's eyes, good monks. Beware, though, of sarabaites. They are "the most detestable kind of monks, who with no experience to guide them, no rule to try them *as gold is tried in a furnace* (Prov 27:21), have a character as soft as lead." With that said, can we imagine anything worse? St. Benedict changes his mind, however, when he describes the fourth kind of monks, the gyrovagues. "In every way they are worse than sarabaites."

St. Benedict regards the sarabaites as anarchists. They live "two or three together, or even alone, without a shepherd, they pen themselves up in their own sheepfolds, not the Lord's." They don't live under an abbot and a rule. For a long time in this country, it has not been out of the ordinary for Benedictine monks to live outside the monastery. Parishes and missions are staffed by two or three monks or even one. A chaplain in a hospital or in the military is physically separated from his community. Benedictine women also find themselves engaged in work that removes them from their communities. These monks and nuns are not sarabaites. The work they are performing is legitimate, and it is blessed by authority. I have never been stationed outside the monastery, but I daydream sometimes about an assignment elsewhere whenever I'm having a rotten day in the monastery. This is when I think like a sarabaite. Wouldn't it be nice to be far away from the abbot? Just think of all the permissions I could presume. If I were away from the monastery, I wouldn't have to get out of bed so early in the morning. There was a parish that our monastery staffed for ten years and then withdrew from because of a personnel shortage. I would have liked being sent there because the rectory was in the same block as the movie theater. "Their law is what they like to do, whatever strikes their fancy."

Whenever I think like a sarabaite, I'm considering my own personal pleasure and nothing else. I forget that the monks away from the monastery are not on vacation. Their work is demanding, and most often it does not end at five o'clock in the afternoon like mine does most days. I suppose you are also tempted to break away from the realities of your responsibilities. Wouldn't you like to call the office and tell them you're sick today? Sick of work. Wouldn't you like to pack your bags and get away from the screaming kids and the house that needs cleaning or the lawn that needs cutting? Oh, for the life of a sarabaite!

A sarabaite, in St. Benedict's day, would have been spotted immediately even if he hadn't been wearing a habit. "They clearly lie to God by their tonsure." A monk used to be identified by the crown of hair that was left encircling his shaved head. The monastic tonsure was a dead giveaway. Nowadays we let our hair grow, but we still have to be cautious about going to places where monks normally aren't seen, places where monks might show that they are "still loyal to the world by their actions"—the kind of world they are supposed to have abandoned. We can let our hair down only so far.

The gyrovague, the fourth kind of monk, is in a class about whom St. Benedict says, "it is better to keep silent than to speak." Gyrovagues, like sarabaites, lead a "disgraceful way of life." They spend "their entire lives drifting from region to region, staying as guests for three or four days in different monasteries." St. Benedict believes that a monk should stay in the monastery to which he has made a commitment. The monk who goes monastery hopping is making a nuisance of himself. Fortunately, there are no genuine gyrovagues these days. Monk visitors are usually attending to some business or staying overnight while on a trip. Monasteries of men and women welcome their brothers and sisters from other Benedictine houses.

St. Benedict does not want to dwell on the matter of monks who give bad example. ''Let us pass them by, then, and with the help of the Lord, proceed to draw up a plan for the strong kind, the cenobites.'' St. Benedict is writing a *Rule* for people who are willing to share a common experience. My profession of vows has bound me to a monastic family. I am a cenobite. Like most of you, I have a family.

The Benedictine Oblate is associated with a particular community within the Order. This relationship with a particular house is a distinctive Benedictine characteristic. Benedictine monks and nuns profess the vow of stability, which binds them to their respective communities for life. This achieves a sense of solidarity and the very real experience of belonging to a family. A Benedictine monk or nun can visit another monastic house where customs and attitudes are familiar. He or she can even live there for a time but the visitor will know that it is not home. Oblates feel the same way about their communities. An Oblate is at home in the community to which he or she has made oblation. Be at home in the monastic family that is yours. You, too, are a cenobite. Love your monastic family and be supportive of it in prayer.

CHAPTER 2

Qualities of the Abbot

Chapter 2 of the *Rule* is clearly a guide to parenting. The very word "abbot" means "father." We monks do not hesitate to describe Benedictine life as familial, but we do complain if we are treated paternalistically by an abbot. In our day we may prefer being brothers of the abbot rather than sons. The truth of the matter is that we are both.

An abbot's image has changed in recent years. Nowadays when the abbot is the celebrant of Mass, we no longer have to kiss his ring before receiving Communion. Newcomers to the monastery were always confused by this ritual in the old days. The abbot sometimes experienced the displeasure of having the stone in his ring licked by the new candidate whose tongue was ready to receive the host but who had forgotten to kiss the ring first. We no longer have to kneel and kiss the abbot's ring whenever we enter his office. Nor are we expected to stand whenever he enters or leaves a room. These examples are just a few of the courtesies or ceremonies that we rendered to the abbot in years past. They were signs of respect for the father of the monastery, but many of them were more medieval than modern. The abbot was treated more like a prince than a father. Nowadays it is easy to be more familiar with an abbot. He is not the awesome person he once was. I think abbots are happy to be relieved of many of the old trappings. Nevertheless, the monk cannot regard the abbot as merely "one of the boys." The abbot is someone special in a community. He is the father of sons who are adults and who want to be treated like adults. Paternalism, not just in the monastery, is undesirable, but the fatherhood of the abbot is absolutely necessary to Benedictine life.

The qualities required of an abbot are no different from those required in other roles of parenting. No abbot, no father or mother, should ever "teach or decree or command anything that would deviate from the Lord's instructions." There is a twofold manner of teaching in both the monastic family and the natural family: words and good example. St. Benedict understands that some members of his family will have to be taught by good example more than by verbal instruction. This is the only way some monks and some children will ever catch on. St. Benedict warns the abbot about hypocrisy. He tells the father to say and do what he means. "If he teaches his disciples that something is not to be done, then neither must he do it."

In dealing with his subjects, St. Benedict suggests that the abbot adapt himself to circumstances and characters. He may have to be "stern as a taskmaster" or "devoted and tender as only a father can be." Knowing how to live with his monks, the abbot "will not only keep the flock entrusted to his care from dwindling, but will rejoice in the increase of a good flock." A monastery will thrive if it is ruled by a reasonable abbot. Although many people belong to a monastery, it is the abbot "to whom more has been entrusted." Monastic history is recalled in terms of what happened or did not happen during the administration of abbots.

In disciplining extremely recalcitrant monks, it may surprise us that St. Benedict resorts to "blows or some other physical punishment." This seems highly unreasonable to us. It wasn't, though, in St. Benedict's day. In a latter chapter of the *Rule*, there is a more temperate reference to the correction of faults. St. Benedict advises the abbot to

> use prudence and avoid extremes; otherwise, by rubbing too hard to remove the rust, he may break the vessel. He is to distrust his own frailty and remember *not to crush the bruised reed* (Isa 42:3). By this we do not mean that he should allow faults to flourish, but rather, as we have already said, he should prune them away with prudence and love as he sees

best for each individual. Let him strive to be loved rather
than feared *(RB* 64:12-15).

I'm certain St. Benedict was an abbot who was loved.

He was an abbot who showed "equal love to everyone."
Some monks, he says, may be more lovable because of their
ideal behavior, but even so, "the abbot should avoid all favoritism in the monastery." Favoritism in all families causes
many serious problems. "Therefore, the abbot is to show equal
love to everyone and apply the same discipline to all according to their merits." This is good advice for all parents.

The role of father in the community is only one of several
roles that St. Benedict expects the abbot to perform. The abbot is also judge, master, servant, shepherd, steward, teacher,
and wise physician. In all these functions, the abbot is en-
couraged to be Christ-like, "to hold the place of Christ in the
monastery."

The abbot will be judged not only by what he has taught
but by how well the monks have responded to his teaching.
"Let the abbot always remember that at the fearful judgment
of God, not only his teaching but also his disciples' obedience
will come under scrutiny." Near the end of this chapter, St.
Benedict again reminds the abbot of the accounting he must
give on judgment day. Fortunately for the abbot, St. Benedict
assures him of an acquittal if it has been proved that the monks
paid no attention to him. St. Benedict knows that the father
of a monastery can accomplish only so much. Although the
abbot is responsible for his monks and must give an account
of their behavior, he will not be condemned "if he has faithfully shepherded a restive and disobedient flock, always striv-
ing to cure their unhealthy ways." Sometimes parents blame
themselves for the way their children turn out. St. Benedict
says, don't do that. If you have really tried, you can't be
blamed.

Chapter 2, while addressing the qualities an abbot should

have, also says something about the kinds of monks who live under the *Rule*. True enough, there are "obedient and docile and patient" monks. There are "upright and perceptive men." But there are monks who are "restive and disobedient," "negligent and disdainful," and "arrogant." The abbot "must know what a difficult and demanding burden he has undertaken: directing souls and serving a variety of temperaments, coaxing, reproving and encouraging them as appropriate. He must so accommodate and adapt himself to each one's character and intelligence . . ."

One of my favorite abbots is St. Aelred of Rievaulx, a twelfth-century English Cistercian who embodies what St. Benedict teaches in chapter 2 of the *Rule*. St. Aelred had this prayer for his community: "May they, Lord, thanks to your Spirit's influence, live at peace, each and all, and with me; may they be well-behaved, kindly disposed; may they obey, help and bear with one another."[1]

St. Aelred spoke and wrote about friendship. As novice master and later as abbot, he was known as a friend. His biographer, Walter Daniel, reports that when he was declining in health and was bedridden, twenty or thirty monks could be found at one time in the abbot's cell. "There was nobody to say to them: 'Away with you. Don't touch the abbot's bed.' "[2] Those who could find room sat on the abbot's bed. Possibly this is the only time in monastic history that monks have dared to sit on an abbot's bed with the abbot in it.

A few years ago a young man came to join our monastery without having done any research on the Benedictines. After being introduced to the abbot, he turned to one of the monks and asked, "What's an abbot?" If anyone intends to live in a Benedictine monastery, it won't take him long to find out what an abbot is.

Oblates who are parents know the demands of their vocation, and they are successful in raising their families if the qualities of parenthood are the same as the qualities asked of an abbot. St. Benedict's closing remark in chapter 2 can be applied to every parent and to anyone who has charges under him or her. "In this way, while always fearful of the future examination of the shepherd about the sheep entrusted to him and careful about the state of others' accounts, he becomes concerned also about his own, and while helping others to amend by his warnings, he achieves the amendment of his own faults."

CHAPTER 3

Summoning the Brothers for Counsel

St. Benedict's monks do not live under a dictatorship or an oligarchy. "As often as anything is to be done in the monastery, the abbot shall call the whole community together and himself explain what the business is; and after hearing the advice of the brothers, let him ponder it and follow what he judges the wiser course." The abbot can make the final decision, but he cannot make it without having first received the advice of the community. When the community is assembled for this purpose, a chapter meeting takes place.

St. Benedict says: "The reason why we have said all should be called for counsel is that the Lord often reveals what is better to the younger." Church law has determined, however, that in our day only those monks who are in final vows may be called to chapter. In St. Benedict's time, monks did not have a temporary period of profession but made perpetual vows upon completion of the novitiate.

"The brothers, for their part, are to express their opinions with all humility, and not presume to defend their own views obstinately." There was a time when chapter meetings were more formal than they are now. Each member, beginning with the seniors, took his turn at expressing an opinion briefly. If a monk had no comment to make, the one next to him spoke, and so the procedure moved down the ranks to the newest member of the chapter. Today there is more opportunity for defending our views "obstinately." Anyone may speak repeatedly by simply raising his hand and being acknowledged. The abbot sometimes has to ask what the rest of us think because certain monks seem to be dominating the meeting.

What are the important matters that the monastic chapter considers? One of them is the admission of new members to the monastery. When I was a novice, we had to present ourselves to the chapter for a midyear deliberation. We were summoned and asked if we wanted to continue in the novitiate. If we were resolved to persevere, the abbot told us to go to the chapel and pray while the chapter considered our requests. After the chapter had discussed us and voted, we were brought back to the meeting, and the abbot told us the favorable and unfavorable impressions we had made on the chapter. I remember one novitiate class being told that it had corporately gained too much weight.

Other matters for the chapter agenda are admissions to temporary and final vows; the founding or closing of a foundation that is dependent on the mother abbey; the granting of independence to such an establishment; construction of new buildings; acceptance or relinquishment of a parish; founding or accepting the administration of a school or other institutions as well as relinquishing them. And the election of an abbot.

St. Benedict wants the abbot to seek advice from the whole community, but he also says, "If less important business of the monastery is to be transacted, he shall take counsel with the seniors only, as it is written: *Do everything with counsel and you will not be sorry afterward* (Sir 32:24)." This small body of advisers is called the "council." The council helps the abbot prepare the agenda for a chapter meeting. It may even advise the abbot against putting one of his own proposals on the agenda. The abbot asks the council's advice about assignments he has under consideration, and it gives advice on other matters that do not have to be brought to chapter.

In chapter 3, St. Benedict reminds the monks to be faithful to the *Rule* and the abbot. And again he warns the abbot to "keep the rule in everything he does" because he will have to give an accounting to God. The abbot must make decisions prudently so that obedience may be reasonable. "Nevertheless, just as it is proper for disciples to obey their master, so it is becoming for the master on his part to settle everything with foresight and fairness." That is why the abbot summons the brothers for counsel.

Seeking advice from others is always helpful in making the right decisions. Don't be afraid to ask. And should you be asked, express your opinion humbly, not obstinately.

CHAPTER 4

The Tools for Good Works

It is not so difficult to understand chapter 4. The *Rule* was written for monks, but the code of behavior that St. Benedict prescribes in this chapter is no different from what is expected of every Christian. There appears to be nothing particularly monastic about chapter 4. The tools for good works are simply the Ten Commandments and the teachings of Christ. Monks are obliged to observe these seventy-four maxims because monks are Christians. Reading chapter 4 is an examination of one's conscience. *"You are not to kill, not to commit adultery; you are not to steal nor to covet* (Rom 13:9); *you are not to bear false witness* (Matt 19:18; Mark 10:19; Luke 18:20). *You must honor everyone* (1 Pet 2:17), *and never do to another what you do not want done to yourself* (Tob 4:16; Matt 7:12; Luke 6:31)." There is nothing new in all of this, is there? At the head of St. Benedict's list is *"Love the Lord God with your whole heart, your whole soul and all your strength, and love your neighbor as yourself* (Matt 22:37-39; Mark 12:30-31; Luke 10:27)." All that follows in the next seventy-three tools for good works leads to that goal of love. There is no need to list all of the tools here. You learned most of them when you studied the catechism. St. Benedict sums up this chapter by saying: "These, then, are the tools of the spiritual craft. When we have used them without ceasing day and night and have returned them on judgment day, our wages will be the reward the Lord has promised: *What the eye has not seen nor the ear heard, God has prepared for those who love him* (1 Cor 2:9)." And in loving God, we cannot fail to love our neighbor. "On these two commandments hang the whole Law and the Prophets also" (Matt 22:40).

When we arrive at tool 44, it appears that St. Benedict is becoming rather morbid. "Live in fear of judgment day and have a great horror of hell. Yearn for everlasting life with holy desire. Day by day remind yourself that you are going to die. Hour by hour keep careful watch over all you do, aware that God's gaze is upon you, wherever you may be." Some people may be inclined to think these admonitions are for monks and nuns only. After all, there is an image of the monastic as someone whose only purpose in life is to make reparation for his or her sins. St. Benedict's admonition to remember one's sins may bolster this image. "Every day with tears and sighs confess your past sins to God in prayer." And *"Do not gratify the promptings of the flesh* (Gal 5:16); hate the urgings of self-will" completes the picture of the monk who is a worm and not a man. Is it any wonder that monks are presumed to hate themselves and their lives in this world and to long to escape from their wretchedness by death?

St. Benedict's severity in this section of chapter 4 should not lead us to believe he wants his followers to live in a state of fear. He is not recommending scrupulosity to anyone. He is simply asking us to be realistic about our fallen nature. We can find great consolation when he tells us the final tool of good works is to "never lose hope in God's mercy."

It is in this part of the *Rule* that reference is made to something about which St. Benedict does appear to be unrealistic. "Prefer moderation in speech and speak no foolish chatter, nothing just to provoke laughter; do not love immoderate or boisterous laughter." There is another stereotype of the monk as someone who is always mirthful. This is the complete opposite of the image of the monk who is digging his own grave. Admittedly, it is probably the free-spirited Franciscan friar, rather than the sedate Benedictine, who became better known for his hilarity. In the Middle Ages, though, some Benedictines gained a reputation for being raucous and downright ribald.

I think we all know people who annoy us with their outlandish sense of humor. Some of them live in monasteries, and some of them live where you do. St. Benedict's attitude about laughter should not convince us that he was a dour old man, a prude, and a kill-joy. What he is asking here is the avoidance of buffoonery.

"The workshop where we are to toil faithfully at all these tasks is the enclosure of the monastery and stability in the community." Oblates have their own workshops, but they use the same tools for good works as we do here in the monastery.

CHAPTER 5

Obedience

"The first step of humility is unhestitating obedience, which comes naturally to those who cherish Christ above all." Forsaking one's own choice in order to obey someone else, to do the will of another, requires humility. Chapter 5 deals with obedience to the abbot, but St. Benedict is of the opinion that obedience to the superior of the monastery is like the obedience we owe to God:

> They [the monks] carry out the superior's orders as promptly as if the command came from God himself. The Lord says of men like this: . . . *Whoever listens to you, listens to me* (Luke 10:16). Such people as these immediately put aside their own concerns, abandon their own will, and lay down whatever they have in hand, leaving it unfinished. With the ready step of obedience, they follow the voice of authority in their actions. Almost at the same moment, then, as the master gives the instruction the disciple quickly puts it into practice in the fear of God; and both actions together are swiftly completed as one.

St. Benedict sees his monks obeying promptly "because of the holy service they have professed, or because of dread of hell and for the glory of everlasting life." Obedience, along with stability and fidelity to monastic life, is a specific vow the monastic makes. Obedience is a clause in the contract the monastic signs. Monks and nuns obey because they have promised to be obedient. Obedience is part of their routine. Also, they know disobedience can lead to hell, and they would prefer going to heaven.

In the next paragraph, it becomes clear that it is not just routine or fear of hell that motivates the obedience of monks.

> It is love that impels them to pursue everlasting life; therefore, they are eager to take the narrow road of which the

Lord says: *Narrow is the road that leads to life* (Matt 7:14). They no longer live by their own judgment, giving in to their whims and appetites; rather they walk according to another's decisions and directions, choosing to live in monasteries and to have an abbot over them. Men of this resolve unquestionably conform to the saying of the Lord: *I have come not to do my own will, but the will of him who sent me* (John 6:38).

St. Benedict brings us back to that first step of humility, to "unhesitating obedience, which comes naturally to those who cherish Christ above all." The monk's obedience is inspired by Christ's obedience to his Father.

Furthermore, the disciples' obedience must be gladly given, for *God loves a cheerful giver* (2 Cor 9:7). If a disciple obeys grudgingly and grumbles, not only aloud but also in his heart, then, even though he carries out the order, his action will not be accepted with favor by God, who sees that he is grumbling in his heart. He will have no reward for service of this kind; on the contrary, he will incur punishment for grumbling, unless he changes for the better and makes amends.

St. Benedict needs to add a warning against grumbling because he knows the nature of monks. Although they choose to live in a monastery and have an abbot over them, monks are still prone to grumbling when orders are given. In the *Rule*, monks are frequently admonished not to grumble. The monk who obeys while grumbling, even interiorly, will merit no reward for his obedience. St. Benedict cannot tolerate grumblers. Neither can God.

Another characteristic about Benedictine obedience is that it is not just the abbot to whom we are to be obedient; St. Benedict wants us to be obedient to one another also (ch. 71). Obeying the boss is one thing, but obeying someone who is your equal is something else.

Our infirmarian was having a problem with one of the elderly monks who refused to take a bath. No amount of coaxing had worked, and the situation was becoming critical—or at least offensive to those of us who dwelt with the old man. The infirmarian sought the intervention of the abbot. Surely, the senior monk who had lived under obedience to more than one abbot in his long monastic career would listen to this one.

"Who are you?" the monk asked when the abbot commanded him to take a bath.

"I'm the abbot."

The old monk was astounded. This seemed incredulous. "How long have you been abbot?"

"I was elected by the community ten years ago," the abbot replied.

"Well, I certainly didn't vote for you."

Nevertheless, the old fellow knew what having an abbot over him meant. He submitted to someone else's decision and direction. He took a bath.

St. Benedict's chapter on obedience seems reasonable. There is nothing irrational in it, no suggestion that his monks will ever be subjected to the demands of blind obedience. St. Benedict is not the kind of abbot, like some of his predecessors, who sent monks out to cultivate stakes planted in the desert.

What St. Benedict said in the Prologue to his *Rule* follows through in chapter 5:

> In drawing up its regulations, we hope to set down nothing harsh, nothing burdensome. The good of all concerned, however, may prompt us to a little strictness in order to amend faults and to safeguard love. Do not be daunted immediately by fear and run away from the road that leads to salvation. It is bound to be narrow at the outset. But as we progress in this way of life and in faith, we shall run on the path of God's commandments, our hearts overflowing with the inexpressible delight of love.

You do not profess monastic obedience, but you are required to be obedient in many ways in your own state of life.

We all learn to "run on the path of God's commandments" by taking that "first step of humility [which] is unhesitating obedience." That's how the race towards heaven is run.

CHAPTER 6

Restraint of Speech

We may wonder if St. Benedict applied the wrong title to chapter 6 of the *Holy Rule*. Perhaps "Restraint of Speech" should be called "Repression of Speech" instead. In his life and teaching, St. Benedict emphasized moderation, but when it comes to speaking he says, "Permission to speak should seldom be granted even to mature disciples, no matter how good or holy or constructive their talk." This hardly seems moderate.

Really, though, things weren't that strict in St. Benedict's monastery. In other chapters of the *Rule*, we can find evidence that the monks were talkative. They exercised their vocal cords more than seldom. In chapter 42, St. Benedict stresses the silence that "monks should diligently cultivate . . . at all times, but especially at night." He appears to be saying that speaking in the daytime is bound to happen but that it should never occur at night.

He tells the monks to make a special effort in Lent (ch. 49) to avoid "needless talking and idle jesting." From reading chapter 6, we know that St. Benedict would prefer that monks abstain from these faults always, but monks have always been human beings (sociable animals), and St. Benedict knew that better than anyone else. Try harder, he says, to be better during Lent.

In chapter 43, dealing with tardiness, St. Benedict insists that monks come to church even when they are late for prayer. "Should they remain outside the oratory, there may be those who would return to bed and sleep, or, worse yet, settle down outside and engage in idle talk." Apparently, he would rather see his monks go back to bed than stay up and "engage in idle talk."

Chapter 48 is another place in the *Rule* where St. Benedict warns about idle talk. The monk should not engage in it when he is supposed to be doing his reading. "Brothers ought not to associate with one another at inappropriate times." This indicates that there must have been appropriate times in which the brothers associated with one another in conversation.

The point St. Benedict wants to make in this chapter is that silence has a reward. If he appears to have some negative attitudes about speech, it is because he sees the greater value of silence. We all need some silence in our lives. We need it in order to be calm, in order to be creative, and in order to communicate with God. You live in a busier world than I do and one in which there is probably a lot more noise. What is good for monks is good for all Christians. A time of silence is necessary for spiritual growth in all of our lives.

CHAPTER 7

Humility

St. Benedict's spiritual doctrine is contained throughout the *Rule*, but it is most evident in the Prologue, "The Tools for Good Works," and chapter 7, the longest chapter of the *Rule*. He begins, "Divine Scripture calls to us saying: *Whoever exalts himself shall be humbled, and whoever humbles himself shall be exalted* (Luke 14:11; 18:14)." These, of course, are the words of our Lord, not St. Benedict's words. Humility is a virtue that every Christian must practice, and in chapter 7 of the *Rule*, St. Benedict teaches his followers how to be humble.

He uses the example of Jacob's ladder to instruct us. Instead of the angels ascending and descending from earth to heaven as in Jacob's vision, St. Benedict sees the two sides of the ladder representing body and soul. There are twelve rungs to this ladder, twelve steps of humility. We ascend the ladder by going up it humbly.

On the first step, we are instructed to keep the fear of God before our eyes and never to forget it. This is the kind of fear that makes us dread the loss of heaven and the pains of hell, but, more importantly, it is a holy fear, a love and respect for God. If we have this kind of fear, we will be in control of our actions.

The second and third steps ask us to submit ourselves to the will of God and the will of another human being. The *Rule* is written for monks who have made a vow of obedience, but monastics are not the only ones who practice obedience. Husbands and wives are obedient to each other. Children are obedient to parents. Everyone is obedient to an employer. Obedience can be difficult at times, but St. Benedict says, be obedient out of love for God, "imitating the Lord of whom the Apostle says: *He became obedient even to death* (Phil 2:8)."

The fourth step acknowledges how difficult obedience can be for us. Even when it is unjust, the climber of the ladder embraces "suffering and endures it without weakening or seeking escape." Persevere to the end.

Step five has the monk confessing his wrongdoing and evil thoughts to the abbot. It was a monastic practice long before St. Benedict's time for a monk to bare his soul to a spiritual father. Nowadays we take our sins to the priest in the sacrament of reconciliation, but St. Benedict and many of the ancient monastic Fathers were not ordained. What St. Benedict is emphasizing in this step is spiritual direction, not sacramental absolution. Alcoholics Anonymous has twelve steps of recovery. The fifth is: "Admitted to God, to ourselves and to another human being, the exact nature of our wrongs.'' Humbly confessing our faults is necessary for every kind of recovery.

The sixth and seventh steps are perhaps the most humbling of all. The monk is expected to be satisfied ''with the lowest and most menial treatment,'' and he should be ''convinced in his heart that he is inferior to all and of less value.'' In terms that are more acceptable to us today, this means, be content with what you have or can afford. Don't think you're better than other people.

''The eighth step of humility is that a monk does only what is endorsed by the common rule of the monastery and the example set by his superiors.'' In his chapter on the abbot, St. Benedict admits that ''a variety of temperaments'' exists in the monastery. He regards the individuality of his monks, but at the same time, for the sake of order in the monastery, he expects them to be conformists. We all know how difficult and humbling that can be sometimes.

Steps nine, ten, and eleven deal with etiquette of speech. Again we see St. Benedict's great concern about his disciples' use of words and laughter. Humble persons will be careful about what they say; they will speak kindly and won't make braying jackasses of themselves.

The twelfth step says a monk should not only be humble, but he should look humble too. ''Whether he sits, walks or stands, his head must be bowed and his eyes cast down.'' Nowadays we would think that someone who went around like that was strange or certainly a casuality risk. The idea is, dont' be ostentatious in your appearance and manners. Don't be arrogant.

Don't be daunted by these twelve steps of humility, St. Benedict says. After ascending them, the climber will ''quickly arrive at that *perfect love* of God which *casts out fear* (1 John 4:18).''

The twelve steps of humility become so natural to us that

we are unaware of our ascent. We count neither the steps nor the costs to our egos. St. Bernard says, "It is better to climb than to count." St. Benedict assures us of this: "Through this love, all that he once performed with dread, he will now begin to observe without effort, as though naturally, from habit, no longer out of fear of hell, but out of love for Christ, good habit and delight in virtue."

CHAPTERS 8–20

The Divine Office

Chapters 8 through 20 of the *Rule* are concerned with the Divine Office. A lot of the material is rubrical, and some of these rubrics are no longer observed in monasteries. In fact, the very structure of the Divine Office as St. Benedict presents it has changed considerably in recent years. Although we may want to overlook these chapters, there are some matters that should not be ignored. These chapters still speak to us about the quality of prayer.

They are situated in the first part of the *Rule.* Before St. Benedict deals with all the practical details in the running of a monastery, he wants to establish prayer as the priority in the monks' lives. The Divine Office is the Work of God, and it is the work to which monks are called above all else. All Christians—lay, clerical, and religious—are called to pray. Monks, however, have an obligation that differs even from that of other religious. Ask a monk what his community's main work is, and he should reply, "The Divine Office." That is the response St. Benedict would want him to give. Once we had a novice who had been in the novitiate of a modern missionary congregation. Those novices had the Divine Office in common only one day a week. On that day he volunteered to work in the kitchen because he did not like praying the Office with other people. He left our novitiate too. He wasn't cut out for our kind of work, the work to which St. Benedict says nothing else should be preferred.

The structure of the Divine Office in the *Rule* is patterned on the practice of monasteries in the city of Rome. St. Benedict also borrowed some customs from the liturgical prayer of Roman basilicas. Monks and nuns remained faithful to this structure of the Divine Office up until the changes implemented by the Second Vatican Council. The spirit of Benedictine prayer remains the same, even though the letter of St. Benedict's law is no longer observed.

One of the hours of the Divine Office, which always appeared in the old Oblate manuals, was suppressed by the Second Vatican Council. There is no more Prime. In medieval monasteries after the praying of Prime, the first hour of daylight, the monks assembled in the chapter house. A section of the *Rule* was read and commented upon by the abbot. Assignments were given for the day, and the officials of the monastery made reports.

In chapter 8, "The Divine Office at Night," which is the first of the chapters in his liturgical code, St. Benedict sets the time for the hour of Vigils. "It seems reasonable to arise at the eighth hour of the night." St. Benedict's reasonableness is shown in two other ways in chapter 8. "By sleeping until a little past the middle of the night, the brothers can arise with their food fully digested." And he gives the monks an "opportunity to care for nature's needs." St. Benedict thinks of everything.

"In the time remaining after Vigils, those who need to learn some of the psalter or readings should study them." If a monk is going to spend his lifetime praying the psalms, he should know them. Father Meinrad, who taught my novitiate class

the psalms, told us repeatedly to "make them your own." He
wanted us to possess the psalms and to be possessed by them.
In St. Benedict's day, the monks not only had to know the
meaning of the psalms, they had to memorize them too.
Psalters were not available for all of the monks.

In addition to praying the psalms at the Night Office, the
monks are to listen to readings. "Besides the inspired books
of the Old and New Testaments, the works read at Vigils
should include explanations of Scripture by reputable and or-
thodox catholic Fathers."

In summer, because of the short nights, there will be only
one reading instead of three (ch. 10). St. Benedict also allows
the shortening of readings and responsories if the monks oversleep on Sunday. "Let special care be taken that this does not
happen, but if it does, the monk at fault is to make due satisfaction to God in the oratory." In chapter 13, St. Benedict instructs the abbot to pray the Lord's Prayer at the end of Lauds
and the end of Vespers "because thorns of contention are likely
to spring up" in monasteries. "Thus warned by the pledge
they make to one another in the very words of prayer: *Forgive
us as we forgive* (Matt 6:12), they may cleanse themselves of this
kind of vice."

Chapter 16 enumerates the seven hours that begin with
Lauds, prayed at dawn, and end with Compline, the bedtime
prayer. Chapter 17 deals with the number of psalms to be sung
at these hours and chapter 18 with the order of psalmody. St.
Benedict concludes chapter 18 with this proviso:

> Above all else we urge that if anyone finds this distribution
> of the psalms unsatisfactory, he should arrange whatever he
> judges better, provided that the full complement of one hun-
> dred and fifty psalms is by all means carefully maintained
> every week. . . . For monks who in a week's time say less
> than the full psalter with the customary canticles betray ex-
> treme indolence and lack of devotion in their service. We
> read, after all, that our holy Fathers, energetic as they were,

did all this in a single day. Let us hope that we, lukewarm
as we are, can achieve it in a whole week.

If St. Benedict considered his monks lukewarm in comparison
with the desert monks, he can no doubt understand why
twentieth-century monks are more lukewarm than sixth-
century monks. It was in the spirit of chapter 18 that our re-
structuring of the Divine Office occurred in modern times. In
our monastery, we pray four hours of the Divine Office, and
the psalter is distributed over a two-week cycle. We have
departed from the letter of the *Rule*, but our appreciation for
the Divine Office has not diminished.

"We believe that the divine presence is everywhere and *that
in every place the eyes of the Lord are watching the good and the
wicked* (Prov 15:3). But beyond the least doubt we should believe this to be especially true when we celebrate the divine
office." These lines from chapter 19 remind us of the decorum we should have at prayer. St. Benedict ends the chapter
this way: "Let us consider, then, how we ought to behave in
the presence of God and his angels, and let us stand to sing
the psalms in such a way that our minds are in harmony with
our voices."

Nowadays it is easier for all of us to keep our minds "in
harmony with our voices" because our voices are praying in
the vernacular. But there are still distractions. Although God
and the angels witness the prayer of monks, the monks can
see and hear only each other when they are in choir. Some
monks want to rush their recitation of the psalms; others want
to drag theirs out. Some monks make rude noises in choir;
others occupy themselves with grooming habits like cleaning
their fingernails or teeth. When we are in choir, we need to
constantly remind ourselves that God and his angels are watching all of this.

Chapter 20, the last in St. Benedict's liturgical code, refers
to the disposition we should have when praying, especially

in the prayer of petition. It seems to refer to private prayer, but the same attitude holds for prayer in common. "Whenever we want to ask some favor of a powerful man, we do it humbly and respectfully, for fear of presumption. How much more important, then, to lay our petitions before the Lord God of all things with the utmost humility and sincere devotion."

Most Oblates have to pray their Divine Office at home, but they are spiritually linked to their communities of monks or nuns who are gathered in choir stalls to praise God in the Divine Office.

The purpose of the Church's renewed Eucharistic liturgy is to provide a more active and intelligent participation for everyone. Oblates do not differ from other members of their parishes in appreciating these liturgical practices. Here is how Oblates do differ: "They strive each day to pray some part of the Divine Office or Liturgy of the Hours, as the circumstances in their lives permit. They strive to appreciate the beauty and spiritual wealth contained in the Psalms which form the core of the Church's prayer" (Guidelines For Oblates of St. Benedict).

CHAPTER 21

The Deans of the Monastery

St. Gregory tells us what happened when St. Benedict's fame spread throughout the region around Subiaco: "A great number of men gathered around him to devote themselves to God's service. Christ blessed this work and before long he had established twelve monasteries there, with an abbot and twelve monks in each of them. There were a few other monks whom he kept with him, since he felt that they still needed his personal guidance."

According to the figures presented by St. Gregory, St. Benedict could have had as many as two hundred sixty-four monks in his monastery at Subiaco. But he believed the ideal monastery should have only twelve monks, so he founded twelve monasteries with twelve monks in each.

In chapter 21 of the *Rule*, however, St. Benedict does make allowance for growth in a monastery. "If the community is rather large, some brothers chosen for their good repute and holy life should be made deans. They will take care of their groups of ten, managing all affairs according to the commandments of God and the orders of their abbot."

The custom of having deans was not something out of the ordinary. St. Pachomius's Egyptian monasteries were large enough to be divided into deaneries. And the Rule of the Master provides two deans for each deanery of monks. The overly cautious Master wants two deans in order for one of them to always be present with his subjects. St. Benedict is not specific in describing the deans' duties. He merely says the job is one of "managing all affairs according to the commandments of God and the orders of their abbot." The Master, as mentioned before, is given to details: "When these deans take charge of a group of ten brothers, they must be so solicitous for them that day or night and at any work whatever they are first of all present with them and work with them no matter what they are doing. Thus whether they are sitting, walking or standing still, by their careful supervision and alert vigilance they must ward off from them the devil's activity."[1]

There was no doubt about it: the monks of the Master's monastery were being followed and they knew it. They could not even escape from the deans when they went to bed. "The deans are to have beds near theirs . . . . And when a brother gets up and does not make his bed properly, as punishment he is not to receive any unmixed wine at the next meal."[2]

Early commentators on the *Rule of St. Benedict* do not shed much light on the role of deans in the Benedictine tradition. We know they granted permissions and made corrections. In later ages, deans supervised the monastic granges, or farms. The deans described in chapter 21 "are to be chosen for virtuous living and wise teaching, not for their rank." St. Benedict says nothing about their ability to spy. It is apparent from the Rule of the Master that the Master intends to employ sleuths as his deans. St. Benedict is more moderate, as he is in everything else. He is only looking for "the kind of men with whom the abbot can confidently share the burdens of his office." It is difficult to imagine the Master's kind of dean functioning in one of St. Benedict's monasteries.

St. Benedict wants a "virtuous" and "wise" man for a dean. "If perhaps one of these deans is found to be puffed up with any pride, and so deserving of censure, he is to be reproved once, twice and even a third time. Should he refuse to amend, he must be removed from office and replaced by another who is worthy." The abbot is still the superior of the monastery, and a dean needs to be reminded that he can be removed from office. Here again we see St. Benedict's use of moderation. He gives the misbehaving dean three warnings, three chances to reform himself. The whole *Rule* shows us how to start over again, and in so many instances St. Benedict provides not only a second chance but even a third.

This chapter speaks to all persons to whom some authority has been delegated. Avoid feelings of self-importance. If you don't, someone will have to remind you that yours is only a sharing in the office of management. You are not the boss.

CHAPTER 22

The Sleeping Arrangements of the Monks

Now St. Benedict is getting down to practical matters. He says that monks are to sleep in separate beds and that they are to use bedding that is "suitable to monastic life." In chapter 55, he will specify what is suitable: "a mat, a woolen blanket and a light covering as well as a pillow." The beds are to be "inspected frequently by the abbot, lest private possessions be found there." Until very recent times, this instruction was followed when the abbot searched our rooms every Lent. He was looking for signs of extravagance. Once he discovered fifty-five pairs of shoes under a bed.

In St. Benedict's day, a straw mattress was used. Paul Warnefrid, a monk of Monte Cassino in a later century, says that feather mattresses were allowed to the sick. I'm grateful that straw mattresses had passed out of usage by the time I entered the monastery. I suffer from hay fever.

I'm also grateful that monks no longer sleep in a dormitory. St. Benedict has other ideas, though. "If possible, all are to sleep in one place, but should the size of the community preclude this, they will sleep in groups of ten or twenty under the watchful care of seniors. A lamp must be kept burning in the room until morning."

In ancient days it was a monastic custom to sleep in a common dormitory. St. Benedict's legislation in this matter is nothing new. Monks worked, prayed, ate, and slept in common. What changed the sleeping arrangements for monks in the West? The influence of monastic orders like the Carthusians and Camaldolese. They were hermits who had their own individual cottages or cells. When Benedictines became more scholarly, this also contributed to the need for private cells. The advantage of having a room of one's own came to be regarded as a necessity and not a luxury. A monk's room is not only a place for sleeping, it is an area where he can experience solitude and be recollected.

"A lamp must be kept burning in the room until morning," St. Benedict says. The reason is obvious. Even monks have to get up in the night. There was another reason for keeping a light burning and for having the monks sleep "under the watchful care of seniors." Precautions had to be taken so that some of these monks would not be tempted by homosexual acts, which were acceptable in the Roman society they had abandoned.

"They sleep clothed, and girded with belts or cords; but they should remove their knives, lest they accidentally cut themselves in their sleep." Sleeping in the habit is another thing that I'm grateful is no longer a practice in monasteries. When I came to the monastery, I was given a night scapular. This was worn to bed—a mini-scapular without a hood on it— as a reminder that I really should be wearing the full habit to bed. One of the monks always wore his night scapular tied to his ankle because he said it choked him when he wore it on his shoulders. Nowadays we don't even have a night scapular around the house to show our young people.

The habit identified the monk, and St. Benedict sees no reason for removing this identity at night. Awake or asleep, the monk is a monk. St. Benedict, practical man that he is, has another reason for sleeping in the habit. "Thus the monks will always be ready to arise without delay when the signal is given; each will hasten to arrive at the Work of God before the others, yet with all dignity and decorum." For St. Benedict, it does not matter if his monks arrive in choir looking as if they have slept in their habits. Just so they are there on time. That is what counts, and if they wear the habit to bed at night, they won't have to waste time putting it on when they get out of bed.

"The younger brothers should not have their beds next to

each other, but interspersed among those of the seniors." Why is this? Again the reason is obvious. The young monks might hatch some mischief if they are together in one area of the dormitory. They might break the grand silence by whispering when they should be sleeping. "Monks should diligently cultivate silence at all times, but especially at night" (ch. 42).

"On arising for the Work of God, they will quietly encourage each other, for the sleepy like to make excuses." Here is advice that pertains to all of us who follow the *Rule*—get out of bed and get going. When monks lived in a dormitory, it was easier for them to encourage one another to get out of bed. The custom when I entered the monastery and for several years thereafter was to have wakers go round to the rooms and rap on the doors. We were expected to respond with "Deo gratias." The waker kept beating on the door until he heard the monk thank God for being wakened. Sometimes the response did not convey much gratitude to either God or the waker.

Wakers were eventually replaced by a buzzer, a battleship horn procured from Army-Navy surplus. Someone had to get up ahead of time to buzz the buzzer, and it was decided this would be a good responsibility for the novices. One year we had a novice who happened to be observing his twenty-first birthday in the week he was assigned to the buzzer. He announced his birthday to the community by waking us with twenty-one blasts of the battleship horn. Now we arise on our own initiative.

In another place in the *Rule*, St. Benedict encourages us to rise from sleep, and this is good advice for all of us. "Let us get up then, at long last, for the Scriptures rouse us when they say: *It is high time for us to arise from sleep* (Rom 13:11). Let us open our eyes to the light that comes from God, and our ears to the voice from heaven that every day calls out this charge: *If you hear his voice today, do not harden your hearts* (Ps 94[95]:8)" (Prologue).

The sleeping arrangements for people who live in monasteries and those of Oblates are bound to differ, but for all of us it is not proper to oversleep or linger in bed if this means we will be late for the Work of God.

CHAPTERS 23–26

The Penal Code

St. Benedict was a holy man, but he did not live with his head in the clouds. Although some people may want to describe a monastery as a heavenly place, St. Benedict lived with monks who were not at all like angels. He knew the monastery was rooted here on earth. It was a place from which to take off for heaven, but no monk, himself included, ever got there alive. It takes us a lifetime to get ready for heaven.

In the last chapter of the *Rule*, St. Benedict says: "The reason we have written this rule is that, by observing it in monasteries, we can show that we have some degree of virtue and the beginnings of monastic life." He counts himself among those who are seeking virtue but who have not yet reached perfection. Members of Alcoholics Anonymous can understand this. Here is what they say about their program of recovery, their rule of life: "No one among us has been able to maintain anything like perfect adherence to these principles. We are not saints. The point is, that we are willing to grow along spiritual lines. The principles we have set down are guides to progress. We claim spiritual progress rather than spiritual perfection."

It is often necessary to admit we are imperfect and to ask forgiveness. Although our sins are personal, some of them offend the society in which we live. St. Benedict has ways of handling an obstinate monk who refuses to acknowledge his wrongdoing in community. There are chapters in the *Rule* known as St. Benedict's penal code.

Chapter 23, "Excommunication for Faults," sets the tone for correction. "If a brother is found to be stubborn or disobedient or proud, if he grumbles or in any way despises the holy rule and defies the orders of his seniors, he should be warned twice privately by the seniors in accord with our Lord's injunction (Matt 18:15-16)." Stubbornness, disobedience, pride, grumbling—St. Benedict dislikes all of these characteristics. His disapproval of them is expressed in other places in the *Rule*. We all know certain kinds of people who make belonging to any organization difficult. When they ignore the rules that bind the group and refuse to listen to its leaders, something has to be done. Such situations are intolerable. St. Benedict, referring to Scripture, recommends two warnings in private by the seniors of the monastery. "If your brother does something wrong, go and have it out with him alone, between your two selves. If he listens to you, you have won back your brother. If he does not listen, take one or two others along with you: the evidence of two or three witnesses is required to sustain any charge" (Matt 18:15-16).

When private confrontation fails, "he must be rebuked publicly in the presence of everyone." By "public" St. Benedict means in front of the whole community. If the monk cannot be humiliated into reforming himself, the next punitive stage is excommunication, "provided that he understands the nature of this punishment." A rebel usually knows he has gone too far when he is kicked out of the group. The unruly student knows he's had it when the scolding teacher points to the door of the classroom. But there are some troublemakers for whom not even excommunication makes an impression. Then there is only one choice left for that kind of monk. Beat some sense into him. St. Benedict says: "If however he lacks understanding, [of excommunication] let him undergo corporal punishment."

In our day, fortunately, abbots no longer submit their problem monks to corporal punishment. None of us has scars on his back. But for St. Benedict flogging was an acceptable method of discipline. He borrowed it from previous monastic leaders, and it lasted beyond his time. In fact, for a long time corporal punishment was employed by the Church at large. Remember the Spanish Inquisition? It excelled in torture.

Cardinal Hugh of St. Cher, a thirteenth-century Dominican, explained the symbolism of a bishop's (and abbot's) staff in this fashion: "The prelate's discipline must be exercised with regard to his delinquent sons; otherwise in vain will he carry the pastoral staff [crosier], in which the three duties of the shepherd are symbolized: they are to be drawn by the upper portion, governed by the middle of the staff, and struck with its lower part."[1]

St. Benedict is not unreasonable in meting out punishment. "There ought to be due proportion between the seriousness of a fault and the measure of excommunication or discipline. The abbot determines the gravity of faults" (ch. 24, "Degrees of Excommunication").

For less-serious faults, the monk is not allowed to eat with his brothers but must take his meals by himself at another time. St. Benedict does not put the monk on bread and water. He allows him to eat the same food the other monks eat, but he is not allowed to eat with them. The wayward monk is excommunicated from the communal meal. In the early Church the catechumen who was preparing for baptism had to leave after the Liturgy of the Word. He could not stay for the Eucharistic banquet because he could not yet partake of it. The errant monk of St. Benedict's monastery is told that he cannot eat with his brothers because he is no longer a part of that assembly. He is excommunicated, excluded until the time when he can again partake of the meal.

St. Benedict permits this monk to attend the Divine Office, the work to which monks should prefer nothing else, but "he will not lead a psalm or a refrain nor will he recite a reading until he has made satisfaction."

Excommunication for more serious faults is established in chapter 25. The monk's fault is so serious that he is kicked out of both the refectory and the oratory. He is even excommunicated from the communal Work of God. No one is to give him a blessing or pay any attention to him. He is cut off from the community. It is as if he doesn't exist. "He will work alone at the tasks assigned to him, living continually in sorrow and penance, pondering that fearful judgment of the Apostle: *Such a man is handed over for the destruction of his flesh that his spirit may be saved on the day of the Lord* (1 Cor 5:5)."

St. Benedict is so serious about the enforcement of excommunication that "if a brother, acting without an order from the abbot, presumes to associate in any way with an excommunicated brother, to converse with him or to send him a message, he should receive a like punishment of excommunication" (ch. 25, "Unauthorized Association with the Excommunicated"). The recalcitrant monk will be less inclined to repent and change his ways if his brothers pamper him while he is under the pain of excommunication.

Excommunication is a harsh thing, and St. Benedict uses it only after other efforts have failed to correct a stubborn, proud, grumbling, disobedient monk. Although he has indicated that there will be nothing harsh in his *Rule*, harshness is in store for the monk who disregards the limits of the law.

Do we ever use excommunication for the wrong reasons? Do we ever excommunicate, exclude people because we think they have little or nothing in common with us? Do we ever impose excommunication upon ourselves because we believe we are so much better than the people with whom we are expected to associate? Members of our family, our parish, our religious communities?

CHAPTER 27

The Abbot's Concern for the Excommunicated

Sometimes parents have to tell a child to leave the table and go to his or her room until told to come out. Our parents, if they didn't use that form of excommunication, used some other. We all grew up having our rights and privileges suppressed as the result of our having behaved improperly. Someone is usually around to correct us when we've been bad. We can lose our merits in the Scouts, be campused in college, or be demoted at work. It is not easy for a parent, a scoutmaster, a college dean, or an employer to restrict us, but this has to be done for our own good. And usually we'll admit afterward, "I really needed that."

Often enough we find ourselves in the position of being the one who imposes the punishment, the excommunication. St. Benedict provides helpful hints for the abbot who must deal with erring monks. All of us who are obligated to correct family members, business associates, or friends can find some guidelines for going about it in chapter 27 of the *Rule*.

"The abbot must exercise the utmost care and concern for wayward brothers, because *it is not the healthy who need a physician, but the sick* (Matt 9:12)." Saying, "I'm concerned about what you did" is a kinder approach than asking, "Why the hell did you do that?" Even when we have been angered by what the person to be corrected has done, we must cool down before making the correction.

St. Benedict recommends that "mature and wise brothers" go to the excommunicated monk and "urge him to be humble as a way of making satisfaction, and *console* him *lest he be overwhelmed by excessive sorrow* (2 Cor 2:7)." This is not a copout on the part of St. Benedict. He knows that a monk who is being punished may be more inclined to listen to someone besides the abbot. In your own families, one parent may have to depend on the other or on someone else in the family to get to first base with a son or daughter. There is always the chance that someone else may be able to do a better job of turning people around than you can. Other avenues have to be approached. And, of course, St. Benedict resorts to prayers. *"Let love for him be reaffirmed* (2 Cor 2:8), and let all pray for him."

In the previous chapters dealing with St. Benedict's penal code, he may have left us with the impression that the abbot should be a severe master who will go to any end in subjecting his disciples to him. He speaks in terms of warnings, public rebuke, excommunication, corporal punishment. Perhaps St. Benedict sounds more like an enraged Puritan elder than the author of a rule noted for its discretion and simplicity. We have to remember that he was a legislator making rules in a period of time much different from ours. No doubt among his monks there were both arrogant Roman aristocrats and undisciplined barbarians who had to be taught not to despise the *Rule* and not to defy the orders of the seniors.

In chapter 27, St. Benedict expresses his feelings about the relationship between the abbot and the rebellious member of the monastery. "It is the abbot's responsibility to have great concern and to act with all speed, discernment and diligence in order not to lose any of the sheep entrusted to him. He should realize that he has undertaken care of the sick, not tyranny over the healthy." The abbot is to follow the example of the Good Shepherd, who left the ninety-nine sheep and went in search of the one stray. When he finds it, he must carry it on his shoulders back to the flock. There is no doubt about St. Benedict's being a caring and loving father.

St. Benedict tells us, love the sinner but abhor the sin. Is there someone in your family or at work who needs correction? Act now, try everything, be patient.

CHAPTER 28

Those Who Refuse to Amend after Frequent Reproofs

St. Benedict is a patient father, but even so, he can endure only so much. His patience can become exhausted. After having tried everything, including prayer, ''the abbot must use the knife and amputate.'' Quoting the First Letter to the Corinthians, St. Benedict says, *''Let him depart* (1 Cor 7:15) lest one diseased sheep infect the whole flock.''

Don't become an enabler.

CHAPTER 29

Readmission of Brothers Who Leave the Monastery

This chapter refers to monks who have left the monastery on their own accord, not those who have been expelled. St. Basil, the great Patriarch of monks in the East, says, ''Surely, everyone who has been admitted to the community and then has retracted his promise should be looked upon as a sinner against God, in whose presence and to whom he pledged his consent

to the pact."[1] The Basilian monk who abandoned the cloister
was never allowed an opportunity to return. For Basil, this
turning away from monastic life was an unpardonable sacri-
lege. "The brethren are justified in never again opening their
door to these persons, even if they should apply for shelter
on some occasion when they are merely in transit."[2] Basil never
wants to see such a monk again, not even as an overnight
guest.

St. Benedict, on the other hand, is more liberal, more compassionate.

> If a brother, following his own evil ways, leaves the monas-
> tery but then wishes to return, he must first promise to make
> full amends for leaving. Let him be received back, but as a
> test of his humility he should be given the last place. If he
> leaves again, or even a third time, he should be readmitted
> under the same conditions. After this, however, he must un-
> derstand that he will be denied all prospect of return.

St. Benedict allows the runaway to return to the monastery. The fugitive monk must, however, admit his error in having abandoned the life to which he had vowed himself. If he
appears earnest, he is received back, but he loses the place he
had in the community when he abandoned it. He is a begin-
ner again.

St. Benedict is so lenient that he allows the monk to be
received back three times "under the same conditions." But
that is the limit. By then it is apparent that the monk is fickle
if he leaves and then asks to be received back a fourth time.
Three strikes and you're out. Monastics who follow the *Rule
of St. Benedict* profess stability. A person who cannot make up
his or her mind is not very stable.

The text of chapter 29 as it appears here seems both con-
cise and precise. Some commentators claim that St. Benedict
originally included those monks who were expelled from the
monastery and wished to return. Hildemar, an interpreter of

the *Rule* in the ninth century, insists that the number three was really not an absolute for St. Benedict. In the twelfth century, Peter the Venerable commented to Bernard of Clairvaux that our Lord had told St. Peter that forgiveness should be extended to seventy times seven. Although the *Rule of St. Benedict* and the Rule of the Master set the limit at three times, it seems tradition extended the number of times an apostate monk could return to the monastery.

St. Bernard, who was a stickler for following the literal interpretation of St. Benedict's *Rule,* was certainly solicitous about the readmission of monks. In a letter to an abbot, Bernard intercedes for a monk whose vocation he has recommended in the first place and who has now departed from the monastery:

> The bearer [of this letter] was lately admitted to your house at my request; but moved by foolishness and instability, he threw off the habit and left you. Because he appears to be sorry and wishes to return to you and humbly begs to be received again, I too beg you for the love of God and myself to give this penitent man a second chance and to admit him once more to your house and the habit.[3]

In a letter to another abbot, Bernard pleads for a fugitive monk who has run away before. The monk feels that he has been wronged, and Bernard takes up his case, asking that he be taken back: "Do not fear that by so doing, by thus preferring mercy to justice, you will displease the merciful and just God."[4]

In chapter 64, St. Benedict will say the abbot "must so arrange everything that the strong have something to yearn for and the weak nothing to run from." Yet there are some people for whom pressures become too great and temptations too attractive. They take flight. When the phone call comes to my home or to yours and the person on the other end asks, "May I come back?"—we reply, "Sure. Come home."

CHAPTER 30

The Manner of Reproving Boys

The *Rule* speaks of disciplining boys, but it says nothing about the training they are to receive in the monastery. Tradition establishes two types of boys who were educated by Benedictine monks from early on: the oblates who matured into full-fledged monks and the alumni who were trained for secular life. Benedictine schools are known to be places where students receive a good education and where discipline is enforced.

The *Rule* makes certain that these boys are kept in line. "Boys up to the age of fifteen should, however, be carefully controlled and supervised by everyone, provided that this too is done with moderation and common sense" (ch. 70). Chapter 45 decrees that children "are to be whipped" for making mistakes in the oratory and chapter 30 recommends "severe fasts" and "sharp strokes" for boys who misbehave. Most of us grew up in an age when physical punishment was inflicted upon children, but, really—"severe fasts" and "sharp strokes" and "whippings?" There is a great difference between a licking and a whipping. Is St. Benedict contradicting himself here? These terms of correction, in our present age anyway, do not seem to be examples of "moderation" and "common sense." If a modern monk or nun treated a young student in this fashion, he or she would be subject to arrest.

The adults in St. Benedict's monastery were also given the rod, but for those who could understand, the weight of excommunication was imposed instead. St. Benedict recognizes that "every age and level of understanding should receive appropriate treatment," but he believes the boys are not old enough to comprehend the seriousness of excommunication.

Therefore, they must "be subjected to severe fasts or checked with sharp strokes so that they may be healed."

Fortunately, we do not have to form our impression of St. Benedict from the sections of the *Rule* dealing with punishment only. From the rest of the *Rule*, we know that he hardly appears to be the kind of man who would starve or batter boys.

Chapter 30 surely applies to parents, educators, and others who are responsible for young people. It teaches them this: keep the kids under control. You can't afford to be controlled by them.

CHAPTER 31

Qualifications of the Monastery Cellarer

The cellarer should be "someone who is wise, mature in conduct, temperate, not an excessive eater, not proud, excitable, offensive, dilatory or wasteful, but God-fearing, and like a father to the whole community." If the abbot is to be the father who looks after the spiritual needs of the monastery, the cellarer is to be the father who provides for the monks' material needs. Although the cellarer has an important position in the monastery, he always has to remember that it was assigned to him by the abbot. St. Benedict tells the cellarer to follow his job description. "Let him keep to his orders."

We have changed some of our opinions about what is worldly and extravagant, but monks must still avoid making unreasonable demands on the people who procure things for them. When we are out of line, we need someone to "reasonably and humbly deny the improper request." When people live in community, it is easy to take too much for granted; it is easy to violate personal poverty by presuming that the community will provide whatever we want.

The cellarer is not responsible for the monks only. "He must show every care and concern for the sick, children, guests and the poor." The cellarer is in charge of the monastery's charitable works. This is another reason why he must have a pleasing personality. He represents the monastery to the outside world.

St. Gregory relates that during a famine, St. Benedict gave away all the food supplies of the monastery. Nothing was left in the storeroom but a little vessel of oil. The cellarer heard St. Benedict's command to give away this last bit of oil too. When St. Benedict asked if this had been done, the cellarer replied, "No. I did not. If I had, there would be none left for the community." St. Benedict was upset, but the disobedient cellarer, in this case, was not dismissed from his job. St. Benedict worked a miracle to teach the selfish cellarer a lesson:

> In the room where they were kneeling there happened to be an empty oil-cask that was covered with a lid. In the course of prayer the cask gradually filled with oil and the lid started to float on top of it. The next moment the oil was running down the sides of the cask and covering the floor. As soon as he was aware of this, Benedict ended his prayer and the oil stopped flowing. Then turning to the monk who had shown himself disobedient and wanting in confidence, he urged him again to strive to grow in faith and humility.

Parents are the cellarers of the home. They frequently have to deny permissions and purchases. Children will usually accept these refusals if the reasons are presented in a careful and gentle way. "If goods are not available to meet a request, he will offer a kind word in reply, for it is written: A kind *word is better than the best gift* (Sir 18:17)." I am sure many of you also find yourselves in this same situation at work. There are times when we all have to say no.

The cellarer "should not be prone to greed, nor be wasteful and extravagant with the goods of the monastery, but should do everything with moderation." There is the possibility that a person in this position can become puffed up with pride. He is awed by the power that has been entrusted to him. Although he is a dispenser of monastery property, he might like to think of himself as the owner of a department store. One person in this position may tend to possessiveness while another is given to prodigality. We had a cellarer once who refused to give a monk an article of clothing because it was the only one of its kind on the shelf. "That's my exact size," the monk told the cellarer. "Yes, but if I give it to you, there will be nothing left for the shelf."

St. Benedict advises the cellarer to regard "all utensils and goods of the monastery as sacred vessels of the altar, aware that nothing is to be neglected." St. Benedict wants his monks to take good care of the things belonging to the monastery. A chalice is not treated carelessly, and the monks should show the same respect for everything else they use. There was a time when, if we broke something, we had to kneel in the refectory with the broken object in our hands. Once a Brother appeared there with a tray of broken dishes. After he had said his prayer of penance for breaking the dishes, he rose to his feet, and in the process he dropped the tray and multiplied the breakage. Another time a monk held out two pieces of a crowbar. He had no reason to be mortified, however, by his destruction of monastery property in this case. We were all impressed by such strength that could break a crowbar in two.

Chapter 31 ends with St. Benedict suggesting that help be given the cellarer if providing for a large community is too much for one man. He wants the cellarer to "calmly perform the duties of his office." And he wants no one to be "disquieted or distressed in the house of God." Every household functions smoothly when the members chip in and help one another.

CHAPTER 32

The Tools and Goods of the Monastery

St. Benedict expects us to be good housekeepers. We monks probably do remarkably well for a bunch of bachelors. If St. Benedict were to show up, however, and give this monastery the white-glove test, he might find some dust. "Whoever fails to keep the things belonging to the monastery clean or treats them carelessly should be reproved."

He is rather fussy about the goods of the monastery, "that is, its tools, clothing or anything else. . . ." He wants the abbot to keep a list of the articles being used in the monastery "so that when the brothers succeed one another in their assigned tasks, he may be aware of what he hands out and what he receives back." Modern-day abbots do not keep an inventory of the things that are being used in the monastery. But monks are still conscious of the care they should take in using the tools and goods of the monastery.

St. Benedict did not like to see things fall apart. When he abandoned Rome and before he went to Subiaco, he and his housekeeper, Cyrilla, lived in a place called Affile. One day a tray she had borrowed from the neighbors fell off the table and broke. St. Gregory records what happened:

> The poor woman burst into tears; she had just borrowed this tray and now it was ruined. Benedict, who had always been a devout and thoughtful boy, felt sorry for her when he saw her weeping. Quietly picking up both the pieces, he knelt down by himself and prayed earnestly to God, even to the point of tears. No sooner had he finished his prayer than he noticed that the two pieces were joined together again, without even a mark to show where the tray had been broken. Hurrying back at once, he cheerfully reassured Cyrilla and handed her the tray in perfect condition.

There is another incident of breakage in St. Gregory's *Life* of St. Benedict. A Goth, who had entered the monastery at Subiaco, was assigned to clearing away weeds at the edge of a lake. The iron blade slipped off the handle of the sickle and flew into the water. St. Benedict repaired the sickle. Taking the handle from the Goth, he threw it into the lake. ''Immediately the iron blade rose from the bottom of the lake and slipped back onto the handle. Then he handed the tool back to the Goth and told him, 'Continue with your work now. There is no need to be upset.' '' Nowadays we have to depend on Elmer's Glue to put things like these back together.

What lesson does this short chapter of the *Rule* have for us in our age of hardware supermarkets? If tools can't be repaired, they can easily be replaced. Even so, St. Benedict wants us to take good care of everything we own and use. He is concerned about the quality of life in a home. He wants us to show some responsibility in the way we live. He is great on order—spiritual order and material order too.

We can profit from the reminders St. Benedict gives us. Whatever is broken he likes to see repaired—the borrowed tray, the Goth's sickle, us. When it comes to caring for human beings, he warns about not ''rubbing too hard to remove the rust [for fear of breaking] the vessel'' (ch. 64).

CHAPTER 33

Monks and Private Ownership

Chapter 33 gets to the point in the first sentence. "Above all, this evil practice must be uprooted and removed from the monastery." Obviously, St. Benedict has a very strong opinion about private ownership. So has Karl Marx. St. Benedict is not at all in favor of monks owning things individually. Not even "a book, writing tablets or stylus—in short, not a single item, especially since monks may not have the free disposal even of their own bodies and wills." St. Benedict prefixes this statement by saying: "We mean that without an order from the abbot, no one may presume to give, receive or retain anything as his own, nothing at all." Permission may be obtained, but we clearly understand that this is not one area in which St. Benedict wants to be particularly lenient.

St. Gregory tells us about a monk St. Benedict assigned to give conferences at a nearby convent:

> After one of these instructions they presented the monk with a few handkerchiefs, which he accepted and hid away in his habit. As soon as he got back to the abbey he received a stern reproof. "How is it," the abbot asked him, "that evil has found its way into your heart?" Taken completely by surprise, the monk did not understand why he was being rebuked, for he had entirely forgotten about the handkerchiefs. "Was I not present," the saint continued, "when you accepted those handkerchiefs from the handmaids of God and hid them away in your habit?" The offender instantly fell at Benedict's feet, confessed his fault and gave up the present he had received.

Until recent times such a practice was followed to the letter of the law in monasteries. When I was being formed in monastic ways, I would have been expected to take a gift of handkerchiefs to my superior and ask his permission to keep and use them. Even if my nose had been running as I made the request.

Failure to practice personal poverty is debilitating to the individual monk, and so is the accumulation of communal wealth. I have been made aware of my responsibility to practice poverty by the following remark which I have heard on more than one occasion: "You monks profess poverty and we lay people live it."

Although St. Benedict does not believe in excess, neither does he want his followers to live in abject poverty. He is sensible. His model of ownership is found in the Acts of the Apostles: "*All things should be the common possession* of all, as it is written, *so that no one* presumes to *call anything his own* (Acts 4:32)." People who live in community use what they hold in common.

There may be members of your own household who have to be reminded that a particular item—the car or the telephone—does not belong to him or her personally. It is for the use of the whole family. Chapter 33 also advises all of us about the procurement of things that are needed and things that are not, what is essential and what is extravagant. It says something about sharing, something about being satisfied with what is provided for us.

CHAPTER 34

Distribution of Goods According to Need

St. Benedict quotes from the same chapter of Acts as he did in the previous chapter of the Rule: "It is written: *Distribution was made to each one as he had need* (Acts 4:35)." He is telling the monks their lifestyle should be like that of the early Christians. "The whole group of believers was united, heart and soul; no one claimed for his own use anything that he had, as everything they owned was held in common" (Acts 4:32-33). Some monks, however, require more goods for reasons of occupation or health or other legitimate needs. St. Benedict does not look upon this as "favoritism" but as "consideration of weaknesses." The modern Benedictine whose needs exceed those of a confrere's is not inclined to think of himself as a weak human being. When he asks the abbot for a computer, it is efficiency and saving time that are on his mind. Making use of the inventions in our technological age is surely not a sign of weakness, he thinks. After all, St. Benedict wants his monks to be practical.

In the beginning of my monastic life, we had no television set. Now we have four. No one had an electric typewriter for his personal use. Now there are a number of them, all under service contract. And in those days who needed a blow dryer for his hair? Certainly not the novices. Their heads were shorn. Cassette players, video machines, computers, microwave ovens—they've all come on the market since I entered the monastery, and they've all been deemed necessary by us monks.

Yet St. Benedict reminds us again that our personal needs are the result of weakness. "Whoever needs less should thank God and not be distressed, but whoever needs more should feel humble because of his weakness, not self-important because of the kindness shown him. In this way all the members will be at peace."

We live in peace with our modern gadgets and see nothing wrong in this. Things began to change with the invention of the printing press. If they had not, we would still be copying texts by hand in the scriptorium. A monastery today needs machines. St. Benedict, in the sixth century, said that a monastery should have "all necessities" within it (ch. 66). Times change and so do needs. But some monks have greater needs than others. The monk who needs more must be cautious about weakening his practice of personal poverty. Living in luxury is an inexcusable weakness for the monk.

Although every monk professes poverty, monasteries are not inhabited by poor people. The corporate wealth of monasteries has come under attack throughout history. The Protestant Reformers were critical of the part our wealth played in the decline of morals and discipline in monastic life. So were two of their contemporaries who did not break with the Church of Rome, Erasmus and St. Thomas More. St. Benedict's insistence that a monastery should be self-sufficient was often carried to extremes when monks procured more than they needed. Although we are more careful about what we accumulate nowadays, we still give the impression of being well off. The truth of the matter is that monks live comfortably, even in those monasteries that are known for their austerity. The carpet and furniture in our lobby were new when Dorothy Day visited my monastery. She made the observation that "No poor man will be at ease coming to your front door." I knew we had just been reprimanded by a saint, but even Dorothy Day, who was espoused to a life of poverty, often had to admit that she and her Catholic Workers were better off materially than the people they fed and clothed.

Fortunately, there are always monks living among us who provide an example of needing less. I can think of Brother Robert who had been a successful farmer before entering the monastery at the age of fifty. His room was bare: a bed, a small table, a chair and a number ten tin can into which he spat tobacco juice. When he died, it didn't take long to dispose of the articles in his room. Sometimes the infirmarian spends days cleaning out a room from which a monk has departed for eternity, leaving everything behind.

In his goodness, St. Benedict realizes that some of us have needs that merit special attention. But he says to me and to you, be certain that your needs are really valid. Don't go to pieces if, for some reason, your needs cannot be met. Don't begrudge your neighbor who appears to have more than you have. "First and foremost, there must be no word or sign of the evil of grumbling, no manifestation of it for any reason at all." He is advising us in chapter 34 that not everyone has to try keeping up with the Joneses.

CHAPTER 35

Kitchen Servers of the Week

St. Benedict begins this chapter by repeating a favorite theme of his: "The brothers should serve one another." In this case he is referring to an essential service from which it is not easy to be excused. "Consequently, no one will be excused from kitchen service unless he is sick or engaged in some important business of the monastery, for such service increases reward and fosters love." For a long time now most monks have been engaged in other businesses of the monastery that have been considered important enough to keep them out of the kitchen. My own community doesn't know how lucky it is that I've never had to take my turn at cooking.

St. Benedict says: "Let those who are not strong have help so that they may serve without distress, and let everyone receive help as the size of the community or local conditions warrant." We have to depend on help from outside in our kitchen. No doubt St. Benedict would approve. It was not uncommon for monasteries to have some lay employees even in his day. St. Benedict wants no one to be oppressed by his work in the monastery. Help is to be sought from other monks or wherever it can be found.

St. Benedict wants the abbot to "regulate and arrange all matters that souls may be saved and the brothers may go about their activities without justifiable grumbling'' (ch. 41). In chapter 35 he recommends that ''an hour before mealtime, the kitchen workers of the week should each receive a drink and some bread over and above the regular portion, so that at mealtime, they may serve their brothers without grumbling or hardship.'' He cannot stand complaining monks, and he likes to see to it that there is no reason for grumbling, even ''justifiable grumbling.''

Saturday was cleanup day in the kitchen. The monk who was completing his turn at cooking had to wash the towels that the monks had used all week to dry their hands and feet. The *lavatorium,* or laver, was located near the refectory in medieval monasteries. This is where the monks washed before meals. Not only did the kitchen server have to launder the monks' towels, he had to wash the feet of all the monks too. ''Both the one who is ending his service and the one who is about to begin are to wash the feet of everyone.'' This is in imitation of our Lord, who washed his disciples' feet at the meal on Holy Thursday. It was an ancient monastic custom. St. Basil told hermits that it was impossible for them to follow this example of Christ's humility and love for the brethren. ''The Lord,'' he said, ''out of the fullness of his abundant love, did not content himself with teaching his disciples by word of mouth, but also gave them a clear and unmistakable proof of his humility and perfect love by girding himself with a towel and washing their feet.''[1] Basil asked the hermits: Whose feet will you wash?

The utensils used for cooking were to be handed over spic and span to the cellarer by the cook at the end of his week's service. The cellarer would then give them to next week's cook. The kitchen at Monte Cassino did not have all the pots and pans that are used in a modern-day monastic kitchen. If it were required of a modern-day monastery cook to turn in all his gear to the cellarer, he would have to start delivery before Saturday.

"On Sunday immediately after Lauds, those beginning as well as those completing their week of service should make a profound bow in the oratory before all and ask for their prayers." The kitchen servers are blessed in and blessed out. Their service to the community is deserving of a blessing.

In a monastic home, as well as in yours, a little help is always appreciated in getting the meals to the table. In both places we should "serve one another in love."

CHAPTER 36

The Sick Brothers

"Care of the sick must rank above and before all else, so that they may truly be served as Christ, for he said: *"I was sick and you visited me* (Matt 25:36), and, *What you did for one of these least brothers you did for me* (Matt 25:40)."

St. Benedict makes space for an infirmary in his monastery. Although modern Benedictines are hospitalized and even though some hospitals are operated by Benedictine Sisters who exercise care for the sick in the manner St. Benedict prescribes, every Benedictine house still has its infirmary for the care of the sick and aged. The infirmarian is assured by St. Benedict that this patient labor will be rewarded. The sick, for their part, are not to make excessive demands on the people looking after them. St. Benedict knew there would always be some monks who would enjoy their poor health by expecting special favors and permissions.

North Americans probably bathe more frequently than any other people on earth. Perhaps even our ancestors, who had to heat their bath water once a week on a wood-burning stove, would have considered St. Benedict's attitude about bathing somewhat strange. He says the sick may bathe "whenever it is advisable, but the healthy, and especially the young, should receive permission less readily." This should not lead us to believe that his monks did not have good hygienic habits. They did wash, but taking a bath—that was something exceptional.

A bath was a luxury, something in which the rich indulged. St. Benedict, no doubt, had another reason for not liking baths. He was aware of the public Roman baths, which were the massage parlors of his day. Paul Warnefrid, the eighth-century Monte Cassino monk and commentator on the *Rule,* believed that St. Benedict wanted the sick to have a bath daily, maybe even two baths if necessary. This is quite lenient. As for the healthy and the young, Warnefrid says there are various opinions. Some monks thought that it was proper to bathe three times a year: at Christmas, Easter, and Pentecost. At any rate, St. Benedict does make a concession to the sick in this matter. He also allows them to eat meat in order to regain their strength. The healthy are to abstain from meat. Once again we see that St. Benedict is a sensible and considerate father of the monastery.

He says the sick are to "be served by an attendant who is God-fearing, attentive and concerned." Brother Alexius, who was our infirmarian when I came to the monastery, was this kind of an attendant. He actually empathized with his patients. After one of us had been treated for a particular ailment, he would follow us around the rest of the day asking, "How is *my* sore throat?" or "How is *my* earache?" or "Do you still have *my* headache?" Brother Alexius was conscientious about dispensing pills. He had every aspirin counted. And there was a counting routine in administering them. How well I remember the times he would follow me to the drinking fountain and tell me, "Now take seven swallows in honor of the Seven Sorrows of Mary."

The monastery infirmary is the place where all of us hope to spend our declining years. My mother, who lived in a nurs-

ing home for the last thirteen years of her life, was often confused about my status in life. Once she asked me if I had a
good job and a good salary. I told her that I didn't get paid
for my work. "I live in a monastery, Mother." She said, "Isn't
it nice that they have places for people like us?"

Chapter 36 speaks of the concern we should have for the
sick, but it also tells us how to behave when we are sick. "Let
the sick on their part bear in mind that they are served out
of honor for God, and let them not by their excessive demands
distress their brothers who serve them."

CHAPTER 37

The Elderly and Children

"**A**lthough human nature itself is inclined to be compassionate toward the old and the young, the authority of the rule
should also provide for them." But this short chapter, apart
from relaxing the dietary practice of the monastery for the old
and the young, is not specific about how they should be
treated. "Since their lack of strength must always be taken into
account, they should certainly not be required to follow the
strictness of the rule with regard to food, but should be treated
with kindly consideration and allowed to eat before the regular hours." Thus ends chapter 37, "The Elderly and Children."

While being solicitous for both the young and the old in
this chapter of the *Rule*, St. Benedict cautions elsewhere that
boys should not waste food by being given too much to eat.
"Young boys should not receive the same amount as their
elders, but less, since in all matters frugality is the rule" (ch.
39). The young are mentioned in other chapters of the *Rule*,
but the old are recognized infrequently. In chapter 63, St. Benedict describes the respect the young monks should have for

their seniors, but a senior monk is not necessarily an aged one. Perhaps it is not necessary to say much about the elderly. They have persevered in the monastery to old age. They have already learned to do the things by which they will profit eternity. It is the young who need to learn how to "progress in this way of life and in faith" (Prologue). The young referred to in chapter 37 are, of course, the boys who dwell in the monastery, some of them sons whose parents have offered them to the monastery.

These days children are abused, and the elderly are neglected. St. Benedict prevents this from happening in his monastery. We, who follow his *Rule,* should "be compassionate toward the old and the young" wherever we live.

CHAPTER 38

The Reader for the Week

"Reading will always accompany the meals of the brothers." This is for the edification and instruction of the monks, not to prevent them from verbally complaining about the meals. "Let there be complete silence. No whispering, no speaking— only the reader's voice should be heard there."

Reading is a weekly assignment, and like serving at table, the reader receives a blessing for the work he will perform. St. Benedict allows the reader to have some "diluted wine" before reading. The reader had been fasting for Communion, and after having received the Eucharist, he went to the refectory to read. There is a danger that a particle of the host might be left in his mouth and he might spit it out while reading. A cup of wine will prevent this from happening. Adding water to the wine is good advice. You can imagine what might occur if the table reader approached the lectern on an empty stomach and under the influence of undiluted wine.

St. Benedict ends the chapter by asking that only those monks who have the ability to read well should be assigned the job. He wants to be certain that the hearers are benefited by the table reading.

Although chapter 38 is addressed to the table reader of the week, St. Benedict reminds us of the concern we should have for the people who are seated at table with us for a meal. "The brothers should by turn serve one another's needs as they eat and drink, so that no one need ask for anything." Serving one another at table is a courtesy that applies in my home and yours. St. Benedict's *Rule* reminds us to be courteous.

CHAPTER 39

The Proper Amount of Food

In chapter 39 we see once more how St. Benedict legislates with common sense and moderation. "Two kinds of cooked food, therefore, should suffice for all the brothers, and if fruit or fresh vegetables are available, a third dish may also be added. A generous pound of bread is enough . . . for both dinner and supper."

I'm sure preparing meals in St. Benedict's day was much easier than cooking for monks in our day. The monks ate only two meals and sometimes, depending on the season of the year, only one. What were the cooked foods they ate? St. Benedict does not name them in chapter 39, but we do know that the cook at Monte Cassino never burned the community's roast. "Let everyone, except the sick who are very weak, abstain entirely from eating the meat of four-footed animals."

Some commentators on monastic observance believe that it was legitimate for monks to eat fowl. Birds have only two legs. Fowl, along with fish, was regarded as suitable abstinence fare in the Middle Ages and for many years after. St. Benedict, however, says nothing about bipeds in the *Rule,* and it seems likely that he would have followed the practices of earlier monastic legislators who banned meat in any form.

If the work "is heavier than usual," the abbot may allow something additional. St. Benedict wants no one to go away from the table hungry. The reason for having two cooked dishes is that "the person who may not be able to eat one kind of food may partake of the other." There will always be something for the monks to eat, even the finicky and those with delicate stomachs. No doubt St. Benedict had them in his monastery too.

In the late Middle Ages, monks, unfortunately, came to be caricaturized as gluttons. Monks were often portrayed as corpulent fanciers of gourmet foods. Gout was a monastic disease.

St. Bernard of Clairvaux wrote to a young man who had abandoned the Cistercians' strict interpretation of the *Rule* and had gone to the Benedictines at Cluny where observance had become lax:

> "Wine and white bread, honeyed wine, and rich foods cater to the body, not the soul. The body but not the soul is fattened from frying pans. Many fathers in Egypt served God over long stretches without even fish. Pepper, ginger, cumin, sage and a thousand other such spices delight the palate but they inflame the passions. Will you place your safety on such things, will you spend your teenage years safely in their midst?"[1]

For a long time many people believed that eating too much meat and spicy food caused the arousal of the passions. This was a good reason for monks to stick to a well-balanced, bland diet. When I came to the monastery, there was a bag of saltpeter on our kitchen shelf. It has since disappeared.

What St. Benedict wants to stress above all in chapter 39 of the *Rule* is the avoidance of overindulging. He does not want a monk to "experience indigestion. For nothing is so inconsistent with the life of any Christian as overindulgence." Indigestion is a common experience for most people in a nation like ours. Isn't it remarkable that we—you and I—can be reminded of this pitfall by an abbot in a sixth-century rule of life? St. Benedict is always speaking to us today.

CHAPTER 40

The Proper Amount of Drink

Many families today have members who are chemically dependent. So have monasteries. There is a stereotyped image of the medieval monk who spends more time in the wine cellar than in the chapel. Visitors who come for tours sometimes ask to see our wine cellar. Everyone knows that monks drink. Therefore, it should not be surprising that some monks are alcoholics.

St. Benedict says, "We read that monks should not drink at all, but since the monks of our day cannot be convinced of this, let us at least agree to drink moderately, and not to the point of excess, for *wine makes even wise men go astray* (Sir 19:2)." Not all monks have succeeded in drinking moderately.

Records of monastic visitations in sixteenth-century England refer to a monastery that owned a tavern in the village where a good part of the community "sought solace." In another monastery, the prior was "a bad-tempered drunkard." Martin Luther castigated monks for excessive drinking. Chaucer and Rabelais ridiculed them.

If monks are depicted as sots in history and literature, they have an even greater reputation for the positive contribution they have made to viticulture. European monasteries produced excellent wines and liqueurs throughout the Middle Ages. The Reformation in Germany and the Revolution in France ended much of this monastic enterprise. But monks, and nuns too, have been able to preserve the tradition, although not many of them are involved commercially nowadays.

When the German Benedictines came to Pennsylvania in the last century, Abbot Boniface Wimmer was discouraged to discover the temperance movement in full swing and an Irish bishop who had evidently taken the pledge. Bishop O'Connor opposed the running of a brewery over which St. Vincent's Abbey had control. Wimmer complained to Pope Pius IX, who said, "Germans and not drinking beer. That is much." "Yes indeed," Wimmer said, "until now we could do so, being young, but when we grow older, we will probably be in necessity to make beer." The Pope replied, "Of course. St. Paul also wrote to St. Timothy he should take a little wine for his weak stomach, and so you must have something."[1]

St. Benedict admits "uneasiness" in specifying the amount of drink. He permits "a half bottle of wine a day" for each monk, advising the abbot to "take great care lest excess or drunkenness creep in." Every abbot knows that precautions will not guarantee complete sobriety in his community. After all, St. Benedict himself says monks cannot be convinced. He also says if the amount of wine has to be reduced or not consumed at all, the monks "should bless God and not grumble."

Quoting First Corinthians, St. Benedict begins chapter 40 in this way: "*Everyone has his own gift from God, one this and another that* (1 Cor 7:7)." Abstinence is a gift. The monk who is a recovering alcoholic knows that he has been blessed by God. So does every other man or woman who is recovering from alcoholism. St. Benedict tells them, "Those to whom God gives the strength to abstain must know that they will earn their own reward."

St. Benedict is by no means a teetotaler, but he does advise moderation in drink and everything else.

CHAPTER 41

The Times for the Brothers' Meals

There is an exercise room in our monastery, and some of the overweight monks use it. Probably none of us would be overweight if chapter 41 of the *Rule* were observed as it is written. Nowadays we eat meals three times a day all year long, and we have two daily community coffee breaks at which leftover desserts are served. We can raid the kitchen whenever we wish, and even though one area of it is locked up at ten o'clock in the evening, we all know where the key is kept. In St. Benedict's day, the monks ordinarily ate only two meals a day, and for a good part of the year they ate only one. And, of course, the *Rule* says nothing about coffee breaks.

"From holy Easter to Pentecost, the brothers eat at noon and take supper in the evening." St. Benedict begins this chapter by setting the times for meals in the paschal season. In this joyous season of the liturgical year, there is no reason for the monks to fast. But: "Beginning with Pentecost and continuing throughout the summer, the monks fast until midafternoon on Wednesday and Friday, unless they are working in the fields or the summer heat is oppressive. On the other days they eat dinner at noon."

St. Benedict is quick to introduce monastic fast days, but he is prudent. "Indeed, the abbot may decide that they should continue to eat dinner at noon every day (including Wednesday and Friday) if they have work in the fields or if the summer heat remains extreme. Similarly, he should so regulate and arrange all matters that souls may be saved and the brothers may go about their activities without justifiable grumbling." Fasting should not be carried to an extreme. He wants to hear no complaints about fasting or anything else that is done in the monastery. How well we know that by now.

"From the thirteenth of September to the beginning of Lent, they always take their meal in the midafternoon." Now St. Benedict has the monks cut down to one meal, and that is in the middle of the afternoon. This was known as the "monastic Lent." When the season of Lent began for the Church universally, the monks continued to eat only one meal, but it was served even later in the day. "Finally, from the beginning of Lent to Easter, they eat towards evening."

St. Benedict ends chapter 41 with some practical advice about dining late. "Let Vespers be celebrated early enough so that there is no need for a lamp while eating, and that everything can be finished by daylight. Indeed, at all times let supper or the hour of the fast-day meal be so scheduled that everything can be done by daylight." There are to be no candlelight suppers in the monastery, even in an age when there are no electric lights. St. Benedict says, eat while you still have the natural light. The table reader will be able to see more clearly what he is reading. The table waiter will see when he is being beckoned, and the rest of the monks will see what they are eating. One commentator has suggested that if the monks ate in the dark, they would be inclined to whisper among themselves and pull shenanigans.

St. Gregory describes an occasion when St. Benedict did not dine before dark:

> Once when the saintly abbot was taking his evening meal, a young monk whose father was a high-ranking official happened to be holding the lamp for him. As he stood at the abbot's table the spirit of pride began to stir in his heart. "Who is this," he thought to himself, "that I should have to stand here holding the lamp for him while he is eating? Who am I to be serving him?" Turning to him at once, Bene-

dict gave the monk a sharp reprimand. "Brother," he said, "sign your heart with the sign of the Cross. What are you saying? Sign your heart!" Then calling the others together, he had one of them take the lamp instead, and told the murmurer to sit down by himself and be quiet.

From this little incident of St. Benedict's eating late, we learn again that exceptions to the rule can be made, but the story reveals once more that there are no exceptions for murmuring monks.

There is another occasion when St. Benedict bent the rule— the night he dined out with his sister:

> His sister Scholastica, who had been consecrated to God in early childhood, used to visit with him once a year. On these occasions he would go down to meet her in a house belonging to the monastery a short distance from the entrance. For this particular visit he joined her there with a few of his disciples and they spent the whole day singing God's praises and conversing about the spiritual life. When darkness was setting in, they took their meal together and continued their conversation at table until it was quite late. Then the holy nun said to him, "Please do not leave me tonight, brother. Let us keep on talking about the joys of heaven till morning."
>
> "What are you saying, sister" he replied. "You know I cannot stay away from the monastery."

She prayed up a rain storm which prevented him from leaving. They continued breaking the night silence until dawn. St. Benedict bent his rules for her sake. In being charitable to his sister, he was not aware that this would be the last time he saw her.

> The next morning Scholastica returned to her convent and Benedict to his monastery. Three days later as he stood in his room looking up toward the sky, he beheld his sister's soul leaving her body and entering the heavenly court in the form of a dove.

In chapter 41 we see again St. Benedict's penchant for establishing good order in his monastery. No doubt you also appreciate having meals served on schedule in your home. Perhaps it is often difficult these days, when there are so many commitments outside of the home, to have the whole family seated together for a meal. St. Benedict thinks eating together is a good communal practice. Perhaps members of your household will have to be reminded that meals should be familial. The story of St. Benedict and St. Scholastica's last meal together on earth illustrates how important it is for families to be together.

CHAPTER 42

Silence after Compline

The silence after Compline should be rigorously enforced. ''On leaving Compline, no one will be permitted to speak further. If anyone is found to transgress this rule of silence, he must be subjected to severe punishment.'' There are exceptions to the rule, however: ''on occasions when guests require attention or the abbot wishes to give someone a command, but even this is to be done with the utmost seriousness and proper restraint.''

For many people silence is a luxury. For Benedictines it is a necessity. That is why people come to Benedictine houses seeking silence, and we are glad to offer them a respite from the noises that surround them in their everyday environment.

In St. Benedict's day, the silence after Compline was especially necessary because that was bedtime. The monks had to catch some sleep before the Office of Vigils. This is the case even today with the Cistercians, who rise between three and four o'clock.

Whenever the Benedictine Order has had to be reformed, the restoration of silence has been given top priority. The first sentence of chapter 42 of the *Rule* indicates that "Monks should diligently cultivate silence at all times, but especially at night." In the next sentence St. Benedict begins outlining the public spiritual reading that precedes Compline, the night prayer. "Accordingly, this will always be the arrangement whether for fast days or for ordinary days. When there are two meals, all the monks will sit together immediately after rising from supper. Someone should read from the *Conferences* [by John Cassian, a fifth-century abbot] or the *Lives* of the Fathers [the wisdom literature of the monks of the East] or at any rate something else that will benefit the hearers." There are certain books of the Bible that he forbids, though. Too much sex and violence. "It will not be good for those of weak understanding to hear these writings at that hour." No doubt he is thinking of the boy oblates, but he may have in mind some of the monks too. These parts of Scripture, he says, "should be read at other times" but not at bedtime.

"On fast days there is to be a short interval between Vespers and the reading of the *Conferences,* as we have indicated. Then let four or five pages be read, or as many as time permits. This reading period will allow for all to come together, in case any were engaged in assigned tasks. When all have assembled, they should pray Compline."

We used to have public reading before Compline. Father Daniel brought down the house one night when he was the prayer leader of the week for the first time in a long time. He had recently been assigned to the abbey after having spent many years in the missions, and he was nervous about getting things right at Divine Office. His breviary had several markers in it with notes on what to do next. After finishing the spiritual reading and about to lead us into Compline, he dropped his breviary, and all his instructions to himself fell

out. "Oh hell!" he said. That night there was no silence before Compline began, and some of us held our sides all through
Compline.

Compline is the last hour of the Divine Office. It is the night
prayer. The day's work has ended, the last of communal prayer
has been said, and now the monk must calmly and quietly
enter the night. Chapter 42 does not impose night silence on
an Oblate, but it does suggest once again that a time of silence
in your life is of great value.

CHAPTER 43

Tardiness at the Work of God or at Table

"On hearing the signal for an hour of the divine office, the
monk will immediately set aside what he has in hand and go
with utmost speed, yet with gravity and without giving occasion for frivolity. Indeed, nothing is to be preferred to the Work
of God." In a Benedictine monastery many different kinds of
work are performed by the individual monks, but their most
significant work is the Work of God. This is the communal
work of a monastery, and St. Benedict wants the monks to be
on time for it. Considering our human weakness, though, he
suggests that the invitatory psalm for Vigils (the first of the
hours) "be said quite deliberately and slowly" for the benefit
of monks who have difficulty getting to church on time, for
monks who are slow about getting out of bed. They are not
late as long as they arrive in the oratory when Psalm 94, the
call to praise, is being recited. Again considering our human
weakness, St. Benedict says, come in even if you are late. You
may have to sit in the last place but come in anyway. "They
should come inside so that they will not lose everything and
may amend in the future."

St. Benedict bends over backward in order to stretch out the time allowed for the monks to arrive in choir.

> At the day hours the same rule applies to anyone who comes after the opening verse and the "Glory be to the Father" of the first psalm following it: he is to stand in the last place. Until he has made satisfaction, he is not to presume to join the choir of those praying the psalms, unless perhaps the abbot pardons him and grants an exception. Even in this case, the one at fault is still bound to satisfaction.

In years gone by, we made satisfaction when we were late for Office by kneeling in the middle of choir and then standing and bowing an apology to each side of choir. This practice has been discontinued, even though monks still come late for Office.

Surprisingly, St. Benedict is more insistent on promptness in the refectory than he is on promptness for chapel attendance. There is no leeway here. "But, if anyone does not come to table before the verse so that all may say the verse and pray and sit down at table together, and if this failure happens through the individual's own negligence or fault, he should be reproved up to the second time."

For St. Benedict a community meal is a kind of liturgy, an extension of the Eucharistic banquet. Meals begin and end with prayer. Jesus served his disciples at the Last Supper, and the monks do the same when they eat. The monastery refectory is a place where monks practice charity. "The brothers should by turn serve one another's needs as they eat and drink, so that no one need ask for anything" (ch. 38).

If a monk is habitually late for meals and makes no effort to change his ways, St. Benedict says the offender should be forced to eat alone. If being separated from the community doesn't teach him a lesson, there is another punishment that will. "His portion of wine should be taken away until there is satisfaction and amendment."

Community meals are so important for St. Benedict that he prohibits monks from presuming "to eat or drink before or after the time appointed." Dining is a communal act. "Moreover, if anyone is offered something by a superior and refuses it, then, if later he wants what he refused or anything else, he should receive nothing at all until he has made appropriate amends." This, commentators say, refers to the breaking of a fast that a superior deems necessary. But the monk, in his pride, says: No! I'll show you! If the monk changes his mind, the superior must say: No. Not until you apologize for your obstinacy.

In chapter 43, St. Benedict speaks to all of us once again about the priority we should have for prayer in our lives. He asks us to be prompt when it's time to pray. And he tells us not to keep other people waiting for us at table. How often those of you who are parents have had to say, "Hurry up. It's time for church" and "Stop fooling around and come to the table." St. Benedict reminds us that the same commands have to be issued to adults sometimes—even to ourselves. St. Benedict helps us to be on time wherever we're supposed to be.

CHAPTER 44

Satisfaction by the Excommunicated

St. Benedict returns to the excommunicated in this chapter. "Anyone excommunicated for serious faults from the oratory and from the table is to prostrate himself in silence at the oratory entrance at the end of the celebration of the Work of God." That is only part one of the monk's making satisfaction. When the abbot tells him, the excommunicated must prostrate himself at the abbot's feet and then before all the brothers, asking their prayers. With this accomplished, the offender is allowed back into choir, but he may not "presume to lead a psalm or a reading or anything else in the oratory without further instructions from the abbot." At the end of every hour of the Divine Office, the monk is instructed to prostrate himself at the place where he prays. All of this is for grave faults.

"Those excommunicated for less serious faults from the table only are to make satisfaction in the oratory for as long as the abbot orders. They do so until he gives his blessing and says: 'Enough.'"

St. Benedict does not wish to prolong the monk's penances, but he is adamant about seeing that they are done.

Whenever we participate in the sacrament of reconciliation, we expect to receive a penance for our sins. The excommunicated monk has to do the penances described in chapter 44 in order to become reconciled with his community. Making satisfaction is both penance and apology. St. Benedict asks that reparation be made for serious faults, and all of us should certainly be considerate enough to beg forgiveness for even the smallest faults by which we offend people. Making satisfaction is not just the monk's responsibility.

CHAPTER 45

Mistakes in the Oratory

The Master, in his Rule, says, "Care must be taken while singing that there is not a lot of frequent coughing or prolonged gasping or constant spitting."[1] St. Benedict does not draw his monks' attention to such crudities when they are at prayer, but he does say, "Should anyone make a mistake in a psalm, responsory, refrain or reading, he must make satisfaction there before all." No doubt there have been times when you wished that the person beside you in church could be called to task for being disruptive, for singing too loudly, or giving a response that is not in unison with the rest of the congregation. Such a person is usually not even aware of how annoying he or she is. St. Benedict wants us to be aware, to be conscious of our mistakes. His monastery is a place where people pray together all the time. They must be polite. They must help one another pray well collectively. The Work of God is something that monks should do with great care because it is the work that they value most highly.

Satisfaction must be made for mistakes, St. Benedict says. "If he does not use this occasion to humble himself, he will be subjected to more severe punishment for failing to correct by humility the wrong committed through negligence." St. Benedict, however, does not indicate the exact manner of satisfaction a monk is to make for a mistake in the oratory, nor the type of punishment that will be administered for not making satisfaction. An apology is appropriate, though—not only to the fellow monks but to God for faulty prayer in God's praise.

St. Benedict is more definite about the boys over whom the monks have charge. "Children, however, are to be whipped for such a fault." Anyone who has been to a boarding school run by Benedictine monks or nuns knows that you can't fool around in church. Benedictines are serious about liturgy.

And so are their Oblates. "Oblates highly esteem the holy sacrifice of the Mass and take an active and intelligent part in the celebration of the sacred mysteries of the altar" (Guidelines For Oblates Of St. Benedict).

CHAPTER 46

Faults Committed in Other Matters

"**If** someone commits a fault while at any work—while working in the kitchen, in the storeroom, in serving, in the bakery, in the garden, in any craft or anywhere else—either by breaking or losing something or failing in any other way in any other place, he must at once come before the abbot and community and of his own accord admit his fault and make satisfaction."

A monastic community, like the members of your own household, needs to be informed when something is broken or lost. An apology is expected from the person who is responsible. If the guilty party conceals the fact and knowledge of the accident or loss is made known by someone else, the offender is usually entitled to a good chewing out. "If it is made known through another, he [the one who broke or lost something] is to be subjected to a more severe correction." Have you ever spanked a child for not telling you about his or her misdeed? Why didn't you tell me? Haven't you asked that in either a bubbling or advanced state of anger?

This explains why the chapter of faults was instituted in monasteries. Rather than go before the abbot "at once" to confess his fault, the clumsy monk, along with his brothers who are prone to disaster, confesses his wrongdoing in a ceremony known as the "chapter of faults," or public *culpa*. We have retained the custom in my monastery. Although other observances have disappeared in the age of updating, *culpa* has remained because monks continue to have faults. We are always breaking things or losing them.

St. Benedict lists certain areas of the monastery where faults are committed: the kitchen, storeroom, bakery, garden. But there are other places, he says, and other faults besides breaking or losing things. Some monks need to apologize for being inexcusably absent from community prayer, for failing to do their part in this community work. Other monks sometimes confess laziness in tending to both prayer and work. Monks have numerous faults that handicap the monastery's operation. A lot of things get broken in the monastery. I broke the vacuum sweeper twice in the same careless way. But it's not just material things that get broken. Charity is destroyed sometimes, and this must be confessed too. Our faults even accompany us when we are away from the monastery. "For faults committed outside the monastery" is often heard at our *culpa*. I always wait for the details, but seldom are they given.

There are certain matters that we cannot admit in public. St. Benedict takes this into account. "When the cause of the sin lies hidden in his conscience, he is to reveal it only to the abbot or to one of the spiritual elders, who know how to heal their own wounds as well as those of others, without exposing them and making them public."

The *Rule of St. Benedict* is designed to help us improve our lives. "Conversion" is the term that best describes this procedure. Benedictines make it a vow. Oblates accept this same responsibility when they promise to live according to the *Rule of St. Benedict*. Conversion is an ongoing process for all of us. It is not accomplished by leaps and bounds. Conversion is a daily practice. It requires perseverance. St. Benedict is realistic when he tells us we have to work at our conversion "until death" (Prologue). We plug along. Admitting failure is a good indication that we are sincere about this work of conversion. St. Benedict wants his followers to be humble and honest enough to admit they are not saints. Yet.

CHAPTER 47

Announcing the Hours for the Work of God

"It is the abbot's care to announce, day and night, the hour for the Work of God. He may do so personally or delegate the responsibility to a conscientious brother, so that everything may be done at the proper time." Chapter 47 imposes upon the abbot the obligation to see that the Divine Office begins on time. A modern abbot does not ring the tower bell to summon his monks to prayer, but chapter 47 does explain why it is the abbot who strikes the gavel or intones "O God come to our assistance" when all the monks have assembled in the choir stalls for the beginning of one of the hours of the Divine Office.

How did the abbot or the "conscientious brother" delegated by him rouse the monks from sleep? In chapter 22, St. Benedict says the monks should sleep in their habits: "Thus the monks will always be ready to arise without delay when the signal is given." What is the signal? Commentators believe a variety of noisemakers were used in pre-Benedictine monasteries, but it is thought that a bell or handbell was used to wake St. Benedict's monks.

St. Pachomius, who had been a soldier in the Roman army, used a trumpet for the signal in his monastery in Egypt. What had worked for calling troops to battle now brought monks to prayer. "And when he has heard the noise of the trumpet, calling to a gathering, let him immediately leave his cell, meditating on something from scripture until he reaches the door of the place of assembly."[1]

The second part of chapter 47 tells us that after the monks in St. Benedict's monastery have assembled for prayer "only those so authorized are to lead psalms and refrains, after the abbot according to their rank. No one should presume to read or sing unless he is able to benefit the hearers; let this be done with humility, seriousness and reverence, and at the abbot's bidding." Not everyone in your parish is expected to be a lector or cantor, nor is every monk in the monastery expected to lead the community in prayer or to read and sing the lessons. In either case, the assignment should be given to someone who will "benefit the hearers."

In medieval monasteries there was an official called the "precentor." He trained the monks who were to sing and read in choir, and he taught reading to the boy oblates who would one day be "authorized to lead psalms and refrains." But "He was on no account to slap their heads or pull their hair."[2] The precentor was expected to be patient with the boy oblates.

One English monastic customary saw the precentor in this light:

> Let the precentor then—who may conveniently also be styled the chief of the singers, the leading singer, the singer who sings remarkably or surpassingly or better than the rest— comport himself in his office which is a source of pleasure and delight to God, the angels and mankind, with such regularity, reverence and modesty; let him bend low with such reverence and respect, let him walk so humbly, let him sing with such sweetness and devotion that all his brethren, both old and young, may find in his behavior and demeanor a pattern for the religious life and the observances required by the rule ("Barnwell Observances").[3]

Indeed, the Benedictines are serious about the manner in which the liturgy is observed.

And in this chapter of the *Rule,* we are again taught the importance of punctuality "that everything may be done at the proper time." St. Benedict expects all of his monks to get to church on time so that prayer may begin. He does not like to keep people waiting. Neither should any of us who follow his *Rule.*

CHAPTER 48

The Daily Manual Labor

Chapter 48 is entitled ''The Daily Manual Labor,'' but St. Benedict does not deal with that subject only. ''The brothers should
have specified periods for manual labor as well as for prayerful reading.'' If work is necessary because ''idleness is the ene-
my of the soul,'' so is reading necessary. Both are important,
and St. Benedict wants the monks' day to be balanced by both.

In St. Benedict's monastery, manual labor was the lot of
most monks. Not many laborsaving and timesaving devices
had been invented by the sixth century. Not everyone, of
course, was engaged in work that was strictly manual. Some
monks were artisans, others copied texts in the scriptorium.
A guestmaster provided for the visitors' needs, someone had
to teach the boy oblates, and someone had to tend for the sick
and aged monks. Work, in whatever form it took, was important.

Practically every renewal of the Benedictine Order throughout history has restored manual labor to the significant place
St. Benedict gave it in monastic life. These days, however,
some Benedictine monastics have to look upon manual labor
as a welcome diversion from other duties.

''When they live by the labor of their hands, as our fathers
and the apostles did, then they are really monks.'' This sentence from chapter 48 follows the one that states, ''They must
not become distressed if local conditions or their poverty
should force them to do the harvesting themselves.'' This
seems to imply that monks did not always work on their own
farms. Monastic leaders before St. Benedict had opposite views
about farming. The monks of Egypt thought that work should
be restricted to one's cell. St. Jerome was disgusted with monks
like the Egyptians who sat in their cells and wove baskets all

day. He believed that if a monk were confined to his cell, his work should be scholarly. Otherwise, he should be out in the fields. The Rule of the Master prohibited farm work. St. Basil, who was greatly admired by St. Benedict, prescribed farming as the most suitable kind of work for monks. Without a doubt, farming was acceptable to St. Benedict too. Farming certainly became a Benedictine tradition.

Twice in this chapter St. Benedict takes into consideration monks who are not physically disposed to doing much manual labor. "All things are to be done with moderation on account of the fainthearted." And "brothers who are sick or weak should be given a type of work or craft that will keep them busy without overwhelming them or driving them away."

St. Benedict watches carefully to see that no one is overburdened by his work. He is concerned about both body and soul. That is why this chapter on work is also attentive to *lectio divina*. The English translation is "prayerful reading" but the more literal meaning of the Latin is "divine reading." St. Benedict wants his monks to read the divine book, the Bible. Reading the Bible is a spiritual exercise, and it should also be a spiritual experience. The monk reads not to research a subject. Reading is feeding his soul. *Lectio* is a kind of communion. It prepares the monk for prayer in common, and it is a private prayer as well. Prayerful reading is unhurried. It is meditative. The text is to be savored. Medieval monks used the term *ruminatio* (chewing the cud) to describe the action of *lectio*.

If someone wishes to read instead of taking his siesta, he must do so quietly. It was the custom to read aloud even in private. The monk was to hear the word spoken exteriorly as well as interiorly. But here again we see the considerateness of St. Benedict—read, but don't disturb your napping neighbor.

Lectio is so necessary for monks that St. Benedict wants two seniors to go around the monastery checking on them during the time scheduled for reading. "Their duty is to see that no brother is so apathetic as to waste time or engage in idle talk to the neglect of his reading, and so not only harm himself but also distract others."

On Sundays the monks of St. Benedict's monastery are to do additional reading. "If anyone is so remiss and indolent that he is unwilling or unable to study or to read, he is to be given some work in order that he may not be idle." Yes, even on Sunday, go find some work if you aren't going to read.

Apparently St. Benedict had to reprove the monks of his time for neglecting *lectio*. Benedictines of today may have an excuse for neglecting *lectio* more frequently than they did in the sixth century. Most Benedictine monasteries and convents are busier places nowadays. It would be impossible for most of us to spend four hours reading every day. We are, nevertheless, conscious of what St. Benedict expects of us with regard to *lectio*. I'm sure your lives have also been enriched by work and prayerful reading. St. Benedict blesses all of us for our faithfulness.

CHAPTER 49

The Observance of Lent

"The life of a monk ought to be a continuous Lent. Since few, however, have the strength for this, we urge the entire community during these days of Lent to keep its manner of life most pure and to wash away in this holy season the negligences of other times." St. Benedict knows that there is only so much he can ask of his followers. If they cannot be penitential throughout the whole year, then they should at least try harder during the Church's penitential season.

During these days, therefore, we will add to the usual measure of our service something by way of private prayer and
abstinence from food or drink, so that each of us will have
something above the assigned measure to offer God of his
own will *with joy of the Holy Spirit* (1 Thess 1-6). In other
words, let each one deny himself some food, drink, sleep,
needless talking or idle jesting.''

The Master, in his Rule, is more interested in the communal
observance of Lent than in how the individual monk intends
to observe it. The Master adds extra communal prayers between all the hours of the Divine Office. As Lent progresses,
the food and drink for the monks continue to diminish. Regard-
ing those monks who happen to be ill during Lent, the Master says, ''Let the abbot see to it that no one is lying or
pretending to be sick.''[1]

Rather than impose a Lenten penance that the whole community must uniformly follow, St. Benedict says, ''Everyone
should, however, make known to the abbot what he intends
to do, since it ought to be done with his prayer and approval.
Whatever is undertaken without the permission of the spiritual father will be reckoned as presumption and vainglory, not
deserving a reward.''

A good Lenten practice for everyone is mentioned in the
previous chapter of the *Rule*. ''During this time of Lent each
one is to receive a book from the library, and is to read the
whole of it straight through. These books are to be distributed
at the beginning of Lent.''

For St. Benedict, conversion should result from our Lenten
penitential practices. ''To wash away in this holy season the
negligences of other times''—that is the purpose of Lent. It is
also a time in which to ''look forward to holy Easter with joy
and spiritual longing.''

CHAPTER 50

Brothers Working at a Distance or Traveling

Monks who are working some distance from the monastery may be excused from attending common prayer, but they may not be excused from praying. They are "to perform the Work of God where they are, and kneel out of reverence for God." This applies likewise to monks who are traveling. Prayer is an obligation and an occupation that St. Benedict wants fulfilled even when the monks are away from the monastery, in the field bringing in the harvest, or on the road. We all need to be reminded not to neglect our prayer.

CHAPTER 51

Brothers on a Short Journey

A monk who is on an errand for the monastery or performing a work of charity and who can be expected home the same day is admonished "not [to] presume to eat outside, even if he receives a pressing invitation, unless perhaps the abbot has ordered it."

St. Gregory describes the consequences of accepting a dinner invitation without St. Benedict's permission. Several monks were out on business, and the hour grew late. "They stopped for a meal at the house of a devout woman they knew in the neighborhood. On their return when they presented themselves to the abbot for the usual blessing, he asked them where they had taken their meal."

The monks told him they hadn't eaten. St. Benedict asked them why they were lying to him. "Did you not enter the house of this particular woman and eat these various foods and have so and so many cups to drink?''

The monks were embarrassed and confessed the faults they had committed when they were outside the monastery. St. Gregory says, ''The man of God did not hesitate to pardon them, confident that they would do no further wrong in his absence, since they now realized he was always present to them in spirit.''

Why is St. Benedict so cautious in allowing his monks to associate with people in the neighborhood? He doesn't want his monks to become so comfortable in other people's homes that they begin to neglect responsibilities in their own home.

An Oblate may have to ask occasionally, ''Am I gone from home too often?'' In this chapter we are all reminded once more of the importance of the family meal, and we are advised not to find excuses for absenting ourselves from it.

CHAPTER 52

The Oratory of the Monastery

St. Benedict had no blueprints in mind for the great monastic churches Benedictines would build after he was gone. I doubt if he would ever have allowed their construction. St. Bede tells us about the church his abbot, St. Benedict Biscop, built in seventh century England:

> Benedict crossed the sea to France to look for masons to build him a stone church in the Roman style he had always loved so much. He found them, took them on and brought them back home with him. So strong was his devotion to St. Peter, in whose honor the scheme was begun, and so fervent his zeal in carrying it out, that within a year of laying the foundations, he had the gable-ends of the church in place and you could already visualize Mass being celebrated in it. When

the building was nearing completion he sent his agents across to France to bring over glaziers—craftsmen as yet unknown in Britain—to glaze the windows in the body of the church and in the chapels and clerestory. The glaziers came over as requested but they did not merely execute their commission: they helped the English to understand and to learn themselves the art of glass-making, an art which was to prove invaluable in making of lamps for the church and many other kinds of vessels. He was also a dedicated collector of everything necessary for the service of the church and altar—sacred vessels and vestments for instance—and saw to it that what could not be obtained at home was shipped over from abroad.[1]

Chapter 52 of the *Rule* provides no guidelines for liturgical furnishings or decorations. St. Benedict merely says, "The oratory ought to be what it is called, and nothing else is to be done or stored there." "Oratory" simply means "a place for prayer."

St. Benedict wants his oratory to be reserved for prayer, nothing else. St. Pachomius allowed his Egyptian monks to manufacture rope in their oratory.

And when he begins to walk into the synaxis [liturgical service] room, going to his place of sitting and standing, he should not tread upon the rushes which have been dipped in water in preparation for the plaiting of ropes . . . nor shall you sit idle in the synaxis, but with quick hand you shall prepare ropes for the warps of mats. . . . Let no one look at another twisting ropes or praying; let him rather be intent on his own work with eyes cast down.[2]

St. Benedict's monks must exercise their crafts and trades in the shops only.

And nothing should be stored in the oratory. The oratory is a prayer room, not a warehouse. The visitation report of a thirteenth-century Irish Cistercian monastery mentions just such an infraction of the *Rule:* "They stored large amounts of grain, hay, flour and other necessities in the church."[3] These Irish monks were guilty of a far more serious offense than turning their church into a barn. Their church was also an arsenal. This was a community that had expelled its abbot and the monks who had been sent over from England to reform the place. The Irish monks of Maigue were unwilling to be reformed. They barricaded themselves in the monastery and made a fort out of it. "They strongly fortified a shelter above the altar with provisions and weapons. . . . Finally, they brought thirty head of cattle on the hoof into the cloister, grazing them on the grass there and on hay stored in the church."[4]

St. Benedict says, "After the Work of God, all should leave in complete silence and with reverence for God, so that a brother who may wish to pray alone will not be disturbed by the insensitivity of another." So much of the *Rule* is concerned with reverence for God and sensitivity for others.

"Moreover, if at other times someone chooses to pray privately, he may simply go in and pray, not in a loud voice, but with tears and heartfelt devotion." Although St. Benedict says much about communal prayer, this chapter commends the practice of private prayer also. He refers to the private prayer that is done in the oratory. "Accordingly, anyone who does not pray in this manner [quietly] is not to remain in the oratory after the Work of God, as we have said; then he will not interfere with anyone else." To "pray with tears" is a figure of speech. He means we should pray with compunction, with reverence. Other people may be in the oratory saying their prayers. Do not disturb them by praying your mantra or rosary or novena out loud. If you must address God vocally, go to a place where only God can hear you.

And don't take your knitting to church. "The oratory ought to be what it is called, and nothing else is to be done or stored there."

CHAPTER 53

The Reception of Guests

St. Benedict knew that monasteries would always have guests. In the Middle Ages, monasteries probably had more guests than we have today. Then the monastery was the only motel available for travelers. "Once a guest has been announced, the superior and the brothers are to meet him with all the courtesy of love. First of all, they are to pray together and thus be united in peace, but prayer must always precede the kiss of peace because of the delusions of the devil." Nowadays we shake hands with visitors at the front door instead of giving them the kiss of peace, and we don't pray with them before letting them in. Although St. Benedict tells us, "All guests who present themselves are to be welcomed as Christ," he is aware that there are certain kinds of guests who come to the monastery to take advantage of the monks. In our day we have been deluded too. Once, I took a guest to the bus depot after a stay of several days at the monastery. I was unaware that his suitcase, which I was carrying, was filled with books that he had snitched from our library.

Once we put up two white-robed young men who informed us that they were disciples of the Lord. The guestmaster offered to wash their robes made from bedsheets. One of the sheets was ripped to pieces in the washing machine, and Father Cletus had to provide the disciple with a new bedsheet. St. Benedict instructs the abbot to "pour water on the hands of the guests, and the abbot with the entire community shall wash their feet." We could have washed the feet of these pilgrims in white. Members of their group don't wear shoes. They walk from place to place barefoot. Like the travelers in St. Benedict's day who walked great distances wearing sandals, these two guests arrived at our monastery with dust on their feet. We

didn't wash their feet, though. Instead, Father Cletus showed
the young men to the showers.

"Great care and concern are to be shown in receiving poor
people and pilgrims, because in them more particularly Christ
is received; our very awe of the rich guarantees them special
respect." It is our human nature, I suppose, that leads us to
fawn over the rich and the famous. St. Benedict reminds us
not to ignore the other people—people who cannot afford to
stay in hotels or motels. Like the destitute family who stopped
at a rectory to ask for assistance. The pastor told them, "Go
to the abbey. The monks will put you up for the night."

In the town where I grew up, our neighbors were Oblates
of St. Benedict. They had this plaque on the wall of their dining room: "Let all guests be received as Christ."

CHAPTER 54

Letters or Gifts for Monks

"In no circumstances is a monk allowed, unless the abbot says
he may, to exchange letters, blessed tokens or small gifts of
any kind, with his parents or anyone else, or with a fellow
monk. He must not presume to accept gifts sent him even by
his parents without previously telling the abbot."

When St. Bede was dying in 735, he said to the monk at
his bedside: "I have a few things in my box—some pepper,
napkins, and incense. Bring them to me so that I can make
some small gifts of what God has given me."[1] The monk who
records this incident does not indicate that St. Bede had his
abbot's permission to keep these things. We can presume that
he did. But did he have the abbot's permission to give them
away? I've often wondered if St. Bede ever felt guilty about
hanging on to these precious items. Pepper can't be grown in

northern England. No doubt it and the incense had to have come all the way from the East. And those napkins—they must have been made from exquisite cloth that was not common in England. Perhaps they were artistically embroidered. St. Bede calls these things "small gifts." I suspect they were costly and he didn't want to be caught dead with them in his cell. That's why he gave them away at the end of his life. Monks will be human, even the ones who are saints.

Oblates, of course, are not bound by the vow of poverty. They are not prevented from giving gifts. But even in this chapter there is an application for the follower of the *Rule* who does not live behind cloister walls. St. Benedict says the abbot, even after he has given permission for a monk to keep a gift, "still has the power to give the gift to whom he will; and the brother for whom it was originally sent must not be distressed, *lest occasion be given to the devil* (Eph 4:27; 1 Tim 5:14)." The lesson for Oblates is: Give from what you have been given. Perhaps there is someone else whose need for the article is greater than your own.

CHAPTER 55

The Clothing and Footwear of the Brothers

"**W**e believe that for each monk a cowl and tunic will suffice in temperate regions; in winter a woolen cowl is necessary, in summer a thinner or worn one; also a scapular for work, and footwear—both sandals and shoes."

The Benedictine habit evolved from the garb worn by monks before St. Benedict's time. He originated the scapular, an apron worn for work. St. Benedict's cowl is a long robe with a hood attached to it. The tunic is worn underneath. Some monks in ages before St. Benedict's wore leather tunics or fleece-lined ones. What we have ended up with is a tunic with a scapular worn over it and a hood attached to the scapular. The cowl, or *cuculla*, is a large robe worn over the habit at Mass and at certain hours of the Office. The *cuculla* came to be recognized as a symbol of solemn profession.

St. Benedict allows his monks to procure underwear when they go on a journey. This was a matter of controversy in ancient days. If the argument about nuns wearing veils or not wearing them seems ridiculous to some people today, we should be thankful that we longer have to debate whether or not monks should wear drawers. Hildemar, a ninth-century monk, said that monasteries in which the monks wore underwear were not praiseworthy. The Benedictine monks of Cluny wore it, and their abbot, Peter the Venerable, fought constantly with the Cistercians in order to defend the practice.

St. Benedict tells his monks that they "must not complain about the color or coarseness" of the habit and that the material used for it should be purchased locally at "a reasonable cost." Although black has become the ordinary color for the Benedictine habit, grey, white, and brown have also been worn. The Cistercians opted for a white tunic and black scapular, and Peter the Venerable had to defend the Benedictines' basic black against Bernard of Clairvaux's opinion that the Cistercian habit was more suitable for followers of St. Benedict. Today most Benedictines wear black, but there are some who wear white or blue or a grey tunic and a black scapular.

The tunic, scapular, and hood are common to all groups of Benedictines, but some hoods are detachable, some scapulars have buttons sewn on the front, the Austrians wear a Peter Pan collar, the Italians of the Cassinese Congregation have a winglike, shaped scapular, the English Benedictines have two wide lapels on their hood that hang over the front of the scapular. The Swiss have a long hood that reaches to the middle of the back. It is referred to as "a potato sack."

St. Benedict, however, is not concerned about fashions. What he has in mind is simply that the monk should look like a monk. He wants the habit to fit properly, and he wants it to be worn all the time—even to bed.

There was a time when Oblates were allowed to wear the Benedictine habit on special occasions. And they could be buried in it. With you, as with us, the important thing is to be a Benedictine. The habit does not necessarily make the Benedictine. Certainly, this is another lesson St. Benedict teaches us.

CHAPTER 56

The Abbot's Table

Chapter 56 is one of those very short chapters in the *Rule*. It is so short that it leaves much unsaid. We are left wondering where the abbot ordinarily takes his meals. The first sentence of this chapter says, "The abbot's table must always be with guests and travelers." In chapter 53, St. Benedict indicates that "the kitchen for the abbot and guests ought to be separate." So, the abbot not only eats with the guests, but their meals are prepared in a separate kitchen. St. Gregory offers no evidence, however, of St. Benedict's dining apart from the monastic community.

In chapter 38 St. Benedict provides the superior an opportunity to say a few words of instruction in the monastic refectory, where silence is normally expected, so the monks can listen to table reading. Is this superior the abbot? If so, then it is clear that he is eating with the monks. Or is this superior one of the seniors who must "always be left with the brothers" because the abbot dines with the guests? One way commentators on the *Rule* have solved the question is to conclude that the abbot ate with the monks whenever no guests were present at the monastery. But chapter 56 recommends that when "there are no guests, it is within his right [the abbot's] to invite any of the brothers he wishes." Does this mean invite them to his table in the monastery refectory or to the dining room where he ordinarily eats with the guests and travelers?

Does it matter where the abbot eats? What is more important is that the poor man be fed, isn't it? To me, this chapter of the *Rule* seems to provide an excuse for abuses by future abbots. If St. Benedict ever shows indiscretion, it is here in chapter 56.

In later ages the abbot's dining room became a banquet hall where he wined and dined only the distinguished visitors to the monastery. The monks, in their own refectory, ate the ordinary fare, but his Lordship served his guests a bountiful and varied menu. Even meat! On high feast days, some of the brethren were invited to dine at the abbot's table; often they were the ministers who had functioned at High Mass on that day. By now it was a definitely established custom for the abbot to take his meals outside the refectory. And he lived in his own grand house and had his own courtyard. Sometimes these opulent accommodations were not the choice of an abbot but were demanded by the nobility or by a bishop. When these dignitaries of the Middle Ages visited an abbey, they expected their abbatial host to receive them and their retinue in the manner to which they were accustomed.

In chapter 53, we see St. Benedict's first act of leniency with regard to the abbot's relationship with the guests. "The superior may break his fast for the sake of a guest, unless it is a day of special fast which cannot be broken. The brothers, however, observe the usual fast." In chapter 56 St. Benedict excuses the abbot from eating with the monks. The abbot needn't fast, he needn't eat with his monks. But the monks should fast, and a senior or two should always eat in the refectory to make certain the monks don't misbehave.

Hubert Van Zeller, in his commentary on the *Rule of St. Benedict*, makes this remark about the eating habits of abbots: "All that can be said is that whenever in history the abbot has decided to abide by the words of the Rule [in Chapter 56] there has been trouble. So much so that more than one General Council of Abbots can be cited as forbidding the abbot to make a regular practice of eating on his own with guests."[1]

Is there any practical advice for Oblates in chapter 56 of the *Rule?* Yes, it is: Be solicitous for the guests who come to your home. We are again reminded of that in the *Rule*.

CHAPTER 57

The Artisans of the Monastery

There never was a time when a "No Artists Need Apply" sign was posted at the monastery gate. History has proved that art and monasticism have gotten along well over the centuries. Monks have themselves been artists and they have patronized the arts. St. Dunstan, a monk who became Archbishop of Canterbury in 959, was a painter, a carver in wood and bone, and worked with gold, silver, iron, and brass. He also did embroidery.

One of Ireland's most precious works of art is the Book of Kells, an illuminated manuscript of the Gospels begun in the eighth century and completed in the ninth. A modern authority in illumination states the Book of Kells should be included among the great wonders of the world. It is the work of monks.

Some monks spent their whole lifetime in the scriptorium making books. It is estimated that one scribe could produce forty books if he lived an average life span. These books were needed for the Divine Office, for the monastic library, for the monks' private *lectio*. When new monasteries were founded, books had to be sent with the monks. In some monasteries, laymen had to be hired as scribes, but it was common for each monastery to have at least twelve monks employed full time in the scriptorium. What were the monks copying in all those years before the invention of the printing press? Scripture, of course, and the Church Fathers, but they were also preserving the literature of classical Greece and Rome as well as the stories and myths of their own ancestors. Books were so highly valued in the monasteries that whenever barbarian tribes were raiding the neighborhood, the books were the first things to be hidden. When Monte Cassino was sacked in 577, the monks fled with their books and left behind the body of St. Benedict.

The Benedictines and Cistercians argued about art and architecture in the eleventh century. The Cistercian St. Bernard of Clairvaux has this to say about the Benedictines of Cluny:

> I will not dwell upon the vast height of their churches, their unconscionable length, their preposterous breadth, their richly polished panelling, all of which distracts the eyes of the worshipper and hinders his devotion. You throw money into your decorations to make it breed. Your candlesticks as tall as trees, great masses of bronze of exquisite workmanship, and as dazzling with their precious stones as the lights that surmount them, what think you, is the purpose of all this? Will it melt a sinner's heart and not rather keep him gazing in wonder? O vanity of vanities—no, insanity rather than vanity.[1]

The Cistercians wanted to simplify their architecture and their art. Abbot Suger, the Benedictine who built the first Gothic church in Europe (for his monastic community of St. Denis in Paris) and who immortalized himself in stained glass prostrated at the feet of our Lady, answered St. Bernard's objections:

> There are those who tell us that a holy mind, a pure heart and a right intent suffice for the ministration of the altar, and I would grant these are the principal, proper and peculiar

qualifications. But I maintain that we should do homage also to the rite of the Holy Sacrifice, as to nothing else in the world, with the outward splendor of holy vessels, with all inward purity and all outward magnificence.[2]

When the Benedictines came to this country in the nineteenth century, Abbot Boniface Wimmer, the first abbot of our Order on American soil, said: "Our monasteries and their schools should be centers of the arts where music, art and accompanying crafts are developed and advanced. Theologically we state that the properties of God are truth, goodness and beauty. I suspect more souls are won to God by beauty than by truth and goodness."[3] Wimmer clearly disagreed with St. Bernard of Clairvaux and reasoned more in line with Abbot Suger for the promotion of art.

St. Benedict says artisans in the monastery "are to practice their craft with all humility, but only with the abbot's permission. If one of them becomes puffed up by his skillfulness in his craft, and feels that he is conferring something on the monastery, he is to be removed from practicing his craft and not allowed to resume it unless, after manifesting his humility, he is so ordered by the abbot."

A monk artist usually doesn't have to read chapter 57 of the *Rule* to be reminded about humility. There is always someone around to humble an artist. Some years ago, an abbey in this country asked a European Benedictine monk to paint a mural in the apse of its church. He chose to depict Adam and Eve before their fall. One day while he was on the scaffold painting, the bishop of the diocese came to look at the monk's work. The bishop was shocked to see a naked man and woman on the ceiling of the abbey church. "Cover them up," he told the monk artist. The artist protested. "But, Your Excellency, look at the Sistine Chapel in Rome. There are nudes in it." "Yes," the bishop said, "but that's art."

About the marketing of crafts, St. Benedict says, "When-

ever products of these artisans are sold, those responsible for
the sale must not dare to practice any fraud. The evil of ava-
rice must have no part in establishing prices, which should,
therefore, always be a little lower than people outside the monastery are able to set.''

This chapter certainly speaks to Oblates who are merchants,
reminding them that products should be made well and sold
at fair prices. It applies to everyone who has a creative talent.
Remember that it is first of all God's gift to you. Now you must
give it to the world.

CHAPTER 58

The Procedure for Receiving Brothers

St. Benedict suggests that someone who wants to enter the
monastery should not be granted ''an easy entry.'' A young
man came to our monastery one Saturday afternoon to inquire
about entering our community. He could not find anyone
around. So he got back in his car and drove the 135 miles back
home. He returned the following Saturday after having written a letter during the week to arrange an appointment with
the vocation director. This was, no doubt, a test of perseverance for him, although not in the exact manner St. Benedict
prescribes.

St. Benedict says the newcomer should keep knocking at
the monastery door for four or five days. If ''he has shown
himself patient in bearing his harsh treatment and difficulty
of entry, and has persisted in his request, then he should be
allowed to enter and stay in the guest quarters for a few days.''
After all that fuss, the candidate can proceed only as far as the
guest house. In St. Benedict's day, however, there was no pe-

riod of candidacy before novitiate. The newcomer spent only a few days in the guest quarters and then entered the novitiate. The treatment St. Benedict gives the newcomer is a screening process. ''As the Apostle says, *Test the spirits to see if they are from God* (1 John 4:1).'' Someone who is sincere about wanting to become a monastic will put up with being denied immediate entrance. That person will keep knocking. The phony will give up and go back to where he or she came from. St. Benedict's procedure for admitting a newcomer might be considered a psychological test.

Nor are Oblates easily admitted. Normally a prospective Oblate reads the literature first, thinks about it, and attends a meeting or two before making a decision. Becoming an Oblate, like becoming a monastic, involves a commitment that one must be willing to make.

After his stay in the guest quarters, St. Benedict allows the newcomer to enter the novitiate ''where the novices study, eat and sleep.'' Once in a while, a modern-day novice who has versed himself in the *Rule* will quote St. Benedict in order to get out of work. He'll say: ''A novice can't be expected to help move that piano. My duties are restricted to studying, eating, and sleeping.'' His knowledge of the *Rule* never makes an impression in an instance like this.

St. Benedict assigns a senior with the ''skill of winning souls'' to look after the novices. His ''concern must be whether the novice truly seeks God and whether he shows eagerness for the Work of God, for obedience and trials.'' Today, when the novice master presents a novice to chapter for permission to continue in the novitiate or to profess vows, he makes his report on how well the novice has met the requirements that were expected of a novice in St. Benedict's monastery.

Although St. Benedict's aim is to establish ''nothing harsh, nothing burdensome'' (Prologue), he remains a realist. Being a follower of St. Benedict's *Rule* does not save us from trial and trouble. ''The novice should be clearly told all the hard-ships and difficulties that will lead him to God.''

During the novitiate the *Rule* is read to the novice three times. If the novice feels that he will not be able to live under the *Rule*, he is given the opportunity to depart. The novice who lasts to the end of the novitiate is then allowed to profess vows. ''But he must be well aware that, as the law of the rule estab-lishes, from this day he is no longer free to leave the monas-tery, nor to shake from his neck the yoke of the rule which, in the course of so prolonged a period of reflection, he was free either to reject or to accept.'' The novices of St. Benedict's day, like our Oblates today, made their final commitment after one year. There was no period of temporary profession. Monks and nuns of the Order of St. Benedict still profess vows, tem-porary and final, in rites that are basically the same as the ceremony St. Benedict outlines in the *Rule*. The rite of obla-tion has its roots there. All of us who are followers of the *Rule of St. Benedict* pray: ''Receive me, Lord, as you have promised and I shall live; do not let me be disappointed in my hope.''

CHAPTER 59

The Offering of Sons by Nobles or by the Poor

''**If** a member of the nobility offers his son to God in the mon-astery, and the boy himself is too young, the parents draw up the document mentioned above; then, at the presentation of the gifts, they wrap the document itself and the boy's hand in the altar cloth. That is how they offer him.''

The document is the vow chart St. Benedict describes in chapter 58.

> When he [the novice who is about to make profession] is to
> be received, he comes before the whole community in the
> oratory and promises stability, fidelity to monastic life, and
> obedience. . . . He states his promise in a document drawn
> up in the name of the saints whose relics are there, and of
> the abbot, who is present. The novice writes out this docu-
> ment himself, or if he is illiterate, then he asks someone else
> to write it for him, but himself puts his mark to it and with
> his own hand lays it on the altar.

Chapter 59 applies to boys who are so young they cannot
read or write or even comprehend what making a mark on the
document entails. They will find out, though, as they grow
older. Their parents have offered them to the monastery. The
parents have made an oblation of their sons at the offertory
of the Mass. This is a practice that would surely guarantee
monastic vocations in our day, but no monastery would ever
get away with it now. Neither would parents.

> As to their property, they [the parents] either make a sworn
> promise in this document that they will never personally,
> never through an intermediary, nor in any way at all, nor
> at any time, give the boy anything or afford him the oppor-
> tunity to possess anything; or else, if they are unwilling to
> do this and still wish to win their reward for making an offer-
> ing to the monastery, they make a formal donation of the
> property that they want to give to the monastery, keeping
> the revenue for themselves, should they so desire.

St. Benedict is asking the parents if they'd like to take out an
annuity. It is surprising to find him functioning like the development director of a modern religious community. "This
ought to leave no way open for the boy to entertain any expectations that could deceive and ruin him." The boy will reach
an age when he realizes that his family has wealth, and he may
be tempted to forsake his monastic vocation. "May God forbid this, but we have learned from experience that it can happen." Therefore, take some precautions, St. Benedict advises

the parents. If the boy's inheritance already belongs to the monastery, he will not be tempted to leave.

"Poor people do the same, but those who have nothing at all simply write the document and, in the presence of witnesses, offer their son with the gifts."

While St. Benedict was still at Subiaco, St. Gregory informs us of two youths who were offered to the monastery:

> It was about this time that pious noblemen from Rome first came to visit the saint and left their sons with him to be schooled in the service of God. Thus Euthicius brought his son Maurus, and the senator Tertullus, Placid, both very promising boys. Maurus, in fact, who was a little older, had already acquired solid virtue and was soon very helpful to his saintly master. But Placid was still only a child.

St. Bede was also only a youngster when he began monastic life. "I was born on the lands of this monastery, and on reaching seven years of age, I was entrusted by my family first to the most reverend Abbot Benedict Biscop and later to Abbot Ceolfrid for my education. I have spent all the remainder of my life in this monastery and devoted myself entirely to the study of the Scriptures."[1]

In offering their little boys to monastic life, these parents gave the Church three admirable saints. Are you encouraging vocations to the Benedictine way of life, especially to the comunity of which you are an Oblate?

CHAPTER 60

The Admission of Priests to the Monastery

St. Benedict devotes two chapters of the *Rule* to priests. In his day most monks were not ordained. Monks before St. Benedict's time also avoided ordination. John Cassian, who had an influence on St. Benedict, said that the monk must avoid women and bishops. Both could draw the monk away from his monastic vocation, away from the community to which he has made a commitment. The one could incite passion and the other ordination.

Monks were expected to live apart from society, but this does not mean that monks ignored society. They practiced the spiritual and corporal works of mercy for all who came to the monastery seeking assistance.

St. Gregory had been a monk before being called to the papacy. In recalling those happy days in the cloister, he said: "When I lived in the monastery, I could avoid idle talk and keep my mind almost continuously fixed on prayer. But once I accepted the pastoral burden, many things required and divided my attention, so that my former recollection became impossible."[1]

St. Benedict and the fathers of an earlier monastic tradition knew that priestly orders would cause the divided attention that St. Gregory experienced. Abba Isaac fled the desert because he was being sought for ordination. His pursuers stopped for the night and let their beast of burden graze in a grassy area. The ass found its way to Isaac's hiding place. In the morning when they went to look for the animal, they found Isaac too. They were about to bind him with ropes and haul him off to a bishop, but the old monk said, "Now I can no longer oppose you since it is perhaps the will of God that I, though unworthy, should receive priestly orders."[2] It was not until the ninth century that abbots in the Church of Rome were expected to be priests. St. Jerome never practiced his priesthood because he feared this would detract from his monastic vocation. Monasticism was understood to be a way of life for lay people, and ordination was an exception.

Chapter 60 of the *Rule* deals with letting in men who are already ordained. "Do not agree too quickly," St. Benedict says with regard to their admission. Perhaps he senses that a priest will have great difficulty adjusting to the change of lifestyle. The priest has been formed in one way and the monk in another. There is a difference of spirituality. Will the priest be able to live a life of stability, or will he want to work outside the monastery where he can exercise a parochial ministry?

St. Benedict seems suspicious of the priest's motives for entering the monastery. If St. Benedict were living in our day when there is a scarcity of parish housekeepers, he might be inclined to believe that a priest who'd been left without a housekeeper was seeking admission to the monastery merely to have someone prepare his meals and do his laundry. Put him off for a while, St. Benedict says, but if the priest persists, let him know "that he will have to observe the full discipline of the rule without any mitigation, knowing that it is written: *Friend, what have you come for?* (Matt 26:50)" A priest who enters a monastery may have to take his turn at cooking, and he may even be assigned to the laundry.

What St. Benedict tells the priest applies to every monk, nun, and Oblate. "He must recognize that he is subject to the discipline of the rule, and not make any exceptions for himself, but rather give everyone an example of humility."

CHAPTER 61

The Reception of Visiting Monks

"**A** visiting monk from far away will perhaps present himself and wish to stay as a guest in the monastery." St. Benedict rolls out the carpet for him—but with the proviso that the monk "does not make excessive demands that upset the monastery." If the visitor is satisfied, "he should be received for as long a time as he wishes." St. Benedict's *Rule* says nothing about putting the monk to work. The Rule of the Master does.

> Therefore, if he does not want to work let the weekly servers and the cellarer tell him to depart, lest the brothers working for their monastery have good reason to resent hospitality given to parasites and loafers and, resorting to murmuring and criticizing, they begin to detest such strangers who, because of their wretched laziness, do not settle down anywhere but visit monasteries under the pretext of religion and remain idle while devouring the bread due to workers.[1]

This applies to laypersons also who come to the Master's monastery as guests. St. Benedict, without imposing a limit to the number of days the visiting monk may relax, does presume that the monk will eventually enter into the life of the community. The Master is more definite. He gives the visiting monk two days in which to rest up. St. Benedict is not as suspicious as the Master. St. Benedict believes that a visiting monk may have been guided to the monastery by the Lord for the purpose of suggesting some reforms. If it becomes obvious, however, that a monk from another monastery is "excessive in his demands or full of faults," St. Benedict says, "he should be politely told to depart." St. Benedict's *Rule* is the essence of politeness. The Master's Rule is not always polite.

A visiting monk may ask to transfer to the monastery of his hosts, and if he is an agreeable sort of person, St. Benedict says: "He should even be urged to stay, so that others may learn from his example, ... The abbot must, however, take care never to receive into the community a monk from another known monastery, unless the monk's abbot consents and sends a letter of recommendation, since it is written: *Never do to another what you do not want done to yourself* (Tob 4:16)."

Have you welcomed the new parishioner or the new member of your club?

CHAPTER 62

The Priests of the Monastery

In chapter 62, St. Benedict instructs the abbot what to do if he wants one of his own monks ordained. And there is a warning to be bestowed upon the monk. "The monk so ordained must be on guard against conceit or pride, must not presume to do anything except what the abbot commands him, and must recognize that now he will have to subject himself all the more to the discipline of the rule. Just because he is a priest, he may not therefore forget the obedience and discipline of the rule, but must make more and more progress toward God."

Of course the monastery in St. Benedict's time needed a priest for the same reason monasteries need priests today. The monastic community has to be served. The monks need the sacraments. This was a legitimate reason for St. Benedict's having a monk ordained. Throughout the Middle Ages there was an increase in the number of monks who were ordained to the priesthood. In time the ordained would far outnumber the unordained. Ordination of monks became an accepted fact, and so did the exercise of priestly ministry, even away from the monastery.

When Benedictinism was transplanted to the United States, there was no doubt about the monks' need to become involved in parishes, missions, and chaplaincies. Many a monk entered his community as a young man, professed vows, was ordained, and then spent the remaining active years of his life in assignments outside the monastery. The monastic community needs priestly services, but so does the Church at large. This has been the American Benedictine tradition.

Chapter 62, although addressed to monks who are priests, applies to everyone else. It says: Avoid conceit, pride, presumption. Be obedient, subject to the *Rule*. Don't be rebellious.

CHAPTER 63

Community Rank

Our Brother Vital had already outlived several of his contemporaries and when another much younger monk died, he commented, "The trouble with this place is that no one dies in seniority." Brother Vital didn't like to see people dying out of rank. St. Benedict doesn't like to see them stepping out of rank. "The monks keep their rank in the monastery according to the date of their entry, . . . When they lead psalms or stand in choir, they do so in the order decided by the abbot or already existing among them."

You are familiar with seniority, too, at the places where you work and in the organizations to which you belong. There is even seniority in families. Older children have a status different from younger children. Seniority is part of good order, and St. Benedict is all for orderliness in his monastery. "For example, someone who came to the monastery at the second hour of the day must recognize that he is junior to someone who came at the first hour, regardless of age or distinction."

Seniority in the monastery is attained by having arrived on the scene first.

St. Benedict does suggest that monks can be promoted. "The virtue of their lives and the decision of the abbot" can have bearing on the position a monk achieves in the monastery. Yet, St. Benedict cautions the abbot "not to disturb the flock entrusted to him nor make any unjust arrangements, as though he had the power to do whatever he wished. He must constantly reflect that he will have to give God an account of all his decisions and actions." A monk should not be given a responsible position merely because he is virtuous. He should also be competent lest he botch up things for the whole community. The abbot must use some common sense in the matter of appointments.

"Absolutely nowhere shall age automatically determine rank. Remember that Samuel and Daniel were still boys when they judged their elders (1 Sam 3; Dan 13:44-62)." In chapter 3, St. Benedict insists that "all should be called for counsel" because "the Lord often reveals what is better to the younger." St. Benedict has confidence in his young monks. When modern-day monks of my generation or older tend to disregard the opinions of junior monks, we need to recall St. Benedict's attitude. The juniors may be telling us something important, and we should be willing to listen. Wouldn't it be wonderful if the young people in every home and in every parish had an opportunity to speak and to be listened to? St. Benedict recommends that we keep open the lines of communication. He also says, "The younger monks, then, must respect their seniors, and the seniors must love their juniors."

St. Benedict moves on to the subject of titles. "When they address one another, no one should be allowed to do so simply by name." For St. Benedict, addressing one another on a first-name basis was a sign of disrespect. When I was a young monk, it certainly was not customary for us to address one another without using the proper titles before our names: Father, Frater (a student for the priesthood), and Brother. In fact, it was forbidden, but of course, it happened, especially among one's peers. In this day most of us in the ranks address one another more informally. It not only seems more modern but more American as well. Even so, the *Rule* still obliges us to show proper respect. The quote from the Letter to the Romans used by St. Benedict in chapter 63 still applies: *"They should each try to be the first to show respect to the other* (Rom 12:10).*"* Keeping this in mind, we may be able to avoid namecalling, which is always disrespectful.

Our old laundryman (and infirmarian), Brother Alexius, had all of our laundry numbers memorized, and he often greeted us with them. "Hello, 94!" or "What can I do for you, 67?" St. Benedict probably would have been aghast to hear monks called by a number. But we were amazed that Brother Alexius could identify all of us in this fashion. We liked to shout out numbers to him, and he would quickly name the monk who had that number stamped on all his articles of clothing.

In this chapter of the *Rule*, St. Benedict provides us with two examples of etiquette. The junior is to ask for a blessing whenever he meets a senior. In our day, both the junior and the senior would find this impractical and unnecessary. The second point of etiquette is the young monk's standing whenever an older monk enters the room and offering the older man his chair. Our parents, long before we had read the *Rule of St. Benedict*, told us to do the same thing.

St. Benedict concludes chapter 63 by saying that "In the oratory and at table, small boys and youths are kept in rank and under discipline." Outside of these places "they should be supervised and controlled until they are old enough to be responsible." Even Maurus and Placid had to be supervised.

In our age of getting ahead, sometimes by stepping over (and on) people, St. Benedict says, stay where you are. If you are worthy of being advanced, you will be. The abbot, for "some overriding consideration," will make a promotion. That will happen in your case too.

CHAPTER 64

The Election of an Abbot

Chapter 2 of the *Rule* is concerned with "The Qualities of an Abbot." In chapter 64, St. Benedict again refers to certain qualities an abbot should possess. But this latter chapter is addressed also to the monks who elect an abbot.

> In choosing an abbot, the guiding principle should always be that the man placed in office be the one selected either by the whole community acting unanimously in the fear of God, or by some part of the community, no matter how small, which possesses sounder judgment. Goodness of life and wisdom in teaching must be the criteria for choosing the one to be made abbot, even if he is the last in community rank.

St. Benedict further says, "May God forbid that a whole community should conspire to elect a man who goes along with its own evil ways." He had been the head of the community at Vicovaro, which had wanted an abbot like that. "Their abbot had recently died, and they wanted the man of God to be their new superior. For some time he tried to discourage them by refusing their request, warning them that his way of life would never harmonize with theirs. But they kept insisting until in the end he gave his consent." The monks of Vicovaro regretted having asked St. Benedict to be their abbot. After they had tried poisoning him, he told them that he'd had enough of their wicked ways. "Did I not tell you at the outset that my way of life would never harmonize with yours?"

When a community attempts to elect an abbot who lacks "goodness of life and wisdom in teaching," St. Benedict says, "If the bishop of the diocese or the abbots or Christians in the area come to know of these evil ways to any extent, they must block the success of this wicked conspiracy, and set a worthy steward in charge of God's house." It would be sinful of them, St. Benedict says, not to prevent the wrong kind of man from ruling.

In the later Middle Ages, it became common for the secular ruler or a bishop to appoint an abbot. And in some instances, an abbot named his own successor. All of this was contrary to the *Rule of St. Benedict*, which emphatically states an abbot must be elected by the monks of the monastery in which there is an abbatial vacancy. Abbot St. Benedict Biscop, on his deathbed in 689, pleaded with his monks to keep the monastery out of his brother's hands. Within Anglo-Saxon law, inheritance might be claimed for a monastery ruled by one's relative. Benedict Biscop said:

> I tell you in all sincerity that as a choice of evils I would far rather have this whole place where I have built the monastery revert forever, should God so decide, to the wilderness it once was, rather than have my brother in the flesh, who has not entered upon the way of truth, succeed me as abbot. Take the greatest care, brothers, never to appoint a man as father over you because of his birth; and always appoint from among yourselves, never from outside the monastery. According to the rule of the great St. Benedict, our founder, and according to the decretals of privileges of this house, you are to meet as a body and take common counsel to discover who has proved himself fittest and most worthy by the probity of his life and the wisdom of his teaching to carry out the duties of this office. You must choose as abbot him whom after kindly scrutiny you all acknowledged to be the best. Then you are to summon the bishop and ask him to confirm the candidate in office with the customary blessing.[1]

Oblates are not involved in the election of an abbot or a prioress, but their prayers are sought when an election is in progress. And we all hope Oblates remember to pray for the superior the monks or nuns have chosen to lead them.

CHAPTER 65

The Prior of the Monastery

Reading chapter 65 of the *Rule* might leave you with the impression that St. Benedict considers the prior a menace to monastic life. As St. Benedict sees it, the problems with a prior, the monk second in command, arise "especially in monasteries where the same bishop and the same abbots appoint both abbot and prior." In our day, the abbot is elected by the community, and he appoints his own prior. This is the arrangement St. Benedict favors. "Let him, with the advice of God-fearing brothers, choose the man he wants and himself make him his prior." The abbot may depose the prior whenever he wishes, even before the prior develops "serious faults, or is led astray by conceit and grows proud, or shows open contempt for the holy rule."

St. Benedict is fearful of priors who become "puffed up by the evil spirit of pride and thinking of themselves as second abbots, usurp tyrannical power and foster contention and discord in their communities." He does not give the prior a detailed job description. He tells the prior what to avoid but not what exactly to do. St. Benedict seems to think deans are more suitable if there has to be a chain of command in the monastery (ch. 21).

Somewhere in monastic history the prior was called "the mother of the monastery"—the abbot, of course, being the father. I can understand this analogy. A monk will go to the prior asking a permission that he knows the abbot will refuse. Or a monk will approach the prior and ask, "How do you think the abbot will react if I do this?" A monk may wish to consult the prior before seeing the abbot about a personal matter, and he is free to do this. There are occasions when the prior and the monk may agree to keep secrets. The prior can be a confidant. But like all mothers, there are times when the prior has to reply, "I'm sorry. You'd better see your father about that." St. Benedict is aware of the consequences when the abbot and prior "pursue conflicting policies."

"The appointment of a prior has been the source of serious contention in monasteries." The prior, although he may disagree with an abbatial policy or command, has to obey. He cannot organize a rebellion among the troops. St. Benedict says, "The prior for his part is to carry out respectfully what his abbot assigns to him, and do nothing contrary to the abbot's wishes or arrangements."

St. Benedict has a good deal of patience with an obstreperous prior. In the *Rule*, St. Benedict suggests that an ordinary monk, in order to shape up, should be admonished twice, the deans three times, and the prior four times. If the prior does not reform, "he is to be deposed from the rank of prior and replaced by someone worthy. If after all that, he is not a peaceful and obedient member of the community, he should even be expelled from the monastery." Enough is enough.

When St. Benedict moved from Subiaco to Monte Cassino, he appointed priors to assist in the governing of the monasteries he had founded. In St. Gregory's biography of St. Benedict, we learn about his appearing in the dreams of the abbot and prior of Terracina, instructing them where to construct the monastery. Although St. Benedict was fearful of what a prior could turn into, he apparently saw some usefulness in establishing the office.

Is chapter 65 of the *Rule* applicable only to the prior of a monastery? I think anyone who is in the position of an assistant can benefit from a reading of this chapter. It's a good warning, a prevention against "envy, quarrels, slander, rivalry, factions and disorders of every kind."

CHAPTER 66

The Porter of the Monastery

"**At** the door of the monastery, place a sensible old man who knows how to take a message and deliver a reply, and whose age keeps him from roaming about." St. Benedict wants a competent and polite monk to be at the door. An older monk seems to fit the bill, one who will always be there. "This porter will need a room near the entrance so that visitors will always find him there to answer them." An older monk is well trained in stability. He will always be there. Perhaps there is also a more pragmatic reason for giving an older monk the job of porter. He is unable to roam about. "As soon as anyone knocks, or a poor [person] calls out, he replies, 'Thanks be to God' or 'Your blessing, please'; then, with all the gentleness that comes from the fear of God, he provides a prompt answer with the warmth of love." This warm greeting reminds us of what St. Benedict writes in chapter 53: "All guests who present themselves are to be welcomed as Christ, for he himself will say: *I was a stranger and you welcomed me* (Matt 25:35)."

St. Benedict expects not just the porter to be stable but all the other monks too. "The monastery should, if possible, be so constructed that within it all necessities, such as water, mill and garden are contained, and the various crafts are practiced. Then there will be no need for the monks to roam outside, because this is not at all good for their souls." Throughout history Benedictine monks and nuns have adhered to the practice of doing for themselves. But nowadays we seem to have greater needs and fewer craftspeople in our communities. We have to go shopping on the outside more often than in former days.

Although times have changed, the *Rule* endures. St. Benedict ends chapter 66 with this instruction: "We wish this rule to be read often in the community, so that none of the brothers can offer the excuse of ignorance." This is the *Rule* to which all of us are committed. You in your way and I in mine.

CHAPTER 67

Brothers Sent on a Journey

"**B**rothers sent on a journey will ask the abbot and community to pray for them." It is good advice that St. Benedict gives to all of us—pray for a safe trip. In his day monks traveled a lot by foot. They were not sheltered from the elements as we are in our modern modes of transportation. And his monks were in greater peril of being beaten and robbed than we are while traveling today. Come to think of it, though, Father Thomas Andrew was robbed of three hundred dollars and an American Express card while on a journey. He was not trudging along some remote, dusty path but was instead sleeping on a train from Nice to Rome. And Father Guy was not only robbed but beaten while waiting for a bus in Barcelona.

St. Benedict is not only concerned that his traveling monks be free from physical harm, he wants them to escape injuries to their souls also. When they return to the monastery, "They ask the prayers of all for their faults, in case they may have been caught off guard on the way by seeing some evil thing or hearing some idle talk." In the previous chapter, St. Benedict recommends that the monastery should be so self-contained that "there will be no need for the monks to roam outside, because this is not at all good for their souls.'' This is the ideal, but St. Benedict is realistic enough to know there will be occasion for the monks to leave the grounds. The abbot may even have to send them on a journey.

St. Benedict does not want the returning monk ''to relate to anyone else what he saw or heard outside the monastery, because that causes the greatest harm.'' If a monk has seen Pa-ree, he might have a hard time settling down back on the farm. If he talks too much about what he has seen in the City of Bright Lights, the other monks are going to start hankering to go there too. When I was a novice, I used to sit on our hill after dark and look at all the lights in the valley—the lights in the several towns surrounding the monastery and all the yard lights on the farms. This created the illusion of a large city. My good friend from college days was living in New York City then, and he was writing me letters about his exciting life in the Big Apple. When I gazed at the Whetstone Valley in the night, I was imagining that Broadway shows and nightclubs were within my reach. In daylight, I had to face reality. All I could see from my hill were hay bales and fields of corn. St. Benedict knows that the more his monks learn about what's going on outside the monastery, the more they'll want to go there.

Nevertheless, we no longer consider it such a risky business, going out into the larger world these days. In our day monks need to travel more frequently and to greater distances than they did in St. Benedict's time. And we are not prohibited from telling about what we saw and heard. If we say nothing about our journeys, people will begin to wonder what we were really up to.

Be careful when you travel. Don't do away from home any of the improper things you would never do at home.

CHAPTER 68

Assignment of Impossible Tasks to a Brother

"A brother may be assigned a burdensome task or something he cannot do. If so, he should, with complete gentleness and obedience, accept the order given him." St. Benedict is speaking of obedience again. In chapter 5 he said, "The first step of humility is unhestitating obedience." Now, in chapter 68, he goes on to say that the monk is allowed an opportunity to explain to his abbot the reasons why obedience is an impossibility. "Should he see, however, that the weight of the burden is altogether too much for his strength, then he should choose the appropriate moment and explain patiently to his superior the reasons why he cannot perform the task. This he ought to do without pride, obstinacy or refusal." This makes sense, doesn't it? I'm sure you have at some time been asked to accomplish a task that you found beyond your capabilities. You know that a polite refusal is more effective than an indignant protestation.

Nowadays in monastic life when there are fewer members in our communities, some of us may be asked to do things for which we have never had the inclination or the talent. I live in fear that I will be asked to prepare breakfast one day a week. Should that happen, I will probably consider placing an order at Wanda's Donut Shop in town the day before rather than attempt to fry eggs or cook oatmeal. More likely, I will have to remind myself of these words in the Prologue to the *Rule*: "What is not possible to us by nature, let us ask the Lord to supply by the help of his grace." This is repeated in chapter 68, when St. Benedict tells the monk who is begging off: "If after the explanation the superior is still determined to hold to his original order, then the junior must recognize that this is best for him. Trusting in God's help, he must in love obey."

The story that is often told to illustrate Benedictine obedience is the one St. Gregory relates in his biography of St. Benedict:

> Once while blessed Benedict was in his room, one of his monks, the boy Placid, went down to get some water. In letting the bucket fill too rapidly, he lost his balance and was pulled into the lake, where the current quickly seized him and carried him about a stone's throw away from the shore. Though inside the monastery at the time, the man of God was instantly aware of what had happened and called out to Maurus: "Hurry, Brother Maurus! the boy who just went down for water has fallen into the lake, and the current is carrying him away."
>
> What followed was remarkable indeed, and unheard of since the time of Peter the apostle. Maurus asked the blessing and on receiving it hurried out to fulfill his abbot's command. He kept on running even over the water till he reached the place where Placid was drifting along helplessly. Pulling him up by the hair, Maurus rushed back to shore, still under the impression that he was on dry land. It was only when he set foot on ground that he came to himself and looking back realized that he had been running on the surface of the water. Overcome with fear and amazement at a deed he would never have thought possible, he returned to his abbot and told him what had taken place.
>
> The holy man would not take any personal credit for the deed but attributed it to the obedience of his disciple.

Maurus's obedience, in this case, was "unhesitating." There was no time to invoke chapter 68. Maurus may not even have been able to swim, but he had no chance of telling St. Benedict that. Trusting in God's help, Maurus lovingly obeyed St. Benedict.

St. Benedict attributed the miracle of walking on water to Maurus's obedience, but "Maurus on the contrary claimed that it was due entirely to his abbot's command. He could not have been responsible for the miracle himself, he said, since he had not even known he was performing it."

Placid will try settling the dispute in the next sentence by exclaiming, " 'When I was being drawn out of the water,' he told them 'I saw the abbot's cloak over my head; he is the one I thought was bringing me to shore.' "

Nevertheless, it was Maurus's obedient act that saved Placid from drowning. Obedience always has its own reward. And often enough we are amazed that miracles occur when we consent to do something that at first seemed burdensome or impossible to do.

If the time should ever come, I will have to trust in God's help with breakfast. Who knows—I may eventually turn out a tasty omelet. What will you do the next time the assignment of an impossible task comes your way?

CHAPTER 69

The Presumption of Defending Another in the Monastery

What prompted St. Benedict to include this chapter in his *Rule* was the Roman custom of having a protector. A commoner often had to protect his interests by seeking the protection of an influential person. The commoner then owed his protector a public expression of gratitude and was forever subject to him. All classes of people were allowed to enter St. Benedict's monastery, and he did not want a monk from the aristocratic class to assume the role of protector for a monk from the lower class. St. Benedict didn't want any godfathers in his monastery.

He says, "Even if they are related by the closest ties of blood," one monk cannot defend another or be his "champion." If there are siblings in the monastery, the older cannot "big brother" the younger or excuse the kid brother if he misbehaves. We can imagine a situation in which several monks,

all with a blood relationship, gang up in defense of a relative
or unite to form their own agenda for the monastery. St. Benedict wants to prevent this from happening. He had good foresight because consanguinity has always been prevalent in
Benedictine communities. This does not mean that monks or
nuns who are related must disregard their familial ties. It
simply means they must avoid any kind of exclusive relationships that are detrimental to their communities.

Chapter 69 of the *Rule* says something to all of us about
avoiding exclusive relationships. Aren't there times when we
are inclined to shun other people in the club to which we belong, at the place where we work, or even in our own family?
Do we ever want to discriminate because of sex or religion or
race? Do we identify only with our own intimate circle of
friends? St. Benedict says that anyone who departs from his
teaching in chapter 69 should "be sharply restrained." Here
is another instance in the *Rule* where he speaks in a firm manner. He means what he says.

CHAPTER 70

The Presumption of Striking Another Monk at Will

It is unlikely that an abbot in modern times would ever give
permission for one monk to strike another. In chapter 70 of
the *Rule,* however, St. Benedict says, "We decree that no one
has the authority to excommunicate or strike any of his brothers
unless he has been given this power by the abbot." In St.
Benedict's day a permission of this kind could be delegated
by the abbot. There may be occasions nowadays when a monk
might wish that this custom had never fallen out of use. Oh,
if only I could knock some sense into Brother So and So!

In the *Rule* we find several instances where St. Benedict prescribes the use of physical punishment. All of this was written in an age that was much different from our own. The Rule of the Master has this to say in regard to monks who have been excommunicated from community observance: ''If the excommunicated brothers show themselves so arrogant that they persist in the pride of their heart and refuse to make satisfaction to the abbot by the ninth hour of the third day, they are to be confined and whipped with rods to the point of death.''[1]

Now that does seem excessive, doesn't it? St. Benedict does not go that far. The Master may have used ''to the point of death'' as a figure of speech. But Shenoute, a fifth-century Egyptian abbot, admitted that one of his monks had died as the result of a severe beating. This was the kind of punishment Shenoute recommended that an abbess use on her delinquent nuns—ten to forty blows on the soles of their feet.

The Irish monks could be beaten for even the slightest infractions. All of the old monastic legislators subjected their monks to corporal punishment for reasons they judged necessary. St. Benedict employs corporal punishment too, but he is moderate in this as he is in everything else.

St. Benedict expects all of his monks to use ''moderation and common sense'' in dealing with the boys in the monastery. And certainly he expects the same from his monks in their relationship with one another. Shenoute used neither moderation nor common sense in handling a monk of his who was but a young boy. The youngster grew homesick and decided that the next time his father came to visit him, he would ask to go home with him. When Shenoute learned of this, he asked the young monk:

> ''Is it true that if your father comes, you will go back with him into the world? The boy laughed, and our father said to him: ''Truly, I will send you to your true father.'' And when he had said this, he sent him away. The young boy

began to sicken, and our father Shenoute was told about it. The brothers then asked him to pray for him so that he might recover, for he was truly in great pain. Our father the prophet said to them: "What concern is he of yours? He wants to go to his father!" When the brothers heard this, they withdrew. On Saturday, which was the seventh day after the young boy became ill, he fell asleep at the ninth hour of the day. They wrapped him in a shroud, took him out, and buried him.[2]

St. Benedict's biographer did not have to record a scene like that one.

St. Benedict practiced moderation and common sense. He understands that tempers will flare and people will have disagreements, but he asks all of us to avoid the extreme anger that leads to physical abuse. "After all, it is written: *Never do to another what you do not want done to yourself* (Tob 4:16)." He has said that to us before.

CHAPTER 71

Mutual Obedience

"**O**bedience is a blessing to be shown by all, not only to the abbot but also to one another as brothers, since we know that it is by this way of obedience that we go to God."

Although the title of this chapter is "Mutual Obedience," St. Benedict is careful to clarify that the supreme authority of the monastery is invested in the abbot and other officials. "Therefore, although orders of the abbot or of the priors appointed by him take precedence, and no unofficial order may supersede them, in every other instance younger monks should obey their seniors with all love and concern. Anyone found objecting to this should be reproved."

What begins as a general statement about the obedience all of the monks owe one to the other evolves into a definition of the specific relationship between the seniors and juniors of the monastery. "If a monk is reproved in any way by his abbot or by one of his seniors, even for some very small matter, or if he gets the impression that one of his seniors is angry or disturbed with him, however slightly, he must, then and there without delay, cast himself on the ground at the other's feet to make satisfaction, and lie there until the disturbance is calmed by a blessing." St. Benedict presumes that a junior will be inclined to offend a senior, and even if the offense is a slight one, the junior must cry "Uncle!"

At the very beginning of Christian monasticism there were no cenobitical communities like the one for which St. Benedict wrote his *Rule.* A man simply went to the desert and placed himself under the direction of an abba. This was a relationship between master and disciple. The obedient young monk was formed by his elder. He did what the abba told him to do. One elder said, "If you see a young monk by his own will climbing up into heaven, take him by the foot and throw him to the ground, because what he is doing is not good for him."[1] St. Benedict, in his community of cenobites, clings to the old concept that the elder must be right and the junior must be wrong. He pulls the junior to the ground. "He must, then and there without delay, cast himself on the ground at the other's feet to make satisfaction, and lie there until the disturbance is calmed by a blessing."

There is another story from the Desert Fathers, though, that reverses this attitude:

> There was an elder who had a well-trained novice living with him, and once, when he was annoyed, he drove the novice out of his cell. But the novice sat down outside and waited for the elder. The elder, opening the door, found him there, and did penance before him, saying: "You are my Father

because your patience and humility have overcome the weakness of my soul. Come back in; you can be the elder and the Father, I will be the youth and the novice: for by your good work you have surpassed my old age."[2]

St. Benedict, in this chapter of the *Rule,* seems to be dead set against giving the juniors a hearing. In chapter 3, however, he seeks their advice. "The reason why we have said all should be called for counsel is that the Lord often reveals what is better to the younger." In chapter 63, he says that rank in the community should be according to entry and not age: "Absolutely nowhere shall age automatically determine rank. Remember that Samuel and Daniel were still boys when they judged their elders (1 Sam 3; Dan 13:44-62)." These statements from other parts of the *Rule* soften the hard blows the young take in chapter 71.

Mutual obedience is sometimes difficult in a monastery. Even a command of the abbot's that may seem absurd is easier to obey than a request from an ordinary monk who has a little bit of authority in the monastery. If he has no authority whatsoever, we might become indignant when he asks our obedience. Is it sometimes like that in your families and at the places where you work? The point St. Benedict wants to make is that we should all live and work together with respect for one another. He is asking for cooperation. He says it is by this kind of mutual obedience "that we go to God." Going to God will be easier if we're not fighting among ourselves or resisting one another along the way.

CHAPTER 72

The Good Zeal of Monks

"**G**et one of the novices to do it." The novices are always available at our beck and call. They seldom leave the grounds, so they're usually on hand to take the places of the professed monks who have to be away. Get a novice to take my place washing dishes, to do housework, to be master of ceremonies at Mass. I once heard a novice flatly refuse to take someone's place on dishes. Apparently the professed monk had depended on this novice too often. "No," the novice said. And some of the monks who heard about this refusal commented that the novice lacked good zeal. We all should realize that it is unfair to take advantage of someone who is always willing to do whatever we want him or her to do for us. We all know people who find it impossible to say no, and it's nice to have them around. There is a difference, though, between having friends we can count on and making slaves out of them. I think the novice was correct in refusing to substitute for the upteenth time. Someone else deserved an opportunity to practice charity. St. Benedict, in chapter 72 of the *Rule*, quotes from the Letter to the Romans: "*They should each try to be first to show respect to the other* (Rom 12:10)." He means each of the monks, not just the novices. St. Paul meant each of the Roman converts.

I suppose it is the same in the organizations to which you belong in your parish and your community. The burden of the work seems to fall on the same people all of the time. This happens in families too. If we aren't officially assigned to something, why volunteer? St. Benedict would like to have volunteers rather than monks who seek their own interests only. "No one is to pursue what he judges better for himself, but instead, what he judges better for someone else." Living in a monastic family or a natural family, belonging to the Altar Society or the American Legion, we should be inclined to help one another.

Things operate more smoothly if everyone is cooperative and helpful, especially in the little things of everyday living. Often enough we witness people making heroic sacrifices in extraordinary circumstances, but getting us to lift a finger in the humdrum business of life is more difficult.

St. Benedict wants his followers to experience "nothing harsh, nothing burdensome" (Prologue) in the way of life he has mapped out for them. We aim at finding work that is suitable and agreeable to the people who enter our monastic houses. Even so, there is plenty of opportunity to do the things we don't like doing. That's part of our life and yours too.

I know of a Benedictine Sister who was her community's cook for over forty years. She was a cheerful person and one who was greatly admired by the other Sisters. She always had a kind word for everyone, and only once in her lifetime had she been heard to complain about anything. That was the day on which she began her assignment in the kitchen. She said, "I just hate cooking." Monks and nuns ordinarily don't spend their lives in work they dislike. But this Sister survived because of her extraordinary good zeal.

Chapter 72 is near the end of the *Rule*, and it sums up everything St. Benedict has taught us about Christian living. "To their fellow monks they show the pure love of brothers; to God, loving fear; to their abbot, unfeigned and humble love. Let them prefer nothing whatever to Christ, and may he bring us all together to everlasting life." In doing all of this we are practicing the "good zeal which separates from evil and leads to God and everlasting life."

St. Benedict sees good zeal in "supporting with the greatest patience one another's weaknesses of body or behavior." We are to answer the needs of the sick and the crippled with whom we live, and we are to show the same zeal for the people with erratic or downright eccentric personalities. We must even be zealous in our love for those in our midst who appear to lack zeal.

St. Aelred listened to a novice's impression of monastic life:

> "It is absolutely marvellous to me that in this monastery three hundred men can obey the commands of one superior, and do everything he says as if they had all agreed among themselves on this one thing, or as if they had heard the voice of God telling them to do it. In fact I seem to find here every perfection that the gospel precepts contain, and everything I read in the teaching of the fathers and the monks of old. . . ."
>
> Aelred replied: "Since you are a novice, I can put all this enthusiasm down to fervour, and not to self-satisfaction! But you must be careful to remember that there is no perfection in this life that may not be cleverly aped by people who are insincere. And I don't want you to be put off by them, when you discover faults in the religious life, as you certainly will."[1]

St. Aelred and St. Benedict both knew that some monks are not capable of attaining a whole lot of zeal, that some won't even try. It's that way everywhere, isn't it? St. Benedict's *Rule* stirs us on and reminds us of the good zeal we should have. That's why we have his *Rule* for our guide.

There are also the many people from whom we learn the meaning of good zeal. You know them in your hometown, and I know them here in the monastery. We monks call them community-minded members. They are the ones who never withdraw from the life of the community. They respond enthusiastically to the kind of question that is asked of monks who profess vows at the ecumenical monastery of Taizé in France: "Will you, always discerning Christ in your brothers, watch over them in good days and bad, in suffering and in joy?"[2]

The good zeal I have observed in my brothers has often saved me from developing a bitter zeal "which separates from

God and leads to hell." At this moment I'm thinking of three deceased confreres whose good zeal followed them into old age. Brother Alexius, when he could no longer work in the laundry or be our infirmarian, learned how to type in his seventies and was given an office job. He was so determined to learn typing that he would exercise his fingers on an imaginary typewriter keyboard while standing in line as we assembled to process into church. Brother Vital, who had become too crippled with arthritis to do carpentry, went to work in the library. He was an old man then, and he seemed to look upon his library assignment as a second career. Father Ildephonse became a hospital chaplain at an age when most monks have been retired for several years. A stroke removed him from the chaplaincy, and he came back to the abbey to work alongside Brother Vital in the library. Although Father Ildephonse was deaf and unable to speak the last five years of his life, he liked being with us at coffee breaks and at picnics. All three of these monks contributed their services to the community until the end. Their zeal for the life of the community and the work of the community never waned.

Monks owe their obedience to the abbot and the superiors appointed by him, but St. Benedict says monks should also be "earnestly competing in obedience to one another." Any organization that follows that principle is bound to stick together and succeed in its purpose. When the need arises, feel welcome to quote the *Rule of St. Benedict* at the meetings of the Altar Society or the American Legion.

CHAPTER 73

This Rule Only a Beginning of Perfection

"The reason we have written this rule is that, by observing it in monasteries, we can show that we have some degree of virtue and the beginnings of monastic life." It is a great consolation that St. Benedict does not expect any of us to become saints by following his *Rule*. He does expect us to make progress, though, in that direction.

If some monks wish to become more assured of attaining "the very heights of perfection," there are other examples to imitate, but for people like us—you and me—the *Rule of St. Benedict* is sufficient as we hasten to our heavenly home. "Then with Christ's help, keep this little rule that we have written for beginners." You and I will always be beginners, but we will reach our destination by following the *Rule of St. Benedict*.

Sources

Oblates of St. Benedict

1. Congress of Abbots, 1984.
2. Correspondence with Kathleen Norris, poet and writer.

CHAPTER 2. Qualities of the Abbot

1. Aelred of Rievaulx, *Treatises, The Pastoral Prayer*, introduction by David Knowles (Spencer, Mass.: Cistercian Publications, 1971) 116–117.
2. _____, *On Spiritual Friendship*, trans. Mary Eugenia Loher, S.S.N.D. (Kalamazoo: Cistercian Publications-Consortium Press, 1974) 13.

CHAPTER 21. The Deans of the Monastery

1. *The Rule of the Master*, trans. Luke Eberle, O.S.B. (Kalamazoo: Cistercian Publications, 1977) 142.
2. *Ibid.* 147.

CHAPTERS 23–26. The Divine Office

1. Maurus Wolter, O.S.B., *The Principles of Monasticism*, ed. and trans. Bernard Sause, O.S.B. (St. Louis: B. Herder Book Company, 1962) 743.

CHAPTER 29. Readmission of Brothers Who Leave the Monastery

1. Basil, *Ascetical Works: The Long Rules*, Fathers of the Church, trans. M. Monica Wagner, C.S.C. (Washington: Catholic University of America Press, 1950) 263.

2. *Ibid.* 264.

3. Bernard of Clairvaux, *The Letters of St. Bernard of Clairvaux,* ed. and trans. Bruno Scott James (Chicago: Henry Regnery Company, 1953) 435.

4. *Ibid.* 102.

CHAPTER 35. **Kitchen Servers of the Week**

1. Basil, *The Long Rules* 252.

CHAPTER 39. **The Proper Amount of Food**

1. Bernard of Clairvaux, *The Letters* 8.

CHAPTER 40. **The Proper Amount of Drink**

1. Colman J. Barry, O.S.B., *Worship and Work* (Collegeville: St. John's Abbey Press, 1956) 15.

CHAPTER 45. **Mistakes in the Oratory**

1. *The Rule of the Master* 207.

CHAPTER 47. **Announcing the Hours for the Work of God**

1. Pachomius, *Pachomian Koinonia,* trans. Armand Veilleux (Kalamazoo: Cistercian Publications, 1981) 2:145.

2. Frank Bottomly, *The Explorer's Guide to the Abbeys, Monasteries and Churches of Great Britain* (Kingswood, Surrey: Kaye & Ward, Ltd., 1981) 140.

3. *Ibid.* 140.

CHAPTER 49. **The Observance of Lent**

1. *The Rule of the Master* 215.

CHAPTER 52. **The Oratory of the Monastery**

1. Bede, "Lives of the Abbots of Wearmouth and Jarrow," *The Age*

of Bede, ed. and trans. D. H. Farmer (Harmondsworth, Middlesex: Penguin Books, Ltd., 1983) 189.

2. Pachomius 145.

3. Stephen of Lexington, *Letters from Ireland 1228–1229,* trans. Barry W. O'Dwyer (Kalamazoo: Cistercian Publications, 1982) 188.

4. *Ibid.* 188.

CHAPTER 54. **Letters or Gifts for Monks**

1. Cuthbert, account of Bede's death, trans. in *Book of Prayer* (Collegeville: St. John's Abbey Press, 1975) 1577.

CHAPTER 56. **The Abbot's Table**

1. Hubert Van Zeller, *The Rule of St. Benedict* (New York: Sheed & Ward, 1958) 351.

CHAPTER 57. **The Artisans of the Monastery**

1. David Knowles, *Christian Monasticism* (London: Weidenfeld and Nicolson, 1969) 81–82.

2. *Ibid.* 82.

3. Boniface Wimmer, quoted in *Sacred Art at St. John's Abbey* (Collegeville: The Liturgical Press, 1980).

CHAPTER 59. **The Offering of Sons by Nobles or by the Poor**

1. Bede, *A History of the English Church and People,* trans. Leo Sherley-Price, rev. R.E. Latham (Harmondsworth, Middlesex: Penguin Books, Ltd., 1968) 336.

CHAPTER 60. **The Admission of Priests to the Monastery**

1. Gregory the Great, "Homilies on Ezekiel," *Book of Prayer,* 1700.

2. Thomas Merton, *The Wisdom of the Desert* (New York: New Directions, 1960) 65.

CHAPTER 61. **The Reception of Visiting Monks**

1. *The Rule of the Master* 240.

CHAPTER 64. **The Election of an Abbot**

1. Bede, *The Age of Bede* 196.

CHAPTER 70. **The Presumption of Striking Another Monk at Will**

1. *The Rule of the Master* 153.
2. Besa, *The Life of Shenoute,* trans. David N. Bell (Kalamazoo: Cistercian Publications, 1983) 79.

CHAPTER 71. **Mutual Obedience**

1. Merton, *The Wisdom of the Desert* 47.
2. *Ibid.* 59.

CHAPTER 72. **The Good Zeal of Monks**

1. Aelred of Rievaulx, *The Mirror of Charity,* trans. Geoffrey Webb and Adrian Walker (London: A.R. Mowbray & Co., 1962) 62.
2. *The Rule of Taizé* (Taizé: Ateliers et Presses de Taizé, 1968) 139.

Statistical Problems

About The Author

A Cambridge, England, mathematician, Mr. L. H. Longley-Cook has made a career as an actuary in England and, since 1949, in the United States. He has written extensively on insurance statistics; their collection, interpretation, and use for determining insurance costs.

In 1968 he retired from the post of Vice-President-Actuary of the Insurance Company of North America and is now Special Lecturer and Research Consultant in the School of Business Administration at Georgia State University.

He is a Fellow of the Royal Statistical Society (England), the Institute of Actuaries, the Casualty Actuarial Society, and a member of other actuarial bodies.

His published books include a two volume actuarial text, *Life and Other Contingencies*, a booklet on *Credibility Theory*, and three mathematical puzzle books—*Work This One Out*, *Fun With Brain Puzzlers*, and *New Math's Puzzle Book*.

COLLEGE OUTLINE SERIES

Statistical Problems

L. H. Longley-Cook

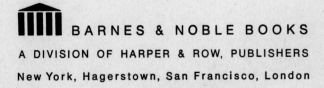 BARNES & NOBLE BOOKS

A DIVISION OF HARPER & ROW, PUBLISHERS

New York, Hagerstown, San Francisco, London

Manufactured in the United States of America

Preface

The development of statistics can be divided into four principal periods. The first three were the early studies of political arithmetic of the seventeenth and eighteenth centuries; the development of frequency distributions in the nineteenth century; and the full exploration of mathematical statistics in the first half of the present century. Over the last two or three decades, statistics has entered its fourth and most exciting period. This has been the result of the spread of quantitative methods from the physical sciences to the social sciences, and to business, government, and the armed services.

It is now fully realized that every branch of the humanities needs statistical techniques to interpret its results. Biometrics has been followed by a whole series of other "—metrics" such as econometrics, sociometrics, etc., each applying statistical techniques to a specialized field. Further, the enormous developments in data processing equipment have enabled studies to be undertaken, particularly in the multivariate field, which were quite impractical a few years ago. Thus, statistics has become the vital tool of the research worker, from the physicist to the psychologist, from the archaeologist to the town-planner.

In addition, in the last two decades, there has been a vast spread of the applications of scientific methods to every type of organization and activity. This has led to a formalization of Decision Mathematics which brings together the techniques of not only statistics but those of applied mathematics, game theory, operations research, organization and methods, actuarial science, and many other fields. As a result, statistics is ceasing to be a specialized field of study but a part of basic education alongside formal mathematics.

Statistics is a very practical subject and it is the aim of this text, with its numerous examples, to provide the reader, not only with an understanding of statistical methods, but with the ability to apply these methods himself in whatever field of endeavor he is personally interested.

L. H. LONGLEY-COOK

Georgia State University

Contents

Statistical Problems

1

Recording Data—Frequency Distributions

1.1. Introduction. We live in a world of uncertainty, and in every field of endeavor, decisions must be made in the face of uncertainty. In this highly competitive age, success is unlikely to be achieved by making guesses, relying on hunches, or even by judgment unsupported by the best data. In business, government, and military affairs, *decision mathematics* has emerged as the essential tool for making proper *judgment decisions*, and *statistics* is a major part of decision mathematics.

Statistics, originally consisting of the collection and tabulation of data concerning the *state*, is now the technical means by which data can be developed and analysed for *intelligent decision making*. The field of its use has extended far beyond state and government services, and it is employed extensively in every branch of science and business.

Because uncertainty is implicit in nearly everything we do, statistics is concerned with *probability distribution models*, *testing of hypotheses*, *significance tests*, and other means of determining the *correctness of our deductions* and the *most likely outcome* of our decisions.

The first step in the analysis of any source of information is the proper collection of statistics—the recording of data. The next step is the display of the recorded data in a form which can be readily interpreted. This chapter will be devoted to the study of these two problems. Statistics is a very practical subject, and a proper understanding of it can be best obtained by constant illustration in the text and the frequent working of examples. The text contains numerous worked examples, and each chapter is followed by a series of problems with, in most cases, detailed solutions.

1

It is often stated that you can use statistics to prove whatever you wish. This is not so, but the brazen use of statistics to mislead is all too common. "Six doctors out of ten recommend brand X." What does this mean? Were a large number of doctors asked which brand they thought best, or were they asked to list any number of different brands they might recommend? The interpretation of the statement depends greatly on the question posed. Perhaps just ten doctors were approached, and if less than six recommended brand X, another ten were tried. The statistician must look beyond the mere statistics he displays to interpret his results.

1.2. Recording Data. The first step in statistical analysis is the recording of data. It may be necessary to make a special study, or the data may be available from records maintained for a purpose other than the statistical investigation to be undertaken. In most cases data will be put on, or will be available on punched cards or tape. However, in the text, we show a limited volume of data in tabular form, similar to a write-out from a tabulating machine or a computer.

To illustrate the type of data which might be recorded, there is set out below, the first three lines of tabulated data concerning a group of students. The data have not been sorted in any order.

Name	Sex	Age	Height	State of Birth	Number of Brothers and Sisters
Adams, John	M	19	6 ft., 2 in.	N.Y.	3
Cowan, Tom	M	22	6 ft., 0 in.	Pa.	0
Brown, Joan	F	18	5 ft., 8 in.	N.Y.	2

Such a tabulation is the "raw material" of any statistical investigation. It must be analysed and displayed if it is to be used to make reasonable deductions or comparisons with other similar data.

1.3. Continuous and Discontinuous Variables. It will be noted that some data are numerical and some are not. The name, sex, and the state are not numerical, although as will be explained later, numbers may be used for recording some *non-numerical data*.

Most of the data used in statistical work are numerical, and items recorded, such as age, height, and number of brothers and sisters, are each called *variables*. Some variables are discontinuous, or discrete in form, for example, the number of brothers and sisters, since the values which the variables can assume are limited to 0, 1, 2, 3, etc. (The term "half brother" does not, of course, have the same meaning as "half a brother." Instructions for any tabulation must explain whether or not half brothers are to be included as brothers.)

While age and height are *continuous variables*, they and other continuous variables have to be recorded in discrete form. Height is usually expressed in feet and inches; it could be measured in some other unit such as centimeters.

1.4. Processing Data. The days of hand tabulation, hand sorting, and calculation on simple calculating machines are a thing of the past for any sizeable investigation. The vast majority of statistical work is carried out by means of electronic data processing equipment, or by punched cards.

For simplicity of recording data when punched cards are used, and to conserve space on the card, non-numerical data may be recorded in an alphabetical or numerical code. Thus, *M* would be used for Male and *F* for Female, or where cards are used, sex and marital status might be indicated in a single code:

1. Male, Single
2. Male, Married
3. Female, Single
4. Female, Married

Similarly, two digits can be used to record states by code.

Although it is rarely necessary to sort data by hand, some understanding of how this can best be done is necessary, and this is explained in the next section. Similarly, short cuts which can be used in the calculation of statistical constants by hand will be included in the text, although such short cuts are of considerably less importance now that most work is done by processing equipment.

In order to study a limited volume of data, the raw data are often arranged in an *array* of descending order of magnitude. The difference between the largest and smallest value is called the *range* of the data.

EXAMPLE 1.1.   The ages of the sixteen members of a bridge club are:

$$37, \ 28, \ 40, \ 47, \ 30, \ 42, \ 38, \ 45,$$
$$47, \ 39, \ 52, \ 25, \ 30, \ 35, \ 29, \ 41$$

Arrange these data in an array of ascending age and determine the range of the data.

Solution.   The array is:

$$25, \ 28, \ 29, \ 30, \ 30, \ 35, \ 37, \ 38,$$
$$39, \ 40, \ 41, \ 42, \ 45, \ 47, \ 47, \ 52$$

and the range is:

$$52 - 25 = 27 \ \text{years}$$

Occasionally, it is necessary to obtain an array for a large volume of data without the help of data processing equipment. In such a case, it is best to select suitable groups of ages, and tabulate for each group the ages of the individual persons in the group.   For the above data the tabulation would be as follows:

Age Group	Individual Ages
20–29	28, 25, 29
30–39	37, 30, 38, 39, 30, 35
40–49	40, 47, 42, 45, 47, 41
50–59	52

The final array can then be written down without difficulty.

$$25, \ 28, \ 29, \ 30, \ 30, \ 35, \ 37, \ 38,$$
$$39, \ 40, \ 41, \ 42, \ 45, \ 47, \ 47, \ 52$$

1.5. Use of a Score Sheet to Tally Data.   With a larger volume of data, there will be a number of persons with the same age, and instead of an array, it is useful to tabulate the *number* of persons at each age. Similar tabulations can be made for other numerical data.

When data are being analyzed without the help of data processing equipment, use is made of a *score sheet* to *tally* the age or other measure of the data. The next example shows how this is done.

EXAMPLE 1.2. The ages of the students in a class are:

19, 20, 23, 25, 21, 19, 19, 18, 20, 20,
17, 23, 19, 21, 22, 18, 20, 19, 20, 21,
21, 18, 20, 19, 21, 20, 17, 18, 22, 19,
22, 20, 19, 22, 20, 21, 19, 20, 19, 18,
22, 18, 22, 20, 22, 19, 20, 23, 22, 26,
21, 19, 20.

Use a score sheet to find the frequency distribution of students by age and determine the range of ages.
Solution.

Age	Tally	Total Number
17	||	2
18	⊬⊬ |	6
19	⊬⊬ ⊬⊬ ||	12
20	⊬⊬ ⊬⊬ |||	13
21	⊬⊬ ||	7
22	⊬⊬ |||	8
23	|||	3
24		0
25	|	1
26	|	1
		53

It will be noted that every fifth tally is drawn on the diagonal across the four preceding tallies to assist in counting. The range of the data is

$$26 - 17 = 9 \text{ years}$$

1.6 Class Intervals. In statistical work, a major problem is how to reduce a large volume of raw data into a form in which the chief characteristics of the data can be studied and comparisons made with other related data. For this reason, the use of arrays for large volumes of data is inappropriate, and frequency distributions are developed which show the distribution of data, not by individual values of such measures as ages, heights, or examination scores, but by ranges of such values. Thus, the tabulating of the residents of a town by age might use age groups 0–5, 6–10, 11–15, 16–20, 21–25, etc., or 0–9, 10–19, 20–29, etc. Such groups are called *classes*. It is important that classes should not overlap and that there should be no gaps between classes. Class intervals need not be of equal size but the graphical display of data and the calculation of statistical constants becomes slightly more difficult when unequal intervals are used.

If height of trees is measured in feet, the class intervals could be 0–9 feet, 10–19 feet, etc., but if height is measured in feet and inches, the class intervals would be 0 feet–9 feet, 11 inches; 10 feet–19 feet, 11 inches, etc. In either case the class intervals can be expressed as, 0 feet–, 10 feet–, 20 feet–, etc.; only the commencing point of each interval being stated, followed by a dash.

When data processing equipment is used, class intervals 0–9 feet, 10–19 feet, etc., are more satisfactory than 1–10 feet, 11–20 feet, etc., because the sorting machines can be instructed to sort by the first digit only in the former case, but not in the latter.

With height measured in feet, the class interval 10 feet to 19 feet includes all true measurements from $9\frac{1}{2}$ feet to $19\frac{1}{2}$ feet, since 9.51 feet would be rounded to 10 feet. $9\frac{1}{2}$ feet is called the *lower class boundary** and $19\frac{1}{2}$ feet the *upper class boundary*. The difference between the upper and the lower class boundary is called the *class size*, width, or interval. In the example being used, the class size is

$$19\frac{1}{2} \text{ feet } - 9\frac{1}{2} \text{ feet } = 10 \text{ feet}$$

The midpoint of a class interval is important, and is obtained by adding the lower and upper class boundaries and dividing by 2. In the example used above, the midpoint is

$$\frac{19\frac{1}{2} + 9\frac{1}{2}}{2} = 14\frac{1}{2} \text{ feet}$$

This is called the *class midpoint* or *class mark*.

It is the custom to record ages as *age last birthday*; hence, the class interval, age 20 to age 29, will include all persons with age last birthday 20 to 29 inclusive. The class boundaries will be *exact* age 20 and *exact* age 30. The class size will be 10 years and the class midpoint will be *exact* age 25.

Class intervals need not commence from zero but must include the lowest and highest values. To choose class intervals, determine the highest and lowest values, and hence, determine the

---

*In this example, 10 feet is sometimes referred to as the lower class *limit*, and 19 feet as the upper class *limit*.

range. If possible, the class intervals should be chosen by dividing the range into a convenient number (about 10 is often suitable) of equal intervals. However, this may not always be possible. The midpoints of class intervals should, if practical, coincide with actual observed data.

EXAMPLE 1.3.   If the data in Example 1.2 is to be displayed in three classes, what class intervals should be used?
Solution.   With 10 ages, equal class intervals must include more than three ages each and the most suitable intervals are

$$16–19$$
$$20–23$$
$$24–27$$

EXAMPLE 1.4.   The results of an examination were as follows:

Marks	Students
40–49	1
50–59	7
60–69	23
70–79	21
80–89	8
90–99	5
	65

Determine the following:

	Solution
1. The number of classes	6
2. The class size	10
3. The lower class boundary of the third class	$59\frac{1}{2}$
4. The class midpoint (or mark) of the fifth class	$84\frac{1}{2}$

EXAMPLE 1.5.   If class intervals for a certain measurement are 0–, 5 inches –, 10 inches –, 15 inches –, and measurements are made to the nearest 1/8 of an inch, what are the class boundaries, size, and midpoint of the second class?
Solution.

Lower class boundary	$4^{15}/_{16}$ inches
Upper class boundary	$9^{15}/_{16}$ inches
Class size	5 inches
Class midpoint	$7^{7}/_{16}$ inches

1.7. Rounding Numbers. Data, whether in the form of a continuous or discontinuous variable, may have been rounded before they reach the statistician, but the statistician may often desire to round numbers to reduce the size of the figures to be tabulated. Thus, the population of the United States at the 1960 Census was 183,285,009. For normal use, no lack of accuracy would result from rounding the figure to the nearest thousand—183,285,000, or even to the nearest hundred thousand—183,300,000. It will be noted that in the latter example, 183,300,000 is the *nearest* hundred thousand, so as to make the approximation as near the true figure as possible. This result is better written as 1.833×10^8 or 183.3 million. The student should avoid recording figures or calculating averages and other statistical constants, to a greater number of digits than are meaningful. Thus, in calculating the average height of the students in a class, 5 ft., 11 in. is a meaningful figure but 5 ft., 11.23 in. includes two places of decimals which are meaningless, since the height of an individual cannot be measured to a tenth or a hundredth of an inch.

The rounding of a number such as 17.50 to the nearest integer presents a dilemma because 17.50 is equally distant from 17 and 18. One practice is to round alternate cases up and down so as to minimize the cumulative rounding error. However, with the increased use of data processing equipment, it is more usual to "round up," to 18 in this case, because this lends itself more readily to machine processing.

EXAMPLE 1.6.   Round the following numbers to the nearest unit, 10 units, and 100 units.   47.73, $392\frac{3}{4}$, $72\frac{1}{8}$, 5321.09, 400, 74.7, 155, 149.5.
Solution.

Units	48	393	72	5321	400	75	155	150
10 Units	50	390	70	5320	400	70	160	150
100 Units	0	400	100	5300	400	100	200	100

1.8. Frequency Distributions. While many types of descriptive statistical distributions are possible, such as distributions according to sex, location, plant genus, color, etc., this book will be concerned mainly with two special types of distribution which have particular importance. These are *frequency distributions* and *time series.* Frequency distributions are discussed in this and in the following chapters. Time series are considered in Chapter 9.

The *frequency* of a variable x is the number of times it occurs, and a *frequency distribution* is an arrangement of numerical data which displays the frequency of the data according to a variable which measures *size or magnitude.* Example 1.2 shows the frequency distribution of a class of 53 students according to age. Example 1.4 shows the frequency distribution of a class of 65 students according to examination marks. It will be noted, as is usually the case, that the marks are grouped into class intervals and the *frequency of each class interval* is shown. Frequency distributions can be displayed in graphical form as in Figures 1.1 and 1.2. In this case the independent variable is measured along the horizontal, or x axis, and the number or frequency, the dependent variable, is measured along the vertical, or y axis.

It should be noted that the class interval grouping is a measure of *size or magnitude* such as age, height, weight, angle, distance, etc. It is not really appropriate to use the term frequency distribution for a non-numerical class measure such as a tabulation of the distribution of population by states, although this term is sometimes used in such cases.

A *frequency histogram* consists of a series of rectangles with bases on the horizontal (x) axis with centers at the class midpoints and length equal to the class interval. The *areas* of the rectangles are proportionate to the class frequencies. When the class intervals are equal in size, the *heights* of the rectangles are also proportionate to the class frequency.

A *frequency polygon* is obtained by joining the midpoint of the top of each rectangle. When the class intervals are equal, it is a graph of class frequency against class midpoint.

In order to compare two frequency distributions, it is useful to increase or decrease the class frequencies so that the total of all class frequencies is the same for both distributions. Such results are usually expressed as percentages of the total for all classes and are called *relative or normalized frequency distributions.*

EXAMPLE 1.7. Draw a frequency histogram and frequency polygon for the data in Example 1.2 and calculate the relative frequency distribution.

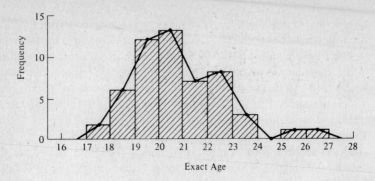

Figure 1.1. Age distribution of a class of students. Frequency histogram and frequency polygon.

Solution.   The histogram and polygon are shown in Figure 1.1. The relative frequency distribution is obtained by dividing the total in each class by 53, the total number of students.

Age* (1)	Number of Students (2)	Relative Frequency Col. (2) ÷ 53
17	2	4%
18	6	11%
19	12	23%
20	13	25%
21	7	13%
22	8	15%
23	3	6%
24	0	0%
25	1	2%
26	1	2%
	53	101%

*Last birthday

The total percentage is 101%, not 100%, because of the rounding of the individual percentages to the nearest one percent.

EXAMPLE 1.8.   The following grouped data show the results of an end of term examination.   Draw the frequency histogram and frequency polygon of the results.

Grade	Number of Students
Under 30	6
30–39	4
40–49	7
50–59	10
60–69	20
70–79	18
80–99	5
100	0
	70

Solution. This is a case of class intervals which are not all the same size, the first and next to last groups being larger than the others. Care must be used in such cases. When the class interval is twice the normal, as in the next to last interval, the length of the rectangle will be twice normal, and hence, the height must be one-half the number of students in order to make the histogram area proportional to the students. The first interval is three times the normal so we make the height one-third the number of students in the class, or 2. This is the same as assuming:

Grade	Number of Students
0–9	2
10–19	2
20–29	2
0–29	6

The histogram and polygon are shown in Figure 1.2.

Remember that for the class 30–39, for example, the lower and upper boundaries are $29\frac{1}{2}$ and $39\frac{1}{2}$ and the midpoint is $34\frac{1}{2}$. The divisions between the rectangles are drawn at these boundaries and the points on the polygon are at the midpoints of the classes.

1.9. Cumulative Frequency Distribution. Sometimes it is desirable to show the distribution of data in a cumulative form. Thus, we may wish to tabulate the number of students scoring less than or more than various scores in the example above. These distributions are called *cumulative frequency distributions* or *ogives* and are obtained by summing the frequency distribution from the top or from the bottom of the table. As with frequency distributions, it is often useful for comparative purposes to develop *relative*

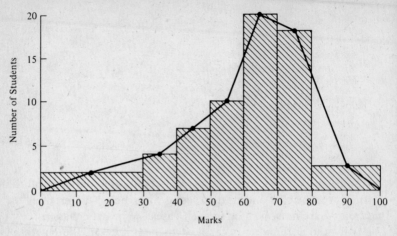

Figure 1.2. Examination results. Frequency histogram and frequency polygon.

cumulative frequency distributions or percentage ogives by expressing the cumulative frequencies as a percentage of the total frequency.

EXAMPLE 1.9. Tabulate "less than" and "and over" ogives for the data in Example 1.8 and graph the results.
Solution.

Marks	Number of Students
Less than 30	6
Less than 40	10
Less than 50	17
Less than 60	27
Less than 70	47
Less than 80	65
100 or less	70

Marks	Number of Students
0 and over	70
30 and over	64
40 and over	60
50 and over	53
60 and over	43
70 and over	23
80 and over	5
Over 100	0

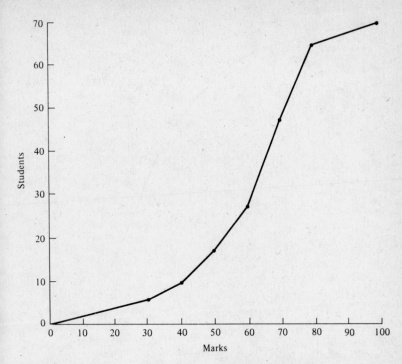

Figure 1.3. Examination results. Cumulative distribution function. "Less than" ogive of the data in Figure 1.2.

The graphs of these distributions (ogives) are shown in Figures 1.3 and 1.4.

1.10. Frequency Curves. In most statistical studies, the data are only a *sample* of a larger *universe* of data. If the whole universe of data were examined, very small class intervals could be used and it would be generally found that the frequency polygon approximates a smooth curve. It is convenient, therefore, to draw a smooth curve which follows the indication of the frequency polygon but does not necessarily pass through any of the actual points of the polygon. Such a curve is called a *frequency curve*. In the same way a smooth ogive can be drawn to fit a cumulative frequency distribution.

Three of the most common shapes of frequency curves are illustrated in the top half of Figure 1.5 and are called *bell-shaped*. Three less usual shapes are shown in the bottom half. However, curves with more than one maximum value can occur.

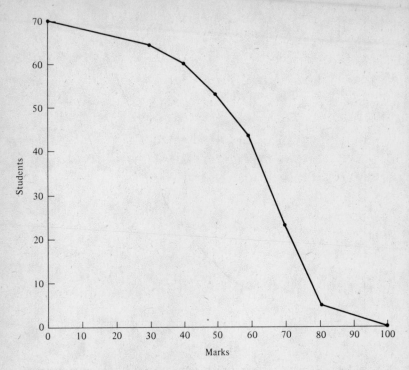

Figure 1.4. Examination results. Cumulative distribution function. "And over" ogive of the data in Figure 1.2.

It will be noted that while the first curve in the top row is symmetrical, the second curve has a "tail" which measured from the highest point, is longer on the right than on the left. Such a curve is stated to be skewed to the right. A discussion of skewness will be found in Section 5.5 of Chapter 5 where the significance of positive (+ ive) and negative (− ive) skewness will be explained.

EXAMPLE 1.10.   Draw a frequency curve for the distribution by age of the students in a class given in Example 1.2.
Solution.   The center points of the top of each rectangle of the frequency histogram are the points of the frequency polygon. These are indicated by dots on graph paper and a smooth curve is drawn passing through these points, keeping the dots as equidistant as possible on either side of the curve, as illustrated in Figure 1.6.

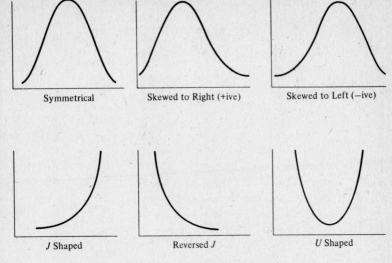

Figure 1.5. Typical frequency curves.

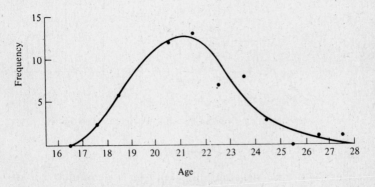

Figure 1.6. Age distribution of a class of students. Smooth frequency curve.

EXAMPLE 1.11. As part of a study of variations in the earth's magnetism over long periods of time, the magnetic inclination of a number of lava flows from volcanic formations in Hawaii were analyzed and correlated with the age of the flows. The following table gives the frequency distribution of these flows by inclination angle. Draw a frequency histogram and a frequency curve of the data.

Inclination Angle	Number of Lava Flows
−10°−	2
0°−	6
10°−	18
20°−	27
30°−	26
40°−	21
50°−	7
60°−	0
	107

Solution. The frequency histogram is given in Figure 1.7, and the frequency curve in Figure 1.8. The dots on the frequency curve are the points of the frequency polygon.

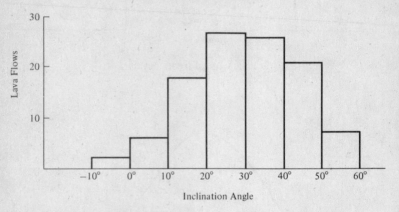

Figure 1.7. Lava flows in Hawaii. Frequency histogram.

Problems

Problem 1.1. List six continuous and six discontinuous variables, not mentioned in the text, which might be used in statistical work.

Problem 1.2. What is the minimum number of digit codes (0 to 9 inclusive) which are needed to record:

    a. Two "yes or no" answers.
    b. Three "yes or no" answers.
    c. One two-choice answer and one three-choice answer.
    d. The day of the month.
    e. The month of the year.
    f. The year.

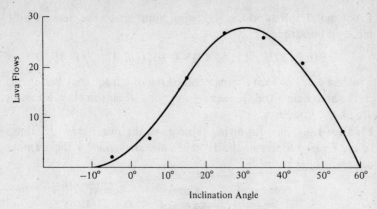

Figure 1.8. Lava flows in Hawaii. Frequency curve.

Problem 1.3. Use a tally score sheet to determine the frequency of the number of words on a line of a page of print. Before you start, write down the shape of the frequency curve you expect to get.

Problem 1.4. By means of a tally sheet, obtain the frequency of the letters of the alphabet in the wording of this sentence. Why do these data not meet the definition of a frequency *distribution* used in this book?

Problem 1.5. Suggest suitable class intervals for a study of the height of male college students when a maximum of nine codes can be used.

Problem 1.6. The following is part of a tabulation of the residents of Pennsylvania in 1960, analyzed according to adjusted gross income:

Adjusted Gross Income Class	Number of Returns
Under $1,000	79,120
$1,000–$1,999	292,734
$2,000–$2,999	376,775
etc.	etc.

For the second class, what are:

(1) the class limits
(2) the class boundaries
(3) the class size
(4) the class midpoint?

Problem 1.7.   Round the following numbers to the nearest unit, ten, and hundred.

$$541.7, \ 17\frac{1}{2}, \ 155.5, \ 4545.4, \ 957, \ 62.47, \ 3/4, \ 85$$

Problem 1.8.   Which is greater, the area of a frequency histogram or the area below the frequency polygon, when the class intervals are all the same size?

Problem 1.9.   The following table gives the number of dwellings in the United States at the 1960 census, analyzed by the number of persons per room.

Number of Persons Per Room	Owner Occupied Dwellings	Renter Occupied Dwellings
	(In thousands)	
0.50 or less	15,292	6,897
0.51 to 0.75	7,702	4,756
0.76 to 1.00	6,953	5,310
1.01 to 1.50	2,180	2,031
1.51 or more	670	1,233
	32,797	20,227

Construct a frequency histogram and a frequency polygon of the distribution of owner occupied dwellings by number of persons per room.   Draw a frequency curve which fits these data. (Note that the class intervals are not all the same size and an assumption must be made as to the upper limit of the last class.)

Problem 1.10.   Using the data of Problem 1.9, develop a frequency distribution for the renter occupied dwellings and for all dwellings.

Problem 1.11.   Tabulate the "less than" cumulative distribution functions for the data in Problem 1.9, for owner occupied, for renter occupied, and for all dwellings, and set out the results in graphic form.

Problem 1.12.   Tabulate and graph the "more than" cumulative distribution functions for the data in Problem 1.9 in the same manner as in Problem 1.11.

Problem 1.13.   Take a pack of shuffled playing cards and deal out successive groups of three cards and tally the resultant frequencies:

**Maximum Number of Cards
in Any Suit**   **Tally   Total**

1 (i.e., all cards of different suits)
2 (i.e., two cards of the same suit)
3 (i.e., three cards of the same suit)

Calculate the relative frequency distribution and draw the frequency polygon. (Try to forecast which group will have the highest frequency before starting the tally.)

Problem 1.14. In a census of the population of the United States, the number of persons at each age is recorded. If a graph of this frequency distribution were drawn, what would be its shape?

Problem 1.15. Suggest statistical distributions which are likely to be:

(*a*)	Bell-shaped—Symmetrical
(*b*)	Bell-shaped—Skewed to right
(*c*)	Bell-shaped—Skewed to left
(*d*)	*J* shaped
(*e*)	Reversed *J*
(*f*)	*U* shaped

Problem 1.16. The following table gives the live births per 1000 native white women, aged 15–44, in the United States in 1964:

Birth	Number
First	30
Second	20
Third	11
Fourth	6
Fifth	4
Sixth	2
Seventh	2
Eighth and Over	3

Draw a frequency polynomial. What is the type of this frequency distribution?

Problem 1.17. Calculate and draw an "or over" ogive from the data in Problem 1.16. Calculate the percentage ogive for this data.

Problem 1.18. Six coins are tossed and the number of heads counted. The result may be any number from 0 to 6. The experiment is performed 100 times, and the results are classified as follows:

Heads	0	1	2	3	4	5	6
Number Observed	2	7	26	29	24	10	2

Draw a graph of this frequency polygon. Has a smooth frequency curve any significance in this case?

Problem 1.19. A true die is rolled 100 times and a tally made of the number of times 1, 2, 3, 4, 5, or 6 comes up. What would be the shape of the frequency distribution?

Problem 1.20. Role two dice 100 times and tally the results. Draw a graph of the frequency polygon. What shape would you expect this polygon to have?

Solutions

Problem 1.1. Continuous: weight, girth, speed, elevation, illumination, miles of highway, etc. Discontinuous: *Number* of very many things such as houses, sales, employees, radios, rooms in a house, children, etc.

Problem 1.2. (*a*) 1, (*b*) 1, (*c*) 1, (*d*) 2, (*e*) 2, (*f*) 2*

*Rarely will there be the need to record more than the last two digits of the year (e.g., 67 for 1967) and in many statistical studies a single digit is sufficient.

Problem 1.3. If there are a full number of words on each line, the frequency curve will be bell shaped, but if short lines in headings and at the end of paragraphs are included in the study, the frequency curve will be skewed to the left.

Problem 1.4. The score sheet will start as follows:

Letter	Tally	Total Number
A	̄N̄N̄ I	6
B	III	3
C	II	2
D	I	1
E	̄N̄N̄ ̄N̄N̄ ̄N̄N̄ I	16
etc.		

Since the letters A, B, C, etc., are not measures of size or magnitude, this is not a frequency *distribution* as defined in Section 1.8. Considerable use can be made of such distributions as this one, particularly when the data are rearranged so that the letter (or other classification such as country, sales outlet, etc.) with the greatest frequency is placed first, the letter with the next greatest frequency is placed second, etc. If we do this, we find the order of letters is:

E, T, N, H, A, O,...

It is interesting to note how close this order, which has been obtained for a small sample, is to the order established for English writing from extensive studies. This order is:

E, T, A, I, S, O, N, . . .

Problem 1.5. It is unlikely that a student will be under 4′6″ or over 6′9″, although an occasional rare case can occur. Suggested class intervals are:

4′6″–, 4′9″–, 5′0″–, 5′3″–, 5′6″–,
5′9″–, 6′0″–, 6′3″–, 6′6″–.

Problem 1.6. The answers are:

(1) $1,000 and $1,999
(2) $999.50 and $1,999.50
(3) $1,000
(4) $1,499.50

However, the statistics collected will not have sufficient accuracy to justify this exactitude and the class boundaries can be taken as $1,000 and $2,000 and the class midpoint as $1,500 without loss of accuracy.

Problem 1.7.

Units	542	18	156	4545	957	62	1	85
Tens	540	20	160	4550	960	60	0	90
Hundreds	500	0	200	4500	1000	100	0	100

Problem 1.8. Consider two neighboring class rectangles *ABCD* and *EFGC* in Figure 1.9. The midpoints of the tops of these rectangles are *X* and *Y*. The portion of the histogram excluded from the area below the polygon is the triangle *EYZ* and this triangle is exactly equal to the triangle *BXZ*, the portion of the area below the polygon excluded from the histogram. Hence, the two areas are equal.

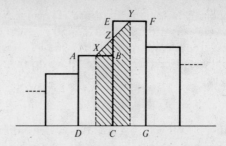

Figure 1.9. Frequency histogram and frequency polygon. Comparison of areas.

Problems 1.9–1.12. These are straightforward and no solutions provided.

Problem 1.13. Class 2 (two cards the same suit) is likely to have the highest frequency.

Problem 1.14. The number of persons at each attained age will generally decrease as the age increases, but owing to fluctuations in the number of births each year, this rule will not be exact and there will be cases where the number of persons at age $x + 1$ is greater than the number of persons at age x.

Problem 1.15.

(*a*) Symmetrical bell-shaped distributions arise from many pure probability concepts such as occur when rolling dice or tossing pennies. Also, many studies in biology (such as distributions by size) will develop curves very close to bell shaped.

(*b*) Bell-shaped distributions skewed to the right occur frequently in studies of wealth, such as distributions of income, size of houses, etc.

(*c*) Bell-shaped distributions skewed to the left are likely to occur in distributions of examination marks, I.Q. scores, etc.

(*d*) *J* shaped distributions will occur only when there is a top limit to the class interval. An example would be the number of games in a world series where the maximum of seven games will be more frequent than the minimum of four games.

(*e*) The number of automobile drivers having 0, 1, 2, 3 or more accidents a year provides an example of a reversed *J* curve.

(*f*) *U* shaped distributions, like *J* distributions, can occur only when there is a top limit to the class interval. An example would be deaths per 100 persons living, classified according to age. The rate of mortality in the first year after birth is higher than in subsequent years, and after about age 25, the rate of mortality increases with each year of age.

Problems 1.16 and 1.17.   Straightforward; no solutions provided.

Problem 1.18.   Because of the discrete nature of the independent variable (the number of heads), a value corresponding to 1.5 heads has no significance. However, a smooth curve does enable the eye to get a clearer picture of the distribution.

Problem 1.19.   Since any number from 1 to 6 is equally likely on the roll of a die, the frequency of each score would be approximately 17 and a frequency polygon would approximate to a straight line.

Problem 1.20.   A symmetrical bell-shaped distribution.

2

The Mean of a Distribution

2.1. Definition. Much statistical data consists of a tabulation of the value of some characteristic for each of a number of individuals or items, for example, the ages of students in a class. The most obvious measure to describe this characteristic of the data is an average value of the variable; in this case the average age of the class. While various averages may be used, the one most frequently employed in statistical work is the *arithmetic mean* or *mean* as it is usually called. This is the arithmetic average obtained by adding up all the individual values and dividing by the number of items. There are other means, such as the geometric mean, described in Chapter 3, but when the term *mean* is used without qualification the arithmetic mean is meant. The mean provides a single value which is typical of the data and is an indication of the *point of central tendency*.

2.2. Calculation of the Mean. With data recorded on punched cards or tape as is usually the case, the calculation of the mean is very simple and straightforward. Data processing equipment can be readily instructed to add all the ages or other characteristic which is being studied. All that remains to be done to calculate the mean is to divide the total by the number of students (or other base as appropriate). With more sophisticated equipment even the division can be performed automatically. However, the student must learn how to calculate the mean of a distribution without the advantage of data processing equipment. Various procedures are available which reduce the work of handling large volumes of data and these procedures are explained in the following examples.

EXAMPLE 2.1. Calculate the mean I.Q. (Intelligent Quotient) of a group of eight students with the following I.Q.'s: 100, 105, 95, 110, 100, 85, 95, 95.

Solution. In this simple example as there are only a few values the direct procedure of adding up the scores can be used.

$$100 + 105 + 95 + 110 + 100 + 85 + 95 + 95 = 785$$

The mean is then obtained by dividing by 8, giving a mean I.Q. of 98. Note that the actual mean is $98\frac{1}{8}$ but when the I.Q.'s of individual students are only given in numbers which are rounded to multiples of 5, anything beyond two significant figures in the result is meaningless.

EXAMPLE 2.2. The number of rooms in owner occupied dwellings in a certain district are available in the form of a listing 5, 3, 8, 4, 5, ... How would you proceed to obtain the mean number of rooms per dwelling?

Solution. The first step is to make a score sheet as illustrated in Chapter 1, Section 1.5. Assumed totals have been included to make the procedure clear.

Number of Rooms in Owner Occupied Dwellings (1)	Number of Dwellings (2)	Total Number of Rooms in Class Col. (1) × Col. (2) (3)
1	1	1
2	4	8
3	13	39
4	54	216
5	96	480
6	86	516
7	41	287
8	33	264
9 and over	0	0
	328	1811

It should be noted that the first column is the class, or independent variable; the second column is the frequency, or dependent variable; and the third column is obtained by multiplying column (1) by column (2). The total of column (3) is the total number of rooms which, when divided by the total of column (2) (the number of dwellings), gives the mean number of rooms.

$$\frac{1811}{328} = 5.5 \text{ rooms}$$

EXAMPLE 2.3. GROUPED DATA. The deaths recorded according to age at death, in an investigation into the mortality of persons insured under annuity contracts were:

Age Group	Number of Deaths
50–54	16
55–59	58
60–64	180
65–69	513
70–74	1075
75–79	1748
80–84	1975
85–89	1569
90–94	600
95–99	183

Ages are recorded as age last birthday. Calculate the mean age at death.

Solution. Age group 50–54 includes all ages from the 50th birthday to the day before the 55th birthday, and hence, the exact age for the midpoint of this class interval is $52\frac{1}{2}$. The midpoint of successive classes is $57\frac{1}{2}$, $62\frac{1}{2}$, $67\frac{1}{2}$, etc. The assumption is made that each death occurs at the age corresponding to the midpoint of the class.

The calculation of the mean then proceeds as follows:

Age Group (1)	Mid-Age Class (2)	Number of Deaths (3)	Col. (2) × Col. (3) (4)
50–54	$52\frac{1}{2}$	16	840
55–59	$57\frac{1}{2}$	58	3,335
60–64	$62\frac{1}{2}$	180	11,250
65–69	$67\frac{1}{2}$	513	$34,627\frac{1}{2}$
70–74	$72\frac{1}{2}$	1075	$77,937\frac{1}{2}$
75–79	$77\frac{1}{2}$	1748	135,470
80–84	$82\frac{1}{2}$	1975	$162,937\frac{1}{2}$
85–89	$87\frac{1}{2}$	1569	$137,287\frac{1}{2}$
90–94	$92\frac{1}{2}$	600	55,500
95–99	$97\frac{1}{2}$	183	$17,842\frac{1}{2}$
		7917	$637,027\frac{1}{2}$

$$\text{Mean age at death} = \frac{637,027\tfrac{1}{2}}{7,917} = 80.5 \text{ years}$$

2.3. Use of Arbitrary Starting Point and Change of Scale. Without a calculating machine the work of calculating the mean age at death in Example 2.3 would be laborious. Two changes in procedure simplify the calculation considerably. The first is the use of an *arbitrary starting point*. Instead of using age zero as the starting point of our calculations, we could call the midpoint of the first class zero. The midpoint of the second class would then be "age" 5 (i.e., $57\tfrac{1}{2} - 52\tfrac{1}{2}$), the next "age" 10, etc. By this means we calculate the mean "age" at death using $52\tfrac{1}{2}$ as age zero. When the calculations are complete, it must be remembered that this assumption has been made and that the mean "age," as calculated, must be increased by $52\tfrac{1}{2}$ to obtain the true age at death. However, it will be found that it simplifies the arithmetic still further if the calculations are made using as "age" zero the mid-age of the class which is near the middle of the range of values. Thus, if $77\tfrac{1}{2}$ is selected as "age" zero, the "age" to be used for the first group will be $52\tfrac{1}{2} - 77\tfrac{1}{2}$ or -25 and the complete range of "ages" will be $-25, -20, -15, -10, -5, 0, 5, 10, 15, 20$.

This compares with

$$0, \; 5, \; 10, \; 15, \; 20, \; 25, \; 30, \; 35, \; 40, \; 45$$

A further simplification can be obtained by *changing the scale*. It will be noted that the "ages" are all multiples of 5. If we use a new scale 5 times larger, the ages in the new units will be

$$-5, \; -4, \; -3, \; -2, \; -1, \; 0, \; 1, \; 2, \; 3, \; 4$$

The arithmetic is now reduced to manageable proportions as will be seen in Example 2.4. It is easy to show mathematically that these procedures do not alter the final result in any way.

EXAMPLE 2.4. Using an arbitrary starting point and a change in scale, calculate the mean age at death for the data given in Example 2.3.

Solution. The starting point will be taken as the mid-age of the group 75–79, i.e., age $77\tfrac{1}{2}$ and the scale of 5 years will be used.

The calculation with these units proceeds as follows:

Age (1)	Midpoint of New Class Unit (2)	Number of Deaths (3)	Col. (2) × Col. (3) (4)
50–54	−5	16	−80
55–59	−4	58	−232
60–64	−3	180	−540
65–69	−2	513	−1026
70–74	−1	1075	−1075
75–79	0	1748	0
80–84	1	1975	1975
85–89	2	1569	3138
90–94	3	600	1800
95–99	4	183	732
		7917	−2953
			+7645
		Total	+4692

$$\text{Mean (in new units)} = \frac{4692}{7917} = .59$$

The mean age is then the starting point, which was $77\frac{1}{2}$, plus the mean in the new units (.59) adjusted to the original scale, that is multiplied by 5, since the unit is 5 years.

$$\begin{aligned}\text{Mean age at death} &= 77.5 + (.59 \times 5) \\ &= 77.5 + 3.0 \\ &= 80.5 \text{ years}\end{aligned}$$

EXAMPLE 2.5.   The following data are available for the incomes of Pennsylvania residents for 1960.

Adjusted Gross Income Classes	Number of Returns	Total Adjusted Gross Income
Under $1,000	79,120	$ 66,374,000
$1,000–$1,999	292,734	440,117,000
$2,000–$2,999	376,775	953,370,000
$3,000–$3,999	436,386	1,530,709,000
$4,000–$4,999	505,013	2,279,477,000
$5,000–$5,999	497,228	2,731,442,000
etc.	etc.	etc.

Calculate the mean income of those residents whose adjusted gross income was less than $5,000. When a portion of the data only is to be used, such data is said to be *truncated*.

Solution. In this example, the data provided give not only the number of returns in each class but also the total adjusted gross income for the class. The table gives an accurate figure for this latter item and this must be used rather than the value obtained by assuming that the midvalue of the class interval is appropriate for the class. Thus, if we had used the midvalue of the class $2,000–$2,999, that is, $2,500, we should have obtained a total adjusted earned income for the class of

$$376,775 \times \$2,500, \text{ or } \$941,940,000$$

compared with the true value of

$$\$953,370,000.$$

While for most classes, the difference will be unimportant, the classes near the end of the table may show remarkably different results. Thus, for the first class, the total based on the midvalue is

$$79,120 \times \$500 = \$39,560,000$$

compared with the true value of

$$\$66,374,000.$$

Adding the number of returns and total adjusted income for all residents with gross incomes less than $5,000, we have:

Adjusted Gross Income Class	Number of Returns	Total Adjusted Gross Income (000 omitted)
Under $1,000	79,120	$ 66,374
$1,000–$1,999	292,734	440,117
$2,000–$2,999	376,775	953,370
$3,000–$3,999	436,386	1,530,709
$4,000–$4,999	505,013	2,279,477
Under $5,000	1,690,028	$5,270,047

$$\text{Mean income} = \frac{\$5,270,047,000}{1,690,028} = \$3,118$$

EXAMPLE 2.6. UNEQUAL CLASS INTERVALS. The 1960 Housing Census of the United States gives the following data on gross rents of renter occupied homes:

Gross Rent	Number of Houses (in thousands)
Less than $20	320
$20–	736
$30–	1,221
$40–	1,755
$50–	2,245
$60	2,555
$70–	2,350
$80–	3,490
$100–	1,693
$120–	973
$150–	406
$200 or more	166

Calculate the mean value of the Gross Rent.

Solution.   The midpoints of the class intervals are:

$10, $25, $35, $45, $55, $65, $75, $90, $110, $135, $175, $250

For the last class interval, judgment must be used in choosing the midpoint, but since the number of houses in the interval is small, the error resulting from a poor choice is unimportant. A mean of $250 is suggested. $65 is an appropriate starting point to assume and $5 intervals. The calculation now proceeds as follows:

Gross Rent (1)	Midpoint of Class (2)	Midpoint with New Starting Point (3)	Midpoint in New Class Scale (4)	No. of Houses (in thousands) (5)	Col. (4) × Col. (5) (6)
Less than $20	$ 10	−$ 55	−11	320	−3,520
$20–	25	−40	− 8	736	−5,888
$30–	35	−30	− 6	1,221	−7,326
$40–	45	−20	− 4	1,755	−7,020
$50–	55	−10	− 2	2,245	−4,490
$60–	65	0	0	2,555	0
$70–	75	10	2	2,350	4,700
$80–	90	25	5	3,490	17,450
$100–	110	45	9	1,693	15,237
$120–	135	70	14	973	13,622
$150–	175	110	22	406	8,932
$200 or more	250	185	37	166	6,142
				17,910	−28,244
					+66,083
					37,839

$$\text{Mean value} = \$65 + \left(\$5 \times \frac{37,839}{17,910}\right)$$

$$= \$65 + (\$5 \times 2.11) = \$76$$

2.4. The Mean of Groups of Data.

It often happens that data are available in grouped form and the means of the individual groups are known. In order to find the mean of the total data combined, it is unnecessary to go back to the original detail since the mean of the combined data is equal to the *weighted average* of the individual data. The use of unweighted averages is incorrect and can produce many misleading results.

EXAMPLE 2.7.   A study is made of the I.Q. (Intelligent Quotient) of students in a certain high school and the following results are obtained:

Grade	Number of Students	Mean I.Q.
9	150	90
10	130	97
11	120	95
12	100	110
	500	

What is the mean I.Q. of the whole school?

Solution.

Grade (1)	Number of Students (2)	Mean I.Q. (3)	Mean I.Q. Weighted by No. of Students Col. (2) × Col. (3) (4)
9	150	90	13,500
10	130	97	12,610
11	120	95	11,400
12	100	110	11,000
	500		48,510

$$\text{Mean I.Q.} = \frac{48,510}{500} = 97$$

It should be noted that the mean of the mean I.Q. values for each of the four grades is

$$\frac{90 + 97 + 95 + 110}{4} = \frac{392}{4} = 98$$

which does not give a correct value for the mean I.Q. of the 500 students. The reason for this is that each grade has been given equal weight and not each student. While this "short cut" will often give a reasonably approximate answer, it will only give the correct answer if the number of students in each class is the same.

2.5. Properties of the Mean.

(*a*) The arithmetic mean is the most commonly used average.

(*b*) It can be readily calculated when data are on punched cards or tape and computed by hand fairly readily from grouped tabulated data.

(*c*) It may be treated algebraically (see below).

(*d*) The sum of the (signed) differences of the individual deviations from the mean is zero. (No other measure has this property.)

(*e*) The sum of the squares of the differences of the individual deviations from the mean is a minimum (e.g., it is less than the sum of the squares computed from any other point).

(*f*) The mean is greatly affected by extreme values.

2.6. Algebraic Properties of the Mean.

If individual values are

$$x_1, x_2, x_3, \ldots, x_i, \ldots, x_n$$

then the mean is

$$x = \frac{1}{n}(x_1 + x_2 + x_3 + \cdots + x_i + \cdots + x_n)$$

The expression in brackets is represented mathematically by

$$\sum_{i=1}^{n} x_i$$

Σ is a capital Greek S, or Sigma, as the letter is called, and indicates summation; $i = 1$ below the sigma gives the item being summed (i) and the first term of the summation (1). The n above the sigma gives the final term.

When the item being summed and the range of terms is clear, the expression is often written simply

$$\Sigma x$$

Hence

$$(1) \quad \bar{x} = \frac{1}{n}\sum_{i=1}^{n} x_i$$

$$(2) \quad \bar{x} = \frac{1}{n}\sum_{i=1}^{n} (x_i - A) + A$$

for any A, which justifies the use of an arbitrary starting point, and

$$(3) \quad \bar{x} = \frac{1}{kn}\sum_{i=1}^{n} (kx_i)$$

for any k, which justifies the use of a change of scale. Writing $\bar{x}$ for A in formula (2) gives

$$\frac{1}{n}\sum_{i=1}^{n} (x_i - \bar{x}) = 0$$

proving property (d).

If $\overline{X}_1$ is the mean of

$$x_1, x_2, x_3, \ldots, x_n \quad (n \text{ terms})$$

and $\overline{X}_2$ is the mean of

$$x_{n+1}, x_{n+2}, \ldots, x_{n+m} \quad (m \text{ terms})$$

then

$$n\overline{X}_1 = \sum_{i=1}^{n} x_i \text{ and } m\overline{X}_2 = \sum_{i=n+1}^{n+m} x_i$$

and hence

$$\frac{n\overline{X}_1 + m\overline{X}_2}{n + m} = \frac{1}{n + m}\sum_{i=1}^{n+m} x_i$$

proving that the mean of grouped data is the weighted average of the means of the individual groups.

Also, for *two groups the same size*, the sum of the means equals the mean of the sums.

For grouped data

$$\text{Mean} = A + \frac{\Sigma f_i d_i}{n} \text{ or } A + C\frac{\Sigma f_i u_i}{n}$$

where

A = the arbitrary origin
C = the class interval

n = the total number of units

f_i = the frequency of class i

d_i = the deviation of the midpoint of class i from the arbitrary origin A

u_i = the deviation of the midpoint of class i, *expressed in class intervals*, from the arbitrary origin A.

Problems

Problem 2.1. The following was the standing of the clubs in the National Hockey League on a certain date:

Club	Won	Lost	Tied	Points
Chicago	38	15	12	88
Toronto	29	25	11	69
Rangers	28	26	12	68
Montreal	27	25	13	67
Detroit	26	35	4	56
Boston	17	39	10	44

Calculate the mean number of games won, lost, and tied, and the mean number of points scored.

Problem 2.2. Explain why the mean number of games won equals the mean number of games lost in Problem 2.1.

Problem 2.3. Show that the mean number of points scored in Problem 2.1 can be obtained by the usual rule (2 for a win, 1 for a tie, and 0 for a loss) from the mean results and explain why this is so.

Problem 2.4. Calculate the mean age of the fifty-three students for which ages are given in Chapter 1, Example 1.2.

   Note. Remember to use an arbitrary starting point— age 20 is suggested. Also remember that the mean age as calculated will be the age last birthday, and hence, one-half must be added to this figure to obtain the true mean age.

Problem 2.5. Calculate the mean number of heads obtained by tossing six coins one hundred times in Problem 1.18. (Again remember to use an arbitrary starting point.)

Problem 2.6. What is the theoretical expected mean number of heads?

Problem 2.7. Calculate the mean inclination angle of lava flows in Hawaii from the data given in Example 1.1..

Problem 2.8. Baseball world series are won by the team which first wins four games. Hence, the number of games in a world series may be 4, 5, 6, or 7. The following table gives the distribution of the number of games in each world series from 1903 to 1961.

Number of games	4	5	6	7	*Total*
Number of series	10	14	15	19 =	58

Calculate the mean number of games played in a series.

Problem 2.9. The following table gives an analysis of the number of reported accidents over the period 1956–1958, among a sample group of automobile drivers in California.

Number of Accidents	Number of Drivers
0	81,714
1	11,306
2	1,618
3	250
4	40
5	7
	94,935

Calculate the mean number of accidents per driver.

Problem 2.10. In Example 1.8, if $54\frac{1}{2}$ is taken as the arbitrary starting point and 10 as the scale unit, what is the midpoint of each class in the new class units.?

Problem 2.11. Calculate the mean grade per student in Example 1.8.

Problem 2.12. What would be an appropriate starting point and scale for the data in Problem 1.9?

Problem 2.13. Calculate the mean number of persons per room in owner occupied dwellings on the basis of the data in Problem 1.9.

Problem 2.14. Calculate the mean number of persons per room in renter occupied dwellings on the basis of the data in Problem 1.9.

Problem 2.15. The following table from a Department of Commerce study of automobile accidents published in 1964 gives the distribution of vehicle-miles by travel speed for day travel on main rural highways:

MPH	Vehicle-miles (000,000 omitted)
22 or less	3
23–32	29
33–37	64
38–42	250
43–47	395
48–52	715
53–57	514
58–62	462
63–72	308
73 or more	39

Calculate the mean travel speed.

Problem 2.16. A study of distribution by sex among litters of pigs gives the following distribution of male pigs in a litter of 5:

Number of Male Pigs	Number of Litters
0	2
1	20
2	41
3	35
4	14
5	4

Calculate the mean number of male pigs in five pig litters.

Problem 2.17. The 1960 housing census of the United States gives the following table of the value of vacant dwellings available for sale:

Value (price asked)	No. of Dwellings (in thousands)
Less than $5,000	51
$5,000–$9,900	97
$10,000–$14,900	138
$15,000–$19,900	104
$20,000–$24,900	42
$25,000 or more	55

Calculate the mean value of these dwellings, assuming the mid-value of the first class interval is $2,450 and the mean value of the last class interval is $32,450.

Problem 2.18. The mean number of physician visits per person per year in the United States for the year July, 1963–June, 1964 is given in the following table. Using population weights given, calculate the mean number of physician visits for the whole population.

Age	No. of Visits	Population (in millions)
Under 15 years	3.8	56
15–24 years	4.3	24
25–44 years	4.5	47
45–64 years	5.0	36
65–74 years	6.3	11
75 + years	7.3	6
		180

Problem 2.19. The following table gives the number of accountants and their average earnings in 1964 from a study of salaries for selected occupations in private industry.

Level of Responsibility	Number	Average Annual Salary
I	4,000	$ 6,250
II	8,500	7,000
III	18,000	8,000
IV	13,000	9,500
V	5,500	11,500

Calculate the average earnings of all accountants in the study.

Problem 2.20. In a study of accident involvement, data is subdivided by type of car, and day and night driving.

| | DAY | | NIGHT | |
	Vehicle-miles (millions)	Accident* Rate	Vehicle-miles (millions)	Accident* Rate
CAR				
Small	33	238	8	668
Low-priced	1,146	215	288	584
Medium-priced	813	196	190	591
High-priced	194	204	44	483
	2,186		530	

*Per 100 million vehicle-miles.

Calculate the accident rate for each class of car for day and night driving combined.

Solutions

Problem 2.1. $27\frac{1}{2}$ $27\frac{1}{2}$ $10\frac{1}{3}$ $65\frac{1}{3}$

Problem 2.2.   The total number of games won must be equal to the total number of games lost, and since the mean number is the total number divided by the number of clubs, the mean number of games won must be equal to the mean number of games lost.

Problem 2.3.   Giving 2 for a win, 1 for a tie, and 0 for a loss, we have

$$(27\frac{1}{2} \times 2) + (27\frac{1}{2} \times 0) + (10\frac{1}{3} \times 1) = 55 + 10\frac{1}{3} = 65\frac{1}{3}$$

the mean number of points scored.

Since this rule applies to the points for *each* individual team, the rule must apply to the sum of the points for all teams. Now the mean in each case is the sum divided by the number of teams and the rule must apply equally well to the means.

Problem 2.4.   20.7 years.   Since ages are recorded at age last birthday, the class midpoint of students age 17 is 17.5.

Problem 2.5.

No. of Heads (1)	Class Scale (2)	Number (3)	Col. (2) × Col. (3) (4)
0	−3	2	−6
1	−2	7	−14
2	−1	26	−26
3	0	29	0
4	1	24	24
5	2	10	20
6	3	2	6
		100	50
			−46
			4

$$\text{Mean} = 3 + \frac{4}{100} = 3.0 \text{ (approximately)}$$

Problem 2.6.   Since heads and tails are equally likely, the theoretically expected number of heads on any throw is $\frac{1}{2}$. Since 6 throws are made at each trial, the expected number of heads is

$$\frac{1}{2} \times 6 = 3$$

Problem 2.7. 30°

Problem 2.8. 5.7 games

Problem 2.9. 0.16 accidents

Problem 2.10. $-4, -2, -1, 0, 1, 2, 3\frac{1}{2}$

Problem 2.11. Using the starting point and scale suggested in the previous problem:

Mark (1)	New Class Midpoint (2)	Number of Students (3)	Col. (2) × Col. (3) (4)
Under 30	-4	6	-24
30–39	-2	4	-8
40–49	-1	7	-7
50–59	0	10	0
60–69	1	20	20
70–79	2	18	36
80–100	$3\frac{1}{2}$	5	$17\frac{1}{2}$
		70	$73\frac{1}{2}$
			-39
			$34\frac{1}{2}$

The mean number of marks is

$$54\frac{1}{2} + \left(10 \times \frac{34\frac{1}{2}}{70}\right) = 59\frac{1}{2}$$

Problem 2.12. Starting point $= .88$ and scale $= .125$. This gives class midpoints of

$$-5, \ -2, \ 0, \ 3, \ 8$$

(if we take the midpoint of the last group as 1.88).

Problem 2.13. Mean $= 0.57$

Problem 2.14. Mean $= 0.71$

Problem 2.15. The midpoint of the 6th group, 50, provides a suitable starting point and it is reasonable to assume 80 as the midpoint of the last group. Using $2\frac{1}{2}$ as a unit, the class midpoints become:

$$-15, \ -9, \ -6, \ -4, \ -2, 0, 2, 4, 7, 12$$

(The first point is not exactly -15, but owing to the small volume of data in this group, this will not affect the results.)

$$\text{Mean speed} = 53 \text{ m.p.h.}$$

Problem 2.16. 2.4 pigs

Problem 2.17. $12,450 + \left(\dfrac{209}{487} \times 5000\right) = \$14,600$

Problem 2.18. 4.6 visits

Problem 2.19. $8,500. The calculated value is $8,474, but in view of the rounding of the original data, the answer should be rounded as indicated.

Problem 2.20. Small: 322. Low-priced: 289. Medium-priced: 271. High-priced: 256.

3

Median, Mode, and Other Averages

3.1. Median. While the mean is the most commonly used average of a distribution and can be obtained readily with data processing equipment, it is not the only measure which can be used to indicate the central tendency of a body of data.

The *median* is defined as the middle value when data are arranged in an array according to size. If there are an even number of values, or if the data are grouped, it is necessary to interpolate to obtain the value of the median. These procedures are illustrated in Examples 3.2 and 3.3. The median divides the frequency histogram into two parts of equal area.

3.2. Interpolation. Interpolation is used extensively in statistical work. In its simplest form it can be very readily understood and applied. Suppose y is a function of x, such that

Value of x	Value of y
20	13.7
30	15.9

It is required to find the value of y corresponding to $x = 26$.

While x increases from 20 to 30, i.e., by 10, y increases from 13.7 to 15.9, i.e., by 2.2. It is reasonable to assume that when x increases from 20 to 26, i.e., by 6, y will increase by six-tenths of 2.2, i.e., by $(6/10) \times 2.2 = 1.3$. Hence, the value of y corresponding to $x = 26$ is

$$13.7 + 1.3 = 15.0$$

The underlying assumption made is that the rate of increase of y is constant over the range from one value of x to the next, or in other words, the graph over this range is a straight line. While in certain circumstances this may not be a sufficiently accurate assumption, it is sufficient for most of the interpolations which are made in statistical work.

When the value required is halfway between the two values of x, the formula gives a figure halfway between the two values of y. Thus

$$\frac{5}{10} \times 2.2 = 1.1$$

and the mean is

$$13.7 + 1.1 = 14.8$$

This result can be obtained also by adding the two values and dividing by 2

$$\frac{13.7 + 15.9}{2} = 14.8$$

EXAMPLE 3.1.   Calculate the median of the following range of numbers:

$$3, \ 4, \ 5, \ 7, \ 8, \ 9, \ 10, \ 12, \ 13, \ 15, \ 17$$

Solution.   There are 11 values in all, and hence, the middle value is the sixth. The sixth value is 9 and this is the median value.

EXAMPLE 3.2.   Calculate the median of the following range of numbers:

$$43, \ 57, \ 81, \ 92, \ 97, \ 105$$

Solution.   There are 6 values in all, and hence there is no middle term. The middle of the range would lie halfway between the third term, 81, and the fourth term, 92. The function increases by $92 - 81 = 11$ over the range from 3 to 4, and hence will increase by half this amount, $11/2$, over half the range. The median is

$$81 + \frac{11}{2} = 86\frac{1}{2}$$

Alternately, the median can be calculated as one half the sum of the two terms.

$$\frac{1}{2}(81 + 92) = 86\frac{1}{2}$$

3.3 Median with Grouped Data. With grouped data, the median will fall in one of the class intervals and although in many cases it may be sufficiently accurate to say that the midpoint of the class is the median, a more accurate procedure is generally used. The class in which the median falls is called the median class, and the assumption is made that individual values in the median class are distributed uniformly over the class. If

L is the lower boundary of the median class
U is the upper boundary of the median class
f_i is the frequency of class i
n is the total frequency
m is the median class

then

$$\text{Median} = L + \frac{\frac{n}{2} - \sum_{0}^{m-1} f_i}{f_m}(U - L)$$

or expressed in words:

$$\text{Median} = \begin{bmatrix} \text{lower boundary} \\ \text{of median class} \end{bmatrix} + \begin{bmatrix} \text{excess of half total} \\ \text{frequency over frequency} \\ \text{below median class} \end{bmatrix}$$

$$\times \begin{bmatrix} \dfrac{\text{median class size}}{\text{median class frequency}} \end{bmatrix}$$

EXAMPLE 3.3. Calculate the median for the following data:

Class	Number of Items (frequency)	Cumulative Frequency
0–	10	10
10–	20	30
20–	30	60
30–	40	100
40–	20	120
50–	10	130
	130	

Solution. The median is halfway between the 65th and 66th value, and from the cumulative frequency table, lies in the fourth class (30–).

$$n = 130 \quad \text{and} \quad \sum_{0}^{m-1} f_i = 60$$

$$\text{Median} = 30 + \left(\frac{65 - 60}{40} \times 10 \right)$$

$$= 30 + \left(\frac{5}{40} \times 10 \right) = 31\tfrac{1}{4}$$

3.4. Mode. Another useful measure of the center tendency is the mode. When there are a number of values at each point or in each class, the point or class with the greatest number is called the mode. When a frequency *curve* has been drawn, the mode is the maximum point on the graph. Occasionally there is no mode or more than one mode.

EXAMPLE 3.4.   Find the mode of the following arrays of data.

(a)   2, 3, 3, 4, 4, 4, 5, 5, 5, 5, 6, 6, 7, 8
(b)   3, 5, 7, 9, 10, 11, 12, 13, 18
(c)   2, 3, 3, 3, 4, 4, 5, 6, 7, 7, 8, 8, 8, 9

Solution.   (a) 5;   (b) none;   (c) 3 and 8.

3.5 Mode for Grouped Data.   It is rarely necessary to use a more accurate figure than the midpoint of the modal class. More than one formula has been suggested for calculating a more accurate mode. The formula now most frequently used is

$$\text{Mode} = M + \frac{1}{2} \left(\frac{c - a}{2b - a - c} \right) C$$

where:

M = the midpoint of the modal class
C = class interval
a = frequency of class immediately below modal class
b = frequency of modal class
c = frequency of class immediately above modal class

This can be expressed in the alternative form:

$$\text{Mode} = L + \left(\frac{b - a}{2b - a - c}\right)C$$

where L = the lower boundary of modal class.

EXAMPLE 3.5. Using the data in Example 3.3, calculate the mode.

Solution. The mode lies in the fourth class and as a first approximation is the midpoint of that class, namely, 35. Calculated more accurately:

$$\text{Mode} = 35 + \frac{1}{2}\left(\frac{20 - 30}{80 - 20 - 30}\right) \times 10$$

$$\text{Mode} = 35 - \frac{1}{2}\left(\frac{10}{30}\right) \times 10$$

$$\text{Mode} = 33.3$$

3.6. Relationship between Mean, Median, and Mode. The median lies between the mean and the mode and is usually approximately one third of the way from the mean to the mode.

$$\text{Mean} - \text{Mode} = 3(\text{Mean} - \text{Median}) \qquad (3.3)$$

With a symmetrical distribution, the mean, median, and mode will all be the same. If the distribution is skewed to the right, the mean will be to the right of the mode. Similarly, if the distri-

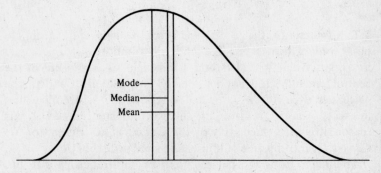

Figure 3.1. Distribution skewed to the right. Relative positions of mean, mode, and median.

bution is skewed to the left, the mean will be to the left of the mode. See Figure 3.1.

EXAMPLE 3.6. Calculate the mean for the distribution in Example 3.3 and show that the above rule is approximately correct in this case.

Solution. The mean is calculated as follows, using 35 as the starting point and 10 as the class interval.

Class (1)	Midpoint of Class Scale (2)	Number of Items (3)	Col. (2) × Col. (3) (4)
0–	−3	10	−30
10–	−2	20	−40
20–	−1	30	−30
30–	0	40	0
40–	1	20	20
50–	2	10	20
		130	−60

$$\text{Mean} = 35 - \left(10 \times \frac{60}{130}\right) = 35 - 4.6 = 30.4$$

$$\text{Median} = 31.3 \text{ (See Example 3.3)}$$

$$\text{Mode} = 33.3 \text{ (See Example 3.5)}$$

The distance between the mean and the mode is 2.9 and one-third of this is 1.0. The distance between the mean and median is 0.9.

3.7. Advantages of the Median and Mode. The *median*, being the point which divides the frequency distribution into two equal areas, has a readily understood significance as a measure of the central tendency. It is not distorted by unusual values and can be calculated even for "open ended" distributions, where all values in excess of a certain figure are thrown into one class. For this reason, it is used extensively by the United States Bureau of the Census for income, size of house, and similar distributions.

The *mode*, being the highest point on the frequency distribution, and hence, the most common value, has obvious significance. It is completely independent of extreme values and can be obtained readily for *small* distributions, if a mode exists. It becomes difficult to calculate for large volumes of data.

Neither the median nor the mode lend themselves readily to mathematical handling, and the values for large groups cannot be obtained from the values for subgroups. They are used less frequently than the mean as measures of central tendency.

3.8. Other Measures of Central Tendency. The following means are comparatively rarely used in statistical work as measures of central tendency.

Geometric Mean
The geometric mean of n numbers, $x_1, x_2, \ldots, x_n$ is the nth root of the numbers all multiplied together.

$$G = \sqrt[n]{x_1 x_2 x_3 \ldots x_n}$$

Harmonic Mean
The harmonic mean is the reciprocal of the mean of the reciprocals of the numbers.

$$\frac{1}{H} = \frac{1}{n} \sum_{i=1}^{n} \frac{1}{x_i}$$

The Root Mean Square
The root mean square (R.M.S.) or *quadratic mean* is the square root of the mean of the squares of the individual values.

$$(\text{R.M.S.})^2 = \frac{1}{n} \sum_{i=1}^{n} x_i^2$$

The Geometric Mean (G) is never less than the Harmonic Mean (H) and the Arithmetic Mean (M) never less than the Geometric Mean.

$$H \leq G \leq M$$

EXAMPLE 3.7.   Calculate the Arithmetic, Geometric, and Harmonic Means, and the Root Mean Square of the two numbers 2 and 8.
Solution.

$$M = \frac{2 + 8}{2} = 5.0$$

$$G = \sqrt{2 \times 8} = \sqrt{16} = 4.0$$

$$\frac{1}{H} = \frac{1}{2}\left(\frac{1}{2} + \frac{1}{8}\right) = \frac{1}{2} \times \frac{5}{8} = \frac{5}{16}$$

$$H = \frac{16}{5} = 3.2$$

$$(\text{R.M.S.})^2 = \frac{1}{2}(2^2 + 8^2) = \frac{1}{2}(4 + 64)$$

$$\text{R.M.S.} = \sqrt{34} = 5.8$$

EXAMPLE 3.8. Calculate the various means specified in Example 3.7 for the five numbers.

$$1, \ 2, \ 3, \ 4, \ 5$$

Solution.

$$M = \frac{1}{5}(1 + 2 + 3 + 4 + 5) = \frac{15}{5} = 3.0$$

$$G = \sqrt[5]{1 \times 2 \times 3 \times 4 \times 5} = \sqrt[5]{120}$$

$$\log 120 = 2.07918$$

$$\log \sqrt[5]{120} = \frac{1}{5} \log 120 = 0.41584$$

$$G = \sqrt[5]{120} = 2.6 \ (\text{approx.})$$

$$\frac{1}{H} = \frac{1}{5}\left(\frac{1}{1} + \frac{1}{2} + \frac{1}{3} + \frac{1}{4} + \frac{1}{5}\right)$$

$$= \frac{1}{5}(1.0 + 0.5 + 0.33 + 0.25 + 0.2)$$

$$= \frac{1}{5}(2.28) = .456$$

$$H = \frac{1}{.456} = 2.2 \ (\text{approx.})$$

$$(\text{R.M.S.})^2 = \frac{1}{5}(1^2 + 2^2 + 3^2 + 4^2 + 5^2)$$

$$= \frac{1}{5} (1 + 4 + 9 + 16 + 25)$$

$$= \frac{1}{5} (55) = 11$$

$$\text{R.M.S.} = \sqrt{11} = 3.3$$

3.9. Quartiles, Deciles, and Percentiles. It will be recalled that the median divides the distribution into two equal parts so that all values on one side are less than the median and all values above are greater than the median.

In the same way, a distribution may be divided by three *quartiles* or nine *deciles* or by ninety-nine *percentiles*. Only a few percentiles are normally used. Thus 5th, 10th, 25th, 75th, 90th, and 95th percentiles might be recorded to give a very full indication of a distribution. The 50th percentile is, of course, the median and the 25th is the first (lower) quartile and the 75th is the third (upper) quartile.

EXAMPLE 3.9. The following table gives the distribution of male pensioners under a private pension plan according to age at nearest birthday on a certain date. Determine the median, quartiles, deciles, and the 5th and 95th percentile points.

Age	Number	Age	Number	Age	Number
60	2	70	5	80	5
61	1	71	6	81	3
62	0	72	9	82	3
63	6	73	9	83	1
64	5	74	7	84	1
65	4	75	7	85	4
66	10	76	4	86	1
67	13	77	8	87	1
68	7	78	6	88	2
69	8	79	7	89	1
				Total	146

Solution. First calculate the percentage distribution and the cumulative percentage distribution.

Age	%	Cumulative %	Age	%	Cumulative %	Age	%	Cumulative %
60	1.4	1.4	70	3.4	41.7	80	3.4	88.3
61	0.7	2.1	71	4.1	45.8	81	2.1	90.4
62	0.0	2.1	72	6.2	52.0	82	2.1	92.5
63	4.1	6.2	73	6.2	58.2	83	0.7	93.2
64	3.4	9.6	74	4.8	63.0	84	0.7	93.9
65	2.7	12.3	75	4.8	67.8	85	2.7	96.6
66	6.8	19.1	76	2.7	70.5	86	0.7	97.3
67	8.9	28.0	77	5.5	76.0	87	0.7	98.0
68	4.8	32.8	78	4.1	80.1	88	1.4	99.4
69	5.5	38.3	79	4.8	84.9	89	0.7	100.1

The difference from 100.0% and cumulative total is due to rounding. The median corresponds to the cumulative 50% point, and is age 72. The quartiles correspond to the cumulative 25%, 50%, and 75% points and are ages 67, 72, and 77. The deciles are ages 65, 67, 68, 70, 72, 74, 76, 78, and 81. The 5th and 95th percentile points are ages 63 and 85.

EXAMPLE 3.10. Using the data in the previous example, determine the mean and the mode. What would be the value of the mode if the approximate relationship referred to in Section 3.6 held?

Solution. The mean age can be calculated either from the original data or the percentage distribution, using age 75 as the arbitrary starting point. The results will be the same.

Unit	Number	Unit × Number	Unit	Number	Unit × Number
−15	2	−30	0	7	0
−14	1	−14	1	4	4
−13	0	0	2	8	16
−12	6	−72	3	6	18
−11	5	−55	4	7	28
−10	4	−40	5	5	25
−9	10	−90	6	3	18
−8	13	−104	7	3	21
−7	7	−49	8	1	8
−6	8	−48	9	1	9
−5	5	−25	10	4	40
−4	6	−24	11	1	11
−3	9	−27	12	1	12

Unit	Number	Unit × Number	Unit	Number	Unit × Number
−2	9	−18	13	2	26
−1	7	−7	14	1	14
			Totals	146	250
					−603
					−353

$$\text{Mean age} = 75 - \frac{353}{146} = 72.6$$

The data has a principal mode at age 67, a secondary mode at $72\frac{1}{2}$ and a number of minor modes.

With a mean of 72.6 and a median of 72 (more accurately, 71.7) the mode would be expected to be approximately:

$$
\begin{aligned}
\text{Mode} &= 72.6 - 3 \times (72.6 - 71.7) \\
&= 72.6 - 2.7 \\
&= 69.9
\end{aligned}
$$

Owing to the multimodal nature of the distribution, this is not close to the principal mode at 67.

Problems

Problem 3.1.　Using the simple interpolation method described in Section 3.2, find the value corresponding to 2.4 of a variable for which the value corresponding to 2.0 is 108 and the value corresponding to 3.0 is 123.

Problem 3.2.　If the value of y corresponding to $x = 10$ is 27 and the value of y corresponding to $x = 20$ is 38, what is the value of x corresponding to $y = 30$?

Problem 3.3.　Given the following table of data, calculate the value of y corresponding to $x = 2.5$ from (1) the values of $x = 1$ and 4; (2) the values of $x = 2$ and 3; (3) the values of $x = 1$ and 3 and (4) the values of $x = 2$ and 4.

x	y
1	256
2	324
3	400
4	484

Problem 3.4.   Explain why the four answers to Problem 3.3 are not the same. Which estimate is the most accurate?

Problem 3.5.   Calculate the median of the data in Example 1.1.

Problem 3.6.   Calculate the median of the data in Example 1.4.

Problem 3.7.   Calculate the median of the data in Example 1.8.

Problem 3.8.   What is the mode of the data in Example 1.2?

Problem 3.9.   What is the mode of the data in Example 1.1?

Problem 3.10.   What is the median and the mode of the data in Example 2.2?

Problem 3.11.   The following data are taken from a sample study made in 1963–4 of total short-stay hospital patients distributed according to age. Calculate the median age and the mode age of patients from these data.

Age	Number of Patients (in thousands)
Under 15	4021
15–24	4083
25–44	7081
45–64	5806
65–74	2299
75 and over	1547
	24837

Problem 3.12.   What is the mean, median, and mode of the following theoretical results of tossing six coins sixty-four times?

Number of Heads	Number of Occurrences
0	1
1	6
2	15
3	20
4	15
5	6
6	1
	64

Problem 3.13.   Find the median and mode of the speeds given in Problem 2.15.

Problem 3.14.   Find the median and mode of the number of male pigs per litter in Problem 2.16.

Problem 3.15. Find the median and mode of the price of dwellings from the data in Problem 2.17.

Problem 3.16. Calculate the Arithmetic, Geometric, and Harmonic Means and the Root Mean Square for the following data.

$$1, \ 1, \ 2, \ 3, \ 4$$

Problem 3.17. Calculate the Harmonic Mean of

$$\frac{1}{2} \text{ and } \frac{1}{4}$$

Express the answer as a fraction.

Problem 3.18. Calculate the Geometric Mean of

$$2^2 = 4, \text{ and } 2^4 = 16$$

What is the answer expressed as a power of 2?

Problem 3.19. What are the quartiles of the data in Problem 3.12?

Problem 3.20. Given that the deciles of a certain distribution are as follows:

0%	10%	20%	30%	40%	50%	60%	70%	80%	90%	100%
0	2	6	14	26	46	70	90	97	99	100

Draw a frequency curve of the distribution.

Solutions

Problem 3.1. $108 + \left(\dfrac{4}{10} \times 15 \right) = 114$

Problem 3.2. $10 + \left(\dfrac{3}{11} \times 10 \right) = 12.7$

Problem 3.3. (1) 370; (2) 362; (3) 364; (4) 364.

Problem 3.4. If the points are plotted on a graph and marked A, B, C, D, then estimate (1) is obtained by drawing a straight line between A and D, (2) between B and C, (3) between A and C, and (4) between B and D.

Since A, B, C, D are not in a straight line, these lines will not all cut $x = 2.5$ at the same point. Estimate (2) is the most accurate because it is based on the two values *nearest* to $x = 2.5$.

Problem 3.5. $38\frac{1}{2}$

Problem 3.6. $69\frac{1}{2} + \dfrac{(32\frac{1}{2} - 31) \times 10}{21} = 70.2$

Problem 3.7. $59\frac{1}{2} + \dfrac{(35 - 27) \times 10}{20} = 63.5$

Problem 3.8. 20

Problem 3.9. With nearly every value different, the data really have no mode but technically it can be said that the data are bimodal with values at 30 and 47.

Problem 3.10.

$$\text{Median} = 4\frac{1}{2} + \dfrac{164 - 72}{96} = 4.5 + .96 = 5.5$$

$$\text{Mode} = 5$$

(With discrete data such as this, it is inappropriate to interpolate for the mode.)

Problem 3.11.

Median. The median class is age 25–44, and since these ages are presumably ages at last birthday (as normally recorded) the lower limit of the median class is age 25 exact (not $24\frac{1}{2}$) and the median age is

$$25 + \left(\dfrac{12418\frac{1}{2} - 8104}{7081}\right) 20 = 37.2$$

Mode. It is tempting to assume that age 25–44 is the modal class since it has the largest number of patients. However, the class intervals are not equal and the number of patients per year of age in the second class is 408 and in the third class 354. Hence, the mode is probably in the range of ages 15 to 24 but it cannot be calculated accurately.

Problem 3.12. Since this data is symmetrical about the number 3, the mean, mode, and median will all be 3 and no calculations are necessary.

Problem 3.13.

$$\text{Median} = 47\frac{1}{2} + \left(\dfrac{1389\frac{1}{2} - 741}{715}\right) \times 5 = 52.0$$

$$\text{Mode} = 50 + \dfrac{1}{2}\left(\dfrac{514 - 395}{1430 - 514 - 395}\right) \times 5 = 50.6$$

Problem 3.14.

$$\text{Median} = 1\tfrac{1}{2} + \frac{58 - 22}{41} = 2.4$$

Since a litter of pigs must contain an exact number, the mode is correctly expressed as 2 rather than 2.3 as developed by formula.

Problem 3.15.

$$\text{Median} = \$9{,}950 + \left(\frac{243\tfrac{1}{2} - 148}{138}\right) \times \$5{,}000 = \$13{,}400$$

$$\text{Mode} = \$12{,}450 + \frac{1}{2}\left(\frac{104 - 97}{276 - 104 - 97}\right) \times \$5{,}000 = \$12{,}700$$

Problem 3.16.

Arithmetic Mean

$$M = \frac{1}{5}(1 + 1 + 2 + 3 + 4) = \frac{11}{5} = 2.2$$

Geometric Mean

$$G = \sqrt[5]{1 \times 1 \times 2 \times 3 \times 4} = \sqrt[5]{24} = 1.9$$

$$\log 24 = 1.38021$$

$$\frac{1}{5}\log 24 = 0.27604$$

$$\text{antilog} = 1.89$$

Harmonic Mean

$$\frac{1}{H} = \frac{1}{5}\left(\frac{1}{1} + \frac{1}{1} + \frac{1}{2} + \frac{1}{3} + \frac{1}{4}\right)$$

$$\frac{1}{H} = \frac{12 + 12 + 6 + 4 + 3}{5 \times 12} = \frac{37}{60} = 0.617$$

$$H = 1.6$$

Root Mean Square

$$(\text{RMS})^2 = \frac{1}{5}(1^2 + 1^2 + 2^2 + 3^2 + 4^2) = \frac{31}{5} = 6.2$$

$$\text{RMS} = 2.5$$

Problem 3.17.

$$\frac{1}{H} = \frac{1}{2}(2 + 4) = \frac{6}{2} = \frac{3}{1}$$

$$H = \frac{1}{3}$$

Problem 3.18.

$$G = \sqrt{2^2 \times 2^4} = \sqrt{2^6} = 2^3 = 8$$

The geometric mean is the third power of 2.

Problem 3.19.

Number of Heads	Number of Occurrences	Cumulative Number of Occurrences
0	1	1
1	6	7
2	15	22
3	20	42
4	15	57
5	6	63
6	1	64

The quartiles correspond to the cumulative number of occurrences of $\frac{1}{4}$, $\frac{1}{2}$ and $\frac{3}{4}$ of 64, namely, 16, 32 and 48. Hence the

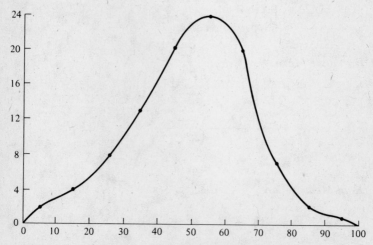

Figure 3.2. Frequency curve. Plotted from decile values.

quartiles are:

$$\text{First Quartile} = 1\frac{1}{2} + \frac{16 - 7}{15} = 2.1$$

$$\text{Second Quartile} = 2\frac{1}{2} + \frac{32 - 22}{20} = 3.0$$

$$\text{Third Quartile} = 3\frac{1}{2} + \frac{48 - 42}{15} = 3.9$$

Problem 3.20.

Percentile Range	Midpoint	Number of Units
0–	5	2
10–	15	4
20–	25	8
30–	35	12
40–	45	20
50–	55	24
60–	65	20
70–	75	7
80–	85	2
90 –100	95	1

See Figure 3.2.

4

Dispersion—Standard Deviation

4.1. Need for a Measure of Dispersion. Two separate sets of data may contain the same number of items and have the same mean but one set may be much more dispersed or spread about the average value than the other. A measure of the *dispersion*, *scatter*, or *variation* from the mean is needed to help define the distribution more fully. The smaller the dispersion, the more typical the mean is of the whole distribution. See Figures 4.1 and 4.2.

Figure 4.1. Dispersion. Small scatter.

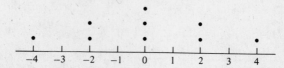

Figure 4.2. Dispersion. Large scatter.

4.2. Measures of Dispersion. A number of measures of dispersion are available.

1. The *Range*. The difference between the largest and the smallest values.
2. The *10–90 Percentile Range*. The difference between the 10th and the 90th percentile points.

Both these measures, as the word range implies, measure the

58

spread from one extreme to the other. The remaining measures of dispersion measure the departure from the mean or median, and hence measure one-half the spread.

3. The *Semi-interquartile Range* or *Quartile Deviation*. One-half the difference between the first and third quartiles.

4. The *Average Deviation from the Mean* or *Mean Deviation*. This is the arithmetic mean (average) of the individual absolute values of the deviations from the mean. See Section 4.6.

5. The *Standard Deviation* or its square, the *Variance*. This is the most generally used measure of dispersion and is discussed in the next section.

6. The *Half-width*. One-half of the width of the frequency curve at a height on the *y* axis equal to one-half of the height of the modal point. (See Figure 4.3.)

In the illustration, *M* is the modal point and *X* is the midpoint of *MO*. *AB* is the "width" of the curve and one-half *AB* equals the "half-width."

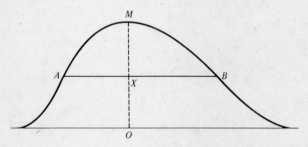

Figure 4.3. Frequency curve. Determination of half-width.

4.3. Standard Deviation—Variance. The *standard deviation* from the mean is the *quadratic mean* or *root mean square* of the deviations from the arithmetic mean. It will be recalled that the mean could be calculated by averaging the distances of the points from any origin. However, the standard deviation can be calculated, without adjustment, only from the *mean as origin*. The standard deviation is represented by the Greek letter σ (sigma).* The *variance* (σ^2) is the square of the standard deviation.

---

*Some texts use s instead of σ. See comments on the use of Latin and Greek letters in Chapter 5, Section 5.10.

With n values, $x_1, x_2, x_3, \ldots, x_n$, the standard deviation is

$$\sigma = \sqrt{\frac{\sum_{i=1}^{n} (x_i - \bar{x})^2}{n}} \tag{4.1}$$

where $\bar{x}$ is the mean value of the x's.

It will be noted that this formula involves (1) calculating the mean, (2) subtracting the mean from each individual value, (3) squaring each of the above results, (4) summing the squares, (5) dividing by the number of items involved, (6) taking the square root of this result. While a machine program can be devised for this procedure, a method of calculation is available which is easier for both machine and hand calculation.

The summation in Formula 4.1 can be written:

$$\sum_{i=1}^{n} (x_i - \bar{x})^2 = \sum_{i=1}^{n} (x_i^2 - 2x_i\bar{x} + \bar{x}^2)$$

$$= \sum_{i=1}^{n} x_i^2 - 2\bar{x} \sum_{i=1}^{n} x_i + n\bar{x}^2$$

$$= \sum_{i=1}^{n} x_i^2 - n\bar{x}^2$$

since

$$\frac{1}{n} \sum_{i=1}^{n} x_i = \bar{x}$$

by definition.

Hence, Formula 4.1 becomes

$$\sigma = \sqrt{\frac{\sum_{i=1}^{n} x_i^2}{n} - \bar{x}^2} \tag{4.2}$$

Since the standard deviation is obtained from a summation of the square of the distances of the individual values from the mean, the above formula is true whatever origin is used for determining the values of the x's. Thus if the values measured from some arbitrary origin A are $d_1, d_2, d_3 \ldots$, so that

$$d_i = x_i - A$$

then Formula 4.2 can be written

$$\sigma = \sqrt{\frac{\sum_{i=1}^{n} d_i^2}{n} - \bar{d}^2} \tag{4.3}$$

where $\bar{d}$ will be the mean calculated from origin A and

$$\bar{d} = \bar{x} - A$$

If A is the mean $\bar{d}^2$ will be zero.

The use of a convenient arbitrary origin often simplifies the arithmetic involved in calculating the mean as will be apparent from the following example.

EXAMPLE 4.1.   Calculate the mean and the standard deviation of the following five values.

$$3, \ 5, \ 6, \ 7, \ 10$$

Solution.   Using Formula 4.1

Item	x	x − x̄	(x − x̄)²
1	3	−3.2	10.24
2	5	−1.2	1.44
3	6	−0.2	.04
4	7	0.8	.64
5	10	3.8	14.44
	31		26.80

$$\text{Mean} = \bar{x} = \frac{\Sigma x}{n} = \frac{31}{5} = 6.2$$

$$\text{Standard Deviation } (\sigma) = \sqrt{\frac{\Sigma (x - \bar{x})^2}{n}} = \sqrt{\frac{26.80}{5}}$$

$$= \sqrt{5.36} = 2.32$$

Using Formula 4.3, and taking 6 as the origin:

Item (1)	Value x (2)	Distance from Assumed Origin d = (x − 6) (3)	Square of Column (3) d² (4)
1	3	−3	9
2	5	−1	1
3	6	0	0
4	7	1	1
5	10	4	16

Divide by number of items.

5) 1   5)27

.2   5.4

$$\text{Mean} = 6 + .2 = 6.2$$

$$\text{Standard Deviation} = \sqrt{\sum \frac{d^2}{n} - \bar{d}^2}$$

$$= \sqrt{5.4 - (0.2)^2}$$

$$= \sqrt{5.36} = 2.32$$

It should be noted carefully that when using an arbitrary origin, the value of the origin has to be added to the average value calculated from that origin to obtain the mean, but no such adjustment is needed when using Formula 4.3 to calculate the standard deviation. In the above example, 6 is added to $\Sigma d/n$ = .2 to obtain the mean, but not to $\sqrt{5.36}$ = 2.32 to obtain the standard deviation.

The square root of a number is frequently required in statistical work. This should be obtained from standard statistical tables.*

EXAMPLE 4.2.   Calculate the mean and standard deviations of the following scores:

25, 17, 33, 18, 10, 15, 22, 20, 18, 21

---

*See: Arkin and Colton, *Tables for Statisticians*, 2nd ed., 1968, Barnes and Noble, College Outline Series.

Solution.   Using 20 as a convenient origin

Item	Score	Deviation from Origin	Square of Deviation
1	25	5	25
2	17	−3	9
3	33	13	169
4	18	−2	4
5	10	−10	100
6	15	−5	25
7	22	2	4
8	20	0	0
9	18	−2	4
10	21	1	1

$$\frac{21}{-22}$$

10) −1
    −0.1

$$10)\overline{341}$$
$$34.1$$

$$\text{Mean} = 20 - 0.1 = 19.9$$

$$\text{Standard Deviation} = \sqrt{34.1 - (0.1)^2}$$
$$= \sqrt{34.09} = 5.84$$

Note the great influence of the extreme values 33 and 10 on the standard deviation.

4.4. Standard Deviation for Grouped Data.   For a large volume of data, Formula 4.3, with zero as origin, is most suitable for calculating the standard deviation when data processing equipment is available. However, data are often grouped in class intervals in order to assist the process of collection, to provide a presentation which can be more readily interpreted, or to assist in the hand calculation of statistical constants, such as the mean and the standard deviation. If the class interval is constant and equal to C, we may write $d_i = Cu_i$ where u_i is the class unit variable having values 0, ±1, ±2, etc. Hence

$$x_i = A + Cu_i$$

where the values of x are taken at the class midpoints, and the arbitrary origin A must be a class midpoint.

Formula 4.3 becomes

$$\sigma = \sqrt{\frac{\Sigma f_i (Cu_i)^2}{n} - \left(\frac{\Sigma f_i Cu_i}{n}\right)^2}$$

$$\sigma = C\sqrt{\frac{\Sigma f_i u_i^2}{n} - \left(\frac{\Sigma f_i u_i}{n}\right)^2} \qquad (4.4)$$

where C = the class interval

n = the total number of units

f_i = the frequency of class i

u_i = the deviation, in class intervals, of the midpoint of class i from the arbitrary origin (which should be a midpoint of a class).

EXAMPLE 4.3. Calculate the standard deviation of the ages of students tabulated in Example 1.2.

Solution. Age 20 is a suitable origin (arbitrary starting point).

Age	Number of Students (f)	Deviation from Origin (d)	Square of Deviation (d^2)	fd	fd^2
17	2	−3	9	−6	18
18	6	−2	4	−12	24
19	12	−1	1	−12	12
20	13	0	0	0	0
21	7	1	1	7	7
22	8	2	4	16	32
23	3	3	9	9	27
24	0	4	16	0	0
25	1	5	25	5	25
26	1	6	36	6	36
	53			53)13	53)181
				0.2	3.42

$$\text{Standard Deviation} = \sqrt{3.42 - (0.2)^2}$$

$$= \sqrt{3.38} = 1.84$$

EXAMPLE 4.4. Calculate the standard deviation of the data of the deaths recorded in Example 2.3.

Solution. Using the midpoint (exact age 77½) of the 6th group as origin and class intervals of 5 years:

Age Group	Number of Deaths (f)	Midpoint of Class Unit (u)	u^2	fu	fu^2
50–54	16	−5	25	−80	400
55–59	58	−4	16	−232	928
60–64	180	−3	9	−540	1620
65–69	513	−2	4	−1026	2052
70–74	1075	−1	1	−1075	1075
75–79	1748	0	0	0	0
80–84	1975	1	1	1975	1975
85–89	1569	2	4	3138	6276
90–94	600	3	9	1800	5400
95–99	183	4	16	732	2928
	7917			4692	22654

Divided by 7917:   .59   2.86

Mean $= 77.5 + (5 \times .59) = 77.5 + 3.0 = 80.5$ years

$$\text{Standard Deviation} = 5\sqrt{2.86 - (.59)^2} = 5\sqrt{2.86 - .35}$$
$$= 5\sqrt{2.51} = 5 \times 1.58 = 7.9 \text{ years}$$

The 5 before the square root sign is the class interval.

4.5. Characteristics of the Standard Deviation. The standard deviation is the root square deviation about the mean. The standard deviation is less than the root square deviation about any point other than the mean. For the normal curve (see Chapter 7), 68.27% of the cases are included in the range from $\bar{x} - \sigma$ to $\bar{x} + \sigma$, that is to say, between the mean less the standard deviation and the mean plus the standard deviation. If the spread is increased to two standard deviations each side of the mean ($\bar{x} - 2\sigma$ to $\bar{x} + 2\sigma$), 95.45% of the cases will be included, and for three standard deviations each side of the mean, virtually all (99.73%) of the cases will be included. It must not be assumed that this is equally true of other distributions, but for many distributions these results will be approximately correct.

The standard deviation places great emphasis on extreme values because all individual deviations are squared in the calculations. Variances (the squares of the standard deviations) are additive. The variance of the sum of two independent variables is the sum of the variances of the two variables.

4.6. Mean Deviation. While the standard deviation is the most generally used measure of dispersion, other measures, enumerated in Section 4.2 are sometimes used. The mean deviation is the average of the deviation, regardless of sign, from the mean.

EXAMPLE 4.5. Calculate the mean deviation for the five values in Example 4.1.
Solution:

Item	x	$x - \overline{x}$	Deviation Regardless of Sign $\lvert x - \overline{x} \rvert$
1	3	-3.2	3.2
2	5	-1.2	1.2
3	6	-0.2	0.2
4	7	0.8	0.8
5	10	3.8	3.8
			9.2

$$\text{Mean deviation} = \frac{9.2}{5} = 1.84$$

It will be noted that the mean deviation 1.84 is less than the standard deviation 2.32. For bell-shaped distributions, the mean deviation is about 80% of the standard deviation (79.79% in the case of the normal curve). While the mean, or average, deviation is normally calculated from the mean, it can be calculated from any other point. It is a minimum if calculated from the median.

4.7. Relationship between Measures of Dispersion. The following empirical relationships hold for many distributions:

(1) Mean deviation = 4/5 (standard deviation)
(2) Semi-interquartile range = 2/3 (standard deviation)

EXAMPLE 4.6. Find the relationship between the mean deviation and standard deviation of the data used for Examples 4.1 and 4.5.
Solution. The standard deviation was found to be 2.32 in Example 4.1, and the mean deviation was found to be 1.84 in

Example 4.5. The mean deviation was therefore

$$\text{mean deviation} = \frac{1.84}{2.32} \times \text{standard deviation}$$

$$\text{mean deviation} = .79 \times \text{standard deviation}$$

This is very close to the empirical figure of 0.8.

4.8. Relative Measures of Dispersion. The measures of dispersion described above are absolute values and are not, therefor, always suitable when comparisons have to be made between two distributions. Thus, a deviation of one ounce in measuring the weight of a man is unimportant; it is vital in measuring the dosage of a drug. A relative measure of dispersion is obtained by dividing the standard deviation by the mean and this is called the

$$\textit{Coefficient of Variation} = \frac{\sigma}{M} \text{ or } \frac{\sigma}{\bar{x}}$$

This measure is *dimensionless*.

EXAMPLE 4.7. What is the coefficient of variation of the five values in Example 4.1?
Solution. In Example 4.1 the mean was found to be 6.2, and the standard deviation was 2.32. Hence, the coefficient of variation = 2.32/6.2 = 0.37.

4.9. Standardized Variables—Standard Scores. When it is necessary to compare an individual value in one distribution with a corresponding individual value in another distribution we have to *standardize* the variables. Thus, if a student scores 80 in one test and 70 in another, it does not necessarily follow that he did better in the first test, relative to the other students in the class. The first test may have been easier. This difficulty of comparison is overcome by calculating a standardized variable

$$\frac{x - \bar{x}}{\sigma}$$

where x is the individual value of the variable, $\bar{x}$ is the mean of the variable and σ is the standard deviation. If the variable is a score in a test, the term *standard score* is often used for this expression.

To compare two distributions, it is useful to draw the relative frequency polynomials (See Chapter 1, Section 1.8) using standardized variables.

EXAMPLE 4.8.   The following are the results of two tests:

	Subject	
	A	**B**
Student X's score	80	70
Mean score of class	70	64
Standard deviation of scores	10	12

Calculate the standard scores for student X in each subject.
Solution.

$$\text{Standard score} = \begin{array}{cc} \textbf{Subject} & \\ \textbf{A} & \textbf{B} \\ \dfrac{80-70}{10} & \dfrac{70-64}{12} \\ = \quad 1.0 & 0.5 \end{array}$$

The student had a better standard score in subject A.   It will be noted that standard scores may be positive or negative.   Scores above the mean are positive, those below, negative.

4.10. Corrections to Standard Deviation

1. *Small samples*
    When a small sample of a larger volume of data is being studied, the standard deviation is sometimes defined by writing $(n - 1)$ for n in the denominator since this is a better estimate of the standard deviation of the population. However, this correction is usually ignored, and when n is greater than 20 or 30, it is unimportant.

2. *Group data*
    The assumption that the data are located at the midpoint of each group is not strictly correct, since with a bell-shaped distribution, more of the data in each group will be nearer the higher point on the curve. Under certain theoretical conditions (where the curve goes gradually to zero in each direction) the correct value of the variance is obtained as follows:

$$\sigma^2 \text{ (correct value)} = \sigma^2 \text{ (from grouped data)} - \frac{C^2}{12}$$

where C is the size of the class interval. This is called *Sheppard's Correction* for variance.

These two corrections are not generally used in practical work, and will not be used in the remainder of this book.

EXAMPLE 4.9. If the values in Example 4.1, namely 3, 5, 6, 7, 10, are a sample of larger data, what is the best estimate of the standard deviation of the population?

Solution. The value given in Example 4.1 was

$$\sqrt{\frac{26.80}{5}} = 2.32$$

The correct value is obtained by substituting $(n - 1) = 4$ for $n = 5$ in the denominator.

$$\sqrt{\frac{26.80}{4}} = 2.59$$

EXAMPLE 4.10. In Example 4.4, the standard deviation of age at death of a group of persons insured under annuity contracts was found to be $5\sqrt{2.51} = 7.9$ years. What is the standard deviation if Sheppard's Correction is applied?

Solution. The variance is the square of the standard deviation and is

$$25 \times 2.51$$

The class interval is 5 years.

Hence, the corrected value of the variance is

$$= (25 \times 2.51) - \frac{25}{12}$$

$$= 25 (2.51 - .08)$$

$$= 25 (2.43)$$

The standard deviation is

$$5\sqrt{2.43} = 5 \times 1.56 = 7.8 \text{ years}$$

It will be noted that the difference from 7.9 years calculated without the correction is very small.

4.11. Charlier's Check.   If the standard deviation is calculated from two different arbitrary origins, the results should be the same; but if they differ, it is difficult to determine where the error lies. Charlier's Check uses two origins, one unit apart, and provides a check on the totals of the columns in the table rather than on the final result, thus simplifying the location of an error. The check is based on the relationship

$$f(u + 1)^2 = fu^2 + 2fu + f$$

Hence
$$\Sigma[f_i(u_i + 1)^2] = \Sigma[f_i u_i^2] + 2\Sigma(f_i u_i) + n$$

where u_i = the deviation, in class intervals, of the midpoint of class i from the arbitrary origin and f_i is the frequency of class i. With the greater use of data processing equipment, the check is rarely used.

EXAMPLE 4.11.   Apply Charlier's Check to the calculation of the standard deviation in Example 4.4.
Solution.

Age Group	Number of Deaths (f)	Midpoint of Class Unit (u)	(u + 1)	(u + 1)²	f(u + 1)²
50–54	16	−5	−4	16	256
55–59	58	−4	−3	9	522
60–64	180	−3	−2	4	720
65–69	513	−2	−1	1	513
70–74	1075	−1	0	0	0
75–79	1748	0	1	1	1748
80–84	1975	1	2	4	7900
85–89	1569	2	3	9	14121
90–94	600	3	4	16	9600
95–99	183	4	5	25	4575
	7,917				39,955

Applying Charlier's Check

$$
\begin{aligned}
\Sigma fu^2 &= 22{,}654 \\
2\Sigma fu = 2 \times 4{,}692 &= 9{,}384 \\
n &= 7{,}917
\end{aligned}
\left.\rule{0pt}{3em}\right\} \text{from previous calculations}
$$

$$\text{Total}\quad \overline{39{,}955}$$

$$\Sigma f(u + 1)^2 = 39{,}955$$

which agree.

Problems

Problem 4.1. The following are the speeds of 10 automobiles passing a certain check point:

$$40, \ 45, \ 45, \ 45, \ 50, \ 50, \ 50, \ 50, \ 55, \ 60$$

Find the range and the 10–90 percentile range from these speeds.

Problem 4.2. Find the semi-interquartile range for the speeds in Problem 4.1.

Problem 4.3. Find the average deviation from the mean of the speeds in Problem 4.1.

Problem 4.4. Find the standard deviation and the variance of the speeds in Problem 4.1.

Problem 4.5. The following were the scores of 100 students in a certain test:

$$19, \ 22, \ 27, \ 30, \ 32, \ 33, \ 35, \ 35, \ 36, \ 37$$
$$37, \ 38, \ 39, \ 40, \ 41, \ 42, \ 44, \ 45, \ 45, \ 45$$
$$46, \ 46, \ 47, \ 47, \ 48, \ 48, \ 49, \ 50, \ 50, \ 51$$
$$51, \ 51, \ 52, \ 52, \ 52, \ 53, \ 54, \ 54, \ 55, \ 56$$
$$57, \ 57, \ 58, \ 58, \ 59, \ 60, \ 60, \ 60, \ 61, \ 62$$
$$62, \ 62, \ 63, \ 63, \ 64, \ 64, \ 65, \ 65, \ 65, \ 65$$
$$65, \ 66, \ 66, \ 67, \ 68, \ 69, \ 70, \ 70, \ 71, \ 71$$
$$71, \ 72, \ 73, \ 74, \ 74, \ 75, \ 76, \ 76, \ 77, \ 77$$
$$77, \ 78, \ 78, \ 79, \ 79, \ 79, \ 80, \ 80, \ 81, \ 81$$
$$82, \ 83, \ 84, \ 86, \ 87, \ 87, \ 90, \ 90, \ 91, \ 93$$

Find the range, the 10–90 percentile range, and the semi-interquartile range of these data.

Problem 4.6. Find the standard and mean deviations of the data in Problem 4.5, grouping the data into ten mark classes so as to simplify the arithmetic.

Problem 4.7. Plot the data in Problem 4.5, and determine the half-width of the distribution.

Problem 4.8. Calculate the Standard Deviation of the data in Example 1.8. (The calculation of the mean will be found in the solution to Problem 2.11. This is an example of unequal intervals and the procedure for calculating the standard deviation under these circumstances is the same as for the mean.)

Problem 4.9. An analysis of the number of traffic violations among a group of drivers over a certain period of time was found to be as follows:

Number of Traffic Violations	Number of Drivers
0	27
1	25
2	12
3	5
4	1
5 and more	0

Calculate the mean and the standard deviation of this distribution.

Problem 4.10. What is the mean deviation of the data in Problem 4.9?

Problem 4.11. The following is the distribution of the number of letters in the words in the paragraph from a novel:

Number of Letters	Number of Words
1	5
2	6
3	10
4	13
5	8
6	3
7	4
13	1

Find the mean, the standard deviation, and the mean deviation of the number of letters in a word.

Problem 4.12. It should be noted that with limited data such as that in the last question, the influence of the single extreme value may be quite large. The range of the data is 12, but if the thirteen letter word is omitted it would be only 6. Calculate the mean, the standard deviation, and the mean deviation of the data in Problem 4.11, omitting the thirteen letter word, and compare the results with the answers to Problem 4.11.

Problem 4.13. The employees of a certain firm receive the following weekly wages:

Wages	Number of Employees
$ 55–	10
65–	12
75–	15
85–	20
95–	14
105–	7
115–	2
125–	0

Calculate the mean and standard deviation of the weekly wages.

Problem 4.14.   What are the coefficients of variation of the data in Problems 4.1, 4.5, 4.9, 4.11, and 4.13?

Problem 4.15.   If the independent variable assumes only positive values, what is the maximum and minimum possible values of the coefficient of variation for a symmetrical distribution?

Problem 4.16.   Draw a relative frequency polygon of the data in Example 4.13, with standardized wages.

Problem 4.17.   The results of three tests taken by a group of 10 students are set out below.   Calculate the standard score of student A in each test.

	Test 1	Test 2	Test 3
A	70	70	70
B	70	65	75
C	65	80	50
D	40	50	60
E	65	75	70
F	75	80	80
G	65	65	65
H	60	70	60
I	50	50	40
J	60	65	60

Problem 4.18.   For what volume of data in a small sample is the error, resulting from using n instead of $n - 1$ in the denominator of the standard deviation, less than 5% of the standard deviation?

Problem 4.19.   What is the effect of applying the Sheppard Correction to the standard deviations in the solutions to Problems 4.5 and 4.13?

Problem 4.20. Calculate the standard deviation of the following milk yield for cows:

Milk Yield for Cow (gallons)	Number of Cows
200– 299	10
300– 399	45
400– 499	90
500– 599	134
600– 699	124
700– 799	74
800– 899	59
900– 999	39
1000–1099	16
1100–1199	3

Check your calculations by Charlier's Check.

Solutions

Problem 4.1. The maximum speed is 60 and the minimum is 40. The range is 60 − 40 or 20 m.p.h. The 10 percentile point lies halfway between 40 and 45 and can be taken to be $42\frac{1}{2}$. Similarly the 90 percentile point can be taken as $57\frac{1}{2}$. The 10–90 percentile range is $57\frac{1}{2} - 42\frac{1}{2} = 15$ m.p.h.

Problem 4.2. The quartiles are 45, 50, and 50, and the interquartile range is 50 − 45, or 5 m.p.h. The semi-interquartile range is $2\frac{1}{2}$ m.p.h.

Problem 4.3. To find the average deviation from the mean, the mean must first be calculated. Using 50 m.p.h. as the arbitrary starting point and class units of 5 m.p.h. gives:

M.P.H.	u (1)	f (2)	fu Col. (1) × Col. (2)
40	−2	1	−2
45	−1	3	−3
50	0	4	0
55	1	1	1
60	2	1	2
		10	−2

$$\text{Mean} = 50 + \left[5 \times \frac{(-2)}{10} \right]$$

$$\text{Mean} = 50 - 1 = 49 \text{ m.p.h.}$$

The average deviation can now be calculated.

M.P.H.	Deviation from Mean (1)	Frequency (2)	Col. (1) × Col. (2)
40	9	1	9
45	4	3	12
50	1	4	4
55	6	1	6
60	11	1	11
		10	42

Average deviation from the mean $= \dfrac{42}{10} = 4.2$ m.p.h.

If the calculation had been made from 50 m.p.h., the median, the answer would have been 4.0 m.p.h., verifying the statement in Example 4.5 that the average deviation from the median is less than the average deviation from the mean.

Problem 4.4. Using the same arbitrary starting point and class intervals as were used in the solution of the previous problem:

M.P.H.	u (1)	f (2)	u² (3)	fu (1) × (2)	fu² (2) × (3)
40	−2	1	4	−2	4
45	−1	3	1	−3	3
50	0	4	0	0	0
55	1	1	1	1	1
60	2	1	4	2	4
		10		−2	12

$$\text{Mean} = 50 + 5\left(\frac{-2}{10}\right) = 49$$

$$\text{Standard Deviation} = 5 \sqrt{\frac{12}{10} - \left(\frac{-2}{10}\right)^2} = 5\sqrt{1.2 - .04}$$

$$\text{Standard Deviation} = 5\sqrt{1.16} = 5 \times 1.08 = 5.4 \text{ m.p.h.}$$

The variance is the square of the standard deviation $= 25 \times 1.16 = 29$.

Problem 4.5. The range is $93 - 19 = 74$. The 10 and 90 percentile points are 37 and $81\frac{1}{2}$ and hence the 10–90 percentile range is $44\frac{1}{2}$. The quartile points are 48, 62, and $74\frac{1}{2}$ and the semi-quartile range is:

$$\frac{74\frac{1}{2} - 48}{2} = 13\frac{1}{4}$$

Problem 4.6. Using $54\frac{1}{2}$ as the arbitrary starting point and 10 as the class interval:

Score	u	f	u²	fu	fu²
10–19	−4	1	16	−4	16
20–29	−3	2	9	−6	18
30–39	−2	10	4	−20	40
40–49	−1	14	1	−14	14
50–59	0	18	0	0	0
60–69	1	21	1	21	21
70–79	2	20	4	40	80
80–89	3	10	9	30	90
90–99	4	4	16	16	64
		100		63	343

$$\text{Mean} = 54\frac{1}{2} + (10 \times .63) = 54.5 + 6.3 = 60.8$$

$$\text{Standard deviation} = 10 \sqrt{\frac{343}{100} - \left(\frac{63}{100}\right)^2}$$

$$= 10\sqrt{3.43 - .40}$$

$$= 10\sqrt{3.03} = 17.4$$

The mean deviation can be calculated without appreciable loss of accuracy from $60\frac{1}{2}$ rather than from 60.8, giving the distances for the mean for each class as $60\frac{1}{2} - 14\frac{1}{2}$, $60\frac{1}{2} - 24\frac{1}{2}$, etc.

Score (1)	Difference from Mean (2)	f (3)	(2) × (3)
10–19	46	1	46
20–29	36	2	72
30–39	26	10	260
40–49	16	14	224
50–59	6	18	108
60–69	4	21	84
70–79	14	20	280
80–89	24	10	240
90–99	34	4	136
		100	1450

$$\text{Mean deviation} = 14.5$$

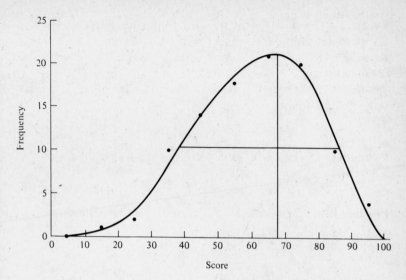

Figure 4.4. Frequency curve. Determination of half-width.

Problem 4.7. The graph is shown in Figure 4.4. Some judgment is needed to draw a smooth curve because the data is not very smooth. The width at one-half the height is seen to be about 48 and the half-width is 24.

Problem 4.8. Standard Deviation $= 10\sqrt{3.9 - (.5)^2} = 19$

Problem 4.9. 1 is the most convenient starting point for the calculation.

$$\text{Mean} = 1 - .03 = .97$$
$$\text{Standard Deviation} = \sqrt{.97 - (-.03)^2} = .98$$

Problem 4.10. Since the mean is very close to 1, the mean deviation can be calculated from 1 rather than from .97 without loss of accuracy. The mean deviation is .74.

Problem 4.11. Using 4 as the arbitrary starting point, the

$$\text{Mean} = 4 - \frac{2}{50} = 3.96 \text{ or } 4.0 \text{ approximately,}$$

and the

$$\text{Standard deviation} = \sqrt{4.32 - (.04)^2} = 2.1 \text{ approximately.}$$

The mean deviation is 1.4 approximately.

Problem 4.12. Using 4 as starting point, the mean = 3.8, the standard deviation = 1.6 and the mean deviation = 1.3. Note that the effect on the standard deviation is greater than on the mean deviation.

Problem 4.13. Using $90 as an arbitrary starting point, and class intervals of $10, the

$$\text{Mean} = \$90 + [10 \times (-.44)] = \$85.60$$

$$\text{Standard Deviation} = 10\sqrt{2.66 - (.44)^2} = 10\sqrt{2.66 - .19}$$

$$= 10\sqrt{2.47} = \$15.70$$

Problem 4.14. The coefficient of variation is the standard deviation divided by the mean $\left(\dfrac{\sigma}{M}\right)$.

Problem Number	Mean	Standard Deviation	Coefficient of Variation
4.1	49	5.4	.11
4.5	60.8	17.4	.29
4.9	.97	.98	1.01
4.11	4.0	2.1	.53
4.13	85.60	15.70	.18

Problem 4.15. If all values of the dependent variable correspond to a certain value (x) of the independent variable, then the mean is x, the standard deviation is zero, and the coefficient of variation is zero. If one-half of the values $(n/2)$ of the dependent variable correspond to $x - t$, and the other half $(n/2)$ to $x + t$, then the mean value is x and the standard deviation is

$$\sqrt{t^2} = t$$

Now t cannot be greater than x, otherwise $x - t$ would be negative. If $t = x$, the mean and the standard deviation of both x and the coefficient of variation is 1. The coefficient of variation must lie in the range

$$0 \leq \text{coefficient of variation} \leq 1$$

Problem 4.16. The calculations required are as follows. From Problem 4.13, the mean is $85.60 and the standard deviation is $15.70.

Wages	Class Midpoint (x)	x − x̄	$\dfrac{x - \bar{x}}{\sigma}$	Number of Employees	Relative Frequency
$ 55–	60	−25.60	−1.63	10	12½%
65–	70	−15.60	−.99	12	15%
75–	80	−5.60	−.36	15	18¾%
85–	90	4.40	.28	20	25%
95–	100	14.40	.92	14	17½%
105–	110	24.40	1.55	7	8¾%
115–	120	34.40	2.19	2	2½%
				80	100%

The frequency polygon is shown in Figure 4.5.

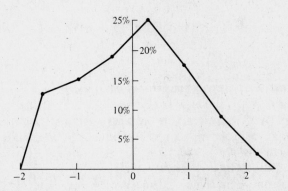

Figure 4.5. Relative frequency polygon with standardized variable.

Problem 4.17. Use 60 or 65 as the arbitrary starting point, and 5 as the class unit.

	Test 1	Test 2	Test 3
Mean score	62	67	63
Standard Deviation	9.8	10.0	11.2
A's Score	70	70	70
A's Standard Score	$\dfrac{8}{9.8}$	$\dfrac{3}{10.0}$	$\dfrac{7}{11.2}$
	= 0.8 =	0.3 =	0.6 approx.

Problem 4.18. The formula for the estimated standard deviation of the population is

$$\sigma = \sqrt{\frac{\Sigma(x - \bar{x})^2}{(n - 1)}}$$

If n is used instead of $(n - 1)$ the error involved will be

$$\sqrt{\frac{\Sigma}{n - 1}} - \sqrt{\frac{\Sigma}{n}}$$

If this is to be 5% of $\sqrt{\Sigma/(n - 1)}$

$$.05 \times \frac{1}{\sqrt{n - 1}} = \frac{1}{\sqrt{n - 1}} - \frac{1}{\sqrt{n}}$$

or

$$\frac{1}{\sqrt{n}} = \frac{.95}{\sqrt{n - 1}}$$

Squaring both sides

$$(n - 1) = .9025n$$

$$.0975n = 1$$

$$n = 10.3$$

If the sample is over 10, the error is less than 5%.

Problem 4.19. The Sheppard Correction decreases the calculated variance by $C^2/12$ when C is the class interval. The variance as calculated in Problem 4.5 was $100 \times 3.03 = 303$, and the corrected value is $303 - 100/12 = 303 - 8 = 295$. The corrected standard deviation is $\sqrt{295} = 17.2$.

The variance as calculated in Problem 4.13 was 247, and the corrected value is $247 - 100/12 = 239$. The correct standard deviation is $\sqrt{239} = \$15.50$.

Problem 4.20. Using 649.5 as the arbitrary starting point, and class intervals of 100 gallons, the calculations are as follows:

Yield	Class Midpoint (u)	Number of Cows (f)	u^2	$(u + 1)^2$	fu	fu^2	$f(u + 1)^2$
200– 299	−4	10	16	9	−40	160	90
300– 399	−3	45	9	4	−135	405	180
400– 499	−2	90	4	1	−180	360	90
500– 599	−1	134	1	0	−134	134	0
600– 699	0	124	0	1	0	0	124
700– 799	1	74	1	4	74	74	296
800– 899	2	59	4	9	118	236	531
900– 999	3	39	9	16	117	351	624

Yield	Class Midpoint (u)	Number of Cows (f)	u^2	$(u+1)^2$	fu	fu^2	$f(u+1)^2$
1000–1099	4	16	16	25	64	256	400
1100–1199	5	3	25	36	15	75	108
		594			388	2051	2443
					−489		
					−101		

$$\text{Check:} \quad \Sigma fu^2 = 2051$$
$$2\Sigma fu = -202$$
$$n = \underline{594}$$
$$2443$$
$$\Sigma f(u+1)^2 = 2443$$

$$\text{Mean Yield} = 649.5 - \left(100 \times \frac{101}{594}\right) = 632 \text{ gallons}$$

$$\text{Standard deviation} = 100 \sqrt{\frac{2051}{594} - \left(\frac{101}{594}\right)^2}$$

$$= 100\sqrt{3.45 - (.17)^2}$$
$$= 100\sqrt{3.45 - .03} = 185 \text{ gallons}$$

5

Moments, Skewness, and Kurtosis

5.1. Moments. In Chapter 2 it was shown that the most obvious single characteristic of a volume of data was the mean, and in Chapter 4 it was shown that the standard deviation provides a measure of the distribution of the data about the mean. It will be noted that the calculation of these two measures involves the summations

$$\frac{\Sigma fx}{n} \quad \text{and} \quad \frac{\Sigma fx^2}{n}$$

respectively, where f is the frequency of the data for value x and n is the total volume of the data. These two summations are the first two terms of the series

$$\frac{\Sigma fx}{n}, \frac{\Sigma fx^2}{n}, \frac{\Sigma fx^3}{n}, \ldots, \frac{\Sigma fx^r}{n}, \ldots$$

These summations are called the first moment, the second moment, the third moment, ..., the rth moment, ... of the data. The moments are normally calculated about the origin but can be calculated about any point. m_r' is the symbol for the rth moment about the origin and m_r is the symbol for the rth moment about the mean. To be explicit, m_r' is described as the "rth moment about zero," and m_r is described as "the rth moment about the mean."

The expressions above are appropriate for grouped data, which is the usual form of data for which moments are calculated. When the data are not grouped, the rth moment becomes

$$m_r' = \frac{\sum_{i=0}^{n} x_i^r}{n}$$

82

EXAMPLE 5.1. Calculate the first four moments of the following distribution:

x	f
0	0
1	10
2	30
3	50
4	80
5	20
6	10
7	0
	200

Solution. The calculations can be made in tabular form as follows:

x	x^2	x^3	x^4	f	fx	fx^2	fx^3	fx^4
0	0	0	0	0	0	0	0	0
1	1	1	1	10	10	10	10	10
2	4	8	16	30	60	120	240	480
3	9	27	81	50	150	450	1350	4050
4	16	64	256	80	320	1280	5120	20480
5	25	125	625	20	100	500	2500	12500
6	36	216	1296	10	60	360	2160	12960
7	49	343	2401	0	0	0	0	0
				200	700	2720	11380	50480

Divide by $n = 200$ 3.5   13.6   56.9   252.4

The first four moments are, $m_1' = 3.5$, $m_2' = 13.6$, $m_3' = 56.9$, and $m_4' = 252.4$. Statistical tables* provide powers of x, but even so, the calculation of the higher moments is laborious. However, moments can be calculated very readily when data processing equipment is available.

5.2. Moments about the Mean. The mean is defined as

$$\bar{x} = \frac{\Sigma fx}{n}$$

---

*See Arkin and Colton, *Tables for Statisticians*, Barnes & Noble, Inc., New York, College Outline Series.

Hence

$$\frac{\Sigma f(x - \bar{x})}{n} = 0$$

and the first moment about the mean m_1 is zero. The variance is defined as

$$\sigma^2 = \frac{\Sigma f(x - \bar{x})^2}{n}$$

and hence, the second moment about the mean is equal to the variance

$$m_2 = \sigma^2$$

The standard deviation σ equals $\sqrt{m_2}$.

The rth moment about the mean is

$$m_r = \frac{\Sigma f(x - \bar{x})^r}{n}$$

EXAMPLE 5.2.   Calculate the first four moments about the mean of the data in Example 5.1.

Solution. From the results of Example 5.1, the mean of the distribution is 3.5, and the calculations can be set out in tabular form as follows:

x	$x - \bar{x}$	$(x - \bar{x})^2$	$(x - \bar{x})^3$	$(x - \bar{x})^4$	f	$f(x - \bar{x})$	$f(x - \bar{x})^2$	$f(x - \bar{x})^3$	$f(x - \bar{x})^4$
1	−2.5	6.25	−15.625	39.0625	10	−25	62.5	−156.25	390.6
2	−1.5	2.25	−3.375	5.0625	30	−45	67.5	−101.25	151.9
3	−0.5	0.25	−0.125	.0625	50	−25	12.5	−6.25	3.1
4	0.5	0.25	0.125	.0625	80	40	20.0	10.00	5.0
5	1.5	2.25	3.375	5.0625	20	30	45.0	67.50	101.2
6	2.5	6.25	15.625	39.0625	10	25	62.5	156.25	390.6
					200	0	270.0	−30.00	1042.4

Divide by $n = 200$ 0   1.35   −0.15   5.21

The first four moments about the mean are, $m_1 = 0$, $m_2 = 1.35$, $m_3 = -0.15$ and $m_4 = 5.21$. It will be noted that the moments about the mean are much smaller than the moments about zero.

The calculation of moments about the mean is particularly laborious when the mean is not a round number, and even when the data processing equipment is used, two steps are required, since the mean must be calculated first. For these reasons, it is best to calculate the moments about an arbitrary origin, and then obtain the moments about the mean from these results by the use of the formulas in the following section.

5.3. Relationship between Moments about Different Origins.

If m_1, m_2, m_3, etc., are the moments about the mean, and m_1', m_2', m_3', etc., are moments about zero or *any other arbitrary origin*, then

$$m_1 = 0$$
$$m_2 = m_2' - (m_1')^2$$
$$m_3 = m_3' - 3m_1'm_2' + 2(m_1')^3$$
$$m_4 = m_4' - 4m_1'm_3' + 6(m_1')^2m_2' - 3(m_1')^4$$

These formulas follow from the expansion of the expressions in Section 5.2. It will be noted that since $\sigma = \sqrt{m_2}$, the second equation can be written

$$\sigma = \sqrt{\frac{\sum_{i=0}^{n} x_i^2}{n} - \bar{x}^2}$$

which in Formula 4.2 in Chapter 4.

EXAMPLE 5.3.   Calculate the first four moments about the mean of the data in Example 5.1 by means of the formulas in Section 5.3.

Solution.   In Example 5.1, the values of the moments about the origin were

$$m_1' = 3.5, m_2' = 13.6, m_3' = 56.9, m_4' = 252.4$$

Hence, by the formulas in Section 5.3

$$m_1 = 0$$
$$m_2 = m_2' - (m_1')^2 = 13.6 - (3.5)^2$$
$$= 13.6 - 12.25$$
$$= 1.35$$
$$m_3 = m_3' - 3m_1'm_2' + 2(m_1')^3$$
$$= 56.9 - (3 \times 3.5 \times 13.6) + 2(3.5)^3$$
$$= 56.9 - 142.8 + 85.75$$
$$= -.15$$

$$m_4 = m_4' - 4m_1'm_3' + 6(m_1')^2 m_2' - 3(m_1')^4$$
$$= 252.4 - (4 \times 3.5 \times 56.9) + (6 \times (3.5)^2 \times 13.6) - 3(3.5)^4$$
$$= 252.4 - 796.6 + 999.6 - 450.2$$
$$= 5.2$$

These values are the same as those obtained in Example 5.2, where the values were calculated directly from the mean.

EXAMPLE 5.4. A coin is tossed until a head comes uppermost. The number of tosses may be 1 (head), 2 (tail, head), 3 (tail, tail, head), or more; 2048 throws are made and the results recorded as follows:

Distribution of heads and tails	Number of tosses	Number of occasions
H	1	1061
TH	2	494
T^{2}H	3	232
T^{3}H	4	137
T^{4}H	5	56
T^{5}H	6	29
T^{6}H	7	25
T^{7}H	8	8
T^{8}H	9	6
		2048

Calculate the first three moments of this distribution about the mean.

Solution. The moments about the arbitrary origin of 3 are first calculated:

d	d^2	d^3	f	fd	fd^2	fd^3
−2	4	−8	1061	−2122	4244	−8488
−1	1	−1	494	−494	494	−494
0	0	0	232	0	0	0
1	1	1	137	137	137	137
2	4	8	56	112	224	448
3	9	27	29	87	261	783
4	16	64	25	100	400	1600
5	25	125	8	40	200	1000
6	36	216	6	36	216	1296
			2048	−2104	6176	−3718

Moments about origin of 3 are

$$m_1' = -\frac{2104}{2048} = -1.027$$

$$m_2' = \frac{6176}{2048} = 3.02$$

$$m_3' = -\frac{3718}{2048} = -1.82$$

The mean is $3 - 1.027 = 1.973$.

The moments about the mean, from the formula in Section 5.3, are

$$m_1 = 0$$

$$m_2 = 3.02 - (-1.027)^2$$
$$= 3.02 - 1.05 = 1.97$$

$$m_3 = -1.82 - 3(-1.027)(3.02) + 2(-1.027)^3$$
$$= -1.82 + 9.30 - 2.17 = 5.31$$

EXAMPLE 5.5. Check the results obtained in Example 5.4, by making the same calculation with zero as origin.
Solution.

x	x^2	x^3	f	fx	fx^2	fx^3
0	0	0	0	0	0	0
1	1	1	1061	1061	1061	1061
2	4	8	494	988	1976	3952
3	9	27	232	696	2088	6264
4	16	64	137	548	2192	8768
5	25	125	56	280	1400	7000
6	36	216	29	174	1044	6264
7	49	343	25	175	1225	8575
8	64	512	8	64	512	4096
9	81	729	6	54	486	4374
			2048	4040	11984	50354

Moments about origin of 0 are

$$m_1 = \frac{4040}{2048} = 1.973$$

$$m_2' = \frac{11984}{2048} = 5.85$$

$$m_3' = \frac{50354}{2048} = 24.59$$

Moments about the mean are

$$m_1 = 0$$

$$m_2 = 5.85 - (1.973)^2$$
$$= 5.85 - 3.89 = 1.96$$

$$m_3 = 24.59 - 3(1.973)(5.85) + 2(1.973)^3$$
$$= 24.59 - 34.63 + 15.36 = 5.32$$

5.4. Moment Generating Function. In theoretical work, considerable use is made of a function called the moment generating function. This function is of the form

$$M_x(\theta) = \sum_{x=0}^{\infty} e^{\theta x} f(x)$$

which when expanded gives

$$M_x(\theta) = 1 + \theta m_1' + \frac{\theta^2}{2!} m_2' + \frac{\theta^3}{3!} m_3' + \cdots$$

The rth moment about the origin is seen to be the coefficient of $\theta^r/r!$

5.5. Skewness. When a distribution is not symmetrical about its mean value, it is said to be *skew*. If the tail of the distribution is longer on the right of the mode, the distribution is said to be *skewed to the right*, or to have *positive skewness*. Similarly, if the tail is longer on the left, the distribution is *skewed to the left*, or has *negative skewness*. (See Figure 3.1).

5.6. Measures of Skewness. The three most common measures of skewness are

(1) $\dfrac{\text{mean} - \text{mode}}{\text{standard deviation}}$

(2) $\dfrac{3(\text{mean} - \text{median})}{\text{standard deviation}}$

$$(3) \quad a_3 = \frac{m_3}{\sqrt{m_2^3}}$$

The first and second measures listed are sometimes referred to as *Pearson's first and second coefficients of skewness*, respectively. It will be noted that if the approximate relationship between the mean, mode, and median (Formula 3.3) is exact, (1) and (2) will be identical.

The third measure is called the *moment coefficient of skewness* (a_3), and since it is calculated from the moments about the mean, it can be readily obtained when data processing equipment is available. The symbol b or β (Greek beta), is sometimes used for a_3^2.

It will be noted that these measures are positive when the distribution is skewed to the right and negative when skewed to the left, justifying the use of the expressions negative and positive skewness.

EXAMPLE 5.6.   Calculate the three measures of skewness listed above for the data in Example 5.1.
Solution.   For these data the mean is 3.5 as calculated in Example 5.1. The data in this example takes on only discrete values 1, 2, 3, etc., but to calculate the mean and mode in order to determine the skewness, it should be assumed that the function is continuous and represents the range 1/2 to 1½, etc.

Using the procedures for calculating the median and mode described in Chapter 3, Sections 3.3 and 3.5, the median is

$$3.5 + \left(\frac{100 - 90}{80}\right) \times 1 = 3.63$$

and the mode is

$$4 + \frac{1}{2}\left(\frac{20 - 50}{160 - 50 - 20}\right) \times 1 = 3.83$$

Hence, the three measures of skewness are

$$(1) \quad \frac{3.5 - 3.83}{\sqrt{1.35}} = \frac{-.33}{\sqrt{1.35}} = -.28$$

$$(2) \quad \frac{3(3.5 - 3.63)}{\sqrt{1.35}} = \frac{3 \times (-.13)}{\sqrt{1.35}} = -.34$$

$$(3) \quad \frac{-0.15}{\sqrt{(1.35)^3}} = \frac{-0.15}{\sqrt{2.46}} = \frac{-0.15}{1.57} = -.096$$

It will be noted that these measures are negative and the distribution is skewed to the left.

EXAMPLE 5.7.   Calculate the moment coefficient of skewness of the data in Example 5.5.
Solution.   For these data $m_2 = 1.96$ and $m_3 = 5.32$
   The moment coefficient of skewness is

$$\frac{m_3}{\sqrt{m_2^3}} = \frac{5.32}{\sqrt{1.96^3}} = \frac{5.32}{\sqrt{7.53}} = \frac{5.32}{2.74} = 1.94$$

The distribution has a marked positive skewness.

5.7. Kurtosis.   Kurtosis is the "peakedness" of a distribution. The *normal curve*, which has been referred to briefly and is described in Chapter 7, is taken as the standard of "peakedness." A curve less peaked than the normal is said to be *platykurtic* and a more peaked curve is said to be *leptokurtic* (see Figure 5.1). The term *mesokurtic* is sometimes used to describe the normal curve.

Like skewness, there is more than one measure of kurtosis. One measure of kurtosis is

$$\frac{Q}{P_{90} - P_{10}}$$

where $Q = 1/2 \, (Q_3 - Q_1)$, the semi-quartile range, and P_{90} and P_{10} are the ninety and the ten percentile points.

The measure based on moments is the *moment coefficient of kurtosis* and makes use of the fourth moment.   It is designated a_4, or b_2, or β_2 (Greek beta).

$$a_4 = \frac{m_4}{m_2^2}$$

For the normal curve, $a_4 = 3$, and hence if $a_4 < 3$ the curve is *platykurtic*, and if $a_4 > 3$ the curve is *leptokurtic*. (Sometimes $a_4 - 3$ is used as the measure of kurtosis.)

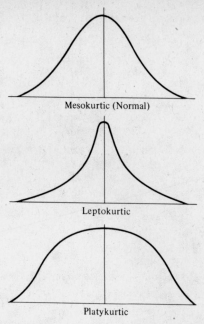

Mesokurtic (Normal)

Leptokurtic

Platykurtic

Figure 5.1. Frequency curves, showing normal, leptokurtic, and platy-kurtic distributions.

EXAMPLE 5.8. Calculate the moment coefficient of kurtosis of the data in Example 5.1. Is the distribution platykurtic or leptokurtic?

Solution. The second and further moments about the mean for these data, were calculated in the solution to Example 5.2. m_2 was 1.35 and m_4 was 5.21. The moment coefficient of kurtosis is

$$\frac{5.21}{(1.35)^2} = \frac{5.21}{1.82} = 2.9$$

Since this is less than 3, the distribution is very slightly platy-kurtic.

EXAMPLE 5.9. Calculate the moment coefficient of kurtosis of the data in Example 5.4.

Solution. Only the first three moments were calculated in the solution to Example 5.4 and hence, the fourth moment must be calculated. Using 3 as an arbitrary origin:

d	d^4	f	fd^4
−2	16	1061	16976
−1	1	494	494
0	0	232	0
1	1	137	137
2	16	56	896
3	81	29	2349
4	256	25	6400
5	625	8	5000
6	1296	6	7776
		2048	40028

$$m_4' = 19.54$$

From the formula in Section 5.3

$$m_4 = m_4' - 4\,m_1'm_3' + 6(m_1')^2\,m_2' - 3(m_1')^4$$
$$= 19.54 - 4(-1.027)(-1.82) + 6(-1.027)^2(3.02)$$
$$- 3(-1.027)^4$$
$$= 19.54 - 4(1.87) + 6(3.185) - 3(1.112)$$
$$= 19.54 - 7.48 + 19.11 - 3.34$$

$$m_4 = 27.83$$

Moment coefficient of kurtosis

$$= \frac{27.83}{(1.96)^2} = \frac{27.83}{3.84} = 7.2$$

The distribution is leptokurtic.

5.8. Dimensionless Moments.   In Chapter 4, Section 4.8, the need for a measure of dispersion which did not depend upon absolute values was explained and the *coefficient of variation* (σ/m) was used for this purpose which is a *dimensionless* function.

When dimensionless moments are needed, the moments about the mean are divided by $(\sqrt{m_2})^r$ and are represented by a_r.

$$a_1 = 0$$

$$a_2 = 1$$

$$a_3 = \frac{m_3}{(\sqrt{m_2})^3} = \frac{m_3}{\sigma^3}$$

$$a_r = \frac{m_r}{(\sqrt{m_2})^r} = \frac{m_r}{\sigma^r}$$

It will be noted particularly that the dimensionless second moment is unity and *not the same* as the dimensionless coefficient of variation.

a_3, *the moment coefficient of skewness*, was introduced in Section 5.6, and a_4, the *moment coefficient of kurtosis*, was introduced in Section 5.7.

EXAMPLE 5.10. What are the first four dimensionless moments of the distribution in Example 5.1, and what are their names?
Solution. The moments about the mean of the distribution in Example 5.1 are

$$m_1 = 0$$
$$m_2 = 1.35$$
$$m_3 = -0.15$$
$$m_4 = 5.21$$
$$\sigma = \sqrt{m_2} = \sqrt{1.35} = 1.16$$

The dimensionless moments of the distribution are

$$a_1 = 0$$
$$a_2 = \frac{1.35}{(1.16)^2} = \frac{1.35}{1.35} = 1$$
$$a_3 = -\frac{0.15}{(1.16)^3} = -\frac{0.15}{1.56} = -0.10$$
$$a_4 = \frac{5.21}{(1.16)^4} = \frac{5.21}{1.81} = 2.88$$

The first two dimensionless moments being always 0 and 1 respectively, have no names. The third dimensionless moment is the moment coefficient of skewness, and the fourth is the moment coefficient of kurtosis.

EXAMPLE 5.11. What are the values of the first four dimensionless moments of the normal curve.

Solution. The first two values are 0 and 1 respectively, as they are for all curves. Since the normal curve is symmetrical, the third dimensionless moment is 0. As stated in Section 5.7 the fourth dimensionless moment of the normal curve is 3. Hence,

$$a_1 = 0$$

$$a_2 = 1$$

$$a_3 = 0$$

$$a_4 = 3$$

5.9. Sheppard's Corrections and Charlier's Check. It will be remembered that in Chapter 4, Section 4.10, the corrected value of the standard deviation, σ^2, for grouped data (*Sheppard's Correction*) was

$$\sigma^2 - \frac{C^2}{12}$$

Similar corrections to higher moments can be applied. If $_g m_1$, $_g m_2$, $_g m_3$, etc., are the moments calculated for grouped data, then the corrected moments are

$$m_1 = {}_g m_1$$

$$m_2 = {}_g m_2 - \frac{1}{12} C^2$$

$$m_3 = {}_g m_3$$

$$m_4 = {}_g m_4 - \frac{1}{2} C^2 {}_g m_2 + \frac{7}{240} C^4$$

As explained in Section 4.10, these corrections will not be used in this book.

Charlier's Check was described in Chapter 4, Section 4.11, and can be extended to higher moments.

$$\Sigma f(u + 1) = \Sigma fu + n$$

$$\Sigma f(u + 1)^2 = \Sigma f(u)^2 + 2\Sigma fu + n$$

$$\Sigma f(u + 1)^3 = \Sigma f(u)^3 + 3\Sigma f(u)^2 + 3\Sigma fu + n$$

$$\Sigma f(u + 1)^4 = \Sigma f(u)^4 + 4\Sigma f(u)^3 + 6\Sigma f(u)^2 + 4\Sigma fu + n$$

Since higher moments are usually calculated by data processing equipment, this check is rarely employed in practice.

5.10. Notation—Universe and Samples. When it is required to distinguish between functions relating to the *total population* or *universe*, and functions relating to a *sample*, Greek letters are used for the universe and Latin letters for the sample. Thus, the moments of the universe are represented by μ (Greek mu) or μ' and skewness and kurtosis of the universe by α_3 and α_4 (Greek alpha). In the same way σ (Greek sigma) is the standard deviation of the universe and s the standard deviation of the sample.

Problems

Moments higher than the first, which establishes the mean, have no significance for very small volumes of data. However, so as to provide tests of the principles involved in the calculation of higher moments without presenting the student with long laborious calculations, some of the following problems are based on very limited data.

Problem 5.1. The ages of children attending a party are

$$2, \ 3, \ 3, \ 4, \ 5$$

What are the first four moments of the ages?

Problem 5.2. What are the first four moments about the mean of the data in Problem 5.1, calculated directly from the mean?

Problem 5.3. Calculate the first four moments about the mean of the data in Problem 5.1, using the relationships between the moments about the mean and the moments about the origin.

Problem 5.4. What are the moment coefficients of skewness and of kurtosis of these data?

Problem 5.5. Is the distribution in Problem 5.1 skewed to the left or the right? Is the distribution platykurtic or leptokurtic?

Problem 5.6. Calculate the first four moments of the data in Problem 5.1, using 3 as origin. Use these results to calculate the first four moments about the mean.

Problem 5.7. In a study of road accidents, the following was the distribution for number of vehicles involved in each accident:

Number of Vehicles	No. of Accident Involvements
1	2241
2	3272
3	264
4	47
5	6
6 or more	3

Calculate the first four moments about the mean of the distribution.

Problem 5.8. What are the mean and standard deviation of the data in Problem 5.7? What are the moment coefficients of skewness and kurtosis?

Problem 5.9. The distribution of days absent during a year among the employees of a small firm are as follows:

No. of Days Absent	Number of Employees
0– 4	5
5– 9	10
10–14	8
15–19	1
20–24	0
25–29	1
	25

Calculate the first four moments of this distribution about the origin.

Problem 5.10. Calculate the first four moments about the mean for the distribution in Problem 5.9.

Problem 5.11. Calculate the first four moments about the mean for the data in Problem 5.9, using an arbitrary origin of 7 and units of 5.

Problem 5.12. What are the mean and the standard deviation of the data in Problem 5.9?

Problem 5.13. What are the moment coefficients of skewness and kurtosis of the data in Problem 5.9?

Problem 5.14. Calculate Pearson's first and second coefficients of skewness for the distribution in Example 3.6. Is the distribution skewed to the left or to the right?

Problem 5.15. What is the percentile measure of kurtosis of the distribution in Example 3.9?

Problem 5.16. What are the first four dimensionless moments of the distribution in Problem 5.1?

Problem 5.17. What are the first four dimensionless moments of the distribution in Problem 5.7?

Problem 5.18. What are the first four dimensionless moments of the distribution in Problem 5.9?

Problem 5.19. What are the first four moments about the mean of the data in Problem 5.9 with Sheppard's Corrections?

Problem 5.20. Apply Charlier's Check of the calculation of the first three moments of the data in Example 5.4.

Solutions

Problem 5.1. The expression for the rth moment is

$$\frac{\sum_{i=0}^{n} \bar{x}_i^r}{n}$$

First moment $= \dfrac{2 + 3 + 3 + 4 + 5}{5} = \dfrac{17}{5} = 3.4 = (m_1')$

Second moment $= \dfrac{2^2 + 3^2 + 3^2 + 4^2 + 5^2}{5}$

$= \dfrac{4 + 9 + 9 + 16 + 25}{5} = \dfrac{63}{5} = 12.6 = (m_2')$

Third moment $= \dfrac{2^3 + 3^3 + 3^3 + 4^3 + 5^3}{5}$

$= \dfrac{8 + 27 + 27 + 64 + 125}{5} = \dfrac{251}{5}$

$= 50.2 = (m_3')$

Fourth moment $= \dfrac{2^4 + 3^4 + 3^4 + 4^4 + 5^4}{5}$

$= \dfrac{16 + 81 + 81 + 256 + 625}{5} = \dfrac{1059}{5}$

$= 211.8 = (m_4')$

Problem 5.2. The mean of the data is 3.4, and the first moment about the mean (m_1) is 0. The second moment about the mean (m_2) is

$$m_2 = \frac{(-1.4)^2 + (-.4)^2 + (-.4)^2 + (.6)^2 + (1.6)^2}{5}$$

$$= \frac{1.96 + 0.16 + 0.16 + 0.36 + 2.56}{5} = \frac{5.20}{5} = 1.04$$

The third moment about the mean (m_3) is

$$m_3 = \frac{(-1.4)^3 + (-.4)^3 + (-.4)^3 + (.6)^3 + (1.6)^3}{5}$$

$$= \frac{-2.744 - .064 - .064 + .216 + 4.096}{5} = \frac{1.440}{5} = 0.29$$

The fourth moment about the mean (m_4) is

$$m_4 = \frac{(-1.4)^4 + (-.4)^4 + (-.4)^4 + (.6)^4 + (1.6)^4}{5}$$

Using tables of fourth powers and rounding to two places of decimals, we have

$$m_4 = \frac{3.84 + .02 + .02 + .13 + 6.55}{5} = \frac{10.56}{5} = 2.11$$

Problem 5.3.

$$m_1 = 0$$

$$m_2 = m_2' - (m_1')^2 = 12.6 - (3.4)^2$$
$$= 12.6 - 11.56$$
$$= 1.04$$

$$m_3 = m_3' - 3m_1'm_2' + 2(m_1')^3$$
$$= 50.2 - (3 \times 3.4 \times 12.6) + 2(3.4)^3$$
$$= 50.2 - (3 \times 42.84) + (2 \times 39.3)$$
$$= 50.2 - 128.5 + 78.6$$
$$= 0.3$$

$$m_4 = m_4' - 4m_1'm_3' + 6(m_1')^2 m_2' - 3(m_1')^4$$
$$= 211.8 - (4 \times 3.4 \times 50.2) + (6(3.4)^2 \times 12.6) - 3(3.4)^4$$
$$= 211.8 - 682.7 + 873.9 - 400.9$$
$$= 2.1$$

These answers, except for the results of rounding, are the same as those calculated in the solution to Problem 5.2.

Problem 5.4.   The moment coefficient of skewness is

$$a_3 = \frac{m_3}{\sqrt{m_2^3}} = \frac{0.3}{\sqrt{(1.04)^3}}$$

$$= \frac{0.3}{1.06} = 0.3$$

The moment coefficient of kurtosis is

$$a_4 = \frac{m_4}{\sqrt{m_2^4}} = \frac{2.1}{\sqrt{1.04^4}} = \frac{2.1}{1.08} = 1.9$$

Problem 5.5.   Since the moment coefficient of skewness is positive, the distribution is skewed to the right. Since the moment coefficient of kurtosis is less than 3, the distribution is platykurtic.

Problem 5.6.   Using 3 as origin, the values become

$$-1, \ 0, \ 0, \ 1, \ 2$$

The moments are

$$m_1' = \frac{-1 + 1 + 2}{5} = \frac{2}{5} = .4$$

$$m_2' = \frac{1 + 1 + 4}{5} = \frac{6}{5} = 1.2$$

$$m_3' = \frac{-1 + 1 + 8}{5} = \frac{8}{5} = 1.6$$

$$m_4' = \frac{1 + 1 + 16}{5} = \frac{18}{5} = 3.6$$

The moments about the mean are

$$m_1 = 0$$
$$m_2 = m_2' - (m_1')^2 = 1.2 - (.4)^2 = 1.2 - .16 = 1.04$$
$$m_3 = m_3' - 3m_1'm_2' + 2(m_1')^3$$
$$= 1.6 - 3(.4)(1.2) + 2(.4)^3$$
$$= 1.6 - 1.44 + .13 = 0.3$$
$$m_4 = m_4' - 4m_1'm_3' + 6(m_1'^2)m_2' - 3(m_1')^4$$
$$= 3.6 - 4(.4)(1.6) + 6(.4)^2(1.2) - 3(.4)^4$$
$$= 3.6 - 2.56 + 1.15 - .08 = 2.1$$

It will be noted that the calculations are less laborious than those used to obtain the same results in Problems 5.2 and 5.3.

Problem 5.7. Using 2 as origin, the calculations are as follows. Owing to the very small size of the last group, the fact that more than 6 vehicles might have been involved in one of the three accidents may be ignored.

d	d^2	d^3	d^4	f	fd	fd^2	fd^3	fd^4
−1	1	−1	1	2241	−2241	2241	−2241	2241
0	0	0	0	3272	0	0	0	0
1	1	1	1	264	264	264	264	264
2	4	8	16	47	94	188	376	752
3	9	27	81	6	18	54	162	486
4	16	64	256	3	12	48	192	768
				5833	−1853	2795	−1247	4511

Dividing by 5833, the total frequency, we have

$$m_1' = -.32$$
$$m_2' = .48$$
$$m_3' = -.21$$
$$m_4' = .77$$

Considerable care with signs will be needed in calculating the moments about the mean.

$$m_1 = 0$$

$$m_2 = .48 - (-.32)^2$$
$$= .48 - .10$$
$$= .38$$

$$m_3 = -.21 - 3(-.32)(.48) + 2(-.32)^3$$
$$= -.21 + .46 - .07$$
$$= .18$$

$$m_4 = .77 - 4(-.32)(-.21) + 6(-.32)^2(.48) - 3(-.32)^4$$
$$= .77 - .27 + .29 - .03$$
$$= .76$$

Problem 5.8. The mean of the distribution is

$$2 - .32 = 1.68$$

The standard deviation is $\sqrt{m_2} = \sqrt{.38} = .62$.

The moment coefficient of skewness is

$$\frac{m_3}{\sqrt{m_2^3}} = \frac{.18}{\sqrt{.38^3}} = \frac{.18}{.23} = .8$$

The distribution is skewed to the right.

The moment coefficient of kurtosis is

$$\frac{m_4}{\sqrt{m_2^4}} = \frac{.76}{(.38)^2} = \frac{.76}{.14} = 5.4$$

The distribution is leptokurtic.

Problem 5.9. The midpoints of the class intervals are 2, 7, 12, 17, and the use of a unit of 5 ages does not appreciably reduce the calculation since the distance of the midpoints from the origin become .4, 1.4, 2.4, 3.4, etc. The calculations proceed as follows:

No. of Days Absent	x	x^2	x^3	x^4	f	fx	fx^2	fx^3 (00)	fx^4 (000)
0– 4	2	4	8	16	5	10	20	0	0
5– 9	7	49	343	2401	10	70	490	34	24
10–14	12	144	1728	20736	8	96	1152	138	166
15–19	17	289	4913	83521	1	17	289	49	84
20–24	22	484	10648	234256	0	0	0	0	0
25–29	27	729	19683	531441	1	27	729	197	531
					25	220	2680	418	805

The calculation of the last two columns has been simplified by the omitting of 2 and 3 digits respectively, as these digits are not significant. It must be remembered to restore these digits in the final result. Thus,

$$m_1' = 8.8$$
$$m_2' = 107$$
$$m_3' = 16.7 \times 100 = 1,670$$
$$m_4' = 32.2 \times 1,000 = 32,200$$

Problem 5.10.

$$m_1 = 0$$
$$m_2 = 107 - (8.8)^2 = 30$$
$$m_3 = 1,670 - 3(8.8)(107) + 2(8.8)^3 = 208$$
$$m_4 = 32,200 - 4(8.8)(1,670) + 6(8.8)^2(107) - 3(8.8)^4$$
$$= 5,000 \text{ (approx.)}$$

Problem 5.11. Using an arbitrary origin, and units of five, the calculation of the moments about the origin is considerably simplified as shown below. It must be remembered to multiply the rth moment by C', that is by 5, 25, 125, and 625, respectively. However, *these multiplications need not be made until the final results are obtained.*

No. of Days Absent	u	u^2	u^3	u^4	f	fu	fu^2	fu^3	fu^4
0– 4	−1	1	−1	1	5	−5	5	−5	5
5– 9	0	0	0	0	10	0	0	0	0
10–14	1	1	1	1	8	8	8	8	8
15–19	2	4	8	16	1	2	4	8	16
20–24	3	9	27	81	0	0	0	0	0
25–29	4	16	64	256	1	4	16	64	256
					25	9	33	75	285

$$m_1' = \frac{9}{25} \times 5 \quad = .36 \times 5$$

$$m_2' = \frac{33}{25} \times 5^2 \quad = 1.32 \times 5^2$$

$$m_3' = \frac{75}{25} \times 5^3 \quad = 3 \times 5^3$$

$$m_4' = \frac{285}{25} \times 5^4 = 11.4 \times 5^4$$

The moments about the mean are

$$m_1 = 0$$

$$m_2 = [1.32 - (.36)^2] \times 5^2 = 1.19 \times 5^2 = 30$$

$$m_3 = [3 - 3(.36)(1.32) + 2(.36)^3] \times 5^3$$
$$= 1.66 \times 5^3 = 208$$

$$m_4 = [11.4 - 4(.36)(3) + 6(.36)^2(1.32) - 3(.36)^4] \times 5^4$$
$$= 8.056 \times 5^4 = 5,035$$

The difference in m_4 as calculated in this solution compared to the result obtained in the solution to Problem 5.10 is due to rounding. In each case the value of m_4 should be stated as 5,000.

Problem 5.12. The mean is m_1' from the solution to Problem 5.9, or 7 (the origin) + m_1' from the solution in Problem 5.11.

$$\text{Mean} = 8.8$$

$$\text{Standard Deviation} = \sqrt{m_2} = \sqrt{30} = 5.5$$

Problem 5.13. The moment coefficient of skewness is 1.3, and the moment coefficient of kurtosis = 5.6.

Problem 5.14. In the solution to Example 3.6, the mean was found to be 30.4, the median 31.3, and the mode 33.3. The standard deviation has to be calculated and this is found to be

$$\sqrt{179} = 13.4$$

Pearson's first coefficient of skewness is

$$\frac{30.4 - 33.3}{13.4} = -\frac{2.9}{13.4} = -.22$$

Pearson's second coefficient of skewness is

$$\frac{3(30.4 - 31.3)}{13.4} = \frac{-2.7}{13.4} = -.20$$

The distribution is skewed to the left.

Problem 5.15. The percentile measure of kurtosis is

$$\frac{Q}{P_{90} - P_{10}}$$

From the solution of Example 3.9, this is

$$\frac{\frac{1}{2}(77 - 67)}{81 - 65} = \frac{\frac{1}{2}(10)}{16} = \frac{5}{16} = .31$$

Problem 5.16. The moments about the mean of the distribution in Problem 5.1 are given in the solution of Problem 5.2.

$$m_1 = 0$$

$$m_2 = 1.04$$

$$m_3 = 0.29$$

$$m_4 = 2.11$$

$\sqrt{m_2} = \sqrt{1.04} = 1.02$, and the dimensionless moments are

$$a_1 = 0$$

$$a_2 = 1$$

$$a_3 = \frac{0.29}{(1.02)^3} = 0.27$$

$$a_4 = \frac{2.11}{(1.02)^4} = 1.95$$

Problem 5.17.

$$a_1 = 0$$

$$a_2 = 1$$

$$a_3 = .77$$

$$a_4 = 5.3$$

Problem 5.18.

$$a_1 = 0$$

$$a_2 = 1$$

$$a_3 = 1.3$$

$$a_4 = 5.6$$

Problem 5.19.   The first four moments about the mean of the data in Problem 5.9 are

$$0, \ 30, \ 208, \ 5000$$

The class interval is 5. The corrected figures are:

$$m_1 = 0$$

$$m_2 = 30 - \left(\frac{1}{12} \times 25\right) = 28$$

$$m_3 = 208$$

$$m_4 = 5000 - \left(\frac{1}{2} \times 25 \times 30\right) + \left(\frac{7}{240} \times 625\right)$$

$$= 5000 - 375 + 18$$

Since 5000 was a rounded figure, the value of m_4 is still approximately 5000.

Problem 5.20. In the solution of Example 5.4, an arbitrary origin of 3 was selected. To apply Charlier's Check to these calculations, the results are now calculated with origin 2.

d	d^2	d^3	f	fd	fd^2	fd^3
−1	1	−1	1061	−1061	1061	−1061
0	0	0	494	0	0	0
1	1	1	232	232	232	232
2	4	8	137	274	548	1096
3	9	27	56	168	504	1512
4	16	64	29	116	464	1856
5	25	125	25	125	625	3125
6	36	216	8	48	288	1728
7	49	343	6	42	294	2058
			2048	−56	4016	10546

Checking:

$$-56 = -2104 + 2048$$

$$4016 = 6176 + 2(-2104) + 2048$$

$$10546 = -3718 + 3(6176) + 3(-2104) + 2048$$

6

Elementary Probability

6.1. Introduction. There are at least four possible methods of defining probability, which may be called briefly:

(1) The Classical definition
(2) The Frequency definition
(3) The "Fair Price" definition
(4) The "Degree of Rational Belief" definition

The *classical theory* dates back to Laplace's principle of *equally possible cases*, now more usually defined as *equally likely alternatives*. Under this definition, probability is an additive function $P(S)$ of the set S, in a given *a priori* space R. It will be noted that this is a purely conceptional mathematical theory. The term *equally likely* is difficult to interpret except in constructed problems involving dice and cards.

For most statistical studies, it is usual to consider probability as the *limiting value of the relative frequency*, when the number of observations is very large. For example, if we throw a die a very large number of times and determine the relative frequency with which each number comes up, we have a set of empirical probabilities which are valid for the particular die used, whether it is loaded or a true die.

Unfortunately, this definition, too, presents problems because, in most practical cases, conditions are not static and it is not possible to repeat a statistical study more than a limited number of times.

Whitworth, whose book *Choice and Chance* is well known, gives the following explanation of the "Fair Price" definition. "The measurement of chance (probability) may be approached *ab initio* from the consideration of the price that may reasonably be paid for 'a gain contingent on some doubtful occurrence.' And to many minds this method appears easier than any other."

The "Degree of Rational Belief" definition presupposes that we have some prior knowledge, and that we are not carrying out our experiments in a vacuum. This credibility approach is especially associated with Bayes' Theorem of *a priori probabilities*.

6.2. Classical Probability.

In the next chapter, we shall consider *probability distributions*, which play an important role in statistical work since they provide valuable mathematical models. In order to understand these distributions some knowledge of classical probability is essential, and this chapter will provide a brief review of the theory.

If an event E can occur in a ways out of a total of n possible equally likely ways, then the probability of the event happening is

$$p = \Pr\{E\} = \frac{a}{n} \tag{6.1}$$

The probability that the event will not happen is

$$q = \Pr\{\text{not } E\} = 1 - p = \frac{n - a}{n} \tag{6.2}$$

$\Pr\{\text{not } E\}$ may be written $\Pr\{\sim E\}$ or $\Pr\{\bar{E}\}$.

$$p + q = 1, \text{ and } \Pr\{E\} + \Pr\{\text{not } E\} = 1$$

EXAMPLE 6.1. What is the probability of throwing a 6 with one die? A 7 with two dice?
Solution. A thrown die can end up with any one of its six sides uppermost. Each is equally likely, so a single die can be thrown in 6 ways. In only one way will a six be uppermost, so that

$$p = \frac{1}{6}$$

If two dice are thrown, each die can end up in six different ways, and since the dice are independent of each other, two dice can be thrown in 6 × 6, or 36, different ways. These are listed below.

1, 1	2, 1	3, 1	4, 1	5, 1	(6, 1)
1, 2	2, 2	3, 2	4, 2	(5, 2)	6, 2
1, 3	2, 3	3, 3	(4, 3)	5, 3	6, 3
1, 4	2, 4	(3, 4)	4, 4	5, 4	6, 4
1, 5	(2, 5)	3, 5	4, 5	5, 5	6, 5
(1, 6)	2, 6	3, 6	4, 6	5, 6	6, 6

The total of the two dice will be 7 in the six ringed cases, and hence the probability of throwing 7 with two dice is

$$\frac{6}{36}, \text{ or } \frac{1}{6}$$

6.3. Relation to Set Theory.   It is sometimes convenient to think of the different ways in which an event can occur as points in a sample space. In a given situation, the *sample space* is defined as all events which can possibly occur. If, in a sample space, there are n equally likely events which can occur, then the probability of each event is $\frac{1}{n}$.   All probabilities lie in the range 0 to 1, 0 indicating an impossible event and 1 a certainty.

If we have two sets in the sample space, E_1 and E_2, then

$E_1 + E_2$ or $E_1 \cup E_2$ (the union of sets A and B) is the set of all elements belonging *either* to E_1 or E_2.

$E_1 E_2$ or $E_1 \cap E_2$ (the intersection of A and B) is the set of all elements belonging *both* to E_1 and to E_2.

From the Venn Diagrams (Figure 6.1) we see that if the events E_1 and E_2 have no points in common or are *mutually exclusive*,

$$\Pr\{E_1 + E_2\} = \Pr\{E_1\} + \Pr\{E_2\}$$

However, if they have points in common, and are not mutually exclusive,

$$\Pr\{E_1 + E_2\} = \Pr\{E_1\} + \Pr\{E_2\} - \Pr\{E_1 E_2\} \quad (6.3)$$

Note that for mutually exclusive events, $\Pr\{E_1 E_2\} = 0$

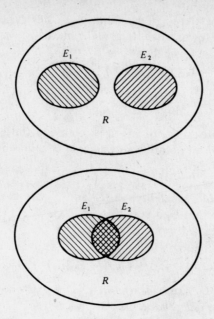

Figure 6.1. Examples of Venn diagrams.

EXAMPLE 6.2. If $E_1 + E_2$ is the sample space, what is the value of $\Pr\{E_1 + E_2\}$?
Solution. Since $E_1 + E_2$ is the whole sample space, $\Pr\{E_1 + E_2\} = 1$.

EXAMPLE 6.3. What is the probability of throwing *either* a double six *or* a three, on the throw of two dice?
Solution. From the table in the solution to Example 6.1, the probability of throwing a double six is 1/36 and the probability of throwing a three is 2/36 (since three can be $2 + 1$ or $1 + 2$). Hence, since these probabilities are mutually exclusive, the required probability is

$$\frac{1}{36} + \frac{2}{36} = \frac{3}{36} = \frac{1}{12}$$

EXAMPLE 6.4. What is the probability of throwing either a single 1 *or* a single 3 on the throw of two dice?
Solution. A single 1 can be thrown in 10 ways. (The first row and the first column in the diagram, less the first case $1 + 1$ which

is not the throw of a *single* 1). Similarly, a single 3 can be thrown in 10 ways. However, these are not mutually exclusive events, since a 1 *and* a 3 can be thrown in 2 ways.

Hence, the required probability is

$$\frac{10}{36} + \frac{10}{36} - \frac{2}{36} = \frac{18}{36} = \frac{1}{2}$$

The same result can be obtained by counting those cases, in the 36 tabulated in the solution to Example 6.1, in which a single 1 or a single 3 occurs.

6.4. Conditional Probability. If E_1 and E_2 are two events, then the probability that E_2 occurs if E_1 occurs is

$$\Pr\{E_2 \mid E_1\}$$

If

$$\Pr\{E_2 \mid E_1\} = \Pr\{E_2\}$$

then E_1 and E_2 are *independent* events. Otherwise they are *dependent*. For *independent* events

$$\Pr\{E_1 E_2\} = \Pr\{E_1\} \Pr\{E_2\} \qquad (6.4)$$

For *dependent* events

$$\Pr\{E_1 E_2\} = \Pr\{E_1\} \Pr\{E_2 \mid E_1\} \qquad (6.5)$$

For three events

$$\Pr\{E_1 E_2 E_3\} = \Pr\{E_1\} \Pr\{E_2 \mid E_1\} \Pr\{E_3 \mid E_1 E_2\}$$

and this reduces to $\Pr\{E_1\} \Pr\{E_2\} \Pr\{E_3\}$ if the three events are all independent.

EXAMPLE 6.5. A bag contains two white and one black ball. What is the probability that first a white ball and then a black ball is drawn from the bag; (1) if the first ball is returned, and (2) if the first ball is not returned to the bag?
Solution. (1) If the first ball is returned we have two independent events. $\Pr\{E_1\}$ (the probability of drawing a white ball) is 2/3, and $\Pr\{E_2\}$ (the probability of drawing a black ball) is 1/3, and

$$\Pr\{E_1 E_2\} = \frac{2}{3} \times \frac{1}{3} = \frac{2}{9}$$

(2) If the ball is not returned, $\Pr\{E_1\}$ is still 2/3, but when the white ball has been drawn, the bag is left with one white and one black ball, so that

$$\Pr\{E_2 \mid E_1\} = \frac{1}{2}$$

$$\Pr\{E_1 E_2\} = \frac{2}{3} \times \frac{1}{2} = \frac{1}{3}$$

6.5. Continuous Probabilities. In the examples used to illustrate the foregoing discrete probabilities, throwing dice and drawing balls from bags have been used. Probability theory, and the formulas given, apply equally to continuous probabilities, but many of the applications require the use of calculus. Given a *probability distribution function*, such as that shown in Figure 6.2, the probability of a value lying between a and b is the area under the curve between the ordinates a and b, expressed as a ratio to the total area under the curve. The probability of an *exact value* a is zero.

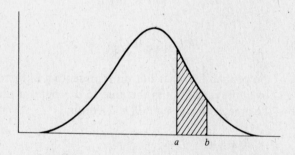

Figure 6.2. Probability distribution function.

EXAMPLE 6.6. In a study of the speeds travelled by automobiles on an expressway, it was found that the speeds of automobiles could be expressed in the form of a triangular distribution shown in Figure 6.3. No automobiles were observed travelling at less than 40 miles per hour. The distribution increased in proportion to the excess over 40 m.p.h. up to 60 m.p.h., the maximum legal speed, and then decreased steadily to 70 m.p.h., the maximum observed. What is the probability that an individual automobile

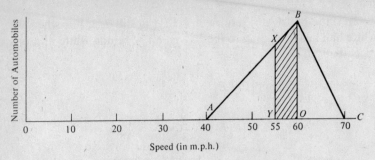

Speed (in m.p.h.)

Figure 6.3. Speeds of automobiles. Probability distribution function.

(1) Is travelling at exactly 60 m.p.h.,
(2) Is travelling above the legal speed limit,
(3) Is travelling between 55 and 60 m.p.h?

Solution.   (1) Since this is a continuous distribution, the probability of an *exact* speed of 60 m.p.h. is zero.

(2) Since the total area under the curve must be unity, the usual formula for the area of a triangle gives

$$\frac{1}{2} \times BO \times (70 - 40) = 1$$

or

$$BO = \frac{2}{30} = \frac{1}{15}$$

The area of the probability distribution representing automobiles travelling above the speed limit is the area to the right of the line BO, that is, the area of the triangle BOC. This is

$$\frac{1}{2} \times BO \times (70 - 60) = \frac{1}{2} \times \frac{1}{15} \times 10 = \frac{1}{3}$$

(3) The area of the probability distribution representing automobiles travelling between 55 and 60 m.p.h. is the shaded area in the illustration. This is

$$\frac{1}{2} \times (BO + XY) \times (60 - 55)$$

now

$$\frac{XY}{55 - 40} = \frac{BO}{60 - 40}$$

so that

$$XY = \frac{15}{20} \times \frac{1}{15} = \frac{1}{20}$$

and the required probability is

$$\frac{1}{2} \times \left(\frac{1}{15} + \frac{1}{20}\right) \times 5 = \frac{1}{2} \times \frac{7}{60} \times 5 = .29$$

6.6. Permutations. In many examples in classical probability, it is necessary to determine the number of *ways* in which an event can occur. For example, in Example 6.1 it was shown that two dice could be thrown in 36 ways. In more complicated problems we often want to know in how many ways can n different objects be taken, r at a time. This is called the number of *permutations* of n things taken r at a time ${}_nP_r$. Since the first thing can be chosen in n ways, the second can be chosen in $n - 1$ ways (from the $n - 1$ remaining things).

$${}_nP_r = n(n - 1)(n - 2)\ldots(n - r + 1)$$

$${}_nP_r = \frac{n!}{(n - r)!} \tag{6.6}$$

where

$$n! = n(n - 1)(n - 2)\ldots 2 \cdot 1$$

and is called *factorial n*.

Factorial n may also be written $\lfloor n$.

$$^-0! = 1 \text{ by definition.}$$

The first few values of $n!$ are

n	n!
1	1
2	2
3	6
4	24
5	120
6	720
7	5040

Statistical tables give values of $n!$, but after the first 10 or 15 values, these become too large to tabulate and log $n!$ is tabulated instead.   Still higher values can be calculated by *Stirling's Approximation*

$$n! \approx \sqrt{2\pi n}\, n^n e^{-n} \qquad (6.7)$$

where *e* is the base of the natural logarithm and equals 2.71828 ...

The *total number* of permutations of *n* things is obtained by putting $r = n$ in Formula 6.6.

$$_nP_n = n! \qquad (6.8)$$

and the number of permutations of *n* things of which r_1 are alike, r_2 are alike, etc., is

$$\frac{n!}{r_1! \times r_2! \times \ldots} \qquad (6.9)$$

EXAMPLE 6.7.   In how many different ways can four cards be drawn from a pack of 52 cards?

Solution.   Four cards can be drawn from 52 cards in $_{52}P_4$ ways.

$$_{52}P_4 = \frac{52!}{(52 - 4)!} = \frac{52!}{48!}$$

$$52! = 52 \times 51 \times 50 \times 49 \times 48!$$

$$\frac{52!}{48!} = 52 \times 51 \times 50 \times 49$$

$$= 6,497,400$$

Alternatively, using logarithms from statistical tables,

$$\log 52! = \quad 67.90665$$

$$-\log 48! = \quad -61.09391$$

$$\overline{\quad\quad 6.81274}$$

$$\text{antilog} = \quad 6,497,000 \; approx.$$

EXAMPLE 6.8.   How many different nine letter words (i.e., arrangements of letters regardless whether they have any meaning) can be formed from the word *statistic*?

Solution.   *Statistic* consists of 9 letters, but *t* appears 3 times, *s* twice and *i* twice. The number of arrangements is

$$\frac{9!}{3! \times 2! \times 2!}$$

$$= \frac{9 \cdot 8 \cdot 7 \cdot 6 \cdot 5 \cdot 4 \cdot 3 \cdot 2 \cdot 1}{3 \cdot 2 \cdot 2 \cdot 2} = 3 \times 7! = 3 \times 5040$$

$$= 15,120$$

6.7. Combinations. In Example 6.7, a four card selection such as Ace of Spades, King of Hearts, Four of Hearts, and Two of Clubs would be counted as different from King of Hearts, Ace of Spades, Four of Hearts, and Two of Clubs. In probability problems we often want to know the number of *combinations* of n objects taken r at a time, *with no regard to the order of arrangement.* This is written

$$_nC_r \quad \text{or} \quad \binom{n}{r}$$

$$\binom{n}{r} = \frac{_nP_r}{r!} = \frac{n!}{r!\,(n-r)!} \qquad (6.10)$$

EXAMPLE 6.9.   How many different sets of five card hands can be dealt from a pack of 52 cards?
Solution.

$$_{52}C_5 = \frac{52!}{5! \times 47!}$$

$$= \frac{52 \times 51 \times 50 \times 49 \times 48 \times 47!}{5 \times 4 \times 3 \times 2 \times 1 \times 47!}$$

$$= 52 \times 51 \times 10 \times 49 \times 2$$

$$= 2,598,960$$

Or using logarithms,

$$\log 52! = 67.90665$$

$$-\log 5! = -2.07918$$

$$-\log 47! = \frac{-59.41267}{6.41480}$$

$$\text{antilog} = 2,599,000 \text{ (approx.)}$$

6.8. Mathematical Expectation. If the probability of an event happening is p and the monetary, or other measure, of amount receivable if the event happens is S, then the expectation is

$$S \times p$$

EXAMPLE 6.10. In a certain game, a player receives 2 points if a spade or club is drawn from a pack and 1 point if a heart is drawn. He has to give up 4 points if a diamond is drawn. What is expectation on each draw?

Solution. The probability of any particular suit being drawn is $1/4$. The player expectation is

$$2\left(\frac{1}{4} + \frac{1}{4}\right) + 1\left(\frac{1}{4}\right) - 4\left(\frac{1}{4}\right) = 1 + \frac{1}{4} - 1 = \frac{1}{4}$$

It should be noted that expectations can be *positive or negative*.

Problems

Problem 6.1. A card is drawn from a regular pack of 52 cards. E_1 is the event of drawing a Heart. E_2 is the event of drawing an Ace or a King.

Describe in words

$$(1) \ \bar{E}_1, \quad (2) \ \bar{E}_2, \quad (3) \ E_1 + E_2,$$
$$(4) \ \Pr\{\bar{E}_1 + E_2\}, \quad (5) \ E_1 E_2,$$
$$(6) \ \Pr\{E_1 \bar{E}_2\}$$

Problem 6.2. Three coins are tossed. E_1 is the event of all turning up heads. E_2 is the event of having at least two tails.

Describe in words each of the following probabilities and calculate their values.

$(1) \ \Pr\{E_1\}, \quad (2) \ \Pr\{\bar{E}_1\}, \quad (3) \ \Pr\{E_2\}, \quad (4) \ \Pr\{\bar{E}_2\},$

$(5) \ \Pr\{E_1 + E_2\}, \quad (6) \ \Pr\{\bar{E}_1 + \bar{E}_2\}, \quad (7) \ \Pr\{E_1 + \bar{E}_2\},$

$(8) \ \Pr\{\bar{E}_1 + E_2\}, \quad (9) \ \Pr\{E_1 E_2\}, \quad (10) \ \Pr\{\bar{E}_1 \bar{E}_2\},$

$(11) \ \Pr\{E_1 \bar{E}_2\}, \quad (12) \ \Pr\{\bar{E}_1 E_2\}$

Problem 6.3. Check the solution to Problem 6.2(5) by Formula 6.3.

$$\Pr\{E_1 + E_2\} = \Pr\{E_1\} + \Pr\{E_2\} - \Pr\{E_1 E_2\}$$

and also Problem 6.2(6), (7), and (8),

$$\Pr\{\bar{E}_1 + \bar{E}_2\}, \Pr\{E_1 + \bar{E}_2\}, \text{ and } \Pr\{\bar{E}_1 + E_2\}$$

Problem 6.4. A bag contains 2 black and 3 white balls. E_1 is the event of drawing a white ball at the first drawing. E_2 is the event of drawing a white ball at the second drawing. The ball drawn is replaced after each drawing. Express in terms of E_1 and E_2 the following probabilities, and evaluate them.

(1) Drawing two white balls.
(2) Drawing two black balls.
(3) Drawing one white and one black ball.

Problem 6.5. Find the solution to Problem 6.4 if the ball drawn is not replaced.

Problem 6.6. If $E_1 + E_2$ is the sample space and $\Pr\{E_1\} = p_1$ and $\Pr\{E_2\} = p_2$, what is the value of $\Pr\{E_1 E_2\}$?

Problem 6.7. Twelve cards are numbered 1 to 12. Two cards are drawn without replacement. What is the probability that the greater of the two numbers drawn exceeds 6?

Problem 6.8. Three men each toss a coin simultaneously to decide who shall pay for dinner. If two heads and a tail come up, the man with the tail pays. Similarly, if two tails and a head came up, the odd man pays. If three heads or three tails come up, they play again. What is the probability that a decision as to who shall pay is reached on the third round of tossing?

Problem 6.9. Bag A contains 5 black balls and 2 red balls. Bag B contains 2 black balls and 3 red balls. I take a ball out of bag A, and without looking at it, place it in bag B. I now shake up bag B and draw out a ball. What is the probability that it is red?

Problem 6.10. Check the result in Problem 6.9 by calculating the probability of drawing a black ball at the second drawing.

Problem 6.11. A certain individual is never early for an appointment, but he may be up to 6 minutes late. The probability of him arriving at his appointment at time t after the due time is proportional to $(6 - t)$ where t is measured in minutes. What is the probability that (1) he will be no more than 1 minute late, (2) that he will be between 3 and 5 minutes late?

Problem 6.12. What are the number of ways in which 8 people may be seated at table?

Problem 6.13. In how many ways can a president, a vice-president, a secretary, and a treasurer be selected for a club with 12 members?

Problem 6.14.   In how many ways can a foursome be selected from 12 members of a golf club?

Problem 6.15.   In how many ways can a pack of 52 playing cards be distributed into four hands of 13 cards each? (Do not evaluate your solution.)

Problem 6.16.   A single die is thrown until a six has come up on two occasions. What is the probability that this will be on the nth throw?

Problem 6.17.   If the die in Problem 6.16 is thrown until a six has come up on *three* occasions, what is the probability that this will be on the nth throw?

Problem 6.18.   Two men roll a die alternately. A wins if he rolls a 5 or 6 before B rolls a 1, 2, or 3. A rolls first. What is the probability that he wins?

Problem 6.19.   Under the conditions of Problem 6.18, what would be B's probability of winning if he rolled first?

Problem 6.20. A wagers B as follows. A will draw two cards from a 52 card pack. If at least one is a spade, B will pay A \$2. If both are from the same suit, A will pay B \$5. If one of them is the King of Hearts, B will pay A \$10. What is A's expectation?

Solutions

Problem 6.1.

    (1) Drawing a Spade, Club, or Diamond.

    (2) Drawing a Queen, Jack, Ten, . . . , or Two.

    (3) Drawing a Heart, an Ace, or a King.

    (4) The probability of drawing a Spade, Club or Diamond or an Ace or King.

    (5) Drawing the Ace of Hearts or the King of Hearts.

    (6) The probability of drawing the Queen of Hearts, the Jack of Hearts, the ten of Hearts, . . . , to the two of Hearts.

Problem 6.2.

    (1) Probability of $HHH = \dfrac{1}{8}$

    (2) Probability of HHT, HTT, or $TTT = \dfrac{7}{8}$

(3) Probability of HTT or $TTT = \dfrac{1}{2}$

(4) Probability of HHH or $HHT = \dfrac{1}{2}$

(5) Probability of $HHH, HTT,$ or $TTT = \dfrac{5}{8}$

(6) Probability of $HHH, HHT, HTT,$ or $TTT = 1$

(7) Probability of HHH or $HHT = \dfrac{1}{2}$

(8) Probability of $HHT, HTT,$ or $TTT = \dfrac{7}{8}$

(9) Probability of HHH *and* (HTT or TTT) $= 0$

(10) Probability of $HHT = \dfrac{3}{8}$

(11) Probability of $HHH = \dfrac{1}{8}$

(12) Probability of HTT or $TTT = \dfrac{1}{2}$

Problem 6.3. $\Pr\{E_1 + E_2\}$ is the answer to (5) and this gives

$$\frac{5}{8} = \frac{1}{8} + \frac{1}{2} - 0 = \frac{5}{8}$$

Similarly for the other three tests.

Problem 6.4. Since the ball drawn is replaced, E_1 and E_2 are independent and $\Pr\{E_1\} = \Pr\{E_2\}$.

(1) $\Pr\{E_1 E_2\} = \Pr\{E_1\}\Pr\{E_1\} = \left(\dfrac{3}{5}\right)^2 = \dfrac{9}{25}$

(2) $\Pr\{\bar{E}_1 \bar{E}_2\} = \Pr\{\bar{E}_1\}\Pr\{\bar{E}_1\} = \left(\dfrac{2}{5}\right)^2 = \dfrac{4}{25}$

(3) $\Pr\{E_1 \bar{E}_2\} + \Pr\{\bar{E}_1 E_2\} = 2\Pr\{E_1\}\Pr\{\bar{E}_1\}$

$$= 2 \times \frac{3}{5} \times \frac{2}{5} = \frac{12}{25}$$

Problem 6.5.

(1) $\Pr\{E_1 E_2\} = \Pr\{E_1\}\Pr\{E_2 \mid E_1\}$

$$= \frac{3}{5} \times \frac{2}{4} = \frac{3}{10}$$

$$(2) \ \Pr\{\bar{E}_1\bar{E}_2\} = \Pr\{\bar{E}_1\} \Pr\{\bar{E}_2 \mid \bar{E}_1\}$$

$$= \frac{2}{5} \times \frac{1}{4} = \frac{1}{10}$$

$$(3) \ \Pr\{E_1\bar{E}_2\} + \Pr\{\bar{E}_1E_2\} = \Pr\{E_1\} \Pr\{\bar{E}_2 \mid E_1\}$$
$$+ \Pr\{\bar{E}_1\} \Pr\{E_2 \mid \bar{E}_1\}$$

$$= \frac{3}{5} \cdot \frac{2}{4} + \frac{2}{5} \cdot \frac{3}{4} = \frac{3}{5}$$

Problem 6.6. From Equation 6.3,

$$\Pr\{E_1 + E_2\} = \Pr\{E_1\} + \Pr\{E_2\} - \Pr\{E_1E_2\}$$

Since $E_1 + E_2$ is the sample space, $\Pr\{E_1 + E_2\} = 1$

$$\Pr\{E_1E_2\} = p_1 + p_2 - 1$$

Problem 6.7.

$$\frac{1}{2} + \left(\frac{1}{2} \times \frac{6}{11}\right) = \frac{17}{22}$$

Problem 6.8.

$$\frac{1}{4} \times \frac{1}{4} \times \frac{3}{4} = \frac{3}{64}$$

Problem 6.9. The probability of a black ball at the first draw is 5/7. In this case bag *B* will contain 3 black and 3 red and the probability of drawing a red ball will be 1/2. The probability of a red ball at the first draw is 2/7 and the probability of a red ball at the next drawing will be 4/6.

Probability of a red ball is

$$\left(\frac{5}{7} \times \frac{1}{2}\right) + \left(\frac{2}{7} \times \frac{4}{6}\right) = \frac{15 + 8}{42} = \frac{23}{42}$$

Problem 6.10. The required probability is

$$\left(\frac{5}{7} \times \frac{1}{2}\right) + \left(\frac{2}{7} \times \frac{2}{6}\right) = \frac{15 + 4}{52} = \frac{19}{42}$$

The sum of the two probabilities is

$$\frac{23 + 19}{42} = 1$$

Problem 6.11.

$$(1) \quad \frac{1}{2}(6 + 5) \div 18 = \frac{11}{36}$$

$$(2) \quad \frac{1}{2}(3 + 1) \times 2 \div 18 = \frac{8}{36} = \frac{2}{9}$$

Problem 6.12.

$$_8P_8 = 8! = 40,320$$

Problem 6.13.

$$_{12}P_4 = \frac{12!}{8!} = 12 \times 11 \times 10 \times 9 = 11,880$$

Problem 6.14.

$$\binom{12}{4} = \frac{12!}{8! \times 4!} = \frac{12 \times 11 \times 10 \times 9}{4 \times 3 \times 2 \times 1} = 495$$

Problem 6.15.   The 52 cards can be arranged in 52! ways, but the arrangement of the cards within each hand will not affect the final results, nor will the arrangement of the four hands. Hence, the answer is

$$\frac{52!}{13! \times 13! \times 13! \times 13! \times 4!}$$

Problem 6.16.   The probability of a six on the nth throw is $1/6$. The probability of one, and only one, six in the preceeding $(n - 1)$ throws is

$$_{n-1}P_1 \times \frac{1}{6} \times \left(\frac{5}{6}\right)^{n-2}$$

$$_{n-1}P_1 = (n - 1)$$

and the total probability is

$$(n - 1)\frac{5^{n-2}}{6^n}$$

Problem 6.17.

$$\frac{(n - 1)(n - 2)}{2} \times \left(\frac{1}{6}\right)^3 \times \left(\frac{5}{6}\right)^{n-3}$$

Problem 6.18.   The probability that A wins on first roll is $2/6 =$ $1/3$. The probability that B wins on his·first roll is equal to the probability that A does not win on first roll $(2/3)$, times the probability that B wins on his roll $(3/6 = 1/2)$. Hence the probability that B wins on his first roll is $1/3$. The probability that neither wins on the first roll is $2/3 \times 1/2 = 1/3$. Let A's total probability of winning be P. Then

$$P = \frac{1}{3} + \frac{1}{3}P$$

since A's probability of winning, after an unsuccessful roll by each player, must be P. Therefore

$$\frac{2P}{3} = \frac{1}{3}$$

or

$$P = \frac{1}{2}$$

Problem 6.19.

$$P = \frac{1}{2} + \frac{1}{3}P$$

therefore

$$\frac{2P}{3} = \frac{1}{2}$$

or

$$P = \frac{3}{4}$$

Problem 6.20.

Event	Probability	A Receives	A's Expectation
At least one Spade	$1 - \dfrac{39 \times 38}{52 \times 51}$	\$ 2	.882
Both from same suit	$\dfrac{12}{51}$	-5	-1.176
King of Hearts	$\dfrac{1}{52}$	10	$\dfrac{.192}{-\ .102}$

A's expectation is approximately -10 cents.

7

Probability Distributions

7.1. Importance of Probability Distributions.   The first five chapters were concerned with developing descriptive measures of empirical frequency distributions.   In many aspects of statistical work, there is the need to find a mathematical model which represents an empirical distribution fairly closely.   In this chapter the principal features of the more commonly used models will be developed.

7.2. Binomial Distribution.   The *binomial* or *Bernoulli distribution* arises naturally when events depend upon a fixed probability of occurrence p, and when the number of trials is limited.   If the probability of an event occurring at any trial is p, and n trials are made, then from Chapter 6, the probability of *exactly x successes* in the n trials is

$$f(x) = \frac{n!}{x!(n-x)!} p^x q^{n-x} \tag{7.1}$$

where

$$q = 1 - p$$
$$x! = x(x-1)(x-2)(x-3)\ldots 1$$

and

$$0! = 1$$

The main properties of the binomial distribution are:

Mean	$\mu = np$
Variance	$\sigma^2 = npq$
Standard Deviation	$\sigma = \sqrt{npq}$
Moment coefficient of skewness	$\alpha_3 = \dfrac{q-p}{\sqrt{npq}}$

Moment coefficient of kurtosis $\alpha_4 = 3 + \dfrac{1 - 6pq}{npq}$

When $p = q$, this distribution is symmetrical and $\alpha_3 = 0$.

EXAMPLE 7.1.   If a coin is tossed 6 times, what is the probability of 0, 1, 2, 3, 4, 5, and 6 heads occurring?
Solution.   (Using Formula 7.1)

$n = 6$, $p = \dfrac{1}{2}$, $q = \dfrac{1}{2}$, and x equals successively, $0, 1, 2, \ldots, 6$

Note since

$$p = q = \frac{1}{2}, \qquad p^x q^{6-x} = \frac{1}{64}$$

for all values of x.

x	x!	(n − x)!	n!	$\dfrac{n!}{x!(n-x)!}$	f(x)
0	1	720	720	1	1/64
1	1	120	720	6	6/64
2	2	24	720	15	15/64
3	6	6	720	20	20/64
4	24	2	720	15	15/64
5	120	1	720	6	6/64
6	720	1	720	1	1/64

It will be noted that the last column adds up to unity, which must be so, since we have included all possible outcomes of tossing the coin six times.

EXAMPLE 7.2.   Six coins are tossed 256 times and the number of times 0, 1, 2, etc., heads occur is exactly equal to the probabilities, i.e.,

No. of Heads	Frequency
0	4
1	24
2	60
3	80
4	60
5	24
6	4
	256

Calculate by the methods of Chapters 2, 4, and 5, the five properties listed in Section 7.2 and show that these are the same as the theoretical values for a binomial distribution with $p = 1/2$ and $n = 6$.

Solution. Use 3 as the arbitrary origin.

d	d^2	d^3	d^4	f	fd	fd^2	fd^3	fd^4
-3	9	-27	81	4	-12	36	-108	324
-2	4	-8	16	24	-48	96	-192	384
-1	1	-1	1	60	-60	60	-60	60
0	0	0	0	80	0	0	0	0
1	1	1	1	60	60	60	60	60
2	4	8	16	24	48	96	192	384
3	9	27	81	4	12	36	108	324
				256	0	384	0	1536

The mean is seen to be 3, the origin selected, and hence,

$$m_1 = 0$$
$$m_2 = 1.5$$
$$m_3 = 0$$
$$m_4 = 6.0$$

$$\text{Mean} = 3$$
$$\text{Variance} = m_2 = 1.5$$
$$\text{Standard Deviation} = \sqrt{m_2} = \sqrt{1.5} = 1.22$$

$$\text{Moment coefficient of skewness} = \frac{m_3}{\sqrt{m_2^3}} = \frac{0}{\sqrt{1.5^3}} = 0$$

$$\text{Moment coefficient of kurtosis} = \frac{m_4}{\sqrt{m_2^4}} = \frac{6.0}{(1.5)^2} = 2.67$$

From the formulas in Section 7.2, putting $p = q = 1/2$, and $n = 6$,

$$\text{Mean} = 3, \text{Variance} = 1.5, \text{Standard Deviation} = 1.22$$

$$\text{Moment coefficient of skewness} = 0$$

$$\text{Moment coefficient of kurtosis} = 3 + \frac{1 - 1.5}{1.5}$$

$$= 3 - \frac{.5}{1.5}$$

$$= 2.67$$

EXAMPLE 7.3.   Three dice are rolled. What is the probability of 0, 1, 2, and 3 sixes?
Solution.   Using Formula 7.1, $n = 3, p = 1/6, q = 5/6$.

x	x!	n!	(n − x)!	$\dfrac{n!}{x!(n-x)!}$	$p^x q^{n-x}$	f(x)
0	1	6	6	1	$125 \div 6^3$	$125 \div 6^3$
1	1	6	2	3	$25 \div 6^3$	$75 \div 6^3$
2	2	6	1	3	$5 \div 6^3$	$15 \div 6^3$
3	6	6	1	1	$1 \div 6^3$	$1 \div 6^3$
						$216 \div 6^3 = 1$

The probabilities of 0, 1, 2, and 3 sixes are

$$\frac{125}{216}, \frac{75}{216}, \frac{15}{216}, \text{ and } \frac{1}{216}, \text{ respectively.}$$

EXAMPLE 7.4.   Three dice are rolled a large number of times, and the relative frequencies of 0, 1, 2, and 3 sixes are found to agree with the probabilities calculated in the previous example. Calculate the properties of the distributions listed in Section 7.2, and show that they are the same as the theoretical values of a binomial distribution with $p = 1/6$ and $n = 3$.
Solution.

x	x^2	x^3	x^4	f	fx	fx^2	fx^3	fx^4
0	0	0	0	125	0	0	0	0
1	1	1	1	75	75	75	75	75
2	4	8	16	15	30	60	120	240
3	9	27	81	1	3	9	27	81
				216	108	144	222	396

$$m_1' = .5$$
$$m_2' = .667$$
$$m_3' = 1.028$$
$$m_4' = 1.833$$

$$m_1 = 0$$
$$m_2 = .667 - .25 = .417$$
$$m_3 = 1.028 - 3(.5)(.667) + 2(.5)^3 = .278$$
$$m_4 = 1.833 - 4(.5)(1.028) + 6(.5)^2(.667) - 3(.5)^4 = .589$$

$$\text{Mean} = .5$$

$$\text{Variance} = .417$$
$$\text{Standard Deviation} = .646$$

$$\text{Moment coefficient of skewness} = \frac{.278}{(.417)^{3/2}} = 1.03$$

$$\text{Moment coefficient of kurtosis} = \frac{.589}{(.417)^{2}} = 3.4$$

From the formulas in Section 7.2, putting $p = 1/6$, $q = 5/6$ and $n = 3$.

Mean = .5,   Variance = .417,   Standard Deviation = .646

$$\text{Moment coefficient of skewness} = \frac{4}{6} \times \frac{1}{.646} = 1.03$$

$$\text{Moment coefficient of kurtosis} = 3 + \frac{36 - 30}{15} = 3 + \frac{6}{15} = 3.4$$

7.3. Applications of the Binomial Distribution. The binomial distribution provides a suitable model for very many statistical distributions which occur in nature, economics, business, psycho-

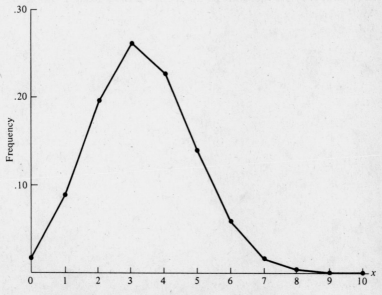

Figure 7.1. Binomial distribution. ($n = 10, p = 1/3$).

logical and educational testing, etc. The binomial is a discrete distribution, and when *n* becomes large it approaches the normal distribution (provided neither *p* or *q* are close to zero). A typical distribution is shown in Figure 7.1.

7.4. The Poisson Distribution. The binomial distribution is not particularly appropriate to statistical studies where an event can occur more than once, for example, automobile accident experience over a *period of time* where a driver may have more than one accident in a year. In this case, the *Poisson distribution* provides a more appropriate model. This distribution is defined by the formula

$$f(x) = \frac{\lambda^x e^{-\lambda}}{x!} \tag{7.2}$$

where *x* takes the discrete values 0, 1, 2, 3, etc. and *e* is the base of the natural logarithm (2.71828 . . .). When λ is small, the distribution is reversed *J* shaped, but when λ is large, the curve is not dissimilar to the binomial. Examples for $\lambda = .5$ and $\lambda = 4$ are shown in Figures 7.2 and 7.3.

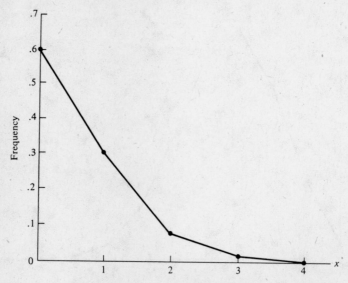

Figure 7.2. Poisson distribution. ($\lambda = .5$).

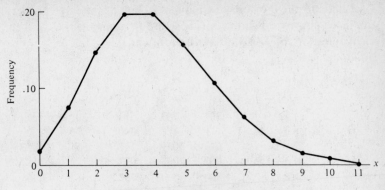

Figure 7.3. Poisson distribution. ($\lambda = 4$).

7.5. Properties of the Poisson Distribution

Mean	μ	$= \lambda$
Variance	σ^2	$= \lambda$
Standard Deviation	σ	$= \sqrt{\lambda}$
Moment coefficient of skewness	α_3	$= \dfrac{1}{\sqrt{\lambda}}$
Moment coefficient of kurtosis	α_4	$= 3 + \dfrac{1}{\lambda}$

If in the binomial distribution, $np = \lambda$ and n approaches infinity, then to keep np finite ($= \lambda$), p must approach zero and q, unity. Under these conditions, the properties of the binomial distribution listed earlier approach those of the Poisson distribution. The Poisson distribution is the limit of the binomial distribution as $n \rightarrow \infty$ and $p \rightarrow 0$.

EXAMPLE 7.5. The Poisson distribution in Figure 7.2 has the following values:

x	f(x)
0	.607
1	.303
2	.075
3	.013
4	.002
	1.000

Calculate, by the methods of Chapters 2, 4, and 5, the five properties listed above and show that these are the same as the theoretical values for the Poisson distribution with $\lambda = .5$.
Solution.

x	x^2	x^3	x^4	f	fx	fx^2	fx^3	fx^4
0	0	0	0	.607	0	0	0	0
1	1	1	1	.303	.303	.303	.303	.303
2	4	8	16	.075	.150	.300	.600	1.200
3	9	27	81	.013	.039	.117	.351	1.053
4	16	64	256	.002	.008	.032	.128	.512
				1.000	.500	.752	1.382	3.068

$$m_1' = .500$$
$$m_2' = .752$$
$$m_3' = 1.382$$
$$m_4' = 3.068$$

Therefore

$$m_1 = 0$$
$$m_2 = .752 - .250 = .5$$
$$m_3 = 1.382 - 3(.5)(.752) + 2(.5)^3$$
$$= 1.382 - 1.128 + .25 = .5$$
$$m_4 = 3.068 - 4(.5)(1.382) + 6(.5)^2(.752) - 3(.5)^4$$
$$= 3.068 - 2.764 + 1.128 - .188$$
$$= 1.24$$

Hence,

Mean $= .5$, Variance $= .5$, Standard Deviation $= .71$

Moment coefficient of skewness $= .5 \div .35 = 1.4$
Moment coefficient of kurtosis $= 1.24 \div .25 = 5$

Substituting .5 for λ in the formulas, the calculated values are

Mean $= .5$, Variance $= .5$ Standard Deviation $= .71$

Moment coefficient of skewness $= \dfrac{1}{.71} = 1.4$

Moment coefficient of kurtosis $= 3 + \dfrac{1}{.5} = 5$

EXAMPLE 7.6.   Calculate the Poisson distribution frequencies for $x = 0, 1, 2, 3$, and 5, when $\lambda = .1$.
Solution.   First calculate the value of $e^{-\lambda}$.

$$\log e = 0.43429$$
$$.1 \log e = 0.04343$$
$$-.1 \log e = 9.95657 - 10$$
$$e^{-.1} = .9048$$

x	λ^x	$e^{-\lambda}$	x!	f
0	1	.9048	1	.9048
1	.1	.9048	1	.0905
2	.01	.9048	2	.0045
3	.001	.9048	6	.0002
5	.00001	.9048	120	.0000

Note, if $\lambda = .1$, the distribution is a steep reversed *J* curve.

EXAMPLE 7.7.   Among the employees of a certain large organization, it is established that, on the average, 2 die each month. Assuming that the distribution of deaths by month follows the Poisson law, what is the probability of 0 deaths in a particular month?
Solution.   The mean of the Poisson distribution is λ. Therefore,

$$\lambda = 2$$

The probability of 0 deaths is $f(0)$ which, from Formula 7.2, equals

$$\frac{\lambda^0 e^{-\lambda}}{0!}$$

Now, $\lambda^0 = 1$, $e^{-\lambda} = e^{-2}$, and $0! = 1$ (see Section 7.2). The probability of 0 deaths equals

$$e^{-2} = .135$$

7.6. Normal Distribution.   The *normal distribution* is one of the most important probability functions. Unlike the binomial and the Poisson distributions, it is *continuous* and always *symmetrical*. The normal distribution is the limiting form of the binomial distribution if *n* is large, provided neither *p* nor *q* are close to zero.

The normal distribution is also called the *normal curve* and the *Gaussian distribution.*

The formula for the normal distribution is

$$y = \frac{1}{\sigma \sqrt{2\pi}} \, e^{-(x - \mu)^2/2\sigma^2} \tag{7.3}$$

where y is the frequency, μ is the mean, and σ the standard deviation. π and e have the values 3.14159..., and 2.71828..., respectively.

When expressed in terms of standard units, where

$$z = \frac{x - \mu}{\sigma}$$

the formula becomes

$$Y = \frac{1}{\sqrt{2\pi}} \, e^{-z^2/2} \tag{7.4}$$

This is the *standard form* and is the equation when the mean is 0 and the variance is 1. The normal curve is shown in Figure 7.4.

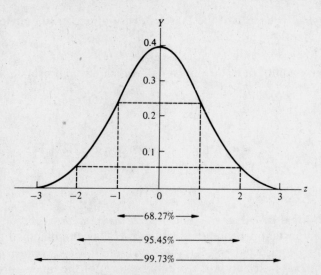

Figure 7.4. Normal distribution (Normal curve).

7.7. Properties of the Normal Distribution.

	Formula 7.3	Formula 7.4
Mean	μ	0
Variance	σ^2	1
Standard Deviation	σ	1
Moment coefficient of skewness	0	0
Moment coefficient of kurtosis	3	3

Using Formula 7.4, the height of the mean is $1/\sqrt{2\pi}$ = .39894. Since the curve is symmetrical, the mean, mode, and median all coincide and

$$\text{Mean Deviation} = \sigma \sqrt{\frac{2}{\pi}} = 0.7979\sigma$$

Further, 68.27% of the total frequency lies within the range $-\sigma$ to σ; 95.45% within the range -2σ to 2σ; and 99.73% within the range -3σ to 3σ.

Since the curve is the limit of the *binomial distribution* when n is large, it provides a model for numerous distributions experienced in all types of statistical work. It can be used as an approximation to the binomial if both *np* and *nq* are greater than 5.

EXAMPLE 7.8. Calculate the values of Y if the standard form of the normal distribution corresponding to $z = -3, -2, -1, -\frac{1}{2}, 0, \frac{1}{2}, 1, 2,$ and 3.

Solution. Since the distribution is symmetrical, the values of Y for negative values of z will be the same as the values for positive values of z and only the latter need be calculated. From Formula 7.4,

$$\log Y = \log \frac{1}{\sqrt{2\pi}} - \frac{1}{2} z^2 \log e$$

The value of $1/\sqrt{2\pi}$ can be found in statistical tables or calculated directly; it is 0.39894. Log e is given in both mathematical and statistical tables. Its value is 0.43429.

z	$\frac{1}{2}z^2$	$\frac{1}{2}z^2 \log e$	$-\frac{1}{2}z^2 \log e$	$\log \dfrac{1}{\sqrt{2\pi}}$	$\log Y$	Y
0	0	0	0	9.6009-10	9.6009-10	.399
$\frac{1}{2}$	.125	0.0543	9.9457-10	9.6009-10	9.5466-10	.352
1	.5	0.2172	9.7828-10	9.6009-10	9.3837-10	.242
2	2.0	0.8686	9.1314-10	9.6009-10	8.7323-10	.054
3	4.5	1.9543	8.0457-10	9.6009-10	7.6466-10	.004

The values of Y for the required values of z are:

z	-3	-2	-1	$-\frac{1}{2}$	0	$\frac{1}{2}$	1	2	3
Y	.004	.054	.242	.352	.399	.352	.242	.054	.004

7.8. Areas and Ordinates of the Standard Normal Curve. To assist in comparing empirical distributions with the normal curve, and to help in drawing conclusions from such distributions, tables have been prepared which give the areas under the *standard normal curve* between the y axis and the parallel line corresponding to any value of z. Tables are also available which give the heights of the y ordinates corresponding to any value of z. Since the area under the total normal curve is unity, the maximum value in the table of areas will be .5000 (See Figure 7.5). A table of areas is given in Table 7.1.

Tables of ordinates may be calculated to agree with a total area of unity, in which case, the ordinate corresponding to $z = 0$ is

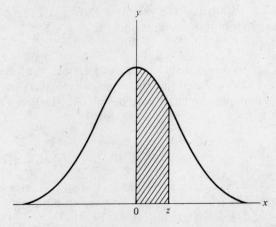

Figure 7.5. Area under the Normal curve.

TABLE 7.1
Area Under Standard Normal Curve

$\frac{x}{\sigma}$	.00	.01	.02	.03	.04	.05	.06	.07	.08	.09
0.0	.0000	.0040	.0080	.0120	.0159	.0199	.0239	.0279	.0319	.0359
0.1	.0398	.0438	.0478	.0517	.0557	.0596	.0636	.0675	.0714	.0753
0.2	.0793	.0832	.0871	.0910	.0948	.0987	.1026	.1064	.1103	.1141
0.3	.1179	.1217	.1255	.1293	.1331	.1368	.1406	.1443	.1480	.1517
0.4	.1554	.1591	.1628	.1664	.1700	.1736	.1772	.1808	.1844	.1879
0.5	.1915	.1950	.1985	.2019	.2054	.2088	.2123	.2157	.2190	.2224
0.6	.2257	.2291	.2324	.2357	.2389	.2422	.2454	.2486	.2518	.2549
0.7	.2580	.2612	.2642	.2673	.2704	.2734	.2764	.2794	.2823	.2852
0.8	.2881	.2910	.2939	.2967	.2995	.3023	.3051	.3078	.3106	.3133
0.9	.3159	.3186	.3212	.3238	.3264	.3289	.3315	.3340	.3365	.3389
1.0	.3413	.3438	.3461	.3485	.3508	.3531	.3554	.3577	.3599	.3621
1.1	.3643	.3665	.3686	.3708	.3729	.3749	.3770	.3790	.3810	.3830
1.2	.3849	.3869	.3888	.3907	.3925	.3944	.3962	.3980	.3997	.4015
1.3	.4032	.4049	.4066	.4082	.4099	.4115	.4131	.4147	.4162	.4177
1.4	.4192	.4207	.4222	.4236	.4251	.4265	.4279	.4292	.4306	.4319
1.5	.4332	.4345	.4357	.4370	.4382	.4394	.4406	.4418	.4430	.4441
1.6	.4452	.4463	.4474	.4485	.4495	.4505	.4515	.4525	.4535	.4545
1.7	.4554	.4564	.4573	.4582	.4591	.4599	.4608	.4616	.4625	.4633
1.8	.4641	.4649	.4656	.4664	.4671	.4678	.4686	.4693	.4699	.4706
1.9	.4713	.4719	.4726	.4732	.4738	.4744	.4750	.4756	.4762	.4767
2.0	.4773	.4778	.4783	.4788	.4793	.4798	.4803	.4808	.4812	.4817
2.1	.4821	.4826	.4830	.4834	.4838	.4842	.4846	.4850	.4854	.4857
2.2	.4861	.4865	.4868	.4871	.4875	.4878	.4881	.4884	.4887	.4890
2.3	.4893	.4896	.4898	.4901	.4904	.4906	.4909	.4911	.4913	.4916
2.4	.4918	.4920	.4922	.4925	.4927	.4929	.4931	.4932	.4934	.4936
2.5	.4938	.4940	.4941	.4943	.4945	.4946	.4948	.4949	.4951	.4952
2.6	.4953	.4955	.4956	.4957	.4959	.4960	.4961	.4962	.4963	.4964
2.7	.4965	.4966	.4967	.4968	.4969	.4970	.4971	.4972	.4973	.4974
2.8	.4974	.4975	.4976	.4977	.4977	.4978	.4979	.4980	.4980	.4981
2.9	.4981	.4982	.4983	.4983	.4984	.4984	.4985	.4985	.4986	.4986
3.0	.49865	.4987	.4987	.4988	.4988	.4989	.4989	.4989	.4990	.4990
3.1	.49903	.4991	.4991	.4991	.4992	.4992	.4992	.4993	.4993	.4993
3.2	.49931									
3.3	.49952									

TABLE 7.1 (continued)

$\dfrac{x}{\sigma}$	.00	.01	.02	.03	.04	.05	.06	.07	.08	.09
3.4	.49966									
3.5	.49977									
3.6	.49984									
3.7	.49989									
3.8	.49993									
3.9	.49995									
4.0	.49997									

.3989; or this ordinate may be taken as unity and other ordinates calculated proportionately. A table in the former scale is given in Table 7.2.

EXAMPLE 7.9. What is the area under the standard normal curve between ordinates minus 0.5 and plus 1.54? What is the area between -0.5σ and $+1.54\sigma$ of the normal curve with mean of 0, height of mean 2, and standard deviation 2?

Solution. Since the curve is symmetrical, the area between -0.5 and 0 is equal to the area between 0 and $+0.5$. Hence, the area required is the sum of the area between 0 and 0.5 and the area between 0 and 1.54. From Table 7.1, this area is .1915 + .4382 = .6297.

The height of the mean of the *standard* normal curve is .3989. If the value of the height of the mean is increased to 2, all areas will be increased in the ratio

$$\frac{2}{.3989} = 5.01$$

Further, the value of the standard deviation of the standard normal curve is 1. If the value of the standard deviation is increased to 2, all areas will be increased in the ratio $2/1 = 2$. Therefore, the area required is

$$.6297 \times 5.01 \times 2 = 6.31$$

EXAMPLE 7.10. If the mean of a normal distribution is 7, the height of the mean is 4.9 and the standard deviation is 4, find the area under the curve between 0 and 10.

TABLE 7.2

ORDINATES (Y) OF A STANDARD NORMAL CURVE AT Z

$z = \dfrac{x}{\sigma}$	.00	.01	.02	.03	.04	.05	.06	.07	.08	.09
0.0	.3989	.3989	.3989	.3988	.3986	.3984	.3982	.3980	.3977	.3973
0.1	.3970	.3965	.3961	.3956	.3951	.3945	.3939	.3932	.3925	.3918
0.2	.3910	.3902	.3894	.3885	.3876	.3867	.3857	.3847	.3836	.3825
0.3	.3814	.3802	.3790	.3778	.3765	.3752	.3739	.3725	.3712	.3697
0.4	.3683	.3668	.3653	.3637	.3621	.3605	.3589	.3572	.3555	.3538
0.5	.3521	.3503	.3485	.3467	.3448	.3429	.3410	.3391	.3372	.3352
0.6	.3332	.3312	.3292	.3271	.3251	.3230	.3209	.3187	.3166	.3144
0.7	.3123	.3101	.3079	.3056	.3034	.3011	.2989	.2966	.2943	.2920
0.8	.2897	.2874	.2850	.2827	.2803	.2780	.2756	.2732	.2709	.2685
0.9	.2661	.2637	.2613	.2589	.2565	.2541	.2516	.2492	.2468	.2444
1.0	.2420	.2396	.2371	.2347	.2323	.2299	.2275	.2251	.2227	.2203
1.1	.2179	.2155	.2131	.2107	.2083	.2059	.2036	.2012	.1989	.1965
1.2	.1942	.1919	.1895	.1872	.1849	.1826	.1804	.1781	.1758	.1736
1.3	.1714	.1691	.1669	.1647	.1626	.1604	.1582	.1561	.1539	.1518
1.4	.1497	.1476	.1456	.1435	.1415	.1394	.1374	.1354	.1334	.1315
1.5	.1295	.1276	.1257	.1238	.1219	.1200	.1182	.1163	.1145	.1127
1.6	.1109	.1092	.1074	.1057	.1040	.1023	.1006	.0989	.0973	.0957
1.7	.0940	.0925	.0909	.0893	.0878	.0863	.0848	.0833	.0818	.0804
1.8	.0790	.0775	.0761	.0748	.0734	.0721	.0707	.0694	.0681	.0669
1.9	.0656	.0644	.0632	.0620	.0608	.0596	.0584	.0573	.0562	.0551
2.0	.0540	.0529	.0519	.0508	.0498	.0488	.0478	.0468	.0459	.0449
2.1	.0440	.0431	.0422	.0413	.0404	.0396	.0387	.0379	.0371	.0363
2.2	.0355	.0347	.0339	.0332	.0325	.0317	.0310	.0303	.0297	.0290
2.3	.0283	.0277	.0270	.0264	.0258	.0252	.0246	.0241	.0235	.0229
2.4	.0224	.0219	.0213	.0208	.0203	.0198	.0194	.0189	.0184	.0180
2.5	.0175	.0171	.0167	.0163	.0158	.0154	.0151	.0147	.0143	.0139
2.6	.0136	.0132	.0129	.0126	.0122	.0119	.0116	.0113	.0110	.0107
2.7	.0104	.0101	.0099	.0096	.0093	.0091	.0088	.0086	.0084	.0081
2.8	.0079	.0077	.0075	.0073	.0071	.0069	.0067	.0065	.0063	.0061
2.9	.0060	.0058	.0056	.0055	.0053	.0051	.0050	.0048	.0047	.0046
3.0	.0044									
4.0	.0001									

Solution. The area table is based on the *standard* normal curve, with mean of 0, height of mean, .3989, and standard deviation of 1. The area required in the example is between (0–7) and (10–7) each side of the mean or between −7 and +3. Further, the standard deviation in the example is 4.

Hence, the area required is between −7/4 of the standard deviation and 3/4 of the standard deviation. That is, between −1.75 and .75 of the *standard* normal curve. From Table 7.1, the area from 0 to 1.75 is .4599, and the area from 0 to .75 is .2734, making .7333 in total.

Now, in the example, the height of the mean is 4.9, compared with .3989 in the standard normal curve, and the standard deviation is 4, compared with 1 in the standard normal curve. Hence the required area is

$$.7333 \times \frac{4.9}{.3989} \times \frac{4}{1} = 36.0$$

EXAMPLE 7.11. A normal curve has mean of 10 and standard deviation of 4. The height of the mean is 8. What is the height of the curve at the following points on the x axis: 0, 3, 6, 9, 12, and 15?

Solution. The values of x, calculated from the mean of 10 are

$$x = -10, \quad -7, \quad -4, \quad -1, \quad 2, \quad 5$$

$$z = \frac{x}{\sigma} = \frac{-10}{4}, \quad \frac{-7}{4}, \quad \frac{-4}{4}, \quad \frac{-1}{4}, \quad \frac{2}{4}, \quad \frac{5}{4}$$

$$= -2.5, \quad -1.75, \quad -1, \quad -.25, \quad .5, \quad 1.25$$

The height of the standard normal curve at these points are, from Table 7.2,

$$.0175, \quad .0863, \quad .2420, \quad .3867, \quad .3521, \quad .1826$$

Since the height of the mean in the example is 8, compared to .3989 in the normal curve, these heights must be multiplied by 8/.3989 or 20.06, giving

x	0	3	6	9	12	15
Height	0.35	1.73	4.85	7.76	7.06	3.66

7.9 Other Theoretical Distributions. There are other theoretical distributions, such as the multinomial and the negative binomial. However, the three distributions discussed in this chapter are by far the most important.

7.10. Fitting Theoretical Distributions. It is most useful to be able to substitute a theoretical model for an empirical distribution. This is usually done by determining (from study of the empirical distribution, from theoretical consideration, or both) the most appropriate model, and then assuming that the mean standard deviation of the empirical distribution are the mean and standard deviation of the model. This is discussed further in Chapter 8.

Problems

Problem 7.1. If the chance of it raining on any day at a certain time of year is 1/3 what are the probabilities of 0, 1, 2, and 3 wet days in a period of three days? Assume that the weather on any day is independent of the weather on any other day, although, in fact, there is usually considerable correlation between the weather on successive days.

Problem 7.2. What are the mean and the standard deviation of the distribution in Problem 7.1?

Problem 7.3. What is the frequency distribution of the score, when two dice are thrown a large number of times?

Problem 7.4. Two dice are thrown ten times, and the number of times the total on the two dice is 4 is recorded. What is the frequency distribution of the number of times this total is recorded, if the experiment is carried out a large number of times? (Express your answer in a formula.)

Problem 7.5. What are the probabilities of 0, 1, and 2 fours, in the previous problem?

Problem 7.6. A pack of eleven cards, numbered 1 to 11 inclusive, is well shuffled; a card is drawn and its number noted. The card is returned to the pack and the procedure repeated. After 8 such drawings, a total of 0, 1, 2, . . . 7 or 8 threes may have been drawn. What is the frequency distribution of the number of threes drawn?

Problem 7.7. What is the mean and the standard deviation of the distribution in Problem 7.6?

Problem 7.8. A real estate broker sells an average of 3 houses a week. Assuming a Poisson distribution, what will be the probability that he will sell exactly 9 houses in 3 weeks? (The answer may be left in formula form.)

Problem 7.9. Calculate the Poisson distribution frequencies for $x = 0, 1, 2, 3, 5, 10$, and 15 for $\lambda = 1$ and for $\lambda = 10$.

Problem 7.10. Among a group of similar automobile drivers, the annual rate of accident involvement is 15%. For each driver in the group, the probability of being involved in an accident on any day is the same. If the accident experience follows the Poisson distribution, what is the proportion of drivers who are accident free, and what is the proportion involved in exactly two accidents in a year?

Problem 7.11. Calculate the properties of the binomial distribution for $p = 1/24$ and $n = 96$ and compare them with the properties of the Poisson distribution for $\lambda = 4$.

Problem 7.12. For what values of λ in a Poisson distribution is the frequency at $x = 0$ greater than the frequency at any other value?

Problem 7.13. What are the differences between the binomial and the normal distributions?

Problem 7.14. What is the breadth of a central segment of the normal distribution which includes (1) 50%, and (2) 75% of the total frequency?

Problem 7.15. What is the height of the ordinate corresponding to the outer edges of the 50% and 75% zones, referred to in Problem 7.14, if the height of the mean is 1?

Problem 7.16. Is the normal distribution leptokurtic or platykurtic?

Problem 7.17. Is the binomial distribution leptokurtic or platykurtic?

Problem 7.18. Is the Poisson distribution leptokurtic or platykurtic?

Problem 7.19. Find the area of the standard normal curve between $z = -.67$ and $z = +.33$.

Problem 7.20. A normal distribution has a mean of $x = 9.6$ and a standard deviation of 2.1. The height of the mean is $y = 11.5$. What is the area under the curve between $x = 9$ and $x = 10$?

Solutions

Problem 7.1. In Formula 7.1, $p = 1/3$, $q = 2/3$, and $n = 3$.

x	x!	(n − x)!	n!	$\dfrac{n!}{x!(n-x)!}$	$27(p^x q^{n-x})$	27 f(x)
0	1	6	6	1	8	8
1	1	2	6	3	5	12
2	2	1	6	3	2	6
3	6	1	6	1	1	1
						27

The probabilities are 8/27, 12/27, 6/27, and 1/27, respectively.

Problem 7.2.

x	x^2	f	fx	fx^2
0	0	8	0	0
1	1	12	12	12
2	4	6	12	24
3	9	1	3	9
		27	27	45

$$\text{Mean} = \frac{27}{27} = 1$$

$$m_2' = \frac{45}{27} = 1\tfrac{2}{3}$$

$$\text{Variance} = 1\tfrac{2}{3} - 1^2 = \tfrac{2}{3}$$

$$\text{Standard Deviation} = \sqrt{\frac{2}{3}} = .82$$

Problem 7.3. From the methods of Chapter 6, the relative frequencies of various scores are:

Scores	2	3	4	5	6	7	8	9	10	11	12
Relative Frequency	1	2	3	4	5	6	5	4	3	2	1

corresponding to the number of ways in which each score can occur.

The probabilities are these relative frequencies divided by the total frequency of 36. It should be noted that the distribution, while based on probabilities, is *not* a binomial distribution.

Problem 7.4. The probability of getting a 4 at a single throw of two dice is (from the answer to Problem 7.3)

$$\frac{3}{36} \text{ or } \frac{1}{12}$$

From Formula 7.1, the frequency distribution of 4 in ten throws is

$$f(x) = \frac{10!}{x!\,(10-x)!} \left(\frac{1}{12}\right)^x \left(\frac{11}{12}\right)^{10-x}$$

This distribution is a binomial distribution.

Problem 7.5. We shall need to evaluate $(1/12)^x(11/12)^{10-x}$ for $x = 0, 1,$ and 2. This is best done by logarithms; $\log 11 = 1.04139$, $\log 12 = 1.07918$.

x (1)	(10 − x) (2)	(10 − x) log 11 (3)	10 log 12 (4)	(3) − (4) (5)	antilog (5) (6)
0	10	10.4139	10.7918	9.6221−10	.4189
1	9	9.3725	10.7918	8.5807−10	.03808
2	8	8.3311	10.7918	7.5393−10	.00346

The calculation then proceeds as follows:

x	x!(10 − x)!	$\frac{10!}{x!(10-x)!}$	$\left(\frac{1}{12}\right)^x \left(\frac{11}{12}\right)^{10-x}$	f(x)
0	10!	1	.4189	.4189
1	9!	10	.03808	.3808
2	2 × 8!	45	.00346	.1557

The required probabilities are .42, .38, and .16.

Problem 7.6. From Formula 7.1, the distribution is

$$\frac{10^8}{11^8}, \quad \frac{8!}{7!1!} \times \frac{10^7}{11^8}, \quad \frac{8!}{6!2!} \times \frac{10^6}{11^8}, \ldots$$

giving a frequency distribution of

No. of threes	Relative Frequency
0	10^8
1	8×10^7
2	28×10^6
3	56×10^5
4	70×10^4
5	56×10^3

No. of threes	Relative Frequency
6	28×10^2
7	8×10
8	1

The probabilities are $\dfrac{1}{11^8}$ times these figures and add to unity.

Problem 7.7. The distribution is binomial with

$$p = \frac{1}{11}, q = \frac{10}{11}, \text{ and } n = 8$$

$$\text{Mean} = 8 \times \frac{1}{11} = .73$$

$$\text{Variance} = 8 \times \frac{1}{11} \times \frac{10}{11} = .66$$

$$\text{Standard Deviation} = \sqrt{.66} = .81$$

Problem 7.8. Since the average rate of sale is 3 houses a week, the average for 3 weeks is 9. Hence, the mean of the distribution for a 3 week period = 9.

The probability of selling exactly 9 houses in 9 weeks is

$$f(9) = \frac{9^9 e^{-9}}{9!}$$

$$= .13$$

Problem 7.9. First calculate the values of $e^{-\lambda}$

$\log e = .043429$	$\log e = 0.43429$
$1 \times \log e = 0.43429$	$10 \times \log e = 4.3429$
$-1 \times \log e = 9.56571 \text{-} 10$	$-10 \times \log e = 5.6571 \text{-} 10$
$e^{-1} = .3679$	$e^{-10} = 4.54 \times 10^{-5}$

For $\lambda = 1$,

x	λ^x	$e^{-\lambda}$	x!	f
0	1	.3679	1	.3679
1	1	.3679	1	.3679
2	1	.3679	2	.1839
3	1	.3679	6	.0613
5	1	.3679	120	.0031
10	1	.3679	3.6×10^6	.0000
15	1	.3679	1.3×10^{12}	.0000

For $\lambda = 10$,

x	λ^x	$e^{-\lambda}$	x!	f
0	1	4.54×10^{-5}	1	.0000
1	10	4.54×10^{-5}	1	.0005
2	100	4.54×10^{-5}	2	.0023
3	1000	4.54×10^{-5}	6	.0076
5	10^5	4.54×10^{-5}	120	.0378
10	10^{10}	4.54×10^{-5}	3.63×10^6	.1251
15	10^{15}	4.54×10^{-5}	1.31×10^{12}	.0347

Problem 7.10. This is a Poisson distribution with mean of .15. Therefore, $\lambda = .15$. The first three terms of the distribution are calculated from Formula 7.2.

$$\log e = 0.43429$$
$$.15 \log e = 0.06514$$
$$-.15 \log e = 9.93486\text{-}10$$
$$e^{-.15} = .861$$

x	λ^x	$e^{-.15}$	x!	f
0	1	.861	1	.861
1	.15	.861	1	.129
2	.0225	.861	2	.010

86% of the drivers will be accident free and one in a hundred will be involved in two accidents during the period of a year.

Problem 7.11.

	Binomial	Poisson
Mean	4	4
Variance	3.83	4
Standard Deviation	1.96	2
Moment coefficient of skewness	4.7	5
Moment coefficient of kurtosis	3.2	3.25

It will be noted how close the two distributions become when p is small.

Problem 7.12. If tables of the Poisson distribution are available, it is seen that for $\lambda = 1$, $f(0) = f(1)$, the required answer is for all values of λ *less than* 1. If tables are not available, it is necessary to calculate the value of λ corresponding to $f(0) = f(1)$. Now

$$f(0) = \frac{\lambda^0 c^{-\lambda}}{0!} = e^{-\lambda}$$

and
$$f(1) = \frac{\lambda c^{-\lambda}}{1!} = \lambda c^{-\lambda}$$

giving $\lambda = 1$ and $f(0)$ will be greater than $f(1)$ for all values of λ less than 1.

Problem 7.13.   The essential difference between the binomial and the normal distributions is that the former is discrete and not symmetrical except when $p = q = .5$, while the latter is continuous and symmetrical.   However, when n is large, the normal distribution provides a close approximation to the binomial distribution, unless p or q are small.

Problem 7.14.   From Table 7.1, it is seen that the ordinate z corresponding to an area of .25 between 0–z of the normal curve is .674.   Hence, the breadth of the central section including 50% of the frequencies is $2 \times .674$ or 1.35σ.   For 75%, the breadth is 2×1.15 or 2.3σ.

Problem 7.15.

Edge of Zone (1)	z (2)	Ordinates from Table 7.2 (3)	Col. (3) ÷ .3989
50%	.674	.318	.80
75%	1.15	.206	.52

It is necessary to divide by .3989 since this figure, and not 1, is the height of the mean in Table 7.2.

Problem 7.16.   The moment coefficient of kurtosis of the normal curve is 3, and by definition, the curve is neither leptokurtic or platykurtic.   It is *mesokurtic*. (See Chapter 5.)

Problem 7.17.   For values of p between .79 and .21, the binomial distribution is platykurtic, and for values outside that range, the distribution is leptokurtic.

Problem 7.18.   The Poisson distribution is always leptokurtic.

Problem 7.19. $.2486 + .1293 = .3779$

Problem 7.20.

$$(.1126 + .0753) \times 2.1 \times \frac{11.5}{.39894} = 11.4.$$

The value, .1126 is obtained by interpolation from Table 7.1.

8

Curve Fitting

8.1. Introduction. It is often necessary to fit a smooth curve to empirical statistical data. The data may be in a form which can be represented fairly closely by one of the probability distributions considered in Chapter 7, or it may be in the form of a continuously increasing or decreasing function. While in many cases these latter functions will be time series, such as the cost of living on December 31st of successive years, this will not always be so. The distance in feet required to stop an automobile by the application of its brakes, plotted against the speed of the automobile when the brakes are first applied, is typical of the kind of increasing or decreasing function arising in statistical work, which is not a time series.

There are two standard methods of curve fitting*: The *graphic method*, where the smooth curve is drawn by hand, and the *formula method*, where an appropriate theoretical curve is assumed and mathematical procedures are used to provide maximum closeness of fit. When fitting a formula to a frequency distribution type of curve, it is usual to *equate the parameters* of the assumed distribution to those of the actual data. For an increasing or decreasing curve, the *method of least squares* is normally employed. Both these methods are explained later in the chapter.

8.2. Theoretical Formulas for Increasing and Decreasing Functions. Just as there are various theoretical probability distributions which can be used as models for empirical probability distri-

---

*There are other methods of *smoothing* data, see, for example, the moving average method in Chapter 9.

butions, so there are theoretical curves which can be used as models for empirical time series and other similar curves. By far the most usual model is the *straight line* which can be expressed by the following formula

(1) Linear $\qquad\qquad\qquad y = a_0 + a_1 x$

Other lines which may be used are

(2) Parabolic or 2nd order $\quad y = a_0 + a_1 x + a_2 x^2$
(3) Cubic or higher order $\quad\ y = a_0 + a_1 x + a_2 x^2 + a_3 x^3 + \cdots$

(4) Hyperbolic $\qquad\qquad\quad \dfrac{1}{y} = a_0 + a_1 x$

(5) Exponential $\qquad\quad \log y = a_0 + a_1 x$
(6) Geometric $\qquad\qquad\quad y = ax^b \text{ or } a + bx^c$

EXAMPLE 8.1. Give an example of each of the formulas, (1), (2), (4), and (5) above, passing through the points $x = 0$, $y = 1$ and $x = 10$, $y = 2$. Tabulate the values of y for $x = 0, 1, 2$, etc., ... 10, and for $x = 20$.

Solution. Formulas (1), (4), and (5) have only two unknowns, a and b, so that, in each case, only one line can be drawn through the two points. Formula (2) has three unknowns, and more than one line can be drawn. For Formula (2), the line selected will be that produced by putting $a_1 = 0$, so that the formula becomes

$$y = a_0 + a_2 x^2$$

For the straight line, by substituting the given values $x = 0$, $y = 1$ and $x = 10$, $y = 2$ in Formula (1) we get

$$1 = a_0$$
$$2 = a_0 + 10a_1$$

Solving,

$$a_0 = 1, \text{ and } a_1 = \frac{1}{10}.$$

Proceeding in the same manner for the other formulas, the following equations are obtained:

(1) Straight line $\qquad y = 1 + \dfrac{1}{10}\,x$

(2) Parabola $\qquad\qquad y = 1 + \dfrac{1}{100}\,x^2$

(4) Hyperbola $\dfrac{1}{y} = 1 - \dfrac{1}{20} x$

(5) Exponential $\log y = (.03010)x$

The actual values are set out below.

x	Straight Line (1)	Parabola (2)	Hyperbola (4)	Exponential (5)
0	1.00	1.00	1.00	1.00
1	1.10	1.01	1.05	1.07
2	1.20	1.04	1.11	1.15
3	1.30	1.09	1.18	1.23
4	1.40	1.16	1.25	1.32
5	1.50	1.25	1.33	1.41
6	1.60	1.36	1.43	1.52
7	1.70	1.49	1.54	1.62
8	1.80	1.64	1.67	1.74
9	1.90	1.81	1.82	1.87
10	2.00	2.00	2.00	2.00
⋮				
20	3.00	5.00	Infinity	4.00

This example shows clearly how very different the results will be according to the formula chosen. Obviously with only two values given, we have no indication of the true shape of the curve, and curve fitting is not really practical.

EXAMPLE 8.2.   In the four curves given above, the value corresponding to $x = 5$ is 1.5 or less. Can an example be constructed where x has a higher value?

Solution.   In the previous example, we arbitrarily made $a_1 = 0$ for the parabola. If a_1 is given a positive value, the value of a_2 will become smaller, and when $a_1 = 1/10$, a_2 will equal 0. Increasing a_1 further, a_2 becomes negative, and the value of the function for $x = 5$ is greater than 1.5.

Thus, if the formula is

$$y = 1 + \frac{1}{5} x - \frac{1}{100} x^2$$

the values of the function are

x	y
0	1.00
5	1.75
10	2.00
20	1.00

It may be noted that, in this case, y attains a maximum value at $x = 10$, and thereafter decreases.

8.3. Graphic Method.

In using the graphic method to fit a smooth curve to empirical statistical data, the data must first be plotted on a large suitable piece of paper. No attempt should be made to make the smooth curve actually pass through the points tabulated; rather, the curve should pass between the points leaving, approximately, an equal number of points on either side of it. The curve should pass as close to the data as possible while remaining smooth. If the data lies approximately on a straight line, a rule may be used, and for other data, a flexible ruler or tracings of suitable smooth curves, if available, are helpful.

EXAMPLE 8.3. The following table gives the thousands of short tons of iron and steel exported by the U.S.A. from 1954 to 1966. Fit a smooth curve to the data by the graphic method.

Year	Short Tons (000)	Year	Short Tons (000)	Year	Short Tons (000)
1954	4,826	1959	7,009	1964	12,051
1955	9,723	1960	11,493	1965	8,934
1956	11,574	1961	12,442	1966	7,776
1957	13,657	1962	7,597		
1958	6,328	1963	9,208		

Solution. The data are plotted in Figure 8.1, and the smooth curve is drawn passing between the values.

EXAMPLE 8.4. The following table gives the observed frequencies of accidents in a four month period in a certain factory.

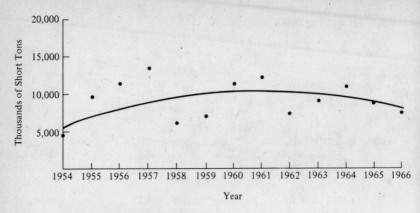

Figure 8.1. Steel exports. Graphic method of curve fitting.

No. of Accidents	Observed Frequency	No. of Accidents	Observed Frequency
0	239	8	–
1	98	9	4
2	57	10	1
3	33	11	–
4	9	12	–
5	2	13	1
6	2		447
7	1		

Fit a smooth curve to these data for accident frequency *3 or greater*.

Solution. The observed and smoothed frequencies are shown in Figure 8.2.

8.4. Equating Parameters. Except in the case of a straight line (when a ruler is used) the graphic method will not produce a curve which is perfectly smooth, and will only provide an approximation to one of the theoretical probability distributions. There are many advantages in fitting a theoretical distribution (rather than a similar hand-drawn smooth curve) to a given body of data. With a theoretical distribution, areas under portions of the curve, and various parameters, can be obtained from tables or readily calculated.

When it is desired to fit a normal, Poisson, or other distribution to given data, the mean and standard deviation of the ob-

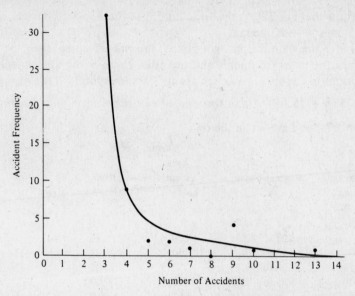

Figure 8.2. Accidents in soap factory. Graphic method of curve fitting.

served data are calculated, and then are used to determine the fitted formula.

EXAMPLE 8.5.   Fit a normal curve to the following distribution of persons in a study of the mortality experience under life insurance policies.

Age Group	Number in Thousands	Age Group	Number in Thousands
0–	51	40–	1,946
5–	38	45–	1,229
10–	53	50–	641
15–	172	55–	290
20–	667	60–	102
25–	1,286	65–	28
30–	1,996	70–	6
35–	2,319	TOTAL	10,824

Solution.   Using $37\frac{1}{2}$ as the origin, and 5 years as the class interval, the mean is found to be 100/10,824, and the variance, 42,210/10,824. These figures for the mean and variance are very close to 0 and 4, respectively, so that for curve fitting we may assume that age $37\frac{1}{2}$ is the mean, and that the standard deviation is $5 \times \sqrt{4} = 10$ years.

Since the data are in age groups, the proper comparison between the observed figures and the fitted curve is the area under sections of the curve. The age group 35– corresponds to the range $-.25$ to $+.25$ for $\frac{x}{\sigma}$, and this and other areas are obtained from Table 7.1 and are set out below.

Age Group	Normal Curve $\frac{x}{\sigma}$	Normal Curve Area from Table 7.1	Fitted Curve	Actual Distribution
0–	∞ to -3.25	.0006	6	51
5–	-3.25 to -2.75	.0024	26	38
10–	-2.75 to -2.25	.0092	99	53
15–	-2.25 to -1.75	.0279	302	172
20–	-1.75 to -1.25	.0655	709	667
25–	-1.25 to $-.75$	.1210	1,310	1,286
30–	$-.75$ to $-.25$	.1747	1,891	1,996
35–	$-.25$ to $+.25$	.1974	2,138	2,319
40–	$+.25$ to $+.75$	.1747	1,891	1,946
45–	$+.75$ to $+1.25$	.1210	1,310	1,229
50–	$+1.25$ to $+1.75$	.0655	709	641
55–	$+1.75$ to $+2.25$	.0279	302	290
60–	$+2.25$ to $+2.75$	.0092	99	102
65–	$+2.75$ to $+3.25$	.0024	26	28
70–	$+3.25$ to ∞	.0006	6	6
		1.0000	10,824	10,824

It will be seen that the normal curve provides a very satisfactory approximation to the actual distribution.

EXAMPLE 8.6. Attempt to fit a Poisson distribution to the full range of data (0–13) in Example 8.4.

Solution. By calculation, the mean of the data is .973 and the variance is 2.44. Since in the Poisson distribution these two parameters are the same, this immediately throws doubt on the likelihood of a satisfactory fit. Further for values of λ greater than unity, the value corresponding to $x = 1$ is greater than the value corresponding to $x = 0$, while the reverse is the case with the data under consideration.

The following table shows three examples of attempting to fit a Poisson curve. In the first example, the value for $x = 0$ has been approximately equated, and in the second and third examples, the total frequencies have been equated. The latter is the more usual procedure. It will be seen that the *tail of the data* is too long to make the Poisson curve suitable.

No. of Accidents	Observed Frequency	Trial Poisson Curves		
		(1) $\lambda = .5$	(2) $\lambda = 1$	(3) $\lambda = 1.5$
0	239	243	164	100
1	98	121	164	150
2	57	30	82	112
3	33	5	27	56
.	.	.	.	.
.	.	.	.	.
6	2	0	0	2
.	.	.	.	.
.	.	.	.	.
10	1	0	0	0
Total	447	400	447	447

8.5. Least Squares Method. If a definition of "*best fitting line*," or "*goodness of fit*" is established, formulas can be designed to determine this line, once its form (straight line, parabola, etc.) has been selected. The definition generally used in statistical work is the *least squares line*.

If the distances D_1, D_2, D_3, etc., parallel to the y axis are measured from the empirical data points to the curve, then the least squares line is the one that makes $D_1^2 + D_2^2 + D_3^2 + \cdots$ a minimum.*

For a straight line,

$$y = a_0 + a_1 x$$

---

*The least squares line is not completely satisfactory because it gives too great a weight to extreme values. Some writers have proposed the least distance line, when $|D_1| + |D_2| + |D_3| + |D_4| + \cdots$ is a minimum. $|D|$ is the distance taken as positive in each case. In the past it has been difficult to calculate this line because of the sign problem, but this can be overcome with modern computers.

fitting N points, (X_1, Y_1), (X_2, Y_2), etc., the sum of the squares of the distances is a minimum if

$$\Sigma Y = a_0 N + a_1 \Sigma X$$
$$\Sigma XY = a_0 \Sigma X + a_1 \Sigma X^2 \qquad (8.1)$$

These two equations are called the *normal equations of the least squares line*.

The corresponding equations for fitting a parabola,

$$y = a_0 + a_1 x + a_2 x^2$$

are

$$\Sigma Y = a_0 N + a_1 \Sigma X + a_2 \Sigma X^2$$
$$\Sigma XY = a_0 \Sigma X + a_1 \Sigma X^2 + a_2 \Sigma X^3 \qquad (8.2)$$
$$\Sigma X^2 Y = a_0 \Sigma X^2 + a_1 \Sigma X^3 + a_2 \Sigma X^4$$

Solving Equations 8.1, the values of a_0 and a_1 are:

$$a_0 = \frac{(\Sigma Y)(\Sigma X^2) - (\Sigma X)(\Sigma XY)}{N(\Sigma X^2) - (\Sigma X)^2}$$

$$a_1 = \frac{N(\Sigma XY) - (\Sigma X)(\Sigma Y)}{N(\Sigma X^2) - (\Sigma X)^2}$$

EXAMPLE 8.7.   Fit a straight line to the following data, for the U.S. Gross National Product, in billions of dollars.

Year	G.N.P.	Year	G.N.P.
1957	441.1	1962	560.3
1958	447.3	1963	590.5
1959	483.7	1964	632.4
1960	503.7	1965	683.9
1961	520.1	1966	743.3

Solution.   Take 1961 as 0 in order to simplify the calculation, which can be set out in tabular form.

Year	u	v	u^2	uv	Fitted Curve $a_0 + a_1 u$
1957	−4	441.1	16	−1764.4	413.0
1958	−3	447.3	9	−1341.9	445.6
1959	−2	483.7	4	−967.4	478.5

Year	u	v	u^2	uv	Fitted Curve $a_0 + a_1 u$
1960	−1	503.7	1	−503.7	511.4
1961	0	520.1	0	0	544.2
1962	1	560.3	1	560.3	577.1
1963	2	590.5	4	1181.0	609.9
1964	3	632.4	9	1897.2	642.8
1965	4	683.9	16	2735.6	675.4
1966	5	743.3	25	3716.5	708.5
Totals	5	5606.3	85	5513.2	5606.3

The normal equations of the least squares are

$$5606.3 = 10 a_0 + 5a_1$$
$$5513.2 = 5a_0 + 85a_1$$

Solving,

$$5606.3 = 10 a_0 + 5a_1$$
$$\underline{11026.4 = 10 a_0 + 170a_1}$$
$$5420.1 = 165a_1$$
$$a_1 = 32.85$$
$$10a_0 = 5606.3 - 164.3 = 5442.0$$
$$a_0 = 544.2$$

EXAMPLE 8.8.   The table below gives the U.S. wholesale price index for all farm products for the period 1955 to 1966. Find the least squares line for these data.

Year	Index	Year	Index
1955	97.9	1961	96.0
1956	96.6	1962	97.7
1957	99.2	1963	95.7
1958	103.6	1964	94.3
1959	97.2	1965	98.4
1960	96.9	1966	102.5

Solution.   The data are so close to a level straight line just below 100, that a level line at the average figure of 98.0 is clearly appropriate. Applying the least squares method, and using a time origin of 1960 and an index origin of 100, the calculations give:

Year	u	v	u^2	uv	Horizontal Line	Least Squares Line
1955	−5	−2.1	25	+10.5	−2.0	−1.89
1956	−4	−3.4	16	+13.6	−2.0	−1.91
1957	−3	−0.8	9	+2.4	−2.0	−1.93
1958	−2	+3.6	4	−7.2	−2.0	−1.95
1959	−1	−2.8	1	+2.8	−2.0	−1.97
1960	0	−3.1	0	0	−2.0	−1.99
1961	1	−4.0	1	−4.0	−2.0	−2.01
1962	2	−2.3	4	−4.6	−2.0	−2.03
1963	3	−4.3	9	−12.9	−2.0	−2.05
1964	4	−5.7	16	−22.8	−2.0	−2.07
1965	5	−1.6	25	−8.0	−2.0	−2.09
1966	6	+2.5	36	+15.0	−2.0	−2.11
	6	−24.0	146	−15.2	−24.0	−24.0

The normal equations of the least squares line are:

$$-24.0 = 12a_0 + 6a_1$$
$$-15.2 = 6a_0 + 146a_1$$

Solving,

$$-24.0 = 12a_0 + 6a_1$$
$$\underline{-30.4 = 12a_0 + 292a_1}$$
$$-6.4 = 286a_1$$
$$a_1 = -.02$$
$$12a_0 = -24.0 + .12$$
$$a_0 = 1.99$$

The least squares line starts at 98.1 in 1955 and drops steadily to 97.9 in 1966.

8.6. Advantages and Disadvantages of Graphic Method.

The principal advantages of the *graphic* or *free hand* method are

1. It is easy to use.
2. No calculations are required.
3. For a straight line, using a ruler, excellent results are quickly obtained.
4. Judgment and a knowledge of the shape of similar data can be brought into play.
5. It is often the only practical method.

The principal disadvantages are:
1. The curve is not completely smooth, except when a ruler is used.
2. The curve is subjective.
3. Two persons will obtain different results.

8.7. Advantages and Disadvantages of Parameter Method. The principal advantages of equating parameters as a means of curve fitting are:
1. The curve is completely smooth.
2. The method produces a curve which is well-known.
3. Tables of areas, ordinates, and various parameters are available for testing the fit and for deducing results concerning the data.
4. It is useful when bodies of similar data have to be compared.
5. There is room for judgment in the choice of the formula and in the selection of the parameters.

The principal disadvantages are:
1. The results are tied to a mathematical formula.
2. The method is more laborious than the graphic.
3. The method can be used only when a suitable curve is available, (however there are many more curves than the three discussed in Chapter 7).

8.8. Advantages and Disadvantages of Least Squares Method. The principal advantages of the least squares method are:
1. The curve is completely smooth.
2. It provides the "best fit."
3. A mathematical formula is easily interpreted.
4. The application of the method is independent of subjective considerations (except for the selection of a straight line or other mathematical formula).
5. The results are convenient for forecasting.

The principal disadvantages are:
1. The results are tied to a mathematical formula, which may not really represent the data.
2. There is no room for judgment.
3. Too much weight is given to unusual values.

8.9. Nonlinear Data. When time series and similar data are of a form which precludes the use of a straight line, other curves, such as a parabola, may be used. However, it is often found that by changing the vertical scale to (for example) a logarithm scale, a close fit by means of a straight line may be obtained. This can be done readily by use of special graph paper ruled for a logarithm scale.

EXAMPLE 8.9.   The following table shows the accumulation of $1,000 at 5 percent interest compounded annually over a period of years. Draw a graph of these figures. Draw a second graph of the logarithm of the amounts, and fit a straight line to the latter results.

Years	Amount	Years	Amount
0	$1,000	60	$18,679
10	1,629	70	30,426
20	2,653	80	49,561
30	4,322	90	80,730
40	7,040	100	131,501
50	11,467		

Solution.   The graph of the original data is given in Figure 8.3. Expressing the amounts in logarithm form, we have:

Years	Amount	Log Amount	Years	Amount	Log Amount
0	$1,000	3.0000	60	18,679	4.2714
10	1,629	3.2119	70	30,426	4.4832
20	2,653	3.4237	80	49,561	4.6951
30	4,322	3.6357	90	80,730	4.9070
40	7,040	3.8476	100	131,501	5.1189
50	11,467	4,0595			

It will be seen from the graph of the log amount against the number of years (as set out in Figure 8.4) that the data now lie on an exact straight line.

8.10 Descriptive Terms for a Straight Line.   In view of the simplicity and the importance of the straight line as a means of representing time series and similar data, the following terms should be noted.

Slope.   The slope of a straight line is the ratio of the vertical to the horizontal distance between two points on the line. (This

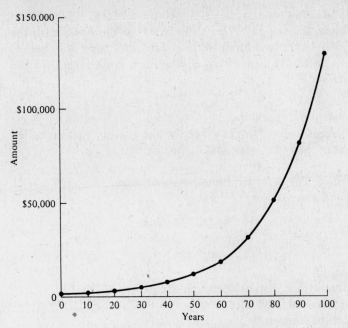

Figure 8.3. Accumulation of $1000 at 5% interest. Normal scale.

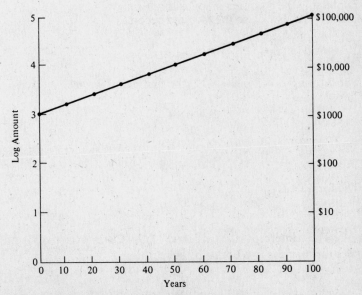

Figure 8.4. Accumulation of $1000 at 5% interest. Logarithm scale.

will be the same whatever two points are selected). For a horizontal line, the slope is 0; for a line at 45° to the horizontal, the slope will be 1; and for a vertical line, the slope will be ∞. When y decreases as x increases, the slope is negative. In the formula

$$y = a_0 + a_1 x$$

the constant a_1 is the slope.

y intercept. The point at which the line cuts the y axis is called the y intercept and this is equal to the constant a_0.

EXAMPLE 8.10. A straight line passes through the points $x = 1$, $y = 2$ and $x = 10, y = 3$. What is

1. The slope of the line,
2. The formula for the line,
3. The y intercept?

Solution.

1. The vertical distance between the two points is $3 - 2 = 1$, and the horizontal distance is $10 - 1 = 9$. The slope is $1/9$.

2. Let the formula be

$$y = a_0 + a_1 x$$

The slope a_1 is $1/9$, so the formula becomes

$$y = a_0 + \frac{1}{9} x$$

Substituting $x = 1$ and $y = 2$ (the first point) we get

$$2 = a_0 + \frac{1}{9}$$

$$a_0 = 2 - \frac{1}{9} = \frac{17}{9}$$

The formula is

$$y = \frac{17}{9} + \frac{1}{8} x$$

3. The y intercept is a_0 which is $17/9$. Check that the formula goes through the two points by substitution.

$$2 = \frac{17}{9} + \frac{1}{9}$$

and

$$3 = \frac{17}{9} + \frac{10}{9}$$

Problems

Problem 8.1.   Two points completely define a straight line, or in other words, only one straight line can be drawn through two given points. How many points define
1. a parabola
2. a cubic
3. a hyperbola?

Problem 8.2.   The slope of a straight line is $1/10$ and the y intercept is 1.
1. What is the formula for the line?
2. What is the value of y corresponding to $x = 0, 5$, and 10?

Problem 8.3.   Find the formula for a parabola passing through the points

$$(x = 0, y = 2) \ (x = 5, y = 3) \ (x = 10, y = 5)$$

Problem 8.4.   Find the values of a_1, a_2 and a_3 in the formula

$$\frac{1}{y} = a_0 + a_1 x + a_2 x^2$$

passing through the three points in Problem 8.3.

Problem 8.5.   The curves in Problem 8.3, and 8.4, both pass through the same three points. What are the values of y corresponding to $x = -5$ and $x = 15$ for the two curves?

Problem 8.6.   The following table from a certain study, gives the rate of daylight accident involvement per hundred million vehicle-miles for passenger automobiles, analyzed by age of car.

Age of Car	Accident Involvement Rate	Age of Car	Accident Involvement Rate
1–1.9	161	6–6.9	251
2–2.9	162	7–7.9	272
3–3.9	193	8–8.9	285
4–4.9	214	9–9.9	300
5–5.9	236	10 and over	396

Make a graphic graduation of these data.

Problem 8.7. A pair of dice are thrown 50 times, and the score for each throw recorded.

Score	Observed Frequency	Score	Observed Frequency
2	1	8	7
3	2	9	6
4	3	10	3
5	6	11	2
6	9	12	0
7	11		

Draw a smooth curve through these data.

Problem 8.8. Use the graphic method to fit a curve to the following data for the mortgage debt outstanding in the U.S.A. at December 31st, for the years shown. Amounts are in billions of dollars.

Year	Mortgage Debt	Year	Mortgage Debt
1940	36.5	1960	206.8
1945	35.6	1961	226.3
1950	72.8	1962	248.6
1955	129.9	1963	274.3
1956	144.5	1964	300.1
1957	156.5	1965	326.2
1958	171.8	1966	347.1
1959	190.8		

Problem 8.9. The following table gives the number of telephone calls for each half-hour on a small office switchboard. Draw a smooth curve through these data.

Time	No. of Calls	Time	No. of Calls
8:30–	10	12:30–	35
9:00–	30	1:00–	22
9:30–	46	1:30–	30
10:00–	56	2:00–	38
10:30–	54	2:30–	60
11:00–	63	3:00–	57
11:30–	52	3:30–	60
12:00–	42	4:00–	58
		4:30–	32

Could a frequency distribution be fitted to these data?

Problem 8.10. A class of 30 students take a certain test and obtain the following scores out of a maximum of 100.

Score	Number of Students	Score	Number of Students
40	5	70	5
50	6	80	5
60	6	90	3

Draw a smooth curve through these data.

Problem 8.11. Students passing a certain examination are analysed according to the number of times they have previously sat for the examination (and failed). The results are as follows:

No. of Failures Prior to Passing	No. of Students
0	40
1	26
2	2
3	2
4 or more	0

Fit a Poisson distribution to these data.

Problem 8.12. Fit a binomial distribution to the data in Problem 8.11.

Problem 8.13. Fit a normal curve to the data in Problem 8.7.

Problem 8.14. Use the method of least squares to fit a straight line to the following data.

x	0	1	2	3	4	5
y	1	2	4	3	5	4

Problem 8.15. The following table gives figures for the average sale per occupied room in hotels. Fit a least squares straight line to these data.

Year	Sale	Year	Sale
1955	$7.50	1963	$9.37
		1964	9.53
1960	9.15	1965	9.71
1961	9.23	1966	10.03
1962	9.35		

Problem 8.16. In the following data, y increases continuously with x. Show that the least squares straight line obtained by

making x the *dependent variable* instead of y is not the same as the normal least squares straight line.

x	0	1	2	4	5	7	9
y	0	2	3	4	7	9	10

Problem 8.17. Why are the two lines obtained in Problem 8.16 different?

Problem 8.18. Fit a least squares straight line to the data in Problem 8.11.

Problem 8.19. The following table gives the amount of ordinary life insurance in force in the U.S.A. (in billions of dollars). Fit a straight line curve to these amounts, and compare the two results.

Year	Amount ($ billions)	Year	Amount ($ billions)
1900	6	1940	79
1910	12	1950	149
1920	32	1960	340
1930	78		

Problem 8.20. Fit the following curve to the data in Problem 8.19, using the least squares method.

$$y = a_0 + a_1 x + a_2 x^2$$

Solutions

Problem 8.1. The number of points required to define a curve is equal to the number of unknown constants, a_0, a_1, etc., in the equation for the curve. The number of points required to define the curves listed in the question are (1) 3; (3) 4; (3) 2. The last answer corresponds to the simple formula of a hyperbola given in Section 8.2. The general hyperbola requires 4 points to define it.

Problem 8.2.

$$1. \ y = 1 + \frac{1}{10} x$$

$$2. \ 1, \ 1\frac{1}{2}, \text{ and } 2.$$

Problem 8.3. The formula for a parabola is

$$y = a_0 + a_1 x + a_2 x^2$$

Substituting the given values

$$2 = a_0$$
$$3 = a_0 + 5a_1 + 25a_2$$
$$5 = a_0 + 10a_1 + 100a_2$$

Hence,

$$1 = 5a_1 + 25a_2$$
$$3 = 10a_1 + 100a_2$$

Solving,

$$50a_2 = 1, a_2 = \frac{1}{50}$$

$$10a_1 = 1, a_1 = \frac{1}{10}.$$

$$y = 2 + \frac{1}{10}x + \frac{1}{50}x^2$$

Problem 8.4.

$$\frac{1}{2} = a_0$$

$$\frac{1}{3} = a_0 + 5a + 25a_2$$

$$\frac{1}{5} = a_0 + 10a_1 \dotplus 100a_2$$

$$\frac{1}{y} = \frac{1}{2} - \frac{11}{300}x + \frac{1}{1500}x^2$$

Problem 8.5.

		x = -5	x = 15
First formula	$y = 2 + \dfrac{1}{10}x + \dfrac{1}{50}x^2$	$y = 2$	$y = 8.0$
Second formula	$\dfrac{1}{y} = \dfrac{1}{2} - \dfrac{11}{300}x + \dfrac{1}{1500}x^2$	$y = 1.43$	$y = 10.0$

Problem 8.6. Note that the center of the age intervals are 1.45, 2.45, etc. The last value is best omitted from the curve fitting because there is no means of estimating the mean age. However, the curve, if projected, should at least reach the value of 396. The fitted curve is shown in Figure 8.5.

Problem 8.7. The plot of the data and the fitted curve are shown in Figure 8.6.

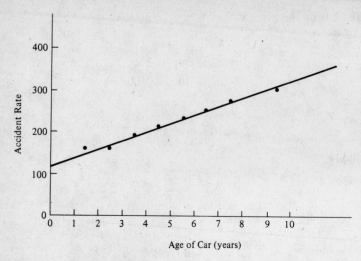

Figure 8.5. Daylight accident rates for passenger automobiles. Analysis
         by age of car.

Problem 8.8.   It must be noted that data for the early years is
given at quinquennial points only.   These must, of course, be
properly spaced out on the *x* axis.   Dates shown on the *x* axis
must indicate (by a footnote or other means) that they are

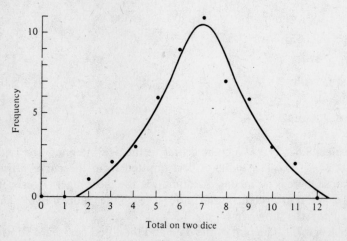

Figure 8.6. Distribution of scores from the throw of two dice.

December 31. This is best achieved as follows:

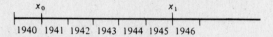

Figure 8.7. Method of indicating data at December 31st of any year.

The values for December 31, 1940 and December 31, 1945 are placed immediately above the points marked as x_0 and x_1.

Problem 8.9. Note that the figures given should be recorded against the midpoint of each interval: 8.45, 9.15, etc.

The distribution has two humps, one in the morning and one after lunch; for this reason none of the frequency distributions discussed in this book could be used. Two hump distribution formulas can however be constructed.

Problem 8.10. In plotting these data remember that the values for scores 30 and 100 are both zero. The smooth curve should not be greater than 1 or 2 at score 30 and must be zero for values above 100.

Problem 8.11. First calculate the mean and variance of the data.

No. of Failures (x)	No. of Students (y)	xy	x^2y
0	40	0	0
1	26	26	26
2	2	4	8
3	2	6	18
4	0	0	0
	70	36	52

$$\text{Mean} = \frac{36}{70} = .51$$

$$\text{Variance} = \frac{52}{70} - (.51)^2$$

$$= .74 - .26 = .48$$

$\lambda = .5$ provides a close fit to both the mean and the variance. The values of the Poisson distribution for this value of λ can be obtained from statistical tables or calculated.

No. of Failures	Observed	No. of Students Fitted	Difference
0	40	42.5	+2.5
1	26	21.2	−4.8
2	2	5.3	+3.3
3	2	0.9	−1.1
4	0	0.1	+0.1
	70	70	0

Problem 8.12. The mean of the data is .51 and the variance is .48. From the formulas for the binomial curve,

$$\text{Mean} = np$$
$$\text{Variance} = npq$$

This gives

$$q = \frac{.48}{.51} = .94$$

Using this figure, we get $p = .06$ and $n = 8$. In view of the small volume of the data (70 observed cases), any attempt to fit the data too closely would be wrong and it will be sufficient to simplify the calculation by assuming $q = .9$, $p = .1$ and $n = 5$, giving

x	x!	(n − x)!	n!	$\dfrac{n!}{x!(n-n)!}$	p^x	q^x	Frequency	Fitted Curve	Observed
0	1	120	120	1	1	.59	.59	41.3	40
1	1	24	120	5	.1	.66	.33	23.1	26
2	2	6	120	10	.01	.73	.07	4.9	2
3	6	2	120	10	.001	.81	.01	0.7	2
4	24	1	120	5	.0001	.9	—	0	0
5	120	1	120	1	.00001	1	—	0	0
							100	70	70

Problem 8.13. Proceed in the usual manner to calculate the mean and standard deviation of the data. (Use 7 as the origin). The mean is 6.86 and the

$$\text{standard deviation} = \frac{207}{50} - (.14)^2 = \sqrt{4.14 - .02}$$

$$= 2.03$$

Using mean of 7 and standard deviation of 2 we have

Point values required	7±	0	1	2	3	4	5
$\dfrac{x}{\sigma}$		0	,5	1.0	1.5	2.0	2.5
Ordinates from Table 7-2			.3989	.3521	.2420	.1295	.0540	.0175

The negative values have been omitted because they are the same as the positive. The sum of the ordinates (positive and negative) is

$$.3989 + 2(.3521 + .2420 + .1295 + .0540 + .0175) = 1.9891$$

The ordinates from Table 7.2 must be increased in the ratio, $50 \div 1.9891 = 25$ approximately, to make the total agree with the curve to be fitted, giving

Score	Frequency Observed	Frequency Fitted	Score	Frequency Observed	Frequency Fitted
2	1	0.4	8	7	8.8
3	2	1,4	9	6	6.1
4	3	3.3	10	3	3.3
5	6	6.1	11	2	1.4
6	9	8.8	12	0	0.4
7	11	10.0			

Problem 8.14.

x	y	x^2	xy	Least squares line
0	1	0	0	1.5
1	2	1	2	2.2
2	4	4	8	2.8
3	3	9	9	3.5
4	5	16	20	4.2
5	4	25	20	4.8
15	19	55	59	

Normal equations for the least square line are

$$19 = 6a_0 + 15a_1$$
$$59 = 15a_0 + 55a_1$$

Solving $\qquad a_0 = 1.52 \qquad a_1 = .66$

The values are set out on the right hand side of the table above.

Problem 8.15. Use 1960 as origin and measure sales in difference from $9.50, to reduce the arithmetic.

Year	u	v	u^2	uv	Least Squares Line From $9.50	From Zero
1955	−5	−2.00	25	$10.00	−$1.74	$7.76
1960	0	− .35	0	0	− .69	8.81
1961	1	− .27	1	− .27	− .48	9.02
1962	2	− .15	4	− .30	− .27	9.23
1963	3	− .13	9	− .39	− .06	9.44
1964	4	+ .03	16	+ .12	+ .15	9.65
1965	5	+ .21	25	+1.05	+ .36	9.86
1966	6	+ .53	36	+3.18	+ .57	10.07
	16	−$2.13	116	$13.39	−$2.16	

$$-2.13 = 8a_0 + 16a_1$$

$$+13.39 = 16a_0 + 116a_1$$

$$a_0 = -.69 \text{ cents}, \qquad a_1 = .21 \text{ cents}$$

Problem 8.16. The equations for the two lines can be calculated in a single tabulation. The point $x = 5$, $\dot{y} = 5$ is used as origin.

(x −5)	(y − 5)	$(x − 5)^2$	(x − 5)(y − 5)	$(y − 5)^2$
−5	−5	25	25	25
−4	−3	16	12	9
−3	−2	9	6	4
−1	−1	1	1	1
0	2	0	0	4
2	4	4	8	16
4	5	16	20	25
−7	0	71	72	84

For the least squares line, with y as the dependent variable,

$$0 = 7a_0 - 7a_1$$
$$72 = -7a_0 + 71a_1$$

whence

$$a_0 = 1.125, \qquad a_1 = 1.125$$

giving

$$(y - 5) = 1.125 + 1.125(x - 5)$$

or

$$y = 0.5 + 1.125x$$

For the least squares line with x as the dependent variable,

$$-7 = 7b_0 + 0$$
$$72 = 0 + 84b_1$$

whence

$$b_0 = -1, \qquad b_1 = .857$$

giving

$$(x - 5) = -1 + .857(y - 5)$$

or

$$x = -0.285 + .857y$$

which may be written

$$y = \frac{1}{.857}x + \frac{0.285}{.857} = .33 + 1.17x$$

Problem 8.17. The reason why the two equations obtained in Problem 8.16 are not identical is because the least squares line is obtained by minimizing the sum of the squares of the distances from the points to the line *measured parallel to the y axis*. In the second set of calculations, the measurements are made parallel to the x axis.

Problem 8.18. The least squares equation is

$$y = 37 - 13x$$

giving values

x	0	1	2	3
Observed	40	26	2	2
Fitted	37	24	11	-2

This is not a satisfactory fit.

Problem 8.19. Use origin 1930 and 10 year intervals for x. The results are:

Year	1900	1910	1920	1930	1940	1950	1960
Actual Figures	6	12	32	78	79	149	340
Straight Line	-41	6	53	100	147	194	241
Straight Line Log	7	13	26	49	93	178	339

Problem 8.20. The formulas for the normal equations are given in Section 8.5.

Using origin year 1930 and 10 year intervals,

Year	u	u^2	u^3	u^4	v	uv	u^2v
1900	−3	9	−27	81	6	−18	54
1910	−2	4	−8	16	12	−24	48
1920	−1	1	−1	1	32	−32	32
1930	0	0	0	0	78	0	0
1940	1	1	1	1	79	79	79
1950	2	4	8	16	149	298	596
1960	3	9	27	81	340	1,020	3,060
	0	28	0	196	696	1,323	3,869

$$696 = 7a_0 + 28a_2$$
$$1,323 = 28a_1$$
$$3,845 = 28a_0 + 196a_2$$

Hence,

$$a_0 = 47.8$$
$$a_1 = 47.2$$
$$a_2 = 12.9$$

giving

Year	1900	1910	1920	1930	1940	1950	1960
Actual Figure	6	12	32	78	79	149	340
Parabola	22	5	14	48	108	194	306

It will be noted that this parabola is less satisfactory than fitting a straight line to the logarithm of the figures.

9

Time Series

9.1. Introduction. In the preceding chapter, mention was made of time series, and it was shown how the method of least squares could be used to fit a straight line, or other mathematical formula, to a series of data which changed with time. *Business*, *economics*, *population studies*, and *weather* are typical of the areas where time series play a vital role for both *recording* and *forecasting*.

The full analysis of a time series is more complex than the simple curve fitting discussed in the previous chapter, because the data are complicated by cyclical and seasonal variations.

9.2. Classification of Time Series Movements. A typical time series is shown in Figure 9.1. It will be seen that while the graph shows an overall *trend* of increasing value with time, there is imposed upon the general trend other variations which, it will be noted, are related to the season of the year.

The *movements* of a time series may be classified as follows:

1. *Secular.* This is the *long term* growth or decline. The determination of this *trend* can be made by the method of least squares (Chapter 8), or by other means discussed in this chapter.

2. *Cyclical.* These are the oscillations, with duration greater than a year, imposed on the data due to swings in the *business cycle or other similar causes.*

3. *Seasonal.* These are the oscillations, which depend on the *season of the year.* Thus, employment is usually higher at harvest time in the country and before Christmas in the cities. Rainfall will be higher at some times of the year than at others. (In some statistics, such as temperature and height of tides, there are even shorter, *daily oscillations.*)

4. *Random.* Empirical time series will be subject also to

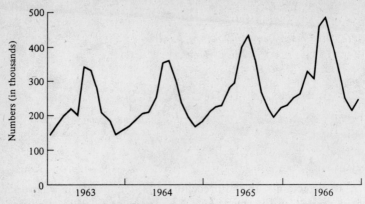

Figure 9.1. U.S. citizens departing the U.S.A. Example of a time series.

chance, and *random* or *irregular variations*. These movements are called *random* or sometimes *residual*.

In the study of time series, the secular or long term trend is usually of greatest interest, but this is not always so. A study of past seasonal movements is needed, for example, to interpret monthly production or other figures as they develop.

EXAMPLE 9.1. Give examples of causes which would lead to the four types of movement listed above.

Solution.

Secular	Population growth
	Inflation of values
	Higher standard of living
Cyclical	Prosperity and slumps
	Changes in fashion
	Sun spot cycle (for weather statistics)
Seasonal	Changes in temperature
	Changes in weather
	Incidence of public and school holidays
Random	Fire or theft losses
	An unseasonal warm Sunday (for automobiles on the road)
	Sudden death of a President
	Declaration of War

9.3. Moving Averages. In order to reduce the effect of random movements on time series data, we may substitute the *average value over a number of recordings*, for each individual value. Thus, if the series is $x_1, x_2, x_3 \ldots$, we could calculate

$$\frac{x_1 + x_2 + x_3}{3}, \frac{x_2 + x_3 + x_4}{3}, \text{etc.}$$

It will be noted that the first term corresponds in time to the individual value x_2, and hence, a moving average shortens the time series at each end. While this is normally unimportant at the beginning of the series, it does make the last recording less recent.

Moving averages using 3, 5, or some other odd number of terms have the advantage that the average figure corresponds to one of the original terms of the series, but in certain cases an even number of terms is more suitable. For example, when it is desired to remove seasonal movements, four quarters or twelve months moving averages should be used. (See next Section.)

EXAMPLE 9.2. The following data give the number of calls made by a salesman over a series of 30 working days.

Day	Calls	Day	Calls	Day	Calls
1	11	11	11	21	9
2	11	12	8	22	12
3	10	13	10	23	7
4	9	14	7	24	12
5	7	15	10	25	7
6	10	16	7	26	10
7	12	17	6	27	11
8	6	18	6	28	11
9	10	19	10	29	10
10	11	20	10	30	9

Plot the graph of these data and of the five day moving average.
Solution.

Day	Calls	5 Day Moving Average	Day	Calls	5 Day Moving Average
1	11		5	7	9.6
2	11		6	10	8.8
3	10	9.6	7	12	9.0
4	9	9.4	8	6	9.8

Day	Calls	5 Day Moving Average	Day	Calls	5 Day Moving Average
9	10	10.0	20	10	9.4
10	11	9.2	21	9	9.6
11	11	10.0	22	12	10.0
12	8	9.4	23	7	9.4
13	10	9.2	24	12	9.6
14	7	8.4	25	7	9.4
15	10	8.0	26	10	10.2
16	7	7.2	27	11	9.8
17	6	7.8	28	11	10.2
18	6	7.8	29	10	
19	10	8.2	30	9	

9.4. Date and Period Data. Data for a time series may be at individual dates, for example, the Dow Jones stock market average on the first of each month; or for a week, month, quarter, or year, for example, the sales of the XYZ company each month. Moving averages will follow the pattern of the original data. Thus, the three month moving average of the price of a stock, using data for January 1, February 1, and March 1, will correspond to February 1. The four month moving average of the price using January 1, February 1, March 1, and April 1 will correspond to February 15th. The three month moving average based on sales for the month of January, February, and March will correspond to the month of February.

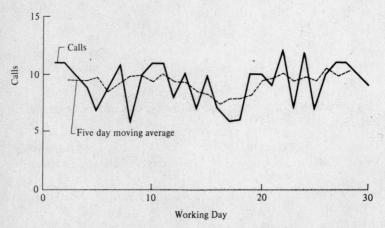

Figure 9.2. Salesman's daily calls. Five-day moving average.

If production and similar data are recorded in quarters of a year, and moving average figures corresponding to quarter years are required, the following formula should be used.

Moving average for quarter

$$= \frac{1}{8} (Q_{-2} + 2Q_{-1} + 2Q_0 + 2Q_1 + Q_2)$$

where Q is the actual quarter's figures and the suffix represents the quarter to be used. If the moving average for the first quarter of any year is required, $Q_0 =$ the first quarter's actual figures, $Q_1 =$ the second quarter's actual figures, $Q_{-1} =$ the last quarter's actual figures for the preceding year, etc.

The corresponding formula for monthly moving averages is

$$\frac{1}{24} \left(M_{-6} + 2 \sum_{x=-5}^{5} M_x + M_6 \right)$$

It should be noted that these formulas produce the same results as taking the mean of two neighboring moving averages, e.g.,

$$\frac{1}{8} (Q_{-2} + 2Q_{-1} + 2Q_0 + 2Q_1 + Q_2)$$

$$= \frac{1}{2} \left[\frac{1}{4} (Q_{-2} + Q_{-1} + Q_0 + Q_1) + \frac{1}{4} (Q_{-1} + Q_0 + Q_1 + Q_2) \right]$$

EXAMPLE 9.3.   Develop six day moving averages for the data in Example 9.2 to correspond with actual days by the method of the previous section.

Solution.   The first figure will correspond to *day 4* and will be

$$\frac{1}{12} [\text{Day } 1 + 2 (\text{Sum of Days 2 to 6}) + \text{Day } 7]$$

Day	6 Day Average	Day	6 Day Average	Day	6 Day Average
4	9.8	12	9.5	20	8.9
5	9.4	13	9.2	21	9.5
6	9.0	14	8.4	22	9.8
7	9.2	15	7.8	23	9.5
8	9.7	16	7.7	24	9.7
9	9.8	17	7.9	25	9.8
10	9.5	18	8.1	26	9.9
11	9.4	19	8.4	27	9.9

9.5. Methods of Determining Trends. There are four principal methods of determining the trend in a time series. These are:

1. *Graphical.* The simplest method of determining a trend is to plot the data on a graph and then to *draw in free hand a smooth curve* which *cuts through the seasonal and other short term variations* and follows the *general trend.* If the curve is approximately a straight line, a ruler can be used to draw it. Flexible rules, which are available from art supply shops, are useful when the data do not approximate to a straight line.

    Advantages.   (1) Simple
                       (2) Not bound to any mathematical formula
                       (3) Excellent results *if done with skill*
    Disadvantages. (1) Requires considerable practice and skill for good results
                       (2) Depends on personal judgment

2. *Semi-Average.* This method is *appropriate only when the trend is approximately a straight line*. The data are divided into two equal (or approximately equal) time ranges. The average value of each range is calculated and plotted at the center point, in time, of each half. These two points are then joined by a straight line which is extended in each direction to span the whole time range.

    Advantages.   (1) Simple
                       (2) Free from judgment
                       (3) Suitable for forecasting
    Disadvantages. (1) Only suitable for a straight line trend
                       (2) Not as satisfactory as the least squares method mentioned below
                       (3) Must be recalculated as new data becomes available

3. *Moving Average.* This method has been described previously in Section 9.3. This method smooths to a limited extent only and provides no definite trend curve for future extrapolation.

    Advantages.   (1) Simple
                       (2) Free from judgment (except in the selection of number of periods averaged)

(3) Can be extended when additional data becomes available without any recalculation

Disadvantages. (1) Not a completely smooth curve

(2) Does not provide a smooth curve over the whole range (ends short of the latest date for which data are available)

4. *Least Squares.* This method is somewhat similar, but more scientific than the semi-average method and can be used for both straight lines and more complicated trend formulas. The method was described in Chapter 8.

Advantages. (1) Free from judgment

(2) Provides the "best fitting curve"

(3) Suitable for forecasting

Disadvantages. (1) Results depend on the assumption of a definite mathematical curve.

(2) The method is rather laborious unless data processing equipment is available

(3) The method gives too much weight to abnormal values

EXAMPLE 9.4. Apply the graphic method to the following data for the sales of a certain periodical over a period of 24 quarters.

Quarter	Sales in Thousands	Quarter	Sales in Thousands	Quarter	Sales in Thousands
1	60	9	90	17	130
2	70	10	100	18	140
3	50	11	120	19	130
4	80	12	110	20	140
5	60	13	120	21	150
6	80	14	130	22	150
7	80	15	140	23	140
8	90	16	140	24	150

Solution. The results of the graphic determination of the trend are shown in Figure 9.3. Note that the judgment determination has been made to show the trend as a curve and not as a straight line.

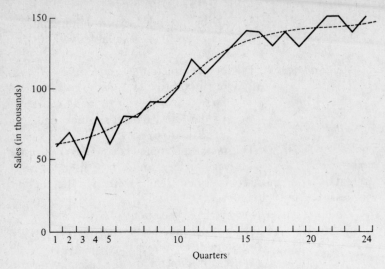

Figure 9.3. Sales of a quarterly periodical. Graphic method of determi-
        nation of trend.

EXAMPLE 9.5.   Apply the semi-average method to determine the
trend of the data in Example 9.4.
Solution.

Quarter	Sales in Thousands	Quarter	Sales in Thousands
1	60	13	120
2	70	14	130
3	50	15	140
4	80	16	140
5	60	17	130
6	80	18	140
7	80	19	130
8	90	20	140
9	90	21	150
10	100	22	150
11	120	23	140
12	110	24	150
	990		1,660

Average ($\div 12$) = 83   = 138

These averages correspond to $6\frac{1}{2}$ and $18\frac{1}{2}$ respectively, the midpoints of the two ranges. The result is shown in Figure 9.4.

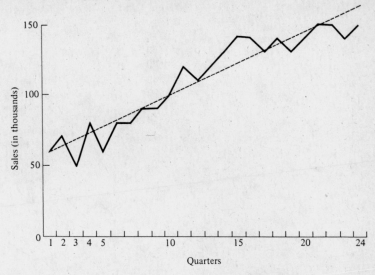

Figure 9.4. Sales of a quarterly periodical. Semi-average method of determination of trend.

EXAMPLE 9.6. Calculate the 4 quarter moving average to determine the trend of the data in Example 9.4.
Solution.

Quarter	Sales in Thousands	4 Period Total	4 Period Average
1	60		
2	70		
3	50	260	65
4	80	260	65
5	60	270	68
6	80	300	75
7	80	310	78
8	90	340	85
9	90	360	90
10	100	400	100
11	120	420	105
12	110	450	113
13	120	480	120
14	130	500	125
15	140	530	133
16	140	540	135
17	130	550	138
		540	135

Quarter	Sales in Thousands	4 Period Total	4 Period Average
18	140		
19	130	540	135
20	140	560	140
21	150	570	143
22	150	580	145
23	140	590	148
24	150		

These results are shown graphically in Figure 9.5.

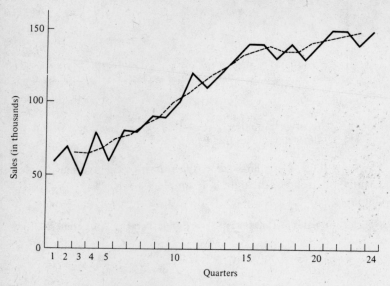

Figure 9.5. Sales of a quarterly periodical. Moving average method of determination of trend.

9.6. Annual Rate of Growth. In many business and similar time series statistics, considerable importance is attached to the rate of growth. For a year x, the rate of growth over the previous year is

$$\frac{f(x) - f(x - 1)}{f(x - 1)} \tag{9.1}$$

where $f(x)$ is the value of the function. Such rates of growth are usually expressed as a percentage. Thus, if sales in 1966 are

$90,000 compared with $80,000 in 1965, the rate of growth of sales in 1966 is

$$\frac{90,000 - 80,000}{80,000} = .125 \text{ or } 12\frac{1}{2}\%$$

It should be noted that if sales (say) followed an exact trend line which was a straight line, the rate of growth over a long period of time would fall. An *exponential* growth line is needed to maintain a steady rate of growth.

EXAMPLE 9.7. The trend line developed in the solution to Example 9.5 was a straight line through the points $(6\frac{1}{2}, 83)(18\frac{1}{2},$ and 138). Obtain a formula for this trend and calculate the *quarterly* rate of growth for the first quarter and the last (24th) quarter, of the trend line figures.
Solution. The formula for a straight line is

$$y = ax + b$$

Substituting the values given,

$$83 = a \times 6\frac{1}{2} + b$$
$$138 = a \times 18\frac{1}{2} + b$$

Subtracting, $\quad\quad 55 = 12a$
$$a = 4.58$$

and $\quad\quad b = 83 - 4.58 \times 6\frac{1}{2}$
$$b = 53.23$$

The trend line is

$$y = 4.58x + 53.23$$

When

$$x = 0, \quad y = 53.23$$
$$x = 1, \quad y = 57.81$$

The quarterly rate of growth for the second quarter is

$$\frac{f(1) - f(0)}{f(0)}$$

which equals

$$\frac{57.81 - 53.23}{53.23} = \frac{4.58}{53.23} = .086 \text{ or } 8.6\%$$

The quarterly rate of growth for the last quarter is

$$\frac{f(24) - f(23)}{f(23)}$$

which equals

$$\frac{163.15 - 158.57}{158.57} = \frac{4.58}{158.57} = 0.29 \text{ or } 2.9\%$$

9.7. Seasonal Variation. Given a volume of monthly data, it may be found that some months of the year are regularly higher or lower than the general average due to seasonal variations. A *seasonal index* is a factor which indicates the average departure from the trend line for any month of the year. Each month will have an index which will be greater than 1 for months with high values of the data and will be less than 1 for months with low values. The average seasonal index for all months should be 1, and hence the total of the seasonal indexes for all the twelve months of the year should be 12. Seasonal indexes are sometimes expressed as percentages. While the above remarks, and what follows, assume monthly data, quarterly and weekly indexes are sometimes used.

If there were no trend, such indexes would be calculated readily by adding up the data for all Januaries, all Februaries, etc., and dividing by the number of years to obtain typical monthly values. Dividing the average value for, say, January, by the average value for all months combined would give the January seasonal index, and similarly for other months.

However, if there is an overall upward trend in data recorded over a series of calendar years, the average value for December will be greater than the average value for January *for this reason alone.* Hence, when trends are involved, an adjustment for trend must be introduced to allow for this in the calculation of seasonal indexes. Four, rather similar, methods are used for calculating seasonal indexes where trends are involved. These are described below.

9.8. Calculation of Seasonal Index.

1. *Average Method.* The procedure described above is carried through and then the February index is divided by 1/12 the annual trend, the March index by 2/12 the annual trend, and so on. The adjusted trend figure will not add up to 12, and each

will be increased or decreased by the ratio of 12 divided by their total to correct this.

Modifications. (1) It is often preferable to express all monthly figures as a percentage of the average monthly figure for the year, before starting the calculations.

(2) Instead of calculating the mean monthly figure for each month, the median is sometimes preferred, omitting unusual extreme values which are probably due to random variation.

2. *Trend Method.* Starting with the trend value, which has previously been calculated (or read off a graph) for each month, the data for each month is expressed as a percentage of the trend value. The averages of the percentages for the respective months then give the required index. As in method 1, if they do not add up to 12 they should be adjusted appropriately.

3. *Moving Average Method.* This method is similar to the trend method, except that the *moving average* is substituted for the trend value.

4. *Link Related Method.* Each month's data can be expressed as a percentage of the previous month. These percentages are links. These links are first calculated for each month's data and then the average February–January link, the average March–February link, etc., are calculated. Suppose the links are:

$$\text{February–January} \quad l_1$$
$$\text{March–February} \quad l_2$$
$$\cdots \cdots$$
$$\text{January–December} \quad l_{12}$$

$l_1 \times l_2 \times l_3 \times \cdots \times l_{12}$ is then calculated. If the data have a trend, this multiplication will not produce unity but the annual trend, say $1 + k$. Each value of l must be multiplied by $1 - k/12$ to adjust for the trend. The adjusted values of l can then be multiplied in succession to produce a series of indexes of seasonal variation based on January as 1, thus

$$\text{January} \qquad 1$$
$$\text{February} \qquad l_1$$
$$\text{March} \qquad l_1 \times l_2$$
$$\cdots \cdots$$
$$\text{December} \qquad l_1 \times l_2 \times \cdots \times l_{11}$$

If necessary the indexes must be increased appropriately to sum to 12.

All four methods normally produce closely similar results, but the actual results will differ because of cyclical movements in the data being treated somewhat differently. No particular method is to be preferred over the others.

EXAMPLE 9.8. The data for U.S. citizens departing the U.S.A. for foreign travel is shown graphically in Figure 9.1. The actual figures are as follows. All numbers are in thousands.

Month	1963	1964	1965	1966	Four Years
January	142	172	207	232	753
February	176	193	225	248	842
March	201	206	234	262	903
April	212	214	278	330	1034
May	200	253	296	308	1057
June	341	356	398	459	1554
July	333	359	433	486	1611
August	283	302	365	396	1346
September	207	238	265	322	1032
October	186	195	224	250	855
November	146	167	195	217	725
December	161	186	221	248	816
	2588	2841	3341	3758	12528

Calculate the trend line by the semi-average method, and calculate the monthly seasonal indexes for the data by the *average method*.

Solution.   Average values for the first and second halves of the experience are

$$\frac{2588 + 2841}{24} \quad \text{and} \quad \frac{3341 + 3758}{24}$$

or,

$$226.2 \quad \text{and} \quad 295.8$$

These correspond to January 1, 1964 and January 1, 1966 respectively, a two-year period.

The annual trend in monthly figures expressed in thousands of travelers is

$$\frac{295.8 - 226.2}{2} = \frac{69.6}{2} = 34.8$$

The average monthly value for the whole 4 years is

$$\frac{2588 + 2841 + 3341 + 3758}{48} = 261$$

The annual trend, as a ratio, is 34.8/261, or 13.3%, and the monthly trend is 13.3%/12 = 1.1%.

The calculation of the seasonal indexes proceeds as follows.

Month (1)	Total 4 Years (2)	Typical Month (3)	Unadjusted Seasonal Index (4)	Trend Adj. (5)	(4) ÷ (5) (6)	Seasonal Index Adj. for Trend (7)
Jan.	753	188	.72	1.000	.72	.76
Feb.	842	210	.80	1.011	.79	.84
Mar.	903	226	.87	1.022	.85	.90
Apr.	1034	259	.99	1.033	.96	1.02
May	1057	264	1.01	1.044	.97	1.03
Jun.	1554	388	1.49	1.055	1.41	1.49
July	1611	403	1.54	1.066	1.44	1.53
Aug.	1346	337	1.29	1.077	1.20	1.27
Sept.	1032	258	.99	1.088	.91	.96
Oct.	855	214	.82	1.099	.75	.80
Nov.	725	181	.69	1.110	.62	.66
Dec.	816	204	.78	1.121	.70	.74
	12,528	3,132			11.32	12.00

Notes. Column (3) is column (2) ÷ 4.

Column (4) is column (3) divided by the monthly average 3132 ÷ 12 = 261. This column could have been calculated by dividing column (2) by the column total ÷ 12.

Column (5) is $[1 + .011 \times (t - 1)]$ where t is the month.

Column (7) is column (6) increased in the ratio 12 ÷ 11.32.

EXAMPLE 9.9. Using the data in Example 9.8, and the trend developed in the solution of that example, calculate the monthly seasonal indexes for the data by the *trend method*.

Solution. The two points for the trend value may be plotted, and values for individual months read off. Alternatively, they may be calculated by the formula for a straight line. If the midpoint of January 1963 is represented by $x = 0$, the midpoint for February 1963 represented by $x = 1$, etc., the two points calculated are $x = 11\frac{1}{2}$ and $x = 35\frac{1}{2}$.

The formula for a straight line is $y = a + bx$. Solving for a and b gives

$$y = 192.85 + 2.9x$$

The trend figures can now be calculated and the actual and trend figures tabulated.

	1963		1964		1965		1966		Average Monthly Percent-age	Seasonal* Index
Month	Trend	A/T†	Trend	A/T	Trend	A/T	Trend	A/T		
Jan.	193	74%	228	75%	262	79%	297	78%	77%	77%
Feb.	196	90	231	84	265	85	300	83	86	86
Mar.	199	101	233	88	268	87	303	86	90	90
Apr.	202	105	236	91	271	103	306	108	102	102
May	204	98	239	106	274	108	309	100	103	102
Jun.	207	165	242	147	277	144	312	147	151	150
July	210	159	245	147	280	155	315	154	154	153
Aug.	213	133	248	122	283	129	318	125	127	126
Sept.	216	96	251	95	286	93	320	101	96	96
Oct.	219	85	254	77	289	78	323	77	79	79
Nov.	222	66	257	65	291	67	326	67	66	66
Dec.	225	72	260	72	294	75	329	75	73	73
									1204	1200

†A/T = Actual divided by Trend.
*Average Monthly Percentage × 1200/1204.

It will be noted that the results are very close to those obtained in Example 9.8.

EXAMPLE 9.10. Use the data in Example 9.8, and the *moving average method* to determine the monthly seasonal index.
Solution. The moving average must be based on 12 month figures, because of the marked season variation. This will produce trend figures corresponding to the *first day of each month*. The mean of the first day of January and February must then be calculated to give the moving average trend for *January* and similarly for other months.

Month	Increase 1964 over 1963	Twelve Month Year Ending	Total	Monthly Trend Month	Value	Actual	A/T
		12/31/63	2588	July 63	217	333	153%
Jan.	30	1/31/64	2618	Aug. 63	219	283	129
Feb.	17	2/28/64	2635	Sept. 63	220	207	94
Mar.	5	3/31/64	2640	Oct. 63	220	186	85
Apr.	2	4/30/64	2642	Nov. 63	222	146	66
May	53	5/31/64	2695	Dec. 63	225	161	72
Jun.	15	6/30/64	2710	Jan. 64	227	172	76
July	26	7/31/64	2736	Feb. 64	229	193	84
Aug.	19	8/31/64	2755	Mar. 64	231	206	89
Sept.	31	9/30/64	2786	Apr. 64	233	214	92
Oct.	9	10/31/64	2795	May 64	234	253	108
Nov.	21	11/30/64	2816	Jun. 64	236	356	151
Dec.	25	12/31/64	2841				

Similarly for the rest of the table. These results are then brought together in a summary and the final seasonal index calculated.

Month	Actual Divided by Trend				Average Monthly Percentage	Seasonal Index
	1963	1964	1965	1966		
Jan.	–%	76%	80%	78%	78%	78%
Feb.	–	84	85	82	84	84
Mar.	–	89	87	86	87	87
Apr.	–	92	102	107	100	100
May	–	108	108	99	105	105
Jun.	–	151	144	147	147	148
July	153	151	155	–	153	154
Aug.	129	125	130	–	128	129
Sept.	94	98	93	–	95	95
Oct.	85	79	78	–	81	81
Nov.	66	66	67	–	66	66
Dec.	72	73	75	–	73	73
					1197	1200

EXAMPLE 9.11. Use the data in Example 9.8, and the *Link Related Method* to determine the monthly seasonal index.
Solution. The links are first calculated and then averaged.

	1963	1964	1965	1966	Average
Feb./Jan.	124%	112%	109%	107%	113%
Mar./Feb.	114	107	104	106	108
Apr./Mar.	105	104	119	126	114
May/Apr.	94	118	106	93	103
Jun./May	171	141	134	149	149
Jul./Jun.	98	101	109	106	103
Aug./Jul.	85	84	84	81	83
Sept./Aug.	73	79	73	81	77
Oct./Sept.	90	82	85	78	84
Nov./Oct.	78	86	87	87	84
Dec./Nov.	110	112	113	114	112
Jan./Dec.	107	112	105	–	108

$$l_1 \times l_2 \times l_3 \times \cdots \times l_{12} = 1.20 = 1 + k$$

$$k = 0.20$$

$$\text{and} \quad \frac{k}{12} = 0.017$$

$$1 - \frac{k}{12} = 0.983$$

Therefore, the links must be multiplied by 0.983 to remove seasonal trend and the calculation proceeds as follows.

Month	Link	Link Adjustment	Adj. Link	Accumulated Links	Monthly Index
Jan.				100%	78%
Feb.	113%	.983	111%	111	86
March	108	.983	106	118	92
April	114	.983	112	132	102
May	103	.983	101	133	103
June	149	.983	146	194	151
July	103	.983	101	196	152
Aug.	83	.983	82	161	125
Sept.	77	.983	76	122	95
Oct.	84	.983	83	102	79
Nov.	84	.983	83	84	65
Dec.	112	.983	110	93	72
				1546	1200

9.9. Seasonally Adjusted Data. Many important national indexes such as production, unemployment, etc., are subject to appreciable seasonal variation. In order to keep a careful watch on cyclical movements, it is necessary to calculate seasonally adjusted figures. Such adjusted figures will include trend, cyclical, and random movements.

9.10. Estimating of Cyclical and Random Movements. Data which has been adjusted for both trend and seasonal movements will reveal the cyclical movements as longer term variations and random movements as short variations often limited to a single month.

9.11. Comparison of Monthly Data. In comparing monthly production and similar data, it is important to remember that the number of working days in a month may vary appreciably owing to the exact length of the month and the incidence of Sundays and holidays. It is often useful to calculate in such circumstances the *production per working day*.

Problems

Problem 9.1. Classify the movements you would expect in a time series from the following causes.
- (1) An earthquake
- (2) A period of deflation
- (3) The football season
- (4) Tornados (as they affect statistics for an individual neighborhood)
- (5) Tornados (as they affect statistics for the whole Middle West of the U.S.)
- (6) Expansion of college enrollment

Problem 9.2. The normal seasonal cycle is one year. Give two examples of shorter cycles which could occur in statistics and state the period of each.

Problem 9.3. Is it true to say that the longer the period used in calculating a moving average, the greater the smoothing? If not, what period is the best for smoothing?

Problem 9.4. The following table gives the value of exports of U.S. merchandise by quarter over the period 1963 to 1966. Smooth these data by calculating the four-quarter moving averages.

		QUARTER		
Year	1	2	3	4
1963	115	134	122	142
1964	142	146	138	162
1965	128	163	148	172
1966	162	169	161	180

(Values are based on an index of 100 for the period 1957–59.)

Compare the smoothness of the original and averaged data by finding the maximum change from one quarter to the next in both cases.

Problem 9.5. The moving averages calculated in the previous problem corresponded to periods halfway between the periods of the original data. Calculate four-quarter moving averages adjusted to agree with the original period.

Problem 9.6. The following were the number of Coast Guard personnel on active duty at June 30th in the years indicated.

Year	1940	1945	1950	1955	1960	1965
Number	13,756	171,192	23,190	28,607	30,616	31,776

To what extent are the variations indicated secular, cyclical, seasonal, and random?

Problem 9.7. For the following data, which are recorded at a certain date and which for a period of time?

(1) Sales of a departmental store.
(2) The Dow Jones average stock price.
(3) The population of the U.S.A.
(4) Unemployment figures.
(5) Company salary figures.
(6) School enrollment.

Problem 9.8. The following data give the enrollment in thousands in institutions of higher education.

Year	1930	1940	1950	1960	1965
Number	1,101	1,494	2,659	3,216	5,500

Plot these data and draw a line fitting them. Explain why all the increase cannot be attributed to secular trend.

Problem 9.9. Fit a least squares curve to the data in Problem 9.8, and compare it to the graphic fitted curve in the answer to Problem 9.8.

Problem 9.10. Calculate by the semi-average method, the straight line trend of the data in Problem 9.8. Compare this result with the answer to Problem 9.9.

Problem 9.11. Which of the four methods for determining trend described in this chapter can be used when the data are not regularly spaced on the time scale?

Problem 9.12. If a certain function has a value of 1,000 at time 0 and an annual rate of growth of 10%, what is

(1) a formula for the function at time t
(2) the value of the function at time $t = \frac{1}{2}$
    and at time $t = 10$ years?

Problem 9.13. The rate of growth for sales, and similar statistics recorded on a monthly basis, is usually in the form of the percentage increase over the *corresponding month for the preceding year*. This is an *annual* rate of growth, since it compares figures for one year with figures for a year previous. It has the advantage of avoiding the difficulties due to seasonal fluctuations. If data were free from all seasonal fluctuations, monthly rates of growth could be calculated by comparing one month with the preceding month. If such a comparison showed a steady monthly rate of growth of 1% what would be the annual rate of growth?

Problem 9.14. If a certain statistic was not subject to appreciable variation from day to day, monthly figures would vary because of the different number of days in the month. What would be the *seasonal index* for such data for

(1) January
(2) February (for a year which is not a leap year)?

Problem 9.15. The following table shows, for the U.S.A., profits and dividends from all manufacturing corporations by calendar quarter, in billions of dollars.

		QUARTER		
Year	1	2	3	4
1963	4.0	5.2	4.8	5.5
1964	5.1	6.1	5.7	6.3
1965	6.2	7.2	6.6	7.5
1966	7.2	8.4	7.4	7.9

Use the Average Method to calculate seasonal indexes for these data.

Problem 9.16. Use the Trend Method to calculate seasonal indexes for the data in Problem 9.15.

Problem 9.17. Use the Moving Average Method to calculate seasonal indexes for the data in Problem 9.15.

Problem 9.18. Use the Link Method to calculate seasonal indexes for the data in Problem 9.15.

Problem 9.19. The data in Problem 9.15 has been analysed for trend and seasonal variation. The residual variation must be due to cyclical or random causes. In which quarter is this residual variation greatest?

Problem 9.20. The following figures give production and working days in a 6 month period.

Month	Production	Working Days
1	8540	22
2	7415	19
3	8265	21
4	8274	21
5	9210	23
6	8107	20

Calculate the production per working day for each month. Which month was most productive per working day?

Solutions

Problem 9.1.

    (1) Random
    (2) Cyclical
    (3) Seasonal
    (4) Random
    (5) Seasonal
    (6) Secular

Problem 9.2.

(1) Travel on public transportation—weekly cycle.
(2) Work load in shops, on telephone exchanges, etc.,
    —daily cycle.

Problem 9.3. If data are subject to only random variations, the longer the period used in calculating the moving average, the greater the smoothing. However, where seasonal variations are predominant, a period equal to, or a multiple of, the seasonal period is best for smoothing.

Problem 9.4. Four-quarter moving averages are

128, 135, 138, 142, 147, 144, 148, 150, 153, 161, 163, 166, 168

The greatest change between successive quarters in the original data is $163 - 128 = 35$. The greatest change between moving averages is $161 - 153 = 8$.

Problem 9.5. For this purpose we use the formula

$$\frac{1}{8} (Q_{-2} + 2Q_{-1} + 2Q_0 + 2Q_1 + Q_2)$$

or we can take the mean of adjacent figures calculated in the previous solution.

QUARTER

Year	1	2	3	4
1963			132	137
1964	140	145	145	146
1965	149	152	157	162
1966	164	167		

Problem 9.6. Since the figures given are at June 30th in quinquennial years, no seasonal movements are involved. The high value in 1945, due to the World War, is random. The steady increase from 1940 to 1965 (ignoring the 1945 figures) is partly secular, and we trust, partly cyclical due to the Korean and Vietnam wars. There is no way to distinguish between the two from the data given.

Problem 9.7.

(1) Sales of a department store will be weekly, monthly, or yearly totals.

(2) Dow Jones average stock price will be the average closing price at the end of a particular day.

(3) The population of the U.S.A. will be as tabulated on a census date and estimated on other dates.

(4) Unemployment figures. These figures can be on a particular date or the average for a month or year. The latter is more usual.

(5) Company salary figures are normally monthly or yearly.

(6) School enrollment. This is usually at the beginning of a term, that is, at a fixed date.

Problem 9.8.   College attendance increase is due to

(1) Population growth—secular.

(2) Birthrate changes some 20 years earlier—cyclical.

(3) Proportion of young people attending college—secular. (However, the present increase cannot continue indefinitely.)

Problem 9.9.

Year	x	y	x^2	xy	Fitted Values
1930	−2	1101	4	−2202	670
1940	−1	1494	1	−1494	1788
1950	0	2659	0	0	2906
1960	1	3216	1	3216	4024
1965	1.5	5500	2.25	8250	4583
	−0.5	13970	8.25	7770	

$$13970 = 5a_0 - 0.5a_1$$
$$7770 = -0.5a_0 + 8.25a_1$$

giving,

$$y = 2906 + 1118x$$

The fitted values are shown above.

Problem 9.10.   Using 1950 as origin and 10 year intervals (as in the solution to Problem 9.9)

Average first 3 dates			Average last 2 dates	
x	y		x	y
−2	1,101		1	3,216
−1	1,494		1.5	5,500
0	2,659			
−3	5,254	*Total*	2.5	8,716
−1	1,751	*Average*	1.25	4,358

The straight line through these two points is

$$y = 2,910 + 1,159x$$

	1930	1940	1950	1960	1965
True Value	1101	1494	2659	3216	5500
Solution 9.9	670	1788	2906	4024	4583
Solution 9.10	592	1751	2910	4069	4648

Problem 9.11.   The graphic, semi-average, and least squares can all be used for non-regular data. The moving-average requires evenly spaced data.

Problem 9.12. The formula for the function is

$$1,000 \times (1.1)^t$$

The values at the two points mentioned are

t	value
$\frac{1}{2}$	1,049
10	2,594

Problem 9.13.

$$(1.01)^{12} - 1 = 12.7\%$$

but $1\% \times 12$ or 12% is often used.

Problem 9.14. There are 365 days in an ordinary year, one-twelfth of this number is 30.417. January has 31 days, so that on the assumptions in the question, the seasonal index for January is

$$\frac{31}{30.417} = 1.019$$

The seasonal index for February is

$$\frac{28}{30.417} = .921$$

Problem 9.15. We must first calculate the trend line. The least squares method will be used.

Year	Quarter	x	y	x^2	xy
1963	1	−7	−2.0	49	+14.0
	2	−6	−0.8	36	+4.8
	3	−5	−1.2	25	+6.0
	4	−4	−0.5	16	+2.0
1964	1	−3	−0.9	9	+2.7
	2	−2	+0.1	4	−0.2
	3	−1	−0.3	1	+0.3
	4	0	+0.3	0	0.0
1965	1	1	+0.2	1	+0.2
	2	2	+1.2	4	+2.4
	3	3	+0.6	9	+1.8
	4	4	+1.5	16	+6.0
1966	1	5	+1.2	25	+6.0
	2	6	+2.4	36	+14.4
	3	7	+1.4	49	+9.8
	4	8	+1.9	64	+15.2
		8	+5.1	344	+85.4

$$5.1 = 16a_0 + 8a_1$$
$$85.4 = 8a_0 + 344a_1$$

Giving

$$a_0 = .197, \; a_1 = .244$$

The trend line is

$$(y - 6) = .197 + .244\,(x - 7)$$

where x is in quarters from first quarter 1963 $= 0$.
The *annual* increase in quarterly amounts is $.244 \times 4 = .976$
The average quarterly amount over the four years is

$$\frac{(6 \times 16) + 5.1}{16} = \frac{101.1}{16} = 6.32$$

The annual trend is

$$\frac{.976}{6.32} \quad \text{or} \quad 15.4\%$$

The quarterly trend is

$$\frac{15.4\%}{4} = 3.9\%$$

The calculation of the seasonal index is as follows:

Quarter	Total 4 Years	Typical Quarter	Unadjusted Seasonal Index	Trend Adj.	(4)÷(5)	Seasonal Index
(1)	(2)	(3)	(4)	(5)	(6)	(7)
1	22.5	5.6	.89	1.00	.89	.94
2	26.9	6.7	1.06	1.04	1.02	1.09
3	24.5	6.1	.97	1.08	.90	.95
4	27.2	6.8	1.08	1.12	.96	1.02
Total	101.1	25.2	4.00		3.77	4.00

Problem 9.16. From the trend formula in the solution to Problem 9.15, we can proceed as follows.

Year	Quarter	Actual	Trend	Actual/Trend
1963	1	4.0	4.49	.89
	2	5.2	4.73	1.10
	3	4.8	4.98	.96
	4	5.5	5.22	1.05
1964	1	5.1	5.47	.93
	2	6.1	5.71	1.07
	3	5.7	5.95	.96
	4	6.3	6.20	1.02
1965	1	6.2	6.44	.96
	2	7.2	6.69	1.08
	3	6.6	6.93	.95
	4	7.5	7.17	1.05
1966	1	7.2	7.42	.97
	2	8.4	7.66	1.10
	3	7.4	7.91	.94
	4	7.9	8.15	.97

Month	1963	1964	1965	1966	Total	Seasonal Index
1	.89	.93	.96	.97	3.75	.94
2	1.10	1.07	1.08	1.10	4.35	1.09
3	.96	.96	.95	.94	3.81	.95
4	1.05	1.02	1.05	.97	4.09	1.02
					16.00	4.00

Problem 9.17. The moving average will be calculated by the formula

$$\frac{1}{8} (Q_{-2} + 2Q_{-1} + 2Q_0 + 2Q_1 + Q_2)$$

to provide a slight variation from the solution in Example 9.10.

Year	Quarter	Actual	Trend	Actual/Trend
1963	1	4.0		
	2	5.2		
	3	4.8	5.01	.96
	4	5.5	5.26	1.05

Year	Quarter	Actual	Trend	$\dfrac{\text{Actual}}{\text{Trend}}$
1964	1	5.1	5.49	.93
	2	6.1	5.70	1.07
	3	5.7	5.94	.96
	4	6.3	6.21	1.01
1965	1	6.2	6.46	.96
	2	7.2	6.73	1.07
	3	6.6	7.00	.94
	4	7.5	7.28	1.03
1966	1	7.2	7.53	.96
	2	8.4	7.68	1.09
	3	7.4		
	4	7.9		

giving seasonal indexes of

$$.94, \ 1.08, \ .95, \ \text{and} \ 1.03$$

Problem 9.18. The links are

Link	1963	1964	1965	1966	Average
2nd/1st	130%	120%	116%	117%	120.8%
3rd/2nd	92	93	92	88	91.3
4th/3rd	115	111	114	107	111.8
1st/4th	—	93	98	96	95.7

$$l_1 \times l_2 \times l_3 \times l_4 = 1.18 = 1 + k$$

$$1 - \frac{k}{4} = .955$$

Quarter	Link	Adj. Links	Accumulated Links	Seasonal Index
1			100.0%	.94
2	120.8	115.4	115.4	1.09
3	91.3	87.2	100.6	.95
4	111.8	106.8	107.4	1.02
			423.4	4.00

Problem 9.19.

Year	Quarter	Trend	Seasonal Index	Seasonally Adj. Trend	Actual	Difference
1963	1	4.49	.94	4.22	4.0	+ .22
	2	4.73	1.09	5.16	5.2	− .04
	3	4.98	.95	4.73	4.8	− .07
	4	5.22	1.02	5.32	5.5	− .18
1964	1	5.47	.94	5.14	5.1	+ .04
	2	5.71	1.09	6.22	6.1	+ .12
	3	5.95	.95	5.65	5.7	− .05
	4	6.20	1.02	6.32	6.3	+ .02
1965	1	6.44	.94	6.05	6.2	− .15
	2	6.69	1.09	7.29	7.2	+ .09
	3	6.93	.95	6.58	6.6	− .02
	4	7.17	1.02	7.31	7.5	− .19
1966	1	7.42	.94	6.97	7.2	− .23
	2	7.66	1.09	8.35	8.4	− .05
	3	7.91	.95	7.51	7.4	+ .11
	4	8.15	1.02	8.31	7.9	+ .41

The last quarter of 1966 shows the greatest variation from the seasonally adjusted trend. However, at the ends of any table, a straight line trend may not be too accurate.

Problem 9.20.

Month	Production	Working Days	Production per Working Day
1	8540	22	388
2	7415	19	390
3	8265	21	394
4	8274	21	394
5	9210	23	400
6	8107	20	405

The sixth month was most productive per working day.

10

Index Numbers, Scores and Rates

10.1. Introduction. An important part of statistical work is the reduction of large volumes of data to forms in which comparisons can be made and deductions drawn. Thus, the mean, standard deviation, and other functions describe a frequency distribution; the trend and seasonal indexes describe a time series.

Index Numbers are statistical measures of groups of related data and are used to compare such data over time, over territory, and in other ways.

Scores are used to compare data, often grouped data, for individuals with the whole class of similar individuals.

Rates are used in vital statistics to provide an index for a non-homogeneous group of data.

10.2. Index Numbers. Index numbers are indicative of various aspects of industry and commerce—cost of living, unemployment, production, wages, etc. They enable us to compare readily, items such as these over periods of time and space. Thus, we have index numbers of the cost of food. Such numbers will vary with the date and also with the area of the country to which they refer. Index numbers normally start with a base of 100 at a particular time for the whole country. It will be seen that index numbers provide time series, discussed in the last chapter, and are subject to analysis as to trend, seasonal movement, etc. Index numbers are often calculated also by territory so that the relative amount of unemployment in different states, for example, may be compared.

10.3. Problems of Constructing Index Numbers. Practically every index number presents special problems which are peculiar to itself, but we can illustrate the nature of these problems by considering one example, the *Consumer Price Index*. Clearly a large number of factors enter into the cost of living: housing, food, transportation, etc. A *weighted average* must be used to represent these costs based on periodic sample studies. If the cost of food goes up 10%, but other costs remain the same, the cost of living goes up by that proportion of 10% which the cost of food bears to the total cost of living. This proportion will vary from family to family, and an average proportion must be used. It will also vary with time and territory and it is here that the major difficulty arises in designing a suitable index number. Further, when the cost of food rises, not all foods go up in price by the same amount. A typical "*market basket*" has to be designed to be representative of the average household's purchase of food. Such a basket will, however, vary with time and if some particular food becomes very expensive, the public will shift to other cheaper alternatives.

EXAMPLE 10.1. An index is to be designed to provide a relative measure of the cost of the hobby of photography. It is suggested that this should consist of (1) the cost of an average camera plus (2) the cost of a roll of film. What would be wrong with such a measure?

Solution. First, in photography the largest portion of the cost of the hobby is that of processing films and this has been entirely ignored in the measure. Second, many films are bought during the lifetime of a camera. The index should be in the form

$$w_1 \times c_1 + w_2 \times c_2 + w_3 \times c_3$$

where c_1, c_2, and c_3 are the cost of cameras, film, and processing; and w_1, w_2, and w_3 are appropriate weights.

10.4. Theoretical Considerations.

The ideal index number should meet certain theoretical tests.

1. *Time Reversal Test.* The base date used for an index number should not affect the index. Thus, if calculations are made for the same index with base dates t_0 and t_1, we have

Actual Date	Base Date t_0	Base Date t_1
		Index Number
t_0	100	N'
t_1	N	100

Then, for consistency, the ratios

$$\frac{100}{N} \quad \text{and} \quad \frac{N'}{100}$$

should be the same.

2. *Factor Reversal Test.* If indexes are constructed of price, quantity, and total value (P_t, Q_t, and V_t) respectively, then for any time t

$$\frac{P_t Q_t}{P_0 Q_0} \quad \text{should equal} \quad \frac{V_t}{V_0}$$

In practice, most indexes come close to meeting these tests but do not meet them exactly.

10.5. Index Weights. For clarity, the following discussion will refer to a price index. The remarks apply equally to other indexes with suitable changes of wording. A *price index* consists of a number of individual prices p_t, where t indicates the time at which the prices are determined. With these prices are associated weights w. If the index at time 0 is 100, the expression

$$100 \times \frac{\Sigma \, wp_n}{\Sigma \, wp_0} \tag{10.1}$$

can be used as the index at time n. If only one item is involved it will be seen that this reduces to

$$\frac{100 \, p_n}{p_0} \tag{10.2}$$

If at time n all items are $(1 + k)$ times the price in year 0, both Formulas 10.1 and 10.2 become

$$100 \, (1 + k)$$

One of the most common methods of selecting the weights is to make them proportional to the quantities purchased (q_0) in the base year. This is called the *base year* or *Laspeyres' index* and may be written

$$\frac{\Sigma \, (q_0 p_n)}{\Sigma \, (q_0 p_0)}$$

Another method is to make the weights proportional to the quantities purchased (q_n) in the year n. This is the *given year* or *Paasche's index*,

$$\frac{\Sigma (q_n p_n)}{\Sigma (q_n p_0)}$$

Two indexes which are more satisfactory than the above, but rather more complicated are the

$$Marshall\text{-}Edgeworth\ index\ =\ \frac{\Sigma (q_0 + q_n) p_n}{\Sigma (q_0 + q_n) p_0}$$

and

$$Fisher's\ Ideal\ price\ index\ =\ \sqrt{\left(\frac{\Sigma q_0 p_n}{\Sigma q_0 p_0}\right)\left(\frac{\Sigma q_n p_n}{\Sigma q_n p_0}\right)}$$

The latter satisfies the time reversal and factor reversal tests.

EXAMPLE 10.2. An index is based on two commodities (A and B) only. The prices and quantities sold in the base year (year 0) and a later year (year n) are

Year	Price (p)		Quantity (q)	
	A	B	A	B
0	150	150	200	100
n	300	150	100	200

If the price index is 100 in year 0, calculate the index in year n for the four indexes described in Section 10.5.
Solution.

Base Year Method (Laspeyres')
$q_0 \times p_t$

Year t	A	B	A + B	Index
0	30,000	15,000	45,000	100
n	60,000	15,000	75,000	167

Given Year Method (Paasche's)
$q_n \times p_t$

Year t	A	B	A + B	Index
0	15,000	30,000	45,000	100
n	30,000	30,000	60,000	133

Marshall-Edgeworth

$$(q_0 + q_n)p_t$$

Year t	A	B	A + B	Index
0	45,000	45,000	90,000	100
n	90,000	45,000	135,000	150

Fisher's Ideal

With this method, the index is the square root of the multiple of the Base year and Given year methods.

Year t	Base Year Index	Given Year Index	Fisher's Ideal Index
0	100	100	$\sqrt{100 \times 100} = 100$
n	167	133	$\sqrt{167 \times 133} = 149$

It will be noted that the Base year method develops a higher index, and the Given year method develops a lower index than the Marshall-Edgeworth or the Fisher methods. This is usually the case because quantities bought tend to increase in the comparatively less expensive items. However, the differences are not normally so marked as in this specially selected example.

EXAMPLE 10.3. A cost of food index is to be constructed from the following six items.

Item	Price 1950	Price 1960	Quantity 1950	Quantity 1960
Bread	7.0	8.1	75	70
Meat	50.5	57.4	23	27
Vegetables	8.4	8.9	67	70
Milk Products	45.3	47.2	10	15
Beverages	61.7	63.8	10	12

Using 1950 as the base year with index of 100, calculate, by the base year method, the index of 1960.

Solution. The calculations can be made as follows.

	p_0	q_0	$p_0 q_0$	p_{10}	q_0	$p_{10} q_0$
Bread	7.0	75	525.0	8.1	75	607.5
Meat	50.5	23	1161.5	57.4	23	1320.2
Vegetables	8.4	67	562.8	8.9	67	596.3
Milk Products	45.3	10	453.0	47.2	10	472.0
Beverages	61.7	10	617.0	63.8	10	638.0
			3319.3			3634.0

$$\text{Index for 1960} = 100 \times \frac{3634.0}{3319.3} = 109.5$$

It is important to realize that in practice most indexes will involve hundreds of items, not just a few as in this example.

EXAMPLE 10.4. Using the data in Example 10.3, calculate, by the given year method, the index for 1960.
Solution. The calculations can be made as follows,

	p_0	q_{10}	$p_0 q_{10}$	p_{10}	q_{10}	$p_{10} q_{10}$
Bread	7.0	70	490.0	8.1	70	567.0
Meat	50.5	27	1363.5	57.4	27	1549.8
Vegetables	8.4	70	588.0	8.9	70	623.0
Milk Products	45.3	15	679.5	47.2	15	708.0
Beverages	61.7	12	740.4	63.8	12	765.6
			3861.4			4213.4
	Index		**= 100**			**= 109.1**

EXAMPLE 10.5. Using the data in Example 10.3, calculate the Marshall-Edgeworth cost-of-food index for 1960, based on 100 for 1950.
Solution. In this index, the weights are the sum of the quantities in the base year and the given year.

	p_0	$q_0 + q_{10}$	$p_0(q_0 + q_{10})$	p_{10}	$q_0 + q_{10}$	$p_0(q_0 + q_{10})$
Bread	7.0	145	1015.0	8.1	145	1174.5
Meat	50.5	50	2525.0	57.4	50	2870.0
Vegetables	8.4	137	1150.8	8.9	137	1219.3
Milk Products	45.3	25	1132.5	47.2	25	1180.0
Beverages	61.7	22	1357.4	63.8	22	1403.6
			7180.7			7847.4
	Index		**= 100**			**= 109.3**

It should be noted that, if the Base and Given year indexes have been calculated, there is no need to go through the complete calculations set out above, since

$$7180.7 = 3319.3 + 3861.4$$
and
$$7847.4 = 3634.0 + 4213.4$$

EXAMPLE 10.6. Using the data in Example 10.3, calculate the Fisher's Ideal index for 1960 based on 100 for 1950.

Solution. Fisher's Ideal index is the square root of the Base year index multiplied by the Given year index.

$$\text{Fisher's Ideal index} = \sqrt{109.5 \times 109.1} = 109.3$$

It will be noted that the differences among the four indexes in Examples 10.3 to 10.6 are small, and are within the range of variation which might be expected from other causes, such as judgment used in determining the items entering into the index.

10.6. Quantity Index Numbers. If, instead of indexes of prices, indexes of production or consumption are required, the most appropriate weights are often the values (prices), and hence the formula for quantity indexes are the same as for price indexes with p and q interchanged.

10.7. Use of the Geometric or Harmonic Means. There are certain theoretical justifications for using the suitably weighted geometric or harmonic means instead of the weighted arithmetic mean in establishing index numbers. These practices are not used widely at present because such indexes are not as easily understood and are more laborious to calculate. They may become more common with the greater use of data processing equipment.

10.8. Cost of Living Adjustments. Many long period time series of income, wages, sales, etc., are difficult to interpret because of changes in the cost of living. For this reason, such figures are sometimes divided by the Consumer Price Index, to provide cost of living adjusted statistics.

10.9. Center of Population. The center of population of the United States is that point upon which the United States would balance if it were a rigid plane without weight and each individual was assumed to have an equal weight. It provides a simple single index to show the shift of the population over long periods of time.

In 1790, the center was 23 miles to the east of Baltimore, in Maryland. From 1820 to 1850, it was in West Virginia; in 1860 and 1870, it was in Ohio; in 1880, it was just southwest of Cincinnati; from 1890 to 1940, it was in Indiana, and since 1950 it has been in Illinois. The center is moving west at about 4 or 5 miles a year.

10.10. Scores.   If a single test is taken by a body of students, the *marks* or *scores* provide a measure of the student's abilities. However, when different tests are involved, it is necessary to adjust the results for the difficulty of the tests. The procedure was explained when *standard scores* were discussed in Chapter 4.

Intelligence tests are designed so that a student with *normal intelligence* will have an intelligence quotient of 100%. If his *intelligence quotient* differs from 100% his mental age is defined as his true or *chronological age* multiplied by this percentage.

$$\text{I.Q.} = \frac{\text{MA}}{\text{CA}} = \frac{\text{mental age}}{\text{chronological age}} \tag{10.3}$$

Intelligence tests are broken down into various subjects; arithmetic, reading, etc.   Quotients for individual subjects can be developed similarly.

10.11. Demography.   Demography is the study of human populations by statistical methods.   The subject is also referred to as *vital statistics*.   In any given population, the ratio of deaths in a year to the total population in the middle of the year is calculated and this is called the death rate.   Similarly, there is a *birth rate*, a *marriage rate*, and a *morbidity* (sickness) *rate*.   The morbidity rate is the ratio of the average number of *people who are sick* at any time (not the average number of people becoming sick).

These rates, called *crude rates*, are not very useful for serious studies.   The reason for this is that the probability of, say, dying varies very greatly with the age.   The *age distribution* of the population being studied will greatly affect the crude death data. This is equally true of births, marriages, and sickness.   For this reason *standardized rates* are used.

If the population is subdivided according to age (or short groups of ages) and the deaths are similarly subdivided, the ratios which these figures develop will be death rates at various ages.   If these death rates are applied to a *standard population* (which may be selected in various ways), a *standardized death rate* is arrived at, which is suitable for properly comparing the mortality of different populations.   Standardized rates are weighted averages of the data analyzed by age.

Fertility rates are usually calculated separately by quinquennial age groups of the mother; overall fertility rates may be obtained by dividing the number of live births in a year by the number of women aged 15 to 44 years.

A *Net Reproductive Rate* of 1000 means that each generation would just replace itself if birth and death rates specified continued indefinitely and there was no migration. Rates above 1000 imply gaining population, rates below imply declining population.

10.12. Population Pyramids. In order to display the distribution of a population by age and sex, a population pyramid is often used as illustrated below

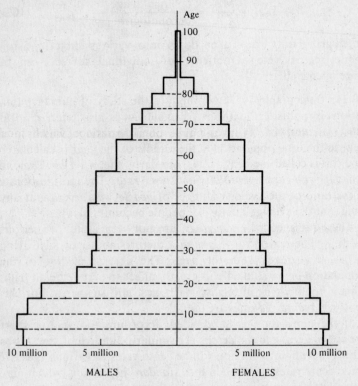

Figure 10.1. Population pyramid. U.S.A. 1966.

10.13. Expectation of Life. A useful measure of overall mortality is the expectation of life, which is the average number of years a person can expect to live according to a certain mortality experience. Expectations of life can be calculated at any age from 0 upwards. Since they do not allow for mortality trends, the calculated expectations normally understate the true expectation. Further, they apply an *average* life, including both healthy and unhealthy. According to the United States census data, the expectations of life at birth were as follows.

Year of Birth	Expectation of Life
1920	54.1
1930	59.7
1940	62.9
1950	68.2
1960	69.7
1965	70.2

In 1965, the expectation of life at birth was 66.8 for men and 73.7 for women.

Problems

Problem 10.1. Indicate the type of statistics for which index numbers are used by the U.S. Government.

Problem 10.2. A certain commodity represents $x\%$ of a price index, and the price of this commodity increases by $y\%$, while all other commodities making up the index remain unchanged. What will be the resulting percentage change in the price index?

Problem 10.3. Over a series of years the prices of all the items making up a certain price index remain unchanged, but an expensive item is purchased less and less each year. What will be the effect on

    (1) Base Year, or Laspeyres' Index
    (2) Given Year, or Paasche's Index?

Problem 10.4. A certain index number has the following values.

1960	1961	1962	1963	1964	1965	1966
105	110	123	128	128	154	165

It is decided to introduce a new base, 1966 = 100, and to recalculate the indexes for the previous years. If the index satisfies the time reversal test, what are the revised values?

Problem 10.5. An index is made up of three items. The weights in year 0 are: A 30%, B 20%, C 50%.

The prices of the items in year 0 and year n are:

Year	0	n
A	54	63
B	42	42
C	49	53

If the index for year 0 is 100, what is the index for year n, using the base year (Laspeyres') method?

Problem 10.6. Use the data of Problem 10.5, and assume weights of A 20%, B 20%, and C 60% in the year n. What is the index in year n, corresponding to 100 in year 0, using the given year (Paasche's) method?

Problem 10.7. Using the data of Problems 10.5 and 10.6, what is the Marshall-Edgeworth index?

Problem 10.8. Show mathematically that Fisher's Ideal price index satisfies the time reversal test.

Problem 10.9. Show mathematically that Fisher's Ideal price index satisfies the factor reversal test.

Problem 10.10. The following table gives the U.S. Gross National Product in billions of dollars for various years and also the Consumer Price Index for the same years. Adjust the G.N.P. to a level Consumer Price, so as to remove the element of inflation for the G.N.P.

Year	1940	1945	1950	1955	1960	1965
G.N.P.	99.7	211.9	284.8	398.0	503.7	683.9
C.P.I.	48.8	62.7	83.8	93.3	103.1	109.9

Problem 10.11. Two cities are 100 miles apart. City A has a population of two million and city B has a population of three million. What is the location of the center of population of the two cities combined?

Problem 10.12. A child aged 8 has an I.Q. of 125. What is his mental age?

Problem 10.13. A statistician goes through the notice of deaths in his local paper each day and analyzes the figures by (1) occupation and (2) age at death. By taking the average age of death over a number of years, he establishes which are the most healthy occupations. List four reasons why his results might not be sound.

Problem 10.14. The *rate of mortality* is defined as the number of people expected to die between age x and $x + 1$ out of a given number of people exactly aged x. The *death rate* at age x is the number of people dying in a year at age x, expressed as a ratio to the number of people living at age x in the middle of the year. Find a relationship between these two rates.

Problem 10.15. Assume the death rates at age 60, 65, and 70 are .03, .04, and .06. What is the crude death rate for a population (A) consisting of 1000 persons aged 60, 500 persons aged 65, and 100 persons aged 70, if they experience the assumed rates? What is the death rate for a population (B) consisting of 500 persons aged 60, 500 aged 65, and 500 aged 70?

Problem 10.16. In the above problem, what would be the standardized death rate if the standard population were as follows?

Age	Population
60	65,000
65	55,000
70	45,000

Problem 10.17. What increments, other than death, cause the population of a territory to change from year to year?

Problem 10.18. What would be the effect on a population pyramid of

    (1) A high rate of immigration

    (2) A declining birthrate?

Assume these features have continued for a long time.

Problem 10.19. The expectation of life at age x is the average number of years a person can expect to live after age x. The function used to represent the expectation of life at age x is

$$\overset{\circ}{e}_x$$

    (1) What will be the average age at death of persons now aged x according to the mortality assumed?

    (2) Does the expectation of life decrease with age?

Problem 10.20. What evidence is there that women live longer than men?

Solutions

Problem 10.1. Indexes are used extensively for *Prices* (Wholesale, Consumer, Retail, etc.) and also for *Production* (both as a measure of *Quantity* and of *Value*).

Problem 10.2.

$$\frac{x}{100} \times y\%$$

Problem 10.3. Since no prices have changed over the years, neither index will have changed.

Problem 10.4.

1960	1961	1962	1963	1964	1965	1966
64	67	75	78	78	93	100

Problem 10.5.

$$\frac{(.3 \times 63) + (.2 \times 42) + (.5 \times 53)}{(.3 \times 54) + (.2 \times 42) + (.5 \times 49)} = 110$$

Problem 10.6.   109

Problem 10.7.   109

Problem 10.8. Assume the prices and quantities of the various items entering into the index are:

	Time 0		Time n	
Price	**Quantity**		**Price**	**Quantity**
p_0	q_0		p_n	q_n

Taking 100 as the index at time 0, Fisher's index at time n is

$$\sqrt{\left(\frac{\Sigma q_0 p_n}{\Sigma q_0 p_0}\right)\left(\frac{\Sigma q_n p_n}{\Sigma q_n p_0}\right)}$$

Taking 100 as the index at time n, Fisher's index at time 0 is obtained by interchanging the suffixes 0 and n.

$$\sqrt{\left(\frac{\Sigma q_n p_0}{\Sigma q_n p_n}\right)\left(\frac{\Sigma q_0 p_0}{\Sigma q_0 p_n}\right)}$$

We see at once that the second expression is the reciprocal of the first, proving time reversal.

Problem 10.9. Proceed as in the previous solution. For the factor reversal test interchange p and q giving

$$\sqrt{\left(\frac{\Sigma p_0 q_n}{\Sigma p_0 q_0}\right)\left(\frac{\Sigma p_n q_n}{\Sigma p_n q_0}\right)}$$

Multiplying this expression by the normal Fisher formula we have,

$$\frac{\Sigma p_n q_n}{\Sigma p_0 q_0} = \frac{\text{Total Value at time } n}{\text{Total Value at time } 0}$$

Problem 10.10. The G.N.P. should be divided by the C.P.I. to produce the adjusted G.N.P. These figures can then be best expressed using an index of 100 for 1940.

Year	1940	1945	1950	1955	1960	1965
$\dfrac{\text{GNP}}{\text{CPI}}$	204.3	338.0	339.9	426.6	488.6	622.3
Adjusted to 100 for 1940	100	165	166	209	239	305

Problem 10.11. We must assume that the center of population of each city is at the center of the city. The center of population of the two cities combined will, by symmetry, lie on the line joining the two cities. Let it be x miles from city A. Then,

$$(2{,}000{,}000 \times 0) + (3{,}000{,}000 \times 100) = 5{,}000{,}000 \times x$$

$$\text{or} \quad x = \frac{300}{5} = 60 \text{ miles}$$

The center of population is 60 miles from city A and 40 miles from city B.

Problem 10.12.

$$\begin{aligned}
\text{Mental Age} &= \text{I.Q.} \times (\text{chronological age}) \\
&= 1.25 \times 8 \\
&= 10 \text{ years}
\end{aligned}$$

Problem 10.13.

(1) *Changes in types of occupation available over the years.* For example, the list would be unlikely to include many old electronic data programmers or any young steam engine drivers.

(2) *Date of entry into occupation classification.* A person has to live quite a time before he becomes a bishop or an orchestra conductor, so that these and similar occupations will show old average ages at death.

(3) *Migration.* People in the higher paid occupations are likely to move to resort type areas on retirement and may not be listed on death.

(4) *Change in occupation class.* Some occupations, such as professional football players, cannot be continued throughout life and all deaths recorded for these classes will be young.

Problem 10.14. Consider 100,000 people all assumed to be exact age x on January 1st of a certain year. Let q_n be the rate of mortality. Then $100,000 \, q_x$ will die in the year and approximately one-half of these will die in the first six months. Hence, the number of people aged x in the middle of the year is approximately

$$100,000 \left(1 - \frac{1}{2} q_x\right)$$

and the death rate is

$$\frac{100,000 \, q_x}{100,000 \left(1 - \frac{1}{2} \, q_x\right)}$$

or

$$\frac{2q_x}{2 - q_x}$$

Problem 10.15.

Age	Death Rate	A Number	Deaths	B Number	Deaths
60	.03	1000	30	500	15
65	.04	500	20	500	20
70	.06	100	6	500	30
		1600	56	1500	65
	Crude Death Rate =		.035		.043

Problem 10.16.

Standardized Population	Death Rate	Deaths
65,000	.03	1,950
55,000	.04	2,200
45,000	.06	2,700
165,000		6,850

Standardized Death Rate = .042

Problem 10.17. Births and migration.

Problem 10.18.

(1) Immigrants normally are heavily weighted in the age 20–30 group, and in men rather than women. Hence, the pyramid

will have a similar base (fewer children) relative to its size at the older ages.

(2) A declining birthrate will also cause a smaller base relative to the higher ages.

Problem 10.19.

(1) $\overset{\circ}{e}_x + x$

(2) Normally, the expectation of life decreases as the age increases, once the first year or so of age is passed. The following figures are from U.S. mortality for the year 1965.

Age	Expectation of Life
0	70.2
1	70.9
2	70.0
10	62.3
20	52.7
50	25.5

Problem 10.20. There is ample statistical evidence that women live longer than men. The expectation of life of women at age 0 is about 7 years longer than men (see figure in text). Further, the very high proportion of women to men at the older ages proves the point.

11

Correlation and Regression

11.1. Introduction. Hitherto we have considered only a single variable and the frequencies, distribution, and analysis thereof. In this chapter, we shall consider the analysis of two variables x and y, and the frequencies with which *pairs of values* occur. This is called *bivariate analysis*.

11.2. Scatter Diagrams. Thirty students sit for two tests in the same subject a month apart. Their scores are

First Test	Second Test	First Test	Second Test
87	80	72	70
80	95	70	63
32	32	62	65
65	72	85	90
55	67	55	47
30	47	45	40
82	82	68	70
90	85	77	73
38	45	68	55
72	80	67	65
60	70	62	58
45	50	52	60
30	30	57	60
90	93	77	85
73	75	80	78

We often desire to examine lists such as these to see what are the relations between the two lists. In this case we note, as we should expect since the tests are in the same subject, that large scores in the first test correspond to large scores in the second test. This is called *positive correlation*. If large scores in one test had corresponded to small scores in the second test this would be *negative correlation.* One way of displaying these results is a *scatter diagram* obtained by plotting the two scores on graph paper.

EXAMPLE 11.1. Plot a scatter diagram for the data given above.
Solution. Each dot represents an individual pair of scores and the results are shown in Figure 11.1.

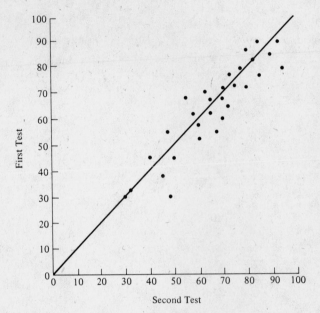

Figure 11.1. Students scores on two tests. Scatter diagram.

We note that the results are positively correlated. When the points are dotted in a haphazard way on the graph, the two functions have *no correlation.*

11.3. Lines of Regression. In Chapter 8 it was shown how the method of least squares could be used to find an approximate value of y in terms of x. Such a fitted curve is called the *line of regression of y on x.*

If the functions x and y are interchanged, we obtain the line of regression of x on y. These two lines are not normally the same. If y is related to x by a formula, a single line through all the points will be both the line of regression of y on x and of x on y. If the curves fitted are straight lines, this is referred to as *linear regression*. The two lines will meet in a point $\bar{x}$, $\bar{y}$, the center of gravity (or centroid) of the data.

EXAMPLE 11.2. Calculate the lines of regression for the data given in Section 11.2.

Solution. Proceeding as in Chapter 8 and using origin of 60 marks for each test, we have

Student	1st Test x − 60	2nd Test y − 60	$(x - 60)^2$	$(x - 60)(y - 60)$	$(y - 60)^2$
1	27	20	729	540	400
2	20	35	400	700	1,225
3	−28	−28	784	784	784
4	5	12	25	60	144
5	−5	7	25	−35	49
6	−30	−13	900	390	169
7	22	22	484	484	484
8	30	25	900	750	625
9	−22	−15	484	330	225
10	12	20	144	240	400
11	0	10	0	0	100
12	−15	−10	225	150	100
13	−30	−30	900	900	900
14	30	33	900	990	1,089
15	13	15	169	195	225
16	12	10	144	120	100
17	10	3	100	30	9
18	2	5	4	10	25
19	25	30	625	750	900
20	−5	−13	25	65	169
21	−15	−20	225	300	400
22	8	10	64	80	100
23	17	13	289	221	169
24	8	−5	64	−40	25
25	7	5	49	35	25
26	2	−2	4	−4	4
27	−8	0	64	0	0
28	−3	0	9	0	0
29	17	25	289	425	625
30	20	18	400	360	324
	287	318	9,424	8,909	9,794
	−161	−136		−79	
	126	182		8,830	

The normal equations for the line of regression of $y - 60$ on $x - 60$ are

$$182 = 30a_0 + 126a_1$$
$$8,830 = 126a_0 + 9,424a_1$$

Giving

$$a_0 = 2.24 \qquad a_1 = .91$$
$$(y - 60) = 2.24 + .91(x - 60)$$

The normal equations of the line or regression of $x - 60$ on $y - 60$ are

$$126 = 30b_0 + 182b_1$$
$$8,830 = 182b_0 + 9,794b_1$$

Giving
$$(x - 60) = -1.44 + .93(y - 60)$$

The two lines of regression cross at the centroid (the center of gravity) of the data and using this point as origin the lines are

$$\bar{y} = .91\bar{x}$$
$$\bar{x} = .93\bar{y}$$

The centroid is

$$x = 60 + \frac{\Sigma x}{n} = 60 + \frac{126}{30} = 64.2$$

$$y = 60 + \frac{\Sigma y}{n} = 60 + \frac{182}{30} = 66.1$$

11.4. Tabulation of Grouped Data. When the volume of data is large, a scatter diagram is not practical and a scatter or *distribution table* must be used. In such a table, the data are grouped in class intervals in a similar way to that used earlier in this book, but since we have two variables, the table is *two dimensional*. The following is a *distribution table* for the data in Section 11.2.

DISTRIBUTION TABLE

Score 1st Test

Score 2nd Test	30-	40-	50-	60-	70-	80-	90-
90-						2	1
80-					2	2	1
70-				3	3	1	
60-			3	2	1		
50-		1		2			
40-	2	1	1				
30-	2						

11.5. Coefficient of Correlation. Let the equation of the lines of regression (referred to the centroid as origin) be

$$\bar{y} = k_1 \bar{x}$$

and

$$\bar{x} = k_2 \bar{y}$$

If they are identical and correlation between the two functions is complete then

$$\frac{1}{k_2} = k_1$$

or

$$k_1 k_2 = 1$$

The *coefficient of correlation* is defined as

$$r = \sqrt{k_1 k_2}$$

If values of x and y are measured from the centroid,

$$r = \frac{\Sigma xy}{\sqrt{(\Sigma x^2)(\Sigma y^2)}} \tag{11.1}$$

This and Formula 11.2 are called *product-moment formulas*. If values are measured from some other origin,

$$r = \frac{n\Sigma xy - \Sigma x \Sigma y}{\sqrt{[n(\Sigma x^2) - (\Sigma x)^2][n(\Sigma y^2) - (\Sigma y)^2]}} \tag{11.2}$$

This formula may be written

$$r = \frac{p}{\sigma_x \sigma_y} \tag{11.3}$$

where

$$p = \frac{\Sigma xy}{n} - \frac{\Sigma x}{n} \cdot \frac{\Sigma y}{n}$$

$$\sigma_x = \frac{\Sigma x^2}{n} - \left(\frac{\Sigma x}{n}\right)^2$$

$$\sigma_y = \frac{\Sigma y^2}{n} - \left(\frac{\Sigma y}{n}\right)^2$$

EXAMPLE 11.3. Apply Formula 11.3 to obtain the coefficient of correlation of the data in Section 11.2.
Solution. In the solution to Example 11.2, $x = 60$, $y = 60$, was

used as an origin. From the figures in that solution

$$\bar{x} = \frac{126}{30} = 4.2$$

$$\bar{y} = \frac{182}{30} = 6.1$$

$$\sigma_x^2 = \frac{9424}{30} - (4.2)^2 = 296.5 \qquad \text{and } \sigma_x = 17.2$$

$$\sigma_y^2 = \frac{9794}{30} - (6.1)^2 = 289.3 \qquad \text{and } \sigma_y = 17.0$$

$$p = \frac{8830}{30} - (4.2)(6.1) = 268.7$$

$$r = \frac{268.7}{(17.2)(17.0)} = .92$$

11.6. Coefficient of Correlation—Grouped Data. The methods of handling grouped data in the calculation of the mean and standard deviation have been explained earlier in the book. Completely similar procedures apply to the calculation of the coefficient of correlation. We may proceed to make the calculation for each group in a single tabulation as in Example 11.4, or, as is more usual, set the working-out in a two dimensional table as in Example 11.5 and 11.6.

EXAMPLE 11.4. Calculate the coefficient of correlation for the grouped data in Section 11.4, using a single column tabulation.
Solution. Using origin of $x = 64\frac{1}{2}$, $y = 64\frac{1}{2}$, and 10 marks as class scale, and writing $x = 64\frac{1}{2} + 10u$ and $y = 64\frac{1}{2} + 10v$

1st Test	2nd Test	u	v	Frequency f	fu	fv	fu²	fuv	fv²
30–	30–	−3	−3	2	−6	−6	18	18	18
30–	40–	−3	−2	2	−6	−4	18	12	8
40–	40–	−2	−2	1	−2	−2	4	4	4
40–	50–	−2	−1	1	−2	−1	4	2	1
50–	40–	−1	−2	1	−1	−2	1	2	4
50–	50–	−1	−1	0	0	0	0	0	0
50–	60–	−1	0	3	−3	0	3	0	0
60–	50–	0	−1	2	0	−2	0	0	2
60–	60–	0	0	2	0	0	0	0	0
60–	70–	0	1	3	0	3	0	0	3

1st Test	2nd Test	u	v	Frequency f	fu	fv	fu²	fuv	fv²
70–	60–	1	0	1	1	0	1	0	0
70–	70–	1	1	3	3	3	3	3	3
70–	80–	1	2	2	2	4	2	4	8
80–	70–	2	1	1	2	1	4	2	1
80–	80–	2	2	2	4	4	8	8	8
80–	90–	2	3	2	4	6	8	12	18
90–	80–	3	2	1	3	2	9	6	4
90–	90–	3	3	1	3	3	9	9	9
				30	2	9	92	82	91

$$\bar{u} = \frac{2}{30} = .067$$

$$\bar{v} = \frac{9}{30} = .300$$

$$\sigma_x^2 = \frac{92}{30} - (.067)^2 = 3.07 - .00 = 3.07$$

$$\sigma_y^2 = \frac{91}{30} - (.300)^2 = 3.03 - .09 = 2.94$$

$$p = \frac{82}{30} - (.067)(.300) = 2.73 - .02 = 2.71$$

$$r = \frac{p}{\sigma_x \sigma_y} = \frac{2.71}{1.75 \times 1.71} = \frac{2.71}{2.99} = .91$$

It should be particularly noted that at no time during the calculations do we return to the true origin or the true units.

EXAMPLE 11.5. Calculate the coefficient of correlation for the grouped data in Section 11.4, using a two dimensional table.
Solution. The two dimensional tabulation proceeds as follows. Comparison should be made with the previous solution. In the main box, the frequency in the various groupings of *u* and *v* from the table in Section 11.4 are shown in the left top corner and the factor *uv* in the right bottom corner. This is done to facilitate

	u	30–	40–	50–	60–	70–	80–	90–				
v		–3	–2	–1	0	1	2	3	f	fv	fv²	fuv
90–	3						2 / 6	1 / 9	3	9	27	21
80–	2					2 / 2	2 / 4	1 / 6	5	10	20	18
70–	1				3 / 0	3 / 1	1 / 2		7	7	7	5
60–	0			3 / 0	2 / 0	1 / 0			6	0	0	0
50–	–1		1 / 2		2 / 0				3	–3	3	2
40–	–2	2 / 6	1 / 4	1 / 2					4	–8	16	18
30–	–3	2 / 9							2	–6	18	18
f		4	2	4	7	6	5	2	30	9	91	82
fu		–12	–4	–4	0	6	10	6	2			
fu²		36	8	4	0	6	20	18	92			

the calculation of the final column. Some texts show fuv in the right hand corner, others include three figures in each box.

$$
\begin{array}{|c|}
\hline
\quad\quad fuv \\
f \\
uv \quad\quad \\
\hline
\end{array}
$$

In this case, the top row would read

$$
\begin{array}{|cc|}
\hline
\quad 12 & \quad\quad 9 \\
2 & 1 \\
6 \quad & 9 \quad \\
\hline
\end{array}
$$

From the table we can read off, $n = 30$, $fu = 2$, $fu^2 = 92$, $fv = 9$, $fv^2 = 91$, $fuv = 82$, and the calculation of the coefficient of correlation proceeds as in the previous example.

EXAMPLE 11,6. The following table gives the analysis of group medical insurance plans in a certain study according to (1) size of plan and (2) loss ratio experience.

Medical Experience Group Plans

Ratio of Actual to Expected Losses	–50%	50–119%	120–199%	200%–
Size of Plan	**Number of Plans**			
Under 50 lives	630	694	368	309
50–99	285	638	294	77
100–499	113	860	307	44
500–	3	232	70	3

Assuming the midpoints of the groups are as follows, calculate the coefficient of correlation between size of group and loss experience.

Size of Plan	Midpoint
Under 50 lives	30
50–99	75
100–499	200
500–	1,000

Ratio of Actual to Expected	
–50%	30%
50%–119%	80%
120%–199%	150%
200%–	250%

Solution. We will use as origin the midpoint of the second class interval for each variable. Units of increment will be 100 employees and 100% so that the modified variables applying to the two attributes of the plans being studied are

Ratio of Actual to Expected Losses

Class Interval	Midpoint	u
–50%	30%	–.5
50%–119%	80%	0
120%–199%	150%	.7
200%–	250%	1.7

Size of Plan

Class Interval	Midpoint	v
Under 50 lives	30	–.45
50–99	75	0
100–499	200	1.25
500–	1,000	9.25

The calculations proceed as follows.

v \ u	−.5	0	.7	1.7	f	fv	fv²	fuv
−.45	630 .225	694 0	368 −.315	309 −.765	2001	−900	405	−211
0	285 0	638 0	294 0	77 0	1294	0	0	0
1.25	113 −.625	860 0	307 .875	44 2.125	1324	1655	2069	292
9.25	3 −4.625	232 0	70 6.475	3 15.725	308	2849	26353	487
f	1031	2424	1039	433	4927	3604	28827	568
fu	−516	0	727	736	947			
fu²	258	0	509	1251	2018			

Taking the figures from the table,

$$\bar{u} = \frac{947}{4927} = .19$$

$$\bar{v} = \frac{3604}{4927} = .73$$

$$\sigma_x^2 = \frac{2018}{4927} - (.19)^2 = .41 - .04 = .37$$

$$\sigma_x = .61$$

$$\sigma_y^2 = \frac{28827}{4927} - (.73)^2 = 5.85 - .53 = 5.32$$

$$\sigma_y = 2.31$$

$$p = \frac{568}{4927} - (.19)(.73)$$

$$= .12 - .14 = -.02$$

$$r = \frac{-.02}{.61 \times 2.31} = -.014$$

showing practically no correlation.

EXAMPLE 11.7.   The following table shows the distribution of 200 individual items.

y \ x	−1	0	1
1	10	20	30
0	20	40	20
−1	30	20	10

Calculate the lines of regression and the coefficient of correlation.

Solution.

y \ x	−1	0	1	f	fy	fy²	fxy
1	10	20	30	60	60	60	20
0	20	40	20	80	0	0	0
−1	30	20	10	60	−60	60	20
f	60	80	60	200	0	120	40
fx	−60	0	60	0			
fx²	60	0	60	120			

The equations for the line of regression of y on x are

$$0 = 120a_0 + 0a_1$$
$$40 = 0a_0 + 120a_1$$

giving

$$a_0 = 0, \text{ and } a_1 = \frac{1}{3}$$

The line of regression of y on x is

$$y = \frac{1}{3}x$$

Similarly, the line of regression of x on y is

$$x = \frac{1}{3}y$$

The coefficient of correlation is

$$\sqrt{\frac{1}{3} \times \frac{1}{3}} = \frac{1}{3}$$

or by Formula 11.1

$$\frac{40}{\sqrt{120 \times 120}} = \frac{1}{3}$$

11.7. Standard Error of Estimation, Coefficients of Determination and Non-Determination. The two basic concepts so far discussed in this chapter are the *regression lines* and the *coefficient of correlation*. Associated with these two concepts are

    (1) Standard Error of Estimation
    (2) Coefficient of Determination
    (3) Coefficient of Non-Determination

The formula for the least square regression line of y on x is

$$y = a_0 + a_1 x$$

This is an estimate of the values of y for each x. The sum of the squares of the differences between actual and estimated y's is

$$\Sigma (y - y_{est})^2$$

and the square root of their average value is

$$s_{y \cdot x} = \frac{\Sigma (y - y_{est})^2}{n} \tag{11.4}$$

This is called the *standard error of estimate* of y on x. Similarly, the standard error of estimate of x on y is

$$s_{x \cdot y} = \frac{\Sigma (x - x_{est})^2}{n}$$

Formula 11.4 may be written for

$$s_{y \cdot x}^2 = \frac{\Sigma y^2 - a_0 \Sigma y - a_1 \Sigma xy}{n} \tag{11.5}$$

The standard error of estimation of y on x is not normally equal to that of x on y. These errors have properties similar to the standard deviation and if n is large, bands one, two, and three times the standard error, measured each side of the line of regression, will contain 68%, 95%, and 99.7% of the sample points.

For any value y we may write

$$y - \bar{y} = (y - y_{est}) + (y_{est} - \bar{y})$$

where $\bar{y}$ is the mean value of y.

It can be shown that

$$\Sigma (y - \bar{y})^2 = \Sigma (y - y_{est})^2 + \Sigma (y_{est} - \bar{y})^2$$

The first term on the right is called the *unexplained variation* and the second term, the *explained variation*. The *coefficient of determination* is

$$\frac{\text{explained variation}}{\text{total variation}} = \frac{\Sigma\,(y_{est} - \bar{y})^2}{\Sigma\,(y - \bar{y})^2}$$

Similarly, the coefficient of *non-determination* is

$$\frac{\Sigma\,(y - y_{est})^2}{\Sigma\,(y - \bar{y})^2}$$

This coefficient of determination is always positive, and for linear correlation it *is the same whether it is calculated for y on x or for x on y.* It is the square of the coefficient correlation.

$$r = \sqrt{\frac{E}{T}} \quad \text{or} \quad \sqrt{1 - \frac{U}{T}}$$

where

$$r = \text{coefficient of correlation}$$
$$E = \text{explained variation}$$
$$U = \text{unexplained variation}$$
$$T = \text{total variation}$$

Considering a single value of y, understanding of the above will be helped by the illustration in Figure 11.2. It must be re-

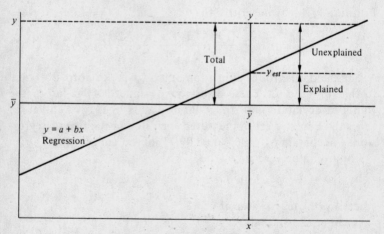

Figure 11.2. Regression. Explained and unexplained variation.

membered that in the equations above we are concerned with the *sum of the squares* of the individual variations.

EXAMPLE 11.8.   Using the data in Example 11.7, calculate
  (a) The standard error of estimation of y on x
  (b) The standard error of estimation of x on y
  (c) The coefficient of determination
  (d) The coefficient of non-determination

Solution.   The line of regression of y on x is

$$y = \frac{1}{3} x$$

Hence, we have

x	−1	0	1	Total
$\overline{y}$	0	0	0	
y_{est}	$-\dfrac{1}{3}$	0	$\dfrac{1}{3}$	
$y_{est} - \overline{y}$	$-\dfrac{1}{3}$	0	$\dfrac{1}{3}$	
$(y_{est} - \overline{y})^2$	$\dfrac{1}{9}$	0	$\dfrac{1}{9}$	
f	60	80	60	200
$f(y_{est} - \overline{y})^2$	$\dfrac{60}{9}$	0	$\dfrac{60}{9}$	13.33

From the solution to Example 11.7

$$fy^2 = 120$$

and since $\overline{y} = 0$,

$$f(y - \overline{y})^2 = 120$$

$$\text{coefficient of determination} = \frac{13.33}{120} = \frac{1}{9}$$

The coefficient of non-determination can be calculated from a table similar to the above, or as

$$1 - (\text{coefficient of determination}) = 1 - \frac{1}{9} = \frac{8}{9}$$

$$\text{coefficient of correlation} = \sqrt{\frac{1}{9}} = \frac{1}{3}$$

11.8. Small Volumes of Data. If we have only two points (x_1, y_1) and (x_2, y_2), a straight line can be drawn through the two points and this would be the line of regression of x on y and of y on x. The coefficient of correlation would be 1. This shows that the formula developed above applies only to a reasonable volume of data and cannot be used without adjustment if the number of points (n) is small. Just as for the standard deviation when n is small, a factor $\sqrt{\dfrac{n}{n-1}}$ is introduced, so for correlation we need a factor $\sqrt{\dfrac{n}{n-2}}$ for small data.

11.9. Spurious or Nonsense Correlation. It does not follow that a high degree of correlation means that there is any direct dependence of one variable on the other. Many examples of high degree of correlation can be found for two variables in time series, without any direct connection between the two; such correlation is called spurious or nonsense correlation. While spurious correlation is most common in time series, it can occur in other statistics.

EXAMPLE 11.9. Give examples of spurious correlation.
Solution. We can take any two variables which are increasing with time. Thus, we could find positive correlation between the population of Cuba and the number of miles flown by passenger airlines. Again, there would be positive correlation between the cost of living and the number of students entering college. As an example of negative correlation, we could relate the number of sleeping car tickets sold, with the average price of a cinema ticket.

11.10 Rank Correlation. In comparing two educational or other tests applied to a small body of students, rank correlation is often useful. The students are ranked in order of their achievement in the two lists, and the difference in rank between the tests D is calculated for each student. ρ, the measure of rank correlation is defined by the equation

$$\rho = 1 - \frac{6\Sigma D^2}{n(n^2 - 1)}$$

This is *Spearman's Formula* for rank correlation.

EXAMPLE 11.10. The following are the scores of a group of 10 students in two tests. Calculate the rank correlation.

Student	Test 1	Test 2
1	87	80
2	80	95
3	32	32
4	65	72
5	55	67
6	35	47
7	82	82
8	90	85
9	38	45
10	72	79

Solution.

Student	Test 1 Grade	Test 1 Rank	Test 2 Grade	Test 2 Rank	D	D²
1	87	2	80	4	2	4
2	80	4	95	1	3	9
3	32	10	32	10	0	0
4	65	6	72	6	0	0
5	55	7	67	7	0	0
6	35	9	47	8	1	1
7	82	3	82	3	0	0
8	90	1	85	2	1	1
9	38	8	45	9	1	1
10	72	5	79	5	0	0
						16

$$\rho = 1 - \frac{6 \times 16}{10(100 - 1)}$$

$$= 1 - \frac{96}{990}$$

$$= 1 - .097$$

$$= .903$$

11.11. Method of Dealing with Ties. If two students score the same in any test, they can both be given the same rank and the next student a rank two places lower (*bracket method*) or they can be given the *mid-rank value*. Thus,

Student	Score	Rank Bracket Method	Rank Mid-Rank Method
1	90	1	1
2	85	2	2.5
3	85	2	2.5
4	80	4	5
5	80	4	5
6	80	4	5
7	75	7	7

11.12. Correlation of Attributes. The methods described above are not suitable when we wish to find the correlation of attributes which do not lend themselves to numerical classification. Such attributes could be straight or curly hair, light or dark skin, married or single status, etc. Often we are concerned with a fourfold table (2 × 2 classifications) but not necessarily so.

The *coefficient of contingency* is obtained by comparing the actual distribution in the cells with the distribution to be expected if there were no correlation. This will be discussed further in Chapter 14.

11.13. Other Coefficients of Correlation. The *coefficient of reliability* is applied to the correlation of two results from the same test applied to students on two different occasions. When correlation is calculated between characteristics of a parent and an offspring it is called the *coefficient of heredity*. Similarly, correlation between husbands and wives is called the *coefficient of assorted mating*.

11.14. Multiple Correlation, Non-Linear Correlation. The principles of correlation can be extended to the correlation between three or more variables and the *coefficient of partial correlation* is the correlation between two variables when the other variables are kept constant.

Just as curves other than a straight line can be used in curve fitting, so formulas may be used for the regression lines which are curves. In this case the correlation is stated to be *non-linear*.

Problems

Problem 11.1. Draw a scatter diagram for the following data and calculate the lines of regression of y on x and x on y. Ages are at nearest birthday.

Case	Age of Husband	Age of Wife
1	30	27
2	30	31
3	29	25
4	29	25
5	28	26
6	28	25
7	27	24
8	27	23
9	26	24
10	26	25

Problem 11.2. What is the centroid of the data in Problem 11.1?

Problem 11.3. Express the lines of regression in Problem 11.1 in terms of the centroid.

Problem 11.4. Calculate the coefficient of correlation of the data in Problem 11.1 from (a) the lines of regression and (b) by the product-moment formula (ignore the correction for small volume).

Problem 11.5. Is the correlation in Problem 11.4 positive or negative, high or low?

Problem 11.6. The following table gives the number of persons employed on farms and the average farm wages per month, with room and board, over the period 1961 to 1966. Calculate the correlation between the two, and state if it is positive or negative, weak or strong, real or spurious.

Year	Employment (in millions)	Wages
1961	6.9	$151
1962	6.7	155
1963	6.5	159
1964	6.1	162
1965	5.6	171
1966	5.2	185

Problem 11.7. The following table gives the expectation of life for different ages. Ignoring the adjustment for small volumes of

data, calculate the correlation between the age and the expectation of life.

Age	Expectation	Age	Expectation
0	70	40	34
10	62	50	26
20	53	60	18
30	43	70	12

Is the correlation spurious?

Problem 11.8. Prepare a distribution table for the data in Problem 11.1 and calculate the coefficient of correlation using this table.

Problem 11.9. The following data refers to a test applied to 200 students at an interval of 1 year.

	First Test				
	50–59	60–69	70–79	80–89	90–100
Second Test 90–100	0	0	0	0	0
80–89	0	10	20	20	0
70–79	10	10	40	10	0
60–69	20	30	10	0	0
50–59	10	10	0	0	0

Calculate the line of regression of the second test on the first test.

Problem 11.10. What is the centroid of the data in Problem 11.9?

Problem 11.11. Show that the line of regression of the second test on the first test in Problem 11.9 goes through the centroid.

Problem 11.12. Calculate the coefficient of correlation for the data in Problem 11.9.

Problem 11.13. What is the coefficient of correlation when the lines of regression are identical?

Problem 11.14. In a correlation study involving a large volume of data, the standard error of estimation of y on x is found to be 1.5. How wide a band must be drawn on either side of the regression line of y on x to include approximately 50% of the points in the scatter diagram.

Problem 11.15. In measuring the distance between the regression line and the edges of the band referred to in the previous question, is the measurement made at right angles to the line of regression or parallel to the y axis?

Problem 11.16. Calculate the standard error of estimation of y on x for the data in Problem 11.1, using Formula 11.5.

Problem 11.17. Check the result of Problem 11.16 by calculating the individual values of $(y - y_{est})$.

Problem 11.18. Calculate the coefficient of determination from the data in Problem 11.1.

Problem 11.19. Calculate the coefficient of correlation for the data in Problem 11.1 from the result of Problem 11.18.

Problem 11.20. Calculate the rank correlation of the following two tests, using the mid-rank method.

		Marks	
Student	**Test 1**	**Test 2**
1	80	92
2	67	70
3	91	78
4	80	92
5	73	74
6	85	83
7	80	76
8	78	76

Solutions

Problem 11.1. Use age 28 and age 25 as origin.

Case	x − 28	y − 25	$(x - 28)^2$	$(x - 28)(y - 25)$	$(y - 25)^2$
1	2	2	4	4	4
2	2	6	4	12	36
3	1	0	1	0	0
4	1	0	1	0	0
5	0	1	0	0	1
6	0	0	0	0	0
7	−1	−1	1	1	1
8	−1	−2	1	2	4
9	−2	−1	4	2	1
10	−2	0	4	0	0
	0	5	20	21	47

To calculate the line of regression of y on x

$$5 = 10a_0 + 0a_1$$
$$21 = 0a_0 + 20a_1$$

giving

$$y - 25 = .5 + 1.05(x - 28), \quad \text{or} \quad 1.05x - y - 3.9 = 0$$

To calculate the line of regression of x on y

$$0 = 10b_0 + 5b_1$$
$$21 = 5b_0 + 47b_1$$

giving

$$x - 28 = -.236 + .472(y - 25), \quad \text{or } x - .472y - 15.964 = 0$$

Problem 11.2.

$$\frac{\Sigma(x - 28)}{n} = 0, \qquad \frac{\Sigma(y - 25)}{n} = .5$$

The centroid is $(x - 28) = 0$, $(y - 25) = .5$, or male age 28, female age 25.5.

Problem 11.3.　　The line of regression of y on x is

$$(y - 25) = .5 + 1.05(x - 28)$$
$$y - 25.5 = 1.05(x - 28)$$
$$\bar{y} = 1.05\bar{x}$$

The line of regression of x on y is

$$\bar{x} = .472\bar{y}$$

Problem 11.4.

(a)　$\sqrt{1.05 \times .472} = \sqrt{.496} = .704$

(b)　$\dfrac{(10 \times 21) - (0 \times 5)}{\sqrt{(10 \times 20 - 0)(10 \times 47 - 25)}} = \dfrac{210}{\sqrt{200 \times 445}}$

$$= \frac{210}{298} = .705$$

The difference is due to rounding.

Problem 11.5.　　The correlation is positive and fairly high.

Problem 11.6.　　Use origin of 6.0 million and $160.

Year	u	v	u^2	uv	v^2
1961	.9	−9	.81	−8.1	81
1962	.7	−5	.49	−3.5	25
1963	.5	−1	.25	−.5	1
1964	.1	2	.01	+.2	4
1965	−.4	11	.16	−4.4	121
1966	−.8	25	.64	−20.0	625
	1.0	23	2.36	−36.3	857

Using the product-moment formula

$$r = \frac{-(6 \times 36.3) - (1.0 \times 23)}{\sqrt{[6 \times 2.36 - (1.0)^2][6 \times 857 - (23)^2]}}$$

$$= \frac{-217.8 - 23}{\sqrt{13.16 \times 4613}}$$

$$= \frac{-240.8}{\sqrt{60707}} = \frac{-240.8}{246.5} = -.98$$

The correlation is negative, strong, and spurious.

Problem 11.7. Use origins of 30 years of age and 40 years of expectation. Use units of 10 years.

u	v	u^2	uv	v^2
-3	3.0	9	-9.0	9.00
-2	2.2	4	-4.4	4.84
-1	1.3	1	-1.3	1.69
0	0.3	0	0	0.09
1	-0.6	1	-0.6	0.36
2	-1.4	4	-2.8	1.96
3	-2.2	9	-6.6	4.84
4	-2.8	16	-11.2	7.84
4	-0.2	44	-35.9	30.62

Coefficient of correlation

$$r = \frac{-(8 \times 35.9) + (4 \times 0.2)}{\sqrt{[(8 \times 44) - 16][(8 \times 30.62) - .04]}}$$

$$= \frac{-287.2 + 0.8}{\sqrt{336 \times 244.9}}$$

$$= \frac{-286.4}{286.9} = -1.00$$

The correlation is very strongly negative. It is not spurious.

Problem 11.8.   Using origin of male age 28, and female age 25,

Wife Age	v	u	Husband Age 26 (−2)	27 (−1)	28 (0)	29 (1)	30 (2)	f	fv	fv²	fuv
31	6						1 12	1	6	36	12
30	5										
29	4										
28	3										
27	2						1 4	1	2	4	4
26	1				1 0			1	1	1	0
25	0		1 0		1 0	2 0		4	0	0	0
24	−1		1 2	1 1				2	−2	2	3
23	−2			1 2				1	−2	4	2
	f		2	2	2	2	2	10	5	47	21
	fu		−4	−2	0	2	4	0			
	fu²		8	2	0	2	8	20			

Using the product-moment formula

$$r = \frac{(10 \times 21) - (0 \times 5)}{\sqrt{[(10 \times 20) - 0][(10 \times 47) - 25]}} = .705$$

Problem 11.9.   Use origins of $64\frac{1}{2}$ for each test and intervals of 10 marks, ($u = $ 1st test, $v = $ 2nd test)

v \ u	−1	0	1	2	f	fv	fv²	fuv
2	0 −2	10 0	20 2	20 4	50	100	200	120
1	10 −1	10 0	40 1	10 2	70	70	70	50
0	20 0	30 0	10 0	0 0	60	0	0	0
−1	10 1	10 0	0 −1	0 −2	20	−20	20	10
f	40	60	70	30	200	150	290	180
fu	−40	0	70	60	90			
fu²	40	0	70	120	230			

The equations for the lines of regression of v on u are

$$150 = 200a_0 + 90a_1$$
$$180 = 90a_0 + 230a_1$$

Giving

$$a_0 = .48, \qquad a_1 = .59$$

and

$$(y - 64\tfrac{1}{2}) = .48 + .59(x - 64\tfrac{1}{2})$$

Problem 11.10.

$$\sum \frac{u}{n} = \frac{90}{200} = .45$$

$$\sum \frac{v}{n} = \frac{150}{200} = .75$$

The centroid is age

$$64.5 + (10 \times .45) \text{ and } 64.5 + (10 \times .75)$$
$$= 69 \text{ and } 72.$$

Problem 11.11.   Substituting in the solution to Problem 11.9.

$$.75 = .48 + (.59 \times .45)$$
$$.75 = .48 + .27$$

proving that the line of regression goes through the centroid.   It will be recalled that the lines of regression meet at the centroid.

Problem 11.12.

$$\frac{(200 \times 180) - (90 \times 150)}{\sqrt{[(200 \times 230) - (90)^2][(200 \times 290) - (150)^2]}}$$

$$= \frac{36000 - 13500}{\sqrt{(46000 - 8100)(58000 - 22500)}}$$

$$= \frac{22500}{\sqrt{(37900)(35500)}}$$

$$= \frac{22500}{36680}$$

$$= .61$$

Problem 11.13.   The correlation is 1.

Problem 11.14.   Since the distribution of the points follows the normal distribution, the width of the band on either side of the line of regression must be

$$.67 \times 1.5 = 1.0 \text{ approx.}$$

Problem 11.15. Parallel to the y axis. Compare Figure 11.2.

Problem 11.16. From Formula 11.5

$$s_{y \cdot x}^2 = \frac{\Sigma(y - 28)^2 - a_0 \Sigma(y - 25) - a_1 \Sigma(x - 28)(y - 25)}{n}$$

$$= \frac{47 - (.5 \times 5) - (1.05 \times 21)}{10}$$

$$= \frac{47 - 2.5 - 22.05}{10}$$

$$= 2.245$$

$$s_{y \cdot x} = 1.5$$

Problem 11.17. The line of regression of y on x is

$$y - 25 = .5 + 1.05(x - 28)$$

Case	x − 28	.5 + 1.05(x − 28)	y − 25	y − y_est	(y − y_est)²
1	2	2.60	2	−.60	.36
2	2	2.60	6	+3.40	11.56
3	1	1.55	0	−1.55	2.40
4	1	1.55	0	−1.55	2.40
5	0	.50	1	+.50	.25
6	0	.50	0	−.50	.25
7	−1	−.55	−1	−.45	.20
8	−1	−.55	−2	−1.45	2.10
9	−2	−1.60	−1	+.60	.36
10	−2	−1.60	0	+1.60	2.56

$$ 10)\overline{22.44}$$
$$ 2.244$$

$$s_{y \cdot x}^2 = 2.244$$

$$s_{y \cdot x} = 1.5$$

Problem 11.18.

$$\bar{y} = .5$$

$$\Sigma(y - \bar{y})^2 = 44.5$$

Explained variation $= \Sigma(y_{est} - \bar{y})^2 = 44.5 - 22.45 = 22.05$

Coefficient of determination $= \dfrac{22.05}{44.5} = .496$

Problem 11.19.   Coefficient of correlation is $\sqrt{.496} = .704$
Problem 11.20.

Student	Rank 1st Test	Rank 2nd Test	D	D^2
1	4	$1\frac{1}{2}$	$2\frac{1}{2}$	6.25
2	8	8	0	0
3	1	4	3	9.00
4	4	$1\frac{1}{2}$	$2\frac{1}{2}$	6.25
5	7	7	0	0
6	2	3	1	1.00
7	4	$5\frac{1}{2}$	$1\frac{1}{2}$	2.25
8	6	$5\frac{1}{2}$	$\frac{1}{2}$	0.25
				25.00

$$\rho = 1 - \frac{6 \times 25}{8 \times 63}$$

$$= 1 - \frac{150}{504}$$

$$= 1 - .30$$

$$= .70$$

12

Sampling Theory

12.1. Introduction. The whole of a particular body of data is called the *population* or *universe*, and a representative portion of this body is called a *sample*. Samples play a very important part in statistical work because it is often impossible or too expensive to analyse the whole population. Information obtained from a sample or a set of samples is useful in the estimation of the unknown population *parameters*, such as the mean, the variance, etc. This is called *statistical inference* or *estimation*. (See Chapter 13). Again, we often wish to compare two samples from the same population to determine the *hypothesis* that certain differences are *significant* or not. This is part of *decision theory* (Chapter 14).

EXAMPLE 12.1. Give examples where it is impossible, impractical, or too expensive to study the whole of a population or universe.
Solution.

(1) In the decennial census of the United States, an attempt is made to enumerate every person and obtain certain basic information such as age, sex, dependents, etc. However, more detailed information relating to such items as income, housing, etc., is obtained from a sample study.

(2) Between censuses, many sample studies are made on such matters as unemployment, population movements, etc.

(3) In the analysis of the production of items from a factory, sample batches are usually tested for conformity to standards rather than the total output. This saves expense.

(4) In biology and other sciences, it is not normally possible to study every item of the population and sample studies are the only available procedure.

12.2. Large and Small Sample Theory. It will be recalled that in calculating a standard deviation and in correlation, certain adjustments had to be made to the formulas when the data was small ($N < 30$). This is equally true in sampling theory. The formulas used for large samples do not apply exactly when N < 30 and the *small sampling theory* has then to be used. The formulas developed in small sampling theory actually apply to samples of all sizes, but they are complex and the more simple formulas for large samples are used whenever practical. The early part of this chapter will be concerned with large samples, and small samples will be discussed in the latter sections.

12.3. Types of Samples. There are several different ways of drawing samples from a population.

(1) *Random sampling.* Each member of the population has an equal chance of being chosen.

(2) *Stratified sampling.* A heterogeneous population may be divided into homogeneous subgroups, and the sample is then drawn from each subgroup in a random manner. The proportions of the subgroups in the sample should equal the proportions of the subgroups in the population.

(3) *Judgment sampling.* This is the deliberate selection of a sample by the statistician, to obtain a representative cross section of the population. This method is often used in the construction of a model to represent the population. The techniques of this chapter do not apply to a judgment sample.

A number of other terms are used to represent variants of these three major divisions, such as, systematic, double, sequential, area, cluster, quota, and proportional.

12.4. Methods of Obtaining Random Samples. In very many problems, each unit has, or can be assigned, a number. People have Social Security numbers, city houses have street numbers, and automobiles have serial numbers and license numbers. The output from a machine can be numbered serially. If each number in our population were written on a slip of paper, and if all the slips were placed in an urn and mixed thoroughly, then by drawing slips from the urn, a random sample of any desired size could be obtained. Many cases can be thought of where this theoretical idea would not be practical, for example, where the whole population is large or innumerable. Often a sample can be obtained by selecting every number with a last digit 4 (say) or with the last two digits 34(say) in the serial number. It is necessary to determine that selection in this way will not involve *bias*, and when this is suspected, a *table of random numbers* should be used instead.

EXAMPLE 12.2. If it were desired to obtain a sample of all telephones in a city, what would be wrong with selecting all numbers ending in the two selected digits (say 34)?

Solution. If a sample of private subscribers were needed, this method would probably prove quite satisfactory, but if a sample of all telephones were desired, this would exclude many large firms whose numbers end in 000.

12.5. Tables of Random Numbers. Tables of random numbers are usually tabulated in blocks of 5 digits. A start may be made with any block on any page. If the serial numbers of the units to be sampled ran from 1 to 700, the last three digits of each block of five digits would be used. Any random number greater than 700 would be ignored, and 1 would be treated as 001, 35 as 035, etc.

EXAMPLE 12.3. How would you use a table of random numbers to select a sample from a population where the serial numbers were six digits?

Solution. Successive pairs of 5 digit numbers from the table would be used, and the first four digits of each ten digit pair would be ignored.

12.6. Sampling with or without Replacement. In the urn procedure described above, each slip drawn from the urn could be replaced after the number on it had been recorded. This gives a random selection process which permits the same number to be selected more than once. Any procedure which does this is called *sampling with replacement*. Provided the population is large, the matter is unimportant, but with a small population, the difference is important. Sampling with replacement enables formulas appropriate for infinite populations to be used.

12.7. Distribution of Sample Means. A number of samples, all of size N, are taken from a certain population, and the mean of each sample is calculated. We then have a new distribution—the distribution of the means of the samples. These sample means have a *normal distribution*, provided the sample size (N) is large, even though the population may not have a normal distribution. The mean of this distribution is μ_p, the mean of the population; and the standard deviation is $\sigma_p/\sqrt{N}$, the standard deviation of the population divided by the square root of the sample size. This standard deviation is called the *standard error* of the sampling distribution of the means.

EXAMPLE 12.4.   A population consists of all numbers from 0 to 99. Samples of 5 numbers are selected by means of a table of random numbers, as follows:

$$51, \ 77, \ 27, \ 46, \ 40$$
$$42, \ 33, \ 12, \ 90, \ 44$$
$$46, \ 62, \ 16, \ 28, \ 98$$
$$93, \ 58, \ 20, \ 41, \ 86$$
$$19, \ 64, \ 08, \ 70, \ 56$$

Calculate the means of these samples, and the mean and standard deviation of these sample means.
Solution.

Adding the number in each sample and dividing by 5, the means of the five samples are

$$48.2, \ 44.2, \ 50.0, \ 59.6, \ 43.4$$

The mean of the means is

$$\frac{48.2 + 44.2 + 50.0 + 59.6 + 43.4}{5} = 49.1$$

The variance is

$$\frac{(.9)^2 + (4.9)^2 + (.9)^2 + (10.5)^2 + (5.7)^2}{5}$$

$$= \frac{.81 + 24.01 + .81 + 110.25 + 32.49}{5}$$

$$= 33.7$$

$$\text{Standard Deviation} = \sqrt{33.7} = 5.8$$

EXAMPLE 12.5.   A population has a mean of 50 and a standard deviation of 30. If a large number of samples each of size 36 are selected, what will be the mean and the standard deviation of the means of the samples.

Solution.

$$\text{Mean} = 50$$

$$\text{Standard Deviation} = \frac{30}{\sqrt{36}} = \frac{30}{6} = 5$$

12.8. Other Sampling Distributions. Consider a proportion p and a large population, obtained by rolling a die or other means, based on the proportion. If samples are taken from this population, the *sampling distribution of proportion of successes* will be p and the standard deviation (standard error) of the distribution will be

$$\sqrt{\frac{p(1-p)}{N}} = \sqrt{\frac{pq}{N}}$$

where $q = 1 - p$.

Although the population is a binomial distribution, the sampling distribution of the proportion is close to normal.

If two independent sets of samples are taken from two separate populations with means μ_1 and μ_2 and standard deviations σ_1 and σ_2 then the mean of the *sums of the means* will be

$$\mu_1 + \mu_2$$

and the mean of the *differences of the means* will be

$$\mu_1 - \mu_2$$

In either case, the standard deviation (standard error) of the distribution of the sums or of the differences of the means will be

$$\frac{\sigma_1^2}{N_1} + \frac{\sigma_2^2}{N_2}$$

where N_1 and N_2 are the sizes of the samples.

For large N the *sampling distribution* of the standard deviation of samples is nearly normal and its standard error is

$$\frac{\sigma}{\sqrt{2N}}$$

EXAMPLE 12.6. Two sets of samples of size 30 and 50 are taken from the population mentioned in Example 12.5. What are

(1) the means and standard deviations of the means of the two sets of samples
(2) the mean and standard deviation of the sampling distribution of the sums of the means
(3) the mean and standard deviation of the sampling distribution of the difference of the means.

Solution.

	Set 1	**Set 2**
Mean	50	50
Standard Deviation	$\dfrac{30}{\sqrt{30}} = 5.5$	$\dfrac{30}{\sqrt{50}} = 4.2$

Sum of Sample Means

$$\text{Mean} = 100$$
$$\text{Standard Deviation} = \sqrt{\frac{30^2}{30} + \frac{30^2}{50}}$$
$$= \sqrt{30 + 18}$$
$$= 6.9$$

Difference of Sample Means

$$\text{Mean} = 0, \text{Standard Deviation} = 6.9$$

EXAMPLE 12.7. Population A consists of the numbers 3 and 5 distributed in equal proportions. Population B consists of the numbers 1 and 5 distributed in equal proportions. Both populations are infinite. A set of samples X of size 50, is taken from population A. They will generally have an approximately equal number of 3's and 5's but any distribution of 3's and 5's totalling 50 is possible. A set of samples, Y of size 100 is taken from population B.

A new set of samples is formed by combining the mean of any one of sample X with the mean of any of sample Y. What is the mean and standard deviation of this distribution?

Solution. For population A, the mean is 4 and the standard deviation is 1. For population B, the mean is 3 and the standard deviation is 2. The mean of the distribution will be

$$\mu_1 + \mu_2 = 4 + 3 = 7$$

The standard deviation will be

$$\sqrt{\frac{\sigma_1^2}{N_1} + \frac{\sigma_2^2}{N_2}} = \sqrt{\frac{1}{50} + \frac{2}{100}} = \sqrt{\frac{2}{50}} = \frac{1}{5}$$

12.9. Correction for Finite Population. If the sample size is N and the population size is M, the mean of the sample distribution of means is still equal to the mean of the population,

$$\mu = \mu_p$$

But for the standard deviation

$$\sigma^2 = \frac{\sigma_p^2}{N} \cdot \frac{M - N}{M - 1}$$

EXAMPLE 12.8.   What is the correction factor to be applied to the standard deviation for a finite population where the population is 100 and the sample size is 10?
Solution.   The correction factor to the variance (σ^2) is

$$\frac{M - N}{M - 1} = \frac{100 - 10}{100 - 1} = \frac{90}{99} = .91$$

The factor to be applied to the standard deviation is

$$\sqrt{.91} = .95$$

EXAMPLE 12.9.   If the population is 100, what size of sample corresponds to a correction factor to the standard deviation of .9?
Solution.

$$\frac{100 - N}{100 - 1} = (.9)^2$$

Hence

$$100 - N = 99 \times .81$$
$$N = 100 - 80$$
$$N = 20$$

12.10. Student's *t*-distribution. It was stated earlier that if the sample size is large, the means of the samples have a normal distribution, even if the population itself is not normal. Even for small samples this is true *if the population has a normal distribution*.

Expressed mathematically,

$$z = \frac{\bar{x} - \mu}{\sigma / N^{1/2}}$$

is a standard normal curve, where μ and σ refer to the population. In most cases σ is unknown and we must substitute

$$\sigma_{est} = \sqrt{\frac{N}{N-1}}\, s$$

where s is the standard deviation of the sample. (See Chapter 4, Section 4.10). The equation

$$t = \frac{\bar{x} - \mu}{s / (N - 1)^{1/2}}$$

is called *Student's t-distribution* and approximates to the normal distribution when N is large.

The t-distribution is not unlike the normal distribution, but for the same area under the curve and the same standard deviation, the peak is lower and the tails are higher. The use of tables of the t-distribution involve the idea of *degrees of freedom*. Expressed simply the number of degrees of freedom is the size of the sample N, minus the number k of *population parameters* (constraints) which must be estimated from the sample observations.

$$\nu = N - k$$

For example, one constraint is involved in estimating the mean since

$$\Sigma (x_i - \bar{x}) = 0$$

12.11. Probable Error. The table for the areas under the normal curve (Chapter 7) enable us to determine the probability of values being within any particular range outside the mean. Thus, from the range $-\sigma$ to $+\sigma$ the probability is 68%, from -2σ to $+2\sigma$ it is 95.5%, and from -3σ to $+3\sigma$ it is 99.7%. The range corresponding to 50% is called the probable error, since values are equally likely to be inside or outside this range. For the normal curve, this range is $-.6745\sigma$ to $+.6745\sigma$.

For the t-distribution, this range is larger. For 10 degrees of freedom the range is $-.700\sigma$ to $+.700\sigma$ and for 5 degrees of freedom the range is $-.727\sigma$ to $+.727\sigma$.

12.12. Table of the *t*-distribution. In using the *t*-distribution, we are normally concerned with the probability that a given value will be outside the range $-x\sigma$ to $+x\sigma$. The probabilities are tabulated in the following form.

Degrees of Freedom	Probability			
	0.50	0.10	0.05	0.01
1	1.000	6.31	12.71	63.66
2	0.816	2.92	4.30	9.92
3	.765	2.35	3.18	5.84
4	.741	2.13	2.78	4.60
5	.727	2.02	2.57	4.03
10	.700	1.81	2.23	3.17
20	.687	1.72	2.09	2.84
∞	.674	1.64	1.96	2.58

EXAMPLE 12.10.   If the number of degrees of freedom is 10, what range of values will include 90% of the total number of means recorded in a large number of sample tests?

Solution.   If 90% of the values are within the range, 10% will be outside the range. Entering the table with probability of .10 and 10 degrees of freedom we obtain a value of 1.81. Hence the required range is

$$-1.81\sigma \text{ to } +1.81\sigma$$

Problems

Problem 12.1.   A library records in the back of its books the date each book is borrowed. It wishes to determine the average number of times a book is borrowed a year. It is suggested that every tenth book on the shelves be taken down and the number of withdrawals in the last 12 months counted. What is wrong with this sampling technique?

Problem 12.2.   A public opinion analyst obtains the opinions of passersby at a busy street corner to try to determine an election result. What would be wrong with this procedure?

Problem 12.3.   At a customs inspection counter at a certain airport, large numbers, 0 to 9, are placed at equal intervals above the counter and baggage is distributed under the numbers according to the next-to-last digit of the baggage ticket. Is this done to provide an equal distribution of the luggage along the counter? Why is the next-to-last digit used?

Problem 12.4. A population consists of five numbers 1, 2, 3, 4, 5. How many different samples of two numbers can be selected? List them.

Problem 12.5. Calculate the mean and standard deviation of the population in Problem 12.4 and the mean and standard deviation of the mean of the samples.

Problem 12.6. How would the answer to Problem 12.5 be altered if the samples were drawn with replacement?

Problem 12.7. The age of the 5,000 male students in a college has a mean of 20.1 and a standard deviation of 2.6 years. If 10 samples of 100 students each are taken, what would be the expected mean of the sample means and the standard deviation of this mean?

Problem 12.8. In the previous problem, if instead of 10 samples of 100 students each, there had been 100 samples of 10 students each, how would the results be affected? (Assume large sample theory applies).

Problem 12.9. How would the result of Problem 12.8 be affected if only 10 samples had been taken instead of 100?

Problem 12.10. In Problem 12.7, what is the expected number of the 10 samples which would have a mean between 20.0 and 21.0?

Problem 12.11. In Problem 12.7, what is the expected number of the 10 samples which would have a mean less than 20.5?

Problem 12.12. From a table of random numbers, the following three samples, each of 10 individual digits, are extracted:

$$5, 2, 4, 3, 0, 6, 1, 0, 2, 9$$
$$1, 4, 5, 0, 3, 4, 5, 9, 1, 1$$
$$7, 0, 9, 5, 5, 9, 6, 4, 6, 0$$

What are the means of the three samples? What is the mean and standard deviation of these means?

Problem 12.13. What is the theoretical mean and standard deviation of the means of three samples of 10 digits taken at random from the digits 0 to 9?

Problem 12.14. A true die is rolled 360 times. What is the probability that a six comes up at least 70 times?

Problem 12.15. In the last problem what is the probability of at least 40 sixes?

Problem 12.16. Two sample studies each of size 25, out of a very large population, produce means of 18.4 and 17.8 respectively. If the standard deviation of the population is 2.0, what is the standard deviation of the sample distribution of these two means?

Problem 12.17. What is the standard deviation of the sample distribution of the difference of the two means in Problem 12.16?

Problem 12.18. What is the probability that the two samples in Problem 12.16 did in fact come from the same large population?

Problem 12.19. What is the probable error of a distribution with a mean of 10.0 and a standard deviation of 2.0?

Problem 12.20. In a t-distribution with 10 degrees of freedom, what range of multiples of the standard deviation will include $92\frac{1}{2}\%$ of the values? How does this compare with the normal curve?

Solutions

Problem 12.1. The books on the shelves are not a proper sample of the total books in the library because they will include all the books never borrowed and only a small percentage of the books in frequent demand. A random sample taken from the books on the shelves will not be a random sample of all the books in the library.

Problem 12.2. (1) The passersby at a busy street corner are not a random sample of the voting public and (2) such a sample is likely to be too small to be of value.

Problem 12.3. The method is likely to produce a reasonable distribution of the luggage and will bring together the luggage of individual passengers since they will usually have the same next-to-last digit.

Problem 12.4. From Chapter 6, the number of samples is

$$\binom{5}{2} = \frac{5!}{2! \times 3!} = \frac{5 \times 4}{2} = 10$$

They are

$$(1,2); \ (1,3); \ (1,4); \ (1,5); \ (2,3);$$
$$(2,4); \ (2,5); \ (3,4); \ (3,5); \ (4,5).$$

Problem 12.5.

Population	Mean = 3	Standard Deviation = $\sqrt{2}$ = 1.4	
Sample	**Mean**	$x - \bar{x}$	$(x - \bar{x})^2$
1, 2	1.5	−1.5	2.25
1, 3	2.0	−1.0	1.00
1, 4	2.5	−0.5	.25
1, 5	3.0	0	0
2, 3	2.5	−0.5	.25
2, 4	3.0	0	0
2, 5	3.5	0.5	.25
3, 4	3.5	0.5	.25
3, 5	4.0	1.0	1.00
4, 5	4.5	1.5	2.25
	10)30.0	0	10)7.50
	Mean = 3.0		Variance = .75

Mean of samples = 3

Standard deviation = $\sqrt{.75}$ = .87

Problem 12.6. With replacement, the samples would be

$$(1, 1); \ (1, 2); \ (1, 3); \ \text{etc.}$$

and we must distinguish between $(1, 2)$ and $(2, 1)$ as otherwise we shall give double weight to $(1, 1); (2, 2);$ etc. The mean of the samples will still be 3 but the standard deviation will be calculated as follows:

Sample	**Frequency**	**Mean**	$f(x - \bar{x})$	$f(x - \bar{x})^2$
1, 1	1	1	−2	4
2, 2	1	2	−1	1
3, 3	1	3	0	0
4, 4	1	4	1	1
5, 5	1	5	2	4
All Other	20	3	0	15*
	25		0	25)25
				1

Mean of samples = 3

Standard Deviation = $\sqrt{1}$ = 1

*From previous table.

Problem 12.7. The mean would be the same as the mean of the population, 20.1, and the standard deviation is

$$\frac{2.6}{\sqrt{100}} = .26$$

Problem 12.8. The mean would be unaltered at 20.1. The standard deviation, by the formula for large samples, would be

$$\frac{2.6}{\sqrt{10}} = .82$$

Problem 12.9. The results would not be altered in any way. The mean and standard deviation of the sample means is the same if there is one or any number of samples.

Problem 12.10. The mean of the means is 20.1 and the standard deviation is .26.

$$20.0 = m - .4\sigma$$
$$21.0 = m + 3.5\sigma$$

From Table 7.1, the area under the normal curve

$$\text{between} -.4\sigma \text{ and } 0 = .155$$
$$\text{between } 0 \text{ and } 3.5\sigma = \underline{.500}$$
$$.655 \; total$$

The probability of a value between 20.0 and 21.0 is .655 and the expected number out of ten samples is 6.55.

Problem 12.11. The area under the normal curve between $-\infty$ and $+1.54\sigma$ is .938. The expected number is

$$10 \times .938 = 9.4 \text{ approx.}$$

Problem 12.12. The means are 3.2, 3.3, and 5.1. The mean of the means is 3.87. The variance is

$$\frac{(.67)^2 + (.57)^2 + (1.23)^2}{3} = .76$$

The standard deviation is

$$\sqrt{.76} = .87$$

Problem 12.13. The mean is 4.5 and the variance is

$$\frac{\dfrac{1}{10} \sum_{r=o}^{9} r^2 - (4.5)^2}{10} = \frac{\dfrac{1}{10} \times 285 - 20.25}{10}$$

$$= \frac{28.5 - 20.25}{10} = .825$$

The standard deviation = $\sqrt{.825}$ = .91

Since this is an example of sampling with replacement, no adjustment is needed for the small size of the sample.

Problem 12.14. This is a sample study of an infinite population of all possible rolls of the dice. The probability of a six is 1/6, so that $p = 1/6$ and $q = 5/6$.

For the sample distribution of the proportion of successes, the mean will be p or 1/6 and the standard deviation is

$$\sqrt{\frac{\dfrac{1}{6} \times \dfrac{5}{6}}{360}}$$

The expected number of sixes will be 360 × 1/6 = 60 and the standard deviation is

$$\sqrt{360 \times \frac{1}{6} \times \frac{5}{6}} = \sqrt{50} = 7.07$$

Since this is a discrete distribution, we want the probability of at least 69.5. Now 69.5 − 60 = 9.5 or 1.34 times the standard deviation. Hence, we want the area of the normal curve from 1.34σ to ∞. From Table 7.1 this is

.50 − .41, or .09 approximately

Problem 12.15. 39.5 is 20.5 from the mean or 2.9σ from the mean. Therefore we need the area under the normal curve between -2.9σ and $+\infty$, or

.4981 + .5000 = .998

Problem 12.16. In each case, the standard deviation is

$$\frac{2.0}{\sqrt{25}} = 0.4$$

Problem 12.17.

$$\sqrt{\frac{(2.0)^2}{25} + \frac{(2.0)^2}{25}} = \sqrt{\frac{8}{25}} = 0.57$$

Problem 12.18. The difference between the means is 0.6 and the standard deviation is 0.57. Hence, the difference is 1.05σ and from Table 7.1, the probability is $2 \times .35$ or .7.

Problem 12.19.

$$.6745 \times 2, \quad \text{or} \quad 1.35$$

Problem 12.20. From the table in Section 12.12, 90% of the values are in the range $\pm 1.81\sigma$ and 95% of the values are in the range $\pm 2.23\sigma$. Interpolating between these values, $92\frac{1}{2}\%$ of the values will lie in the range $\pm 2.0\sigma$. For the normal curve, the range is $\pm 1.78\sigma$.

13

Estimation

13.1. Introduction. Often the only information we can obtain about a population is from a study of samples taken at random from it. *Statistical inference*, or statistical *estimation theory*, is the procedure by which population parameters are estimated from a study of samples.

13.2. Biased and Unbiased Estimates. It was shown in the last chapter that the theoretical mean of the sampling distribution of the means is equal to the mean of the population. When this is true for any parameter, the statistic is referred to as an *unbiased estimator*.

The theoretical mean of the sampling distribution of variances is equal to

$$\frac{N-1}{N} \sigma^2$$

where σ^2 is the population variance, and N is the sample size. Here, a sample variance is a *biased estimator* of the population variance, but an unbiased estimator of

$$\frac{N-1}{N} \sigma^2$$

Put another way,

$$\frac{N}{N-1} \sigma_s^2$$

(where σ_s^2 is a sample variance, or the mean of a number of sample variances) is an unbiased estimator of the population variance σ^2.

13.3. The *k*-statistics. It will be recalled from Chapter 5 that
the moments of a distribution about the origin were m_1', m_2', m_3'
and m_4' and were 0, m_2, m_3 and m_4 about the mean.

The corresponding moments of an *individual sample* will be
approximations to the population moments, but if the sample is
not large, better approximations will be the following functions
called *k-statistics*.

Sample k-statistic	Estimate of Population Statistic
$k_1 = \bar{x} = m_1'$	μ_1'
$k_2 = N\sigma^2/(N - 1) = Nm_2/(N - 1)$	μ_2
$k_3 = N^2 m_3/(N - 1)(N - 2)$	μ_3
k_4	$\mu_4 - 3\mu_2^2$

where

$$k_4 = \frac{N^2}{(N - 1)(N - 2)(N - 3)} [(N + 1)m_4 - 3(N - 1)m_2^2]$$

These are unbiased estimators.

Where N is large,

$$k_2 = m_2, \quad k_3 = m_3 \quad \text{and} \quad k_4 = m_4 - 3m_2^2$$

EXAMPLE 13.1.   Which of the following are unbiased estimators
and which are biased estimators of the population parameters?

1. The mean of a sample as an estimator of the mean of the
population.

2. The median of a sample as an estimator of the mean of the
population.

3. The variance of a sample as an estimator of the variance
of the population.

Solution.   The mean and median are both unbiased estimators;
this was shown for the mean in the previous chapter, and since
the sample distribution of the means is a normal curve, it will be
equally true of the median. The variance is a biased estimator.

EXAMPLE 13.2.   What is an unbiased estimator of the standard
deviation of a population?

Solution.   Since the variance is an unbiased estimator of

$$\frac{N - 1}{N} \sigma^2$$

then it follows that the variances times $\dfrac{N}{N-1}$ is an unbiased estimator of σ^2 and hence,

$$\sqrt{\frac{N}{N-1}}\ \sigma_s$$

is an unbiased estimator of the standard deviation of the population.

13.4. Consistent Estimates. Consistent estimates of a parameter are estimates which become more accurate as the sample size increases. In technical language, an estimate is consistent if the probability that it differs from the true value by less than a given amount, however small, tends to unity as $N \to \infty$. The estimators discussed in this chapter are all consistent.

13.5. Point and Interval Estimates. Estimates can be stated in the form of a single value such as 4.32 or a range of values $4.32 \pm .13$. The first is called a *point estimate*, the latter, an *interval estimate*. Clearly, the interval estimate is more satisfactory because it not only indicates the *probable value* but also the *reliability* of the estimate.

13.6. Confidence Limits and Intervals. For large samples ($N \geq 30$), the sampling distribution of the mean is approximately normal, so that we can expect to find any actual mean within the range $\mu - \sigma$ and $\mu + \sigma$ in about 68% of the samples. Using Table 7.1, we can choose any appropriate percentage and determine the range in which we may expect to find the mean of a sample. The chosen percentage is called the *confidence level*. Thus, for 50% confidence level, the *confidence interval* is

$$\mu - .67\sigma \text{ to } \mu + .67\sigma$$

These two values are called the *confidence limits*. The factor .67 is called the *confidence coefficient* (z_c). The following table gives the confidence coefficients for given confidence levels in a normal distribution.

Normal Curve

Confidence Level	Confidence Coefficient (z_c)	Confidence Level	Confidence Coefficient (z_c)
99.73%	3.00	95%	1.96
99%	2.58	90%	1.64
98%	2.33	80%	1.28
97%	2.17	75%	1.15
96%	2.05	68.27%	1.00
95.45%	2.00	50%	.67

What estimate can we make of the mean of the whole population and what confidence can we attach to it? We have already seen that the mean of the sample means is an unbiased estimator of the population, and for an infinite population, the population mean is

$$\overline{X} \pm z_c \frac{\sigma}{\sqrt{N}} \tag{13.1}$$

where $\overline{X}$ is the sample mean and σ is the standard deviation of the population. However, σ is unknown and we use instead the sample estimate σ_s. N is the sample size.

For a finite population, the formula becomes

$$\overline{X} \pm z_c \frac{\sigma}{\sqrt{N}} \sqrt{\frac{N_p - N}{N_p - 1}}$$

where N_p is the population size.

For a small sample ($N < 30$) these formulas will over-estimate the reliability of the estimate and Formula 13.1 becomes,

$$\overline{X} \pm t_c \frac{\sigma}{\sqrt{N - 1}}$$

where t is obtained from Student's t-distribution.

EXAMPLE 13.3. (1) Which is the more reliable estimate, $4.32 \pm .03$ or $4.32 \pm .13$?

(2) Which is the more reliable estimate, $4.32 \pm .13$ or $8.32 \pm .13$?

Solution. (1) For a given confidence level, $4.32 \pm .03$ is more reliable than $4.32 \pm .13$. If the confidence level is 90%, the former implies that there is a 90% probability that the true value does not depart from the estimate of 4.32 by more than .03, while the latter implies that there is a 90% probability that the true value does not depart from the estimate by more than .13.

(2) Although, in the second example, the confidence intervals have the same breadth in both cases, this breadth, when expressed as a percentage of the estimate, is greater in the former case and hence 4.32 ± .13 is less reliable than 8.32 ± .13. This will be made clearer when we consider estimates such as

$$1 \pm 1 \quad \text{and} \quad 100 \pm 1$$

The former has the confidence interval of 0 to 2, which does not provide a particularly accurate estimate; the latter has an interval 99 to 101, which is a fairly close estimate.

EXAMPLE 13.4.   For a large sample, if the mean is

$$9.8 \pm .07$$

for a 95% confidence level, what is it for an 80% confidence level? *Solution.*   For a 95% confidence level, the confidence coefficient is 1.96. For an 80% confidence level, it is 1.28. Hence, the value for an 80% confidence level is

$$9.8 \pm \frac{1.28}{1.96} \times .07$$

or

$$9.8 \pm .05$$

EXAMPLE 13,5.   What is the confidence coefficient for confidence level 97.5%?
Solution.   From the table, the coefficient for 97% is 2.17, and for 98% it is 2.33. Interpolating, we have for 97.5%

$$\frac{2.17 + 2.33}{2} = 2.25$$

Alternatively, entering Table 7.1 with

$$\frac{.975}{2} = .4875$$

we get a figure of 2.24. The latter is the correct figure, but the former is a reasonable approximation.

EXAMPLE 13.6.   If the value of the mean of a population, estimated from a sample of size 100 is

$$8.12 \pm 2.5$$

what would you expect the estimate to be, based on a sample of size 200?

Solution.   From Formula 13.1 the first estimated value is

$$\overline{X} \pm z_c \frac{\sigma}{\sqrt{100}}$$

and the second estimated value is

$$\overline{X} \pm z_c \frac{\sigma}{\sqrt{200}}$$

We will expect $\overline{X}$ and σ to be the same in both cases, hence the new value will be

$$8.12 \pm \frac{\sqrt{100}}{\sqrt{200}} \times 2.5$$

or

$$8.12 \pm 1.8$$

EXAMPLE 13.7.   If the probable error of a certain statistic which is distributed normally is 2.0, what is the 90% confidence interval?
Solution.   It was explained in the previous chapter (Section 12.11) that the probable error is the 50% confidence level which has a confidence coefficient of .67. A 90% confidence level has a confidence coefficient of 1.64. Hence, the 90% confidence interval is the mean value plus or minus

$$2.0 \times \frac{1.64}{.67} = 4.9$$

13.7. Confidence Intervals for Other Statistics.   We have seen that for a sample size N, the confidence intervals for the population mean is

$$\overline{X} \pm z_c \frac{\sigma}{\sqrt{N}}$$

For some common statistics, the confidence intervals are

Proportions $P \pm z_c \sqrt{\dfrac{pq}{N}}$ (13.2) where P is the proportion of successes in a sample size N, and p is the population proportion of successes, and $q = 1 - p$. For a large sample, it is generally satisfactory to write P for p giving

$$P \pm z_c \sqrt{\frac{P(1 - P)}{N}}$$

For a finite population, Formula 13.2 becomes

$$P \pm z_c \sqrt{\frac{pg}{N}} \sqrt{\frac{N_p - N}{N_p - 1}}$$

Difference of Means

$$\overline{X}_1 - \overline{X}_2 \pm z_c \sqrt{\frac{\sigma_1^2}{N_1} + \frac{\sigma_2^2}{N_2}} \qquad (13.3)$$

Sums of Means

$$\overline{X}_1 + X_2 \pm z_c \sqrt{\frac{\sigma_1^2}{N_1} + \frac{\sigma_2^2}{N_2}}$$

Standard Deviation

$$s \pm \frac{z_c \, \sigma_s}{\sqrt{2N}}$$

if the population is normally distributed.

EXAMPLE 13.8.   A sample of 200 employees of a large company indicated that 65% thought the company's promotion procedures were satisfactory. Find the 50%, 95% and 99% confidence limits for the proportion of all employees who were satisfied with the promotion procedures.
Solution.

$$\sqrt{\frac{pq}{N}} = \sqrt{\frac{.65 \times .35}{200}} = \sqrt{.00114} = .034$$

For 50% confidence limits we have

$$.65 \pm (.67 \times .034)$$

or $\qquad\qquad .65 \pm .02$

For 95% confidence limits we have

$$.65 \pm (1.96 \times .034)$$

$$.65 \pm .07$$

For 99% confidence limits we have

$$.65 \pm (2.58 \times .034)$$
$$.65 \pm .09$$

EXAMPLE 13.9.   A sample of 50 male students in University A gives a mean height of 72.1 inches and standard deviation of 3.0 inches. A sample of 100 male students in University B gives a mean height of 71.0 inches and a standard deviation of 2.0 inches. Find the 95% confidence limits of the difference in the mean height of the male students of the two universities.

Solution.   From Formula 13.3 the difference in the means is

$$72.1 - 71.0 = 1.1 \text{ inch}$$

$$z_c \sqrt{\frac{\sigma_1^2}{N_1} + \frac{\sigma_2^2}{N_2}} = 1.96 \sqrt{\frac{(3.0)^2}{50} + \frac{(2.0)^2}{100}}$$

$$= 1.96 \times .47$$

$$= 0.9$$

Difference in the means $= 1.1 \pm 0.9$.

13.8. Choice of Size of Sample.   It can be readily seen that the larger the sample, the narrower is the confidence interval for any specified confidence limits. Hence, in planning a sample study, the size of the sample will depend on the confidence interval and the confidence limits desired. It will also depend on cost and feasibility.

EXAMPLE 13.10.   The mean and standard deviation of a large population are approximately 10.0 and 1.0, respectively. What sized sample should be used to determine the mean within a confidence interval $\pm$ 0.1 with 90% confidence?

Solution.   The confidence interval is

$$\bar{X} + z_c \frac{\sigma}{\sqrt{N}}$$

Hence,

$$0.1 = z_c \frac{1.0}{\sqrt{N}}$$

For 90% confidence,

$$z_c = 1.64$$

$$0.1 = 1.64 \times \frac{1.0}{\sqrt{N}}$$

$$\sqrt{N} = \frac{1.64 \times 1.0}{0.1} = 16.4$$

$$N = (16.4)^2 \text{ or } 269$$

Problems

Problem 13.1. Six scores, chosen at random from a large body of students taking a certain test, are

$$73, 84, 70, 83, 65, 75$$

Determine unbiased and efficient estimates of (1) the true mean and (2) the true standard deviation.

Problem 13.2. Compare the sample standard deviation with the estimated standard deviation of the population in the previous problem.

Problem 13.3. How large must a sample be for the unbiased estimate of the standard deviation of the population to differ from the sample standard deviation by less than $2\frac{1}{2}\%$?

Problem 13.4. What is the median of the sample scores in Problem 13.1? Is this an unbiased estimate of the mean of the population? Is this an efficient estimate?

Problem 13.5. A sample of size 10 of a certain population is

$$6.8, 7.0, 7.2, 7.4, 7.5, 7.5, 7.6, 7.8, 8.0, 8.2$$

Calculate the k-statistics of this sample and use them to estimate the parameters of the population.

Problem 13.6. What is an estimate of the mean and standard deviation of the means of 20 samples, each of size 10, taken from the population referred to in the previous problem?

Problem 13.7. A person, wishing to estimate the true value of a certain stock, takes the price on the New York stock market on January 1st as his first estimate. As his second estimate he takes the mean of the price on January 1st and January 2nd, and as his third estimate he takes the mean of the price on the first three days of the year and so on. Would this provide a consistent estimate?

Problem 13.8. A statistic is stated to have a value of 13.8 ± 1.5. What additional information is needed to interpret this statement?

Problem 13.9. A true die is rolled. What are the confidence levels for the following statements of the value expected to be observed?

$$(1) \ 3.5 \pm 1.0$$
$$(2) \ 3.5 \pm 2.0$$
$$(3) \ 3.5 \pm 3.0$$

Problem 13.10. What is the confidence coefficient for the normal curve corresponding to a 25% confidence level?

Problem 13.11. There are 100 students in a particular age group in a school. A random sample of 50 students shows a mean I.Q. of 105 and a standard deviation of 10. At a 50% confidence level, what is the mean I.Q. of the group?

Problem 13.12. How would the solution to the above problem be modified if the sample were only 5 students?

Problem 13.13. If a certain statistic has a value of 13.2 ± 1.0 at 75% confidence level, what is the confidence level corresponding to a value of 13.2 ± 2.0?

Problem 13.14. What is the probable error of the statistic 13.2 referred to in the previous problem?

Problem 13.15. A study shows that among 100 persons reaching age 65, 3 die within a year. If these persons can be considered a random sample of the population, what is the confidence limits of the percentage, 3%, as applied to all persons reaching age 65, (1) at 99% confidence level, and (2) at 50% confidence level?

Problem 13.16. A poll reports that 54% of the electorate will vote for candidate A. If the poll is based on a random sample, and none of the electorate change their mind between the poll and the election, and everyone votes, what is the probability that candidate A will obtain at least 50% of the votes if the poll is based on (a) 100 people, (b) 1000 people?

Problem 13.17. In Problem 13.16, how large a poll is needed to give a 90% probability of A obtaining at least 50% of the votes?

Problem 13.18. Random sample statistics of 100 married men and of 200 married women show that they average 12 and 15 days of sickness a year respectively. The standard deviation of these figures are 4 and 6 respectively. Find for 90% confidence limits, the mean number of combined days of sickness of a husband and wife.

Problem 13.19. From a random sample study it is found that 10% of men and 70% of women like soap operas. If the studies are based on 100 men and 100 women, what, at the 99.73% confidence level, is the difference between the two percentages?

Problem 13.20. What are the confidence levels that the standard deviations in Problem 13.18 do not differ from the true population standard deviations by more than 10%.

Solutions

Problem 13.1. An unbiased and efficient estimate of the mean of the population is the mean of the sample,

$$\frac{73 + 84 + 70 + 83 + 65 + 75}{6} = \frac{450}{6} = 75$$

An unbiased and efficient estimate of the variance of the population is

$$\frac{N}{N - 1} \sigma_s^2 = \frac{\Sigma (x - \bar{x})^2}{N - 1}$$

$$= \frac{(-2)^2 + (9)^2 + (-5)^2 + (8)^2 + (-10)^2 + (0)^2}{5}$$

$$= \frac{4 + 81 + 25 + 64 + 100}{5} = 55$$

An unbiased and efficient estimate of the standard deviation is

$$\sqrt{55} = 7.4$$

Problem 13.2.

Sample variance $= \dfrac{4 + 81 + 25 + 64 + 100}{6} = 46$

Sample standard deviation $= \sqrt{46} = 6.8$
Estimated standard deviation of population $= 7.4$

Problem 13.3. We require to find the value of N such that

$$\sqrt{\frac{N}{N - 1}} < 1.025$$

Evaluating for $\sqrt{\dfrac{N}{N-1}} = 1.025$ we have

$$N = (N-1)\,1.051$$
$$.051N = 1.051$$
$$N = 20.6$$

For $N = 20.6$, the unbiased estimate of the standard deviation of the population is $2\frac{1}{2}\%$ greater than the sample standard deviation. If the difference is to be less than $2\frac{1}{2}\%$, the sample must be of size 21 or more.

Problem 13.4. The two middle values are 73 and 75. The median is therefore 74. This is an unbiased but not an efficient estimate of the mean of the population.

Problem 13.5. The sum of the ten values is 75.0 and hence,

$$k_1 = \bar{x} = 7.5$$

Measuring from the mean, we have

$x - \bar{x}$	$(x - \bar{x})^2$	$(x - \bar{x})^3$	$(x - \bar{x})^4$
-0.7	.49	$-.343$	.240
-0.5	.25	$-.125$	.063
-0.3	.09	$-.027$	.008
-0.1	.01	$-.001$	.000
0	0	0	0
0	0	0	0
0.1	.01	.001	.000
0.3	.09	.027	.008
0.5	.25	.125	.063
0.7	.49	.343	.240
0	1.68	0	.622

$$m_2 = .168$$
$$m_3 = 0$$
$$m_4 = .062$$

$$k_2 = \frac{10}{9} \times .168 = .19$$

$$k_3 = 0$$

$$k_4 = \frac{100}{9 \times 8 \times 7}[(11 \times .062) - 3 \times 9 \times (.168)^2]$$

$$k_4 = 2.0\,[.68 - .76] = -.16$$

These are unbiased estimators of μ_1', μ_2, μ_3, and $\mu_4 - 3\mu_2^2$

Problem 13.6. The mean of the one sample is 7.5 and this is the only estimate available of the mean of the population. Hence, the estimate of the mean of the means of the 20 samples is 7.5.

The estimate of the standard deviation of the population is $\sqrt{k_2} = \sqrt{.19} = .44$. The standard deviation of the 20 sample means will be

$$\frac{\sigma}{\sqrt{10}} = \frac{.44}{3.16} = .14$$

Remember that N is the size of the sample, not the number of samples. The latter does not affect the result.

Problem 13.7. The price of a stock on various days will not provide a homogeneous group of data and the adding of additional data from a time series such as this will not meet the definition of a *consistent* estimate, since there is neither a *true value* to which the series of estimates can converge nor will the estimates approach any selected value in the manner described in Section 13.4.

Problem 13.8. We require to know the confidence level used in determining the confidence interval 1.5. Is it a 50% figure, a 90% figure, or what? Sometimes a 50% level is assumed when no limit is stated.

Problem 13.9. (1) The value 3.5 ± 1.0 includes 3 and 4 only. The probability of the die coming up 3 or 4 is 1/3. Hence, the confidence level is $33\frac{1}{3}\%$.

For (2) the confidence level is $66\frac{2}{3}\%$ and for (3) it is 100%.

Problem 13.10. The value of the confidence coefficient for a confidence level of 25% cannot be obtained from the table in Section 13.6, and reference must be made to Table 7.1 giving the areas under the normal curve. For 25% confidence level, 75% of the values will be outside the limits: $37\frac{1}{2}\%$ below the confidence limits and $37\frac{1}{2}\%$ of the values above them. Since the areas tabulated are for one side of the curve only, we need z corresponding to the area $(.50 - .375)$ or $.125$. This area corresponds to $z = 0.32$. It will be noted that this value of z is approximately 1/2 the value for a 50% confidence level.

Problem 13.11.   The estimated mean is

$$105 \pm .67 \frac{10}{\sqrt{50}} \sqrt{\frac{100 - 50}{100 - 1}}$$

$$= 105 \pm .67 \frac{10}{\sqrt{50}} \frac{\sqrt{50}}{\sqrt{99}}$$

$$= 105 \pm 0.7$$

Problem 13.12.   With only 5 students, the sample would be "small" and the formula used in the solution to the previous problem could not be used. Student's *t*-formula would apply.

Problem 13.13.   We are given that

$$z_c \frac{\sigma}{\sqrt{N}} = 1.0$$

for a 75% confidence level. Hence,

$$\frac{\sigma}{\sqrt{N}} = \frac{1.0}{1.15}$$

For a confidence interval of ±2.0

$$z_c \frac{1.0}{1.15} = 2.0$$

or $z_c = 2 \times 1.15 = 2.3$

From the table in Section 13.6 this figure corresponds to a confidence level of 98%.

Problem 13.14.   For the probable error $z_c = .67$, hence, the confidence interval is

$$13.2 \pm \left(\frac{1.0}{1.15} \times .67 \right)$$

$$= 13.2 \pm .58$$

The probable error is .58.

Problem 13.15.   For 99% confidence level, the confidence limits are

$$.03 \pm 2.58 \sqrt{\frac{pq}{N}}$$

$$.03 \pm 2.58 \sqrt{\frac{.03 \times .97}{100}}$$

or $\qquad = .03 \pm .04$

For 50% the limits are

$$.03 \pm .67 \sqrt{\frac{.03 \times .97}{100}}$$

$$= .03 \pm .01$$

Problem 13.16. The confidence limits are

$$.54 \pm z_c \sqrt{(.54)(.46)/N}$$

For $N = 100$ this gives

$$.54 \pm z_c(.050)$$

The candidate will fail to be elected if his percentage of votes is less than $.54 - .04$, not if it is greater than $.54 + .04$. Hence, while we equate

$$.50 = .54 - z_c(.050)$$

to obtain the value of z_c, we must not take the resultant confidence level as the probability of election.

$z_c = .8$ in this case, which corresponds to a 58% confidence level. The probability of not being elected is only $1/2 \ (1 - .58)$ or .21 and the probability of election is .79.

For $N = 1000$ we have

$$.54 \pm z_c \times .016$$

giving $z_c = 2.5$ when equated to .50, which corresponds to the 99% confidence level. The probability of election is $99\frac{1}{2}\%$.

Problem 13.17. For a 90% chance of being elected, we need only an 80% confidence level since errors of estimation on the high side will not affect the results.

$$.50 = .54 - 1.28 \times \frac{.50}{\sqrt{N}}$$

$$\sqrt{N} = \frac{1.28 \times .50}{.04} = 16$$

$$N = 256$$

Problem 13.18.   The confidence limits are

$$27 \pm z_c \sqrt{\frac{\sigma_1^2}{N_1} + \frac{\sigma_2^2}{N_2}}$$

$$= 27 \pm 1.64 \sqrt{\frac{16}{100} + \frac{36}{200}}$$

$$= 27 \pm 1.64 \times .58$$

$$= 27 \pm .95$$

Problem 13.19.

$$(.70 - .10) \pm 3.00 \sqrt{\frac{.10 \times .90}{100} + \frac{.30 \times .70}{100}}$$

$$= .60 \pm 3.00 \times .055$$

$$= .60 \pm .16$$

or $60\% \pm 16\%$

Problem 13.20.   The percentage error is

$$\frac{z_c \dfrac{\sigma}{\sqrt{2N}}}{\sigma}$$

Equating this to 10%

$$\frac{z_c}{\sqrt{2N}} = .1$$

or, $z_c = .1 \times \sqrt{200}$ for men; $.1 \times \sqrt{400}$ for women.   That is, $z_c = 1.41$ for men; 2.00 for women, giving confidence levels of 84% and 95½% respectively.

14

Decision Theory

14.1. Tests of Hypotheses. In the application of statistics to the solution of many problems, we make a *statistical hypothesis* or *decision* about the population, and then proceed to *test the decision* from a sample study. If the sample study shows that the observed results differ from what would be expected on our hypotheses to a considerably greater extent than would be expected by mere chance, then we say the difference is *significant*. Procedures which enable such decisions to be made are called *tests of hypotheses* or *tests of significance*.

14.2. The Null Hypothesis. One of the most useful procedures in decision theory is to make an hypothesis which we can later reject or *nullify*. We can then accept the *alternative* to the null hypothesis. It must be understood that we can never *disprove* the null hypothesis or prove the alternative. We can only say that either the null hypothesis is untrue or a very improbable event has occurred.

EXAMPLE 14.1.   A coin is tossed 100 times and it is found that it comes up tails 60 times. What null hypothesis should be used to determine whether the coin is balanced? (In other words, that a chance of a head or tail is 1/2.)
Solution.   We assume that the coin is balanced and then examine the probability of 60 tails occurring in 100 tosses.

14.3. Level of Significance. It is customary to use a level of significance of 5% or 1%. With a level of 5%, for example, we accept an hypothesis if our test shows a 95% chance of its being correct. In this case, the test will show that the chance that the null hypothesis is correct is 5% or less. Similarly, with a 1% level of significance, the percentages are 99% and 1%.

14.4. Type I and Type II Errors. Pure chance will occasionally give test results which cause us to reject an hypothesis when it should be accepted. This is called a Type I Error. If, however, we accept an hypothesis which should be rejected, this is a Type II Error. Sometimes one type of error is more serious than the other, and where necessary, tests must be designed to reflect this.

14.5. One and Two-Tailed Tests. We are usually concerned with testing the significance of the departure of an observed value from the value indicated by our hypothesis. This involves finding the area under the normal curve which represents a departure either above or below the assumed figure. In other words, we are concerned with measuring the *two tails* of the normal curve. In some cases, we are interested in a difference in one direction only. In this case, we use a one-tailed test.

EXAMPLE 14.2.   Give an example where a one-tailed test would be used.
Solution.   In Problem 13.16, a poll reported 54% of the electorate voting for candidate *A* and we calculated the probability, under certain assumptions, that he would be elected. If we wished to test the hypothesis that candidate *A* would be elected, we would be concerned with the observed value (54%) being more than 4 percentage points above the true value, but not with it being more than 4 percentage points below the true value.

14.6. Significance Levels. These are determined by the areas under the normal curve.

Significance Level	Critical Value (z) Two-Tailed Test	One-Tailed Test
1%	2.58	2.33
5%	1.96	1.64
10%	1.64	1.28

Other values can be calculated from Table 7.1.

It will be noted that the value of z for x% significance under a two-tailed test is equal to that for $(100 - x)$% confidence in the table in the previous chapter, since both are calculated from the normal curve. The value of z for $x\%$ significance under a one-tailed test is equal to that for $2x\%$ significance under a two-tailed test. For small samples, the values of z must be adjusted as described in Chapter 12. (Section 12.10, Student's t-distribution.)

14.7. Step-by-Step Test Procedures. The procedures in testing an hypothesis are as follows—

1. Decide on a theoretical model for the population.
2. Decide on the statistical hypothesis to be tested.
3. Decide on a statistic to be calculated from the observations for the purpose of testing.
4. Calculate the significance level of the test.
5. Make a subjective conclusion based on the test.

EXAMPLE 14.3. Use the data of Example 14.1, where a coin came up tails 60 times in a 100 tosses, to determine if the coin was balanced.

Solution. The theoretical model we select is that the probability p of a tail on any throw is the same as the probability of a tail on any other throw. The statistical hypothesis to be tested is that the probability p is equal to $1/2$, that is, that the coin is balanced. The statistic to be calculated is the probability of 60 or more tails in 100 tosses.

On our hypothesis, the mean number of tails should be 50 with a standard deviation of $\sqrt{100 \times .5 \times .5} = 5$. Since the normal curve is continuous, and we use it as an approximation to a discrete distribution, 60 or more tails must be interpreted as $59\frac{1}{2}$ or more. We have to calculate the probability of a departure from the mean of $59.5 - 50 = 9.5$ or more.

This is 1.9σ, which for a one-tailed test has a significance level of 2.9%. Using a two-tailed test, we would calculate the probability of (60 of more) or (40 or less) tails which would be 5.8%. We now come to the subjective conclusion that in the light of these low significance levels it is unlikely that the coin is balanced.

EXAMPLE 14.4. What is the null hypothesis and the alternative hypothesis in the above example?

Solution. The null hypothesis is $p = 1/2$. The alternative hypothesis is $p > 1/2$. On the basis of the one-tailed test, the null hypothesis is rejected at the 3% significance level.

EXAMPLE 14.5.   If we accept the hypothesis that the coin is balanced and it is in fact unbalanced, what type of error is involved?
Solution.   This is a Type II error.

14.8. Sample Differences.   If we have two samples, we can test whether they come from the same population by using the null hypothesis that the two populations are the same.   Similar tests can be used with proportions.

EXAMPLE 14.6.   An I.Q. test is applied to two groups of 100 students, all the same age.   If the mean I.Q.'s are 105 and 110 for the two samples, and the standard deviation of I.Q.'s is assumed to be 20, test the assumption that the two groups can be assumed to come from the same population.
Solution.   The difference in the means is 5 and the standard deviation of the difference is (by Formula 13.3)

$$\sqrt{\frac{\sigma^2}{N_1} + \frac{\sigma^2}{N_2}} = \sqrt{\frac{20^2}{100} + \frac{20^2}{100}} = \sqrt{\frac{800}{100}} = 2.8$$

The difference is

$$\frac{5}{2.8} \sigma = 1.8\sigma$$

This is a two-tailed test and the significance level is 7%.   It is not unreasonable to assume that the two groups came from the same population.

14.9. Chi-Square Test.   This test is used to determine the significance of the differences between observed and expected frequencies, where the expected frequencies are based on some hypothesis.   In this test, the statistic calculated is

$$\chi^2 = \sum \frac{(o_i - e_i)^2}{e_i} \tag{14.1}$$

where the summation is made over the events for which observed and expected statistics are available.   For event i, o_i is the observed frequency and e_i the expected frequency. χ is the Greek letter chi, and the test is called the chi-square test.

Values of χ^2 are tabulated in statistical tables for various *de-*

grees of freedom. (See Chapter 12, Section 12.10.) Some typical values are given below.

Values of χ^2

Degrees of Freedom	.20	.10	.05	.01
1	1.6	2.7	3.8	6.6
2	3.2	4.6	6.0	9.2
3	4.6	6.3	7.8	11.3
4	6.0	7.8	9.5	13.3
5	7.3	9.2	11.1	15.1
10	13.4	16.0	18.3	23.2
20	25.0	28.4	31.4	37.6

Where an $h \times k$ table is involved, the number of degrees of freedom is

$$v = (h - 1)(k - 1) - m$$

where m is the number of population parameters which have to be estimated for the sample statistics.

For discrete data, a correction known as *Yates' correction* should be used which changes Formula 14.1 to

$$\chi^2 = \sum \frac{(|o_i - e_i| - .5)^2}{e_i} \qquad (14.2)$$

where $|o_i - e_i|$ is the positive value of $o_i - e_i$.

EXAMPLE 14.7. In a certain mortality investigation, the observed number of deaths and the expected number of deaths according to a certain mortality table were—

Age Group	Actual Deaths	Expected Deaths
20–	58	47
30–	78	80
40–	96	117
50–	101	115
60–	46	36

Can the lives in the actual mortality investigation be considered as a sample from the population of the lives used to prepare the mortality table?

Solution.

Age Group	Actual Deaths	Expected Deaths	A − E	(A − E)²	$\dfrac{(A - E)^2}{E}$
20−	58	47	+11	121	2.57
30−	78	80	− 2	4	.05
40−	96	117	−21	441	3.77
50−	101	115	−14	196	1.70
60−	46	36	+10	100	2.78
	379	395	−16		$\chi^2 = 10.87$

Since the expected deaths were taken from a separate mortality table, no population parameters have been calculated and the number of degrees of freedom is 5. χ^2 at the 10% significance level is 9.2, and at the 5% significance level it is 11.1.

Hence, the hypothesis can be accepted at the 10% significance level, but not at the 5% significance level.

EXAMPLE 14.8. How would the above results be affected by the Yates correction?

Solution. Since the number of actual deaths is discrete, $(A - E)$ should be corrected as follows—

Age Group	|A−E|	|A−E| −.5	(|A−E| −.5)²	$\dfrac{(\vert A - E \vert - .5)^2}{E}$
20−	11	10.5	110	2.34
30−	2	1.5	2	.03
40−	21	20.5	420	3.59
50−	14	13.5	182	1.58
60−	10	9.5	90	2.50
				10.04

$$\chi^2 = 10.04$$

The conclusion is unaltered.

14.10. Computing χ^2 in a 2 × 2 Contingency Table. The observed frequencies in a study which involves two classifications of each of two variables can be set out in a contingency table as follows—

	I	II	Total
A	a_1	a_2	N_A
B	b_1	b_2	N_B
Total	N_1	N_2	N

If there is no correlation between the two variables, we shall expect the N_1 values in I to be distributed between A and B in the same proportion as the total. That is, we shall expect a_1 to be equal to

$$\frac{N_A}{N} \times N_1$$

and similarly for the other values. From this and the three other similar equations we can show that

$$\chi^2 = \frac{N(a_1 b_2 - a_2 b_1)^2}{N_1 N_2 N_A N_B} \tag{14.3}$$

With Yates' correction this becomes

$$\chi^2 = \frac{N(\,|\,a_1 b_2 - a_2 b_1\,| \, - \, \frac{1}{2}N)^2}{N_1 N_2 N_A N_B}$$

EXAMPLE 14.9. A company using a door-to-door sales procedure is testing a new sales approach, and has the following results on a comparative test under otherwise identical conditions.

	Sales	No Sales	Total Visits
Old Approach	84	116	200
New Approach	98	102	200
Total	182	218	400

Use the χ^2 test to determine the significance of the observed difference.

Solution. The expected frequencies from the combined data are

$$a_1 = b_1 = 91$$

$$a_2 = b_2 = 109$$

Calculating χ^2 directly,

$$\chi^2 = \frac{(84 - 91)^2}{91} + \frac{(98 - 91)^2}{91} + \frac{(116 - 109)^2}{109} + \frac{(102 - 109)^2}{109}$$

$$= .54 + .54 + .45 + .45$$

$$= 1.98$$

Alternatively, using Formula 14.3,

$$\chi^2 = \frac{400[(84 \times 102) - (98 \times 116)]^2}{182 \times 218 \times 200 \times 200} = 1.98, \text{ as before.}$$

$$\nu = (h - 1)(k - 1) = (2 - 1)(2 - 1) = 1$$

so that we have one degree of freedom.

Since $1.6 < 1.98 < 2.7$ we conclude that the new approach has significance at the 20% level, but not at the 10% level. It seems probable that the new approach has not significantly improved the results, but further tests are desirable.

14.11. 2×3 and Larger Contingency Tables. From Formula 14.1

$$\chi^2 = \sum \frac{(o - e)^2}{e} = \sum \frac{o^2}{e} - 2\sum \frac{oe}{e} + \sum \frac{e^2}{e}$$

$$= \sum \frac{o^2}{e} - 2\Sigma o + \Sigma e$$

In any contingency table, $\Sigma o = \Sigma e = N$
Hence,

$$\chi^2 = \sum \left(\frac{o^2}{e}\right) - N \tag{14.4}$$

14.12. Coefficient of Contingency and Correlation of Attributes.
The *coefficient of association or contingency* is a useful measure of association between two or more attributes. It is defined as

$$C = \sqrt{\frac{\chi^2}{\chi^2 + N}}$$

The larger the value of C, the greater the association. The maximum value of C is

$$\sqrt{\frac{k - 1}{k}}$$

where k is the number of rows and columns in the contingency table. C is always less than 1.

Another useful measure is the *correlation of attributes* which is defined as

$$r = \sqrt{\frac{\chi^2}{N(k-1)}}$$

The value is always less than 1.

EXAMPLE 14.10. From Example 14.9, calculate the coefficient of contingency and the correlation of attributes.

Solution. The coefficient of contingency is

$$C = \sqrt{\frac{\chi^2}{\chi^2 + N}}$$

where

$$\chi^2 = 1.98 \quad \text{and} \quad N = 400$$

giving

$$C = \sqrt{\frac{1.98}{401.98}} = \sqrt{.0049} = .07$$

The correlation of attributes is

$$r = \sqrt{\frac{1.98}{400(2-1)}} = .07$$

Problems

Problem 14.1. A die is to be rolled 216 times and the number of times a six comes up counted. It is decided to accept the hypothesis that the die is true if the number of sixes is any number from 31 to 41 and to reject this hypothesis if the number of sixes is 30 or less or 42 or more. List the step by step test procedures. Why is this test procedure faulty?

Problem 14.2. In Problem 14.1, what is the probability of rejecting the hypothesis that the frequency of sixes is 1/6 when it is actually correct.

Problem 14.3. In Problem 14.1, what range of values should be chosen to avoid rejecting the hypothesis that the frequency of sixes is 1/6 at the 5% significance level?

Problem 14.4. How many times should the die in Problem 14.1 be rolled if a 10% departure from the expected number of sixes (on the assumption of a frequency of 1/6) is to correspond to the 10% significance level?

Problem 14.5. To test whether a student has any knowledge of a subject, he is set 6 true or false questions and told to guess if he does not know the answer. The hypothesis is made that if 4 or more answers are right the student has some knowledge of the subject.

What is the probability that a student who guesses the answer to all 6 questions makes this score?

Problem 14.6. There are 100 questions in a multiple choice (5 answer) test, so as to discourage guessing, the score is calculated by the following formula

$$R - \tfrac{1}{4}W$$

where R equals the number of correct answers and W the number of wrong answers. The passing score is 50. A student knows the answer to 40 questions. Of the remaining 60, he knows that in 20 only two out of the 5 possible answers are correct. He has no means of guessing the correct answer to the remaining 40 questions. If he uses a random method of guessing the 20 questions, where he can exclude answers he knows to be wrong, what is the probability that he will pass the examination?

Problem 14.7. 300 balls are drawn at random from a bag with replacement after each drawing. The hypothesis is made that there are two black balls for each red ball, and this is accepted if the number of red balls drawn is in the range 90 to 110. Calculate the probability of a Type I error. What is the significance level of this test?

Problem 14.8. If, in Problem 14.7, suppose there were in fact three black balls for every two red balls in the bag. What is the probability of accepting the two black balls to one red ball hypothesis when it should be rejected (Type II error)?

Problem 14.9. Illustrate the results of Problems 14.7 and 14.8 graphically.

Problem 14.10. If a two-tailed test has a critical value of $2 \times \sigma$, what is the significance level? What is the significance level if it is a one-tailed test?

Problem 14.11. Students in two classes take the same test. The results are

Class	No. of Students	Mean Score	Standard Deviation
A	50	58	10
B	40	62	8

At what level of significance are the results different?

Problem 14.12.   If in the previous study, the figures had referred to two random samples of the same class, sub-division *B* having been given an extra hour a week of study, and we wanted to know if the additional study time had significantly improved the results, what difference would be made in the test?

Problem 14.13.   Two samples have identical means.   Can we conclude they must come from the same population?

Problem 14.14.   A die is rolled 360 times and the results are tabulated.

Face	1	2	3	4	5	6
Frequency	46	65	71	70	56	52

Use the chi-square test to determine if the die is true.

Problem 14.15.   If instead of a manufactured die, in the previous problem, a home-made die had been used, how would the answer be altered?

Problem 14.16.   If the die in Problem 14.14 were rolled twice as many times and the identical frequency distribution resulted, would this increase, leave unchanged, or decrease the significance level of the test?

Problem 14.17.   Prove Formula 14.3 algebraically.

Problem 14.18.   Use the chi-square method on the data in Example 14.3.

Problem 14.19.   Calculated chi-square for the following contingency table.   (Ignore the Yates correction.)

	Hair Color			
	Fair	Dark	Redhead	Totals
Boys	40	50	10	100
Girls	60	30	10	100
	100	80	20	200

What is the significance level of these differences?

Problem 14.20.   What is the coefficient of contingency for the data in the previous problem?

Solutions

Problem 14.1.   The step-by-step test procedures are— ·

1. The theoretical model is that the probability of throwing a six on any roll is the same.

2. The statistical hypothesis to be tested is that the chance of a six is 1/6 on any roll.

3. Calculate the probability that the number of sixes lie outside the range from 31 to 41 in 216 rolls.
4. Calculate the significance level of this test.
5. Make a subjective conclusion based on the test.

The test procedure is faulty because it will test only the proper frequency of the distribution of sixes. It applies no test to the other faces of the die. The die might be so weighted that the frequencies for the various faces were—

Face	1	2	3	4	5	6
Frequency	1/8	1/4	1/8	1/12	1/4	1/6

Problem 14.2. $Np = 36$ and $Nq = 180$ and the normal approximation to the binomial may be used.

$$\mu = Np = 36$$
$$\sigma = \sqrt{Npq} = \sqrt{30} = 5.48$$

On a continuous scale, the test applied is that the range 30.5 to 41.5 equals $\mu \pm \sigma$. From Table 7.1 the area is .68. Hence, the probability that the hypothesis will be rejected when it is in fact true is .32.

Problem 14.3. For a two-tailed test, the critical value for a 5% significance level is 1.96 (see Section 14.6).

$$1.96 \times 5.48 = 10.7$$

The range of values should be 26 to 46 inclusive.

Problem 14.4. For a 10% departure, the range is

$$Np \pm \frac{1}{10} Np$$

For a two-tailed test, the critical value for 10% significance level is 1.64. Therefore

$$1.64\sigma = \frac{1}{10} Np$$

$$1.64\sqrt{Npq} = \frac{1}{10} Np$$

$$2.69N \times \frac{1}{6} \times \frac{5}{6} = \frac{1}{100} N^2 \left(\frac{1}{6}\right)^2$$

$$N = 2.69 \times 5 \times 100 = 1345$$

The number of required rolls is approximately 1,350.

Problem 14.5. For a student who guesses, the probability of a correct reply to an individual question is 1/2. The probability of 4 or more questions right is

$$\frac{6.5}{1.2}\left(\frac{1}{2}\right)^2\left(\frac{1}{2}\right)^4 + \frac{6}{1}\left(\frac{1}{2}\right)\left(\frac{1}{2}\right)^5 + \left(\frac{1}{2}\right)^6$$

$$= \frac{15 + 6 + 1}{64} = \frac{22}{64} = .34$$

Hence, the probability of rejecting the assumption that the student is guessing when this assumption in fact is correct is .34. (A Type I error.)

Problem 14.6. Of the twenty questions he can guess at, he gets 1 for a correct answer and $-1/4$ for an incorrect answer. In order to pass, he must guess 12 or more correctly, since

$$12 - \frac{(20 - 12)}{4} = 10$$

$Np = 10$ and $Nq = 10$ so that the binomial approximation may be used.

$$\sqrt{Npq} = \sqrt{20 \times 1/4} = \sqrt{5} = 2.24$$

$$\frac{(2 - .5)}{2.24} = .67$$

The area under the normal curve between $.67\sigma$ and ∞ is .25. Hence, the probability he will pass is .25. The same result is obtained by summing the terms of the binomial expansion.

Problem 14.7. For a Type I error, the hypothesis is rejected when it should be accepted.

$$p = 1/3 \qquad Np = 100 \qquad Nq = 200$$

$$\sqrt{Npq} = \sqrt{\frac{200}{3}} = \sqrt{66.7} = 8.17$$

The accepted range is $Np \pm 10.5$ or

$$\frac{10.5}{8.17}\sigma = 1.285\sigma$$

The area of the normal curve outside this range is $[1 - (2 \times .4)] = .2$. The probability of a Type I error is .2. The significance level of the test is 20%.

Problem 14.8. For a Type II error, the hypothesis is accepted when it should be rejected. This means that the test gives a value in the range 90 to 110.

$$p = 2/5 \qquad Np = 120 \qquad Nq = 180$$
$$\sqrt{Npq} = \sqrt{120 \times 3/5} = \sqrt{72} = 8.49$$
$$(120 - 110.5) = 9.5 = \frac{9.5}{8.49}\sigma \quad \text{or} \quad 1.12\sigma$$

The probability of a Type II error is

$$1 - .37 - .5 = .13$$

Problem 14.9.

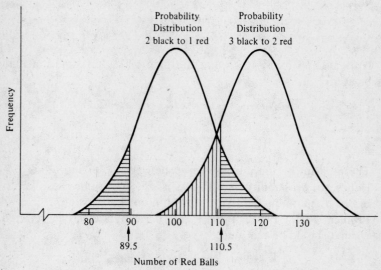

Figure 14.1. Illustration of Type I and Type II Errors.

The horizontal shading represents the answer to Problem 14.7, and the vertical shading represents the answer to Problem 14.8. Note that in one case, two tails of the curve are involved, and the other case, only one tail.

Problem 14.10. (1) 4.6%   (2) 2.3%

Problem 14.11. The null hypothesis is that both classes came from the same population. The closest approximation to the standard deviation of the population of the two classes combined will be approximately 9.

$$\text{Difference in mean} = 62 - 58 = 4$$

The standard deviation of the difference is

$$\sqrt{\frac{q^2}{N_1} + \frac{q^2}{N_2}} = \sqrt{3.65} = 1.91$$

$$\text{critical value} = \frac{4}{1.91} = 2.09$$

For a two-tailed test, this gives a significance level of 4%.

Problem 14.12. In this case, a one-tailed test should be used and the significance level would be 2%.

Problem 14.13. First, a Type II error may be involved and the hypothesis may be accepted when it should be rejected. Second, while the means of the two samples may be the same, the standard deviation or the skewness may be so markedly different that it is improbable that the two samples come from the same population.

Problem 14.14.

Face	1	2	3	4	5	6
Observed Frequency	46	65	71	70	56	52
Expected Frequency	60	60	60	60	60	60
$o - e$	-14	$+5$	$+11$	$+10$	-4	-8
$\lvert o - e \rvert - 1/2$	13.5	4.5	10.5	9.5	3.5	7.5
$[\lvert o - e \rvert - 1/2]^2$	182.3	20.3	110.3	90.3	12.3	56.3

Since the expected value is the same for each face we may sum $[\lvert o - e \rvert - 1/2]^2$ before dividing by e

$$\chi^2 = \sum \frac{[\lvert o - e \rvert - 1/2]^2}{e} = \frac{471.5}{60} = 7.86$$

Since the total observed and expected frequencies are the same, the number of restraints is 1, and the number of degrees of freedom is 5. The observed differences are significant at the 20% significance level but not at the 10% significance level. Since most die are true, we would not assume from this result that the die was untrue without further testing.

Problem 14.15. If the maker was skilled at cutting a die, we would probably come to the same conclusion. If however, the

maker was poorly skilled we might well conclude the die was untrue. This illustrates the importance of the subjective conclusion
which is the last step in decision theory (see Section 14.7).

Problem 14.16.   The values of $(o - e)$ would be approximately
doubled (the Yates correction makes the doubling not exact) and
so would e. Since the numerators of the terms in χ^2 are squared
but not the denominators, the value of χ^2 would be larger and
consequently the significance level would be a smaller figure.
χ^2 becomes 16.5 and the die is untrue at the 1% significance level.

Problem 14.17.   For the left top square, the actual value is a_1
and the expected value is

$$\frac{N_A}{N} \times N_1$$

$$(o_1 - e_1) = a_1 - \frac{(a_1 + a_2)(a_1 + b_1)}{N}$$

$$= \frac{a_1(a_1 + a_2 + b_1 + b_2) - (a_1 + a_2)(a_1 + b_1)}{N}$$

$$= \frac{a_1 b_2 - a_2 b_1}{N}$$

$$\frac{(o_1 - e_1)^2}{e_1} = \frac{(a_1 b_2 - a_2 b_1)^2}{N N_A N_1}$$

$$\chi^2 = \sum \frac{(o - e)^2}{e} = \frac{1}{N}(a_1 b_2 - a_2 b_1)^2$$

$$\cdot \left(\frac{1}{N_A N_1} + \frac{1}{N_A N_2} + \frac{1}{N_B N_1} + \frac{1}{N_B N_2}\right)$$

$$= \frac{1}{N}(a_1 b_2 - a_2 b_2)^2$$

$$\cdot \frac{N_B N_2 + N_B N_1 + N_A N_2 + N_A N_1}{N_1 N_2 N_A N_B}$$

$$= \frac{1}{N}(a_1 b_2 - a_2 b_1)^2 \frac{N_B N + N_A N}{N_1 N_2 N_A N_B}$$

$$= \frac{N(a_1 b_2 - a_2 b_1)^2}{N_1 N_2 N_A N_B}$$

Problem 14.18.

$$o_1 = 60 \qquad o_2 = 40 \qquad e_1 = e_2 = 50$$

$$\chi^2 = \frac{(\,|\,60 - 50\,|\, - .5)^2}{50} + \frac{(\,|\,40 - 50\,|\, - .5)^2}{50}$$

$$= 3.61$$

The degrees of freedom are $(2 - 1) \times (2 - 1) = 1$ and hence the test is significant at just about the 5% significance level (Section 14.9). This agrees with the result obtained in Example 14.3 using the two-tailed test. Note that the square of 1.9, the standard score, in the solution to Example 14.3, is equal to χ^2. This is always true when only two categories are involved.

Problem 14.19. The expected values are

	Hair Color			
	Fair	**Dark**	**Redhead**	**Totals**
Boys	50	40	10	100
Girls	50	40	10	100
Totals	100	80	20	200

Calculating χ^2 directly—

$$\frac{(40 - 50)^2}{50} + \frac{(50 - 40)^2}{40} + \frac{(10 - 10)^2}{10} + \frac{(60 - 50)^2}{50}$$

$$+ \frac{(30 - 40)^2}{40} + \frac{(10 - 10)^2}{10}$$

$$= 9.0$$

or using Formula 14.4

$$\frac{40^2}{50} + \frac{50^2}{40} + \frac{10^2}{10} + \frac{60^2}{50} + \frac{30^2}{40} + \frac{10^2}{10} - 200$$

$$= 9.0$$

The number of degrees of freedom is $(3 - 1) \times (2 - 1) = 2$, indicating a significance level of 1%.

Problem 14.20. The coefficient of contingency is

$$\sqrt{\frac{9}{9 + 200}} = \sqrt{\frac{9}{209}} = .21$$

Index